PEN AND PENCIL SKETCHES IN INDIA

JOURNAL
OF
A TOUR IN INDIA.

PEN AND PENCIL SKETCHES IN INDIA

JOURNAL OF A TOUR IN INDIA.

BY GEN. GODFREY CHARLES MUNDY,

GOVERNOR OF JERSEY, AND AUTHOR OF 'OUR ANTIPODS

THIRD EDITION.

WITH MANY ILLUSTRATIONS

GYAN

Published by

GYAN

Gyan Publishing House
5, Ansari Road
Daryaganj, New Delhi-110002
Phone: 011-47034999, 9811692060
E-mail: books@gyanbooks.com

Distribution Network
gyanbooks.com
India, USA, Canada, UK, Australia, France

ISBN : 978-81-212-4559-3 (HB)
First Published, 1858

2nd Impression 2020

Printed at: Gyan Press, Delhi.

Pen and Pencil Sketches in India.

JOURNAL

OF

A TOUR IN INDIA.

By GEN. GODFREY CHARLES MUNDY,

GOVERNOR OF JERSEY, AND AUTHOR OF 'OUR ANTIPODES.

THIRD EDITION.

WITH MANY ILLUSTRATIONS.

LONDON:
JOHN MURRAY, ALBEMARLE STREET.
1858.

TO

GENERAL LORD VISCOUNT COMBERMERE,

UNDER WHOSE AUSPICES,

AND

IN WHOSE SOCIETY,

THE FOLLOWING TOUR WAS PERFORMED,

This Journal

IS INSCRIBED AS A SMALL TRIBUTE OF RESPECT AND GRATITUDE,

BY

THE AUTHOR.

PREFACE.

A British Sage has pronounced that "every man, who will take the trouble of describing in simple language the scenes of which he has been a spectator, can afford an instructive and amusing narrative." No such public-spirited motive, however, influenced the pen or pencil of the writer of the following pages. On the contrary, the manuscript journal and portfolio, from which these slight and unpretending 'Sketches of a Tour' have been well-nigh *verbatim* and *lineatim* extracted, were most selfishly and unambitiously scribbled for his own amusement, and (undutiful confession!) as a sort of promised sop held out to allay epistolary expectations at home: and it was not until a year after his return to England, that, prompted by the encouragement of perhaps partial friends, and finally rendered desperate by what may almost be said to have amounted to a paternal mandate, he found himself—correcting the proofs.

He has simply described scenes and characters as they appeared, incidents as they occurred, and anecdotes as they were related to him. The number of engravings being necessarily restricted, he has for the most part selected those bearing on Indian sporting, as presenting more of novelty to the English eye than the more hackneyed subjects of landscape.

Should the reader then be disposed, in some idle hour, to accompany the author in his flying tour through India, he is hereby promised, if not "Good Entertainment," at least "Expeditious Travelling;"—and though he fail to be satisfied with his vehicle, he may see enough of an interesting country to induce a wish for a second journey—under the guidance of a more able conducteur.

GLOSSARY.

Anna, a coin; the 16th part of a rupee.
Ankoos, goad to drive the elephant.

Bungalow, thatched house.
Bhause, short-winged hawk.
Bheiree, long-winged ditto.
Begum, Mahomedan princess.
Bunneer, shopkeeper.
Bowlee, a well.
Bagheecha, fruit garden.
Bund, embankment.
Burkindass, armed attendant.
Burra Sahib, great man; chief.
Buckshees, a gift.
Bhistey, water carrier.
Budjerow, decked passage boat.
Beauliah, small decked boat.

Chobdar, mace bearer.
Cummerbund, waist cloth.
Cheraug, small Indian lamp.
Choor! Choor! stop thief!
Chokee, police station.
Chuprassee, upper servant.
Charpoy, low bed, or stretcher.
Chupâtties, unleavened cakes.
Chowrie, fly-flapper formed of the tail of a Thibet cow, and only used by persons of high rank.
Chick, thin curtain made of thread and strips of bamboo.
Chout, one-fourth of the revenue claimed by conquerors of the soil.
Chunam, cement made of shells.
Coolie, man of low caste.

Dâk, travelling-post in palankeen.
Dâk Hurkarah, post messenger.
Dewanee Khâs, hall of audience.
Durbar, Indian levee or council.
Dekkanee, belonging to the Deccan, a province of India.
Dhâllee, basket of garden stuff.

Fakir, holy mendicant.
Florikan, bird of the bustard tribe.

Guddee, Hindoo throne.
Gongwalas, villagers.
Gurrah, earthenware vessel.
Gram, species of vetch.
Ghoont, mountain pony.
Goru, teacher, or priest.
Guzzul or Gazele, an erotic ode.

Hackery, cart.
Houdah, *Anglicè* — elephant's castle.
Haremzadeh, savage — literally Filho da Puta.
Hakim, physician.
Hurkarah, messenger.
Hookam, order or command.
Hafiz, the Horace of the Persians.

Jheel, lake.
Jemadar, sepoy sergeant; upper servant.
Jhool, elephant's housings.
Jaghire, territory.
Jampaun, mountain sedan-chair.
Jât, race or tribe.

Jehanum, Pluto's realm.

Kookaree, knife worn by the Nepaulese.
Khodabund! Maraj! titles of respect.
Khanaut, wall of a tent.
Kuskus, a fragrant grass.
Khansamah, butler.
Khalâmuts, bards.
Kutwâal, police officer.
Kucker, barking deer.
Keemcab, brocade.
Kitmutgar, table attendant.
Killar, a fortress.
Kurwar, coarse cloth.
Khilaut, dress of honour.
Kutcherrie, court of justice.

Lal Purdah, great red curtain.
Lâl Sherâb, Claret.

Mahout, elephant's driver.
Musnud, Mussulman throne.
Mut, temple.
Michaun, platform of bamboo.
Mussalgee, torch-bearer.
Minar, *Anglicè*, minaret.
Musjed, *Anglicè*, mosque; Mahomedan place of worship.
Maungee, boatswain.
Mooluck, kingdom.
Mussuck, sheep-skin water-bag.

Nullah, brook, or small river.
Nautch, Indian dance.
Nautch Lôg, dancers.
Nuzzar, an offering, or gift of homage.
Nusseeb, fate.

Paun, betel-nut.
Paundan, vessel holding paun.
Patarras, a pair of boxes slung on a bamboo.
Pâl, servant's tent.
Pariah, *in this sense*, a wild dog.
Purdah, curtain.
Punkah, large fan hung from the ceiling.
Puharrees, mountaineers.
Pillau, Khawaub, Eastern dishes, almost as well known as curry.

Qui-hi, or Koee-hui, Who's there? or, Who waits?—a summons for servants in Bengal, and applied as a sobriquet to the Anglo-Bengâlese.

Rām-Rām! Hindoo salutation.
Routee, sleeping tent.

Sirdar-bearer, head bearer.
Shuter-suwar, camel courier.
Shikkaree, native hunter.
Seikh, Hindoo sect.
Shemianah, canopied entrance.
Serwans, camel drivers.
Syces, Indian grooms.
Suwarree, a cavalcade.
Suwar, horseman or trooper.
Serai, public building for the reception of caravans or travellers.
Sahib, a gentleman; sir.
Sunderbunds, forest tract in the Delta of the Ganges.
Suppoose, chimney of the hookah.
Sircar, a native writer.
Schroff, banker.

Tom-tom, Indian drum.
Tattee, screen of grass placed in a window, and cooled by water.
Toofaun, hurricane.
Tope, a grove.
Tumâsha, grand display.

Vina, species of guitar.
Vakeel, ambassador.
Videri, a dark-coloured compound metal.

Zenāna, seraglio.

CONTENTS.

CHAPTER I.

CHAPTER II.

CHAPTER III.

CHAPTER IV.

CHAPTER V.

CHAPTER VI.

CHAPTER VII.

CHAPTER VIII.

CHAPTER IX.

CHAPTER X.

CHAPTER XI.

CHAPTER XII.

LIST OF ILLUSTRATIONS.

SCENE NEAR HURDWAR.

A party of sportsmen entering a marsh in search of a tiger. Three of them (sportsmen), together with the pad-elephants, proceed in line to beat the covert, whilst a fourth occupies a commanding station (in the left distance of the picture) in order to intercept the retreat of the tiger to the wood-jungle. In the foreground, under a cotton-tree, a male and female tiger are in the act of devouring a hog-deer, when they are suddenly disturbed by the approach of one of the sportsmen—the female retires sulkily, whilst the male seems inclined to resent intrusion.

In the distance is the first range of the Himalaya mountains near Hurdwar.

SKETCHES IN INDIA.

CHAPTER I.

Palankeen-travelling — Rogonâthpore — Hazarebaug — Sortie of tigers — Journey resumed — Benares — Allahabad — Hermitage of a Fakir — Hautgong — Cawnpore — Onah — An Anglo-Indian camp — Khamutgunge — Young Prince of Lucknow — Exchange of presents — Noelgunge — Futtygunge — the King of Oude — Lucknow — Entry into Lucknow — Breakfast with the King — Dil Koosha — Constantia — Lucknowee field-sports — Mussulman manners — The Imaum-Barree — Royal feast — Fireworks — British Resident's country seat — Wild-beast fights — The King's conjuror — Leave Lucknow — Naubutgunge — Nannemow — Merun-ke-Serai — Ruins of Kanoge — Futtyghur — Antelope-hunt.

The Commander-in-Chief having determined upon a tour of inspection of the military stations in the Upper Provinces during the cooler months of the year, his lordship left Calcutta, with two or three officers of his suite, on the 1st of November, 1827. The remainder of the general and personal staff were directed to join him by the end of the month, at Cawnpore, a considerable town and station, about 650 miles from Calcutta, where the Head-quarters Camp was to be assembled previous to the commencement of our march.

The Dâks, *i. e.* posting in palankeens, being duly laid by the Postmaster-General, it was arranged that we should travel in parties of three, one day intervening between each party, in order to allow time for the bearers at the several stages to return to their posts.

Captain Macan (the Persian interpreter), Colonel Dawkins (a brother aide-de-camp), and myself, formed one of the travelling trios; and snugly ensconced in our palankeens, we turned our backs upon the city of palaces on the evening of the 20th of November.

To those uninitiated into the mysteries of Indian travelling, the prospect of a journey of 600 miles, night and day, in a hot climate, enclosed in a sort of coffin-like receptacle, carried on the shoulders of men, is somewhat alarming; but to one more accustomed to that method of locomotion the palankeen would, perhaps, prove less fatiguing and harassing, for a long journey, than any other conveyance. The horizontal or reclining position is naturally the most easy to the body; and the exhaustion consequent upon a journey in the heat of the day, generally secures to the traveller as much sleep during the cooler hours of the night as the frequent interruptions of the bearers at the several stages will allow him to enjoy. I had laid in a good store of tea, sugar, and biscuits, a novel, some powder and shot, a gun, and a sword, and plenty of blankets as a defence against the coldness of the night. Our baggage consisted of a dozen boxes (patarras) appended to bamboos, and carried by men; which, with two torch-bearers (mussalgees) to each palankeen, completed our cavalcade.

On the 22nd, at 4 P. M., we reached Rogonâthpore, a small village near which is situated one of those stage bungalows, erected by government, for the accommodation of travellers, along the great military road to Benares and Allahabad. Here we fell in with a family of our acquaintance travelling southward with all their household, equipages, &c., and they treated us with a rather more plentiful and luxurious meal than our palankeen stores could have afforded us.

Just above the village of Rogonâthpore there is a group of lofty rocks, of a conical form, and thickly clothed with brushwood, a very favourite resort of bears. The servant at the bungalow informed us that a young officer, who had preceded us about six weeks, ascended the rocks with his gun, and in about an hour shot two bears, carrying off their skins in triumph on the roof of his palankeen. Colonel D. and myself walked over the rocks in the evening, and we distinctly saw one of these uncouth-looking animals climbing up the face of the crags; but he was far out of shot-range.

Nov. 24th, 7 A.M., reached Hazarebaug, a small station, about 220 miles from Calcutta. It is a healthy spot; the earth sandy and rocky, presenting a strong contrast to the loamy and alluvial soil of Southern Bengal.* From Rogonâthpore to Hazarebaug the road runs through an almost uninterrupted jungle, swarming with wild beasts. At this place we met with a hospitable friend, who stored our palankeens with provisions, after giving us a capital breakfast.

At 11 o'clock at night we entered the famous pass of Dunghye. The road bears the appearance of a deep sandy ravine; the banks are rocky and woody, and in many places quite overhung by the forest-trees. We had accomplished about half the defile, when I was suddenly and rudely awakened from a dozing sleep by the shock of my palankeen coming to the ground, and by the most discordant shouts and screams. I jumped out to ascertain the cause of the uproar, and found, on inquiry, that a foraging party of tigers—probably speculating upon picking up a straggling bearer—had sprung off the rocks, and dashed across the road, bounding between my palankeen and that of Colonel D., who was scarcely ten yards a-head! The bearers of both palankeens were all huddled together, bellowing like bedlamites, and the mussalgees waving their torches most vehemently. On mustering our forces we discovered that two of our patarra-bearers were missing, and, fearing that the tigers might intercept them, we despatched four men with spare torches to bring them on. Meanwhile my friend and myself, having brought our palankeens together, armed ourselves with patience and a pair of pistols to await the result. The whole incident, with the time and scene, was highly interesting and wild, with just enough of the awful to give an additional piquancy. The night was dark and stormy, and the wind roared among the

* Therm. 55° at 6 A.M.;—30 degrees lower than when we left Calcutta.

trees above our heads: the torches cast a red and flickering light on the rocks in our immediate neighbourhood, and just showed us enough of the depths of the forest to make the background more gloomy and unfathomable. The distant halloos of the men who were gone in search of their comrades came faintly and wildly upon the breeze; and the occasional shots that we fired rang through the rocky jungle with an almost interminable echo. In about three-quarters of an hour our bearers joined us, together with the two patarra-bearers. These latter, hearing the vociferations of our men, and guessing the cause, had quietly placed their boxes on the ground, about a mile in the rear of us, and, seating themselves on their heels, had determined not to proceed until the break of day.

All being reported present, we resumed our journey, the men keeping up their screaming chorus, to scare our unwelcome visitors, whom I several times fancied I heard rustling among the brushwood on the road-side, as though they were moving on our flanks in order to cut off any straggler who might drop astern. I never saw bearers go more expeditiously, or in more compact order, every man fearing to be the last in the cavalcade.* A sheet would have covered the whole party! The tigers, if they had calculated upon one of our number for their evening meal, must have gone supperless to their lair, for we mustered all our 24 men in the morning. A dâk hurkarah (post messenger) had been carried off in the same spot two days before, probably by the same family of tigers, which, according to the bearers' account, consisted of two old ones and three cubs.

Nov. 27th.—Arrived at Benares at 5 A.M., and were hospitably received by Mr. Princep, master of the Mint, who freighted our palankeens with plentiful stock for the morrow. We were here shocked to learn the death of Colonel Macdonald, one of the party that had preceded us. He was seized with an apoplectic fit on getting out of his

* It is said that a tiger lying in wait for a string of passengers usually selects the last of the party.

palankeen, and expired soon after. There is no country in the world where the demise of one of a small circle is regarded with so much apathy as in India. Sickness, death, and sepulture follow upon each other's heels, not unfrequently within the four-and-twenty hours; and memory of the departed—except among nearer and dearer friends, whose feelings are beyond the influence of climate and circumstances—scarcely outlives the week. By the death of Colonel Macdonald, we lost a courteous, kindhearted, and agreeable companion, and the very outset of our journey was clouded with evil auspices.

28*th*.—Reached Allahabad early in the morning, after having been much retarded by a paucity of bearers. Among those that we did succeed in procuring, many of the poor fellows had their shoulders galled like those of over-worked post-horses in England. At 3 P. M. we called a halt, and combined breakfast, dinner, and supper in one meal; and taking for our motto "Sufficient for the day," &c., bravely devoured our last fowl and loaf, though we had two days' journey to perform, without a chance of falling in with any more of our hospitable countrymen.

In the evening, there being much rain, the roads became very deep and slippery, and the bearers proportionately slow and sulky. To crown the whole, our torches were extinguished, and the men at length put us down under a tree, from whence even the vast consideration of two rupees (four times the usual à boire) could not induce them to move.

29*th*, 6 A.M.—Awoke, and, with the Commander-in-Chief's recommendation to hasten our progress staring me in the face, found myself and palankeen planted under the same ill-omened tree, and the bearers all huddled round, shivering and jibbering, and looking as though they had taken as firm root to the spot where they had squatted the night before as the venerable banyan which overshadowed us. With the assistance of a few rupees, and (shall I confess it?) a little gentle corporal persuasion, we resumed our journey, and at 10 A.M. drew up at the picturesque, though ruined hermitage of an old Mussulman fakir. Here we overhauled our haversacks, and found our whole store to amount to six small biscuits.

Divided rations; and with the assistance of our reverend host, who boiled some water for us, made tea, and, seating ourselves on some ancient Mussulman tombs, devoured our frugal breakfast. After tipping the holy anchorite a few annas,* and receiving his blessing in return, we proceeded.

One P.M. we passed through Hautgong, a strange ruinous old town, surrounded with extensive fortifications, in a state of dilapidation, and the most magnificent groves of tamarind-trees. Here a large pariah dog took a fancy to our party, and, with no other food than a couple of hard-boiled eggs, followed us the whole way to Cawnpore, a distance of nearly 80 miles.

30*th.*—At 4 P.M. we at length reached our destination, having been two days longer than usual on the road, and most heartily tired of palankeens and bearers. We found our tents pitched in the "compound," or enclosure, of Sir S. Whittingham, the General of the division. The Commander-in-Chief had arrived the day before. Our heavy baggage, servants, horses, and dogs were here awaiting us. I missed, however, the joyous welcome of my favourite terrier; and learnt with sorrow that he had met with his quietus on the march, by having unadvisedly disputed a sheep's shank with a foraging hyena, who not only secured the bone of contention, but left nothing but poor Hector's head to tell the story of his sad fate. Flebilis occidit!

Cawnpore being one of the largest military stations in India, his Excellency remained there six days, during which time our mornings were employed in regimental and brigade reviews, and our evenings agreeably consumed by the dinners, balls, and plays with which the hospitable inhabitants entertained the Head-quarters party.

December 6*th.*—At daybreak we commenced our first march towards Lucknow, the metropolis of the Nawaub,

* A small coin, 16 to the rupee.

commonly called King, of Oude.* Having crossed the Ganges, which river forms the boundary between the English and Oude territories, we found the Head-quarters camp ready pitched for our reception near the village of Onah, twelve miles from Cawnpore.

As we galloped up the main street of the camp, his Excellency was saluted by a deputation from the King of Lucknow, who had sent a suite of tents, with elephants, horses, and servants, for his accommodation.

And here let me furnish the reader with a glimpse of Head-quarters camp. As it is invariably pitched in the same order, one description will suffice for it under all circumstances. The main street, about 50 feet wide, consisting of from 20 to 30 large double-poled tents, as symmetrically ranged as the houses of Portland Place, is set apart for the Commander-in-Chief, the general and personal staff, and any visitors of distinction, who, bringing, like the snail, their houses with them, may sojourn for a while at Head-quarters. The two larger marquees, situated midway up the street, facing each other, and distinguished by spacious shemmianas, or canopied porticoes, are the private and public, or durbar, tents of his Excellency. The street is, by the care of the Quartermaster-General, levelled and cleared of brushwood, and sentries are posted to prevent the intrusion of the "profanum vulgus." Immediately in rear of the main line of tents are pitched those of the office-clerks, servants, and kitchens, and behind them the horses of the officers are piqueted in line. A little further back is spread out, in a wilderness of canvas alleys, the camp bazaar, where individuals of every trade, to meet

* Oude was (until, for value received, acknowledged as an independent kingdom by the all-powerful Company) a province of the Mogul or Delhi empire; and the Nawaub Vizier of Lucknow was, as the title literally signifies, the deputy or vicegerent of the Emperor. Ostensibly his Nabobship has been promoted from the rank of servant to that of lord: virtually, he has only changed masters: for, like all other native potentates who have admitted British residents at their courts, he is so strictly supervised, that he can scarcely add an extra wife or two to his establishment, much less enact any important state measure, without the interference of his super-attentive allies.

the exigencies of the Burra-luscar,* are to be found. A long double line of picqueted horses marks the station of the cavalry escort; the infantry guard has its canvas cantonment at the opposite extremity of the camp; and its extreme outskirts are occupied by a crowd of elephants and camels, who, released from their burthens, are enjoying themselves after their respective natures: the former animal covering himself with dust, and fanning himself with a branch, whilst he devours his delicate "tiffen," consisting of a dozen meal-cakes, each as big as the top of a bandbox, with half a peepul-tree, timber included, by way of légumes; the latter beasts lazily chewing the cud as they lie round on the spot where they were unloaded, or browsing on the bushes within reach of their long necks. The number of souls now assembled in Head-quarters camp is computed at nearly 5000.

The immense catalogue of what would in western nations be termed luxuries, but which in an Indian camp are mere necessaries, would astonish our more hardy campaigners in Europe. To those of our party who had experienced the hardships of a Peninsula bivouac, the contrast must have appeared almost antipodean.

It would, perhaps, be worth while to record, as well as I can remember, the matériel and personnel of my camp equipment; an humble captain and single man, travelling on the most economical principles. One double-poled tent, one "routee" or small tent, a "pâl" or servants' tent, two elephants, six camels, four horses, a pony, a buggy, and 24 servants, besides mahouts, serwâns or camel-drivers, and tent-pitchers.

8*th*.—Soon after reveille beating, as is usual in Indian marches, we mounted our horses and continued our journey. The camp was pitched near the village of Khamutgunge. About a mile from it we discerned a large and glittering cavalcade drawn up on the road; which proved to be the young prince of Oude, attended by his minister, and a numerous train of courtiers, horse and infantry

* Great camp.

troops, and vagabonds of every description, who were come to give a ceremonious welcome to the Commander-in-Chief. On first gaining sight of them we resigned our Arabs to the attendant "syces," and mounted our elephants, forming them in a line of 15 abreast. The band and a squadron of his Majesty's 11th Dragoons, and a like number of a Native Cavalry regiment, preceded us as we advanced to meet the heir-apparent of Lucknow. The two cavalcades approached, met, and blended themselves into one; an impenetrable cloud of dust, the never-failing accompaniment of an Indian suwarree, veiling the rencontre of the British and Mussulman chiefs from the gaze of the spectators. The young Prince having quitted his own howdah for that of the Commander-in-Chief, the whole procession rushed on together in one compact mass of about 40 elephants. The two escorts led the way, followed by a pedestrian crowd of chôbdars, or mace-bearers, standards, heralds calling the high-sounding titles of the boy-prince, and led horses richly caparisoned. On front, flanks, and rear, we were surrounded by a cloud of picturesque-looking cavaliers, who were constantly employed in displaying their horsemanship and dexterity in the use of the spear and sword, by curvetting and careering at each other in mimic jousts, with the most noble disregard of banks, ditches, and uneven ground.

The whole scene was highly interesting and striking. The dark and close-serried column of elephants caparisoned with flowing jhools of coloured cloth and brocade, deeply fringed; the splendid howdahs of the Mussulmans, many of them panelled with plates of silver and gilt; the complete contrast of the splendid shawls, and ample flowing drapery of the natives, with the stiff, angular, scarlet coats of the English, as the wearers, riding side by side, conversed courteously from their lofty seats; add to this the wild, fierce, and disorderly array of the Lucknow cavalry, compared with the disciplined regularity of our own escort; the discordant clashing of the British and native bands of music, which seemed vying with each other for the mastery in sound, and the continual glitter of hundreds of banneroles of gold and silver tissue; and we were in possession of materials for amusement and interest which were scarcely exhausted ere we arrived at the camp.

On reaching the tents of the Prince we were invited to partake of a vile breakfast, prepared in the European style, but with the Indian concomitants of nauching and singing, the performers occupying one end of the tent. After breakfast we were conducted to another tent, where the usual presents from His Majesty of Oude to the Commander-in-Chief were displayed. They consisted of shawls, tissues, &c. How absurd is this interchange of presents still kept up between the Honourable Company's and Native Courts! Individuals, at least on the English side, are not suffered to retain what is presented to them; the British Residents taking a list of the articles, and all being sold on the account of the government. Thus it may frequently occur that the native potentates receive again as presents the same shawls which, a few months before, they had bestowed upon a servant of the Honourable Company. The abolition, however, of this ridiculous and troublesome system is, I believe, in agitation.

Before we quitted the Prince's tent our necks were severally ornamented with a heavy silver-tinsel necklace,—value perhaps five rupees;—on the receipt of which we departed to our own encampment.

Dec. 9th.—The camp moved to Noelgunge, a march of twelve miles. The Prince accompanied us, and with his suite breakfasted with the Commander-in-Chief. He was preceded by a train of servants bending under a savoury load of curries, cawâbs, and pillaus. The young Mussulman ate but little, looked frightened, and only drank a little sherbet, which was occasionally handed to him by a diminutive, copper-coloured Ganymede, who stood behind him.

At Futtygunge, where we encamped the following day, we were met by the King of Oude's grand falconer, with about 20 hawks of both the long and short winged species. He showed us some capital sport, flying them at plovers, paddy-birds, and kites. It was wonderful to see with what ease the bhause, or short-winged hawk, brought down the kite, a much larger and apparently stronger bird than itself. The bheiree, or long-winged, were flown at herons, but failed to strike one.

Dec. 11*th.*, therm. 73. This day having been declared auspicious by the soothsayers for the entry of the Commander-in-Chief into Lucknow, we mounted our elephants at an early hour, and started on our march towards the city. About two miles from the town we encountered his Majesty of Oude, accompanied by a numerous and splendid retinue. The King and the Commander-in-Chief, after a fraternal embrace, continued their march in the same howdah. Our cavalcade was most formidably augmented by this last reinforcement, and it must have presented an imposing spectacle to the myriads of lookers-on as we entered the city. The king, Nuseer-ood-Deen Hyder, is a plain, vulgar-looking man of about 26 years of age, his stature about 5 feet 9 inches, and his complexion rather unusually dark. His Majesty's mental endowments, pursuits, and amusements, are by no means of an elevated or dignified order; though his deficiencies are in some measure supplied by the abilities and shrewdness of his minister, who is, however, an unexampled rogue, displaying it in his countenance with such perspicuity of development as would satisfy the most sceptical unbeliever in Lavater. He is detested by all ranks, with the exception of his royal master, who reposes the most perfect confidence in him.

I remarked that the attendant, who sat behind him in the howdah, kept his finger twisted in the knot of his lord's sword, as though he feared the possibility of some wronged wretch snatching it out of the scabbard, from the roof or window of the overhanging houses, and making free with the wearer's head,—which act, par parenthèse, would be doing the state some service.

The streets of Lucknow are extremely narrow, so much so as in some places scarcely to admit more than one elephant to pass at a time. The houses, from the windows of which were displayed silks and draperies, were, as well as the streets, thickly crowded with spectators; some of them employed in greeting their sovereign with profound salaams; the greater proportion, however, consisting of wretched-looking beggars, who followed the cavalcade vociferating for charity, and greedily scrambling for the handfuls of rupees which were from time to time thrown by the King, the Commander-in-Chief, and the Resident, among the multitude. It was curious to see with what care the elephants avoided treading upon or injuring some of these paupers, who, in eager pursuit of the scattered largesse, fearlessly threw themselves under the feet of these animals, the slightest touch of which would have shattered a limb. A few coins thrown on the roof of a house sometimes caused the most amusing scramble, and I saw more than one of the gleaners roll into the street upon the heads of the gaping crowd below.

In some of the narrow passes the crush was awful; the elephants trumpeting, jhools and ladders tearing and crashing; and now and then the projecting roof or veranda of a house carried away by the resistless progress of these powerful animals. The strongest elephants and most determined mahouts held the first places in the cavalcade, next to the King, the Commander-in-Chief, and the Resident. The princes royal were not unfrequently most unceremoniously jostled; and as for the minister, he was generally among the "unplaced."

I was mounted, with Colonel D., upon an elephant who, though perfectly quiet, was the terror of his brethren, by reason of the length and sharpness of his tusks, which (contrary to the usual custom of the country) had not been cut off short. He had been sent as a present to the Commander-in-Chief by the King of Siam, and was a foot higher than any elephant in the procession.

On arriving at the palace we sat down to breakfast with his Majesty and his courtiers. The King was splendidly attired in a tunic of green velvet, and girded with a costly shawl. He wore a diademed turban, and his person was profusely ornamented with necklaces, earrings, and armlets of the most brilliant diamonds, emeralds, and pearls. After breakfast we adjourned to the state-chamber, an ill-proportioned, indifferent room. The throne is, however, beautifully decorated with embroidery in seed-pearl. Here his Majesty presented the Commander-in-Chief with his portrait, set in diamonds, and suspended to a string of pearls and emeralds; and the staff, after having the honour of being severally presented to the King, were each, as on a former occasion, gratified with a silver halter.

After taking leave we mounted our elephants and proceeded to the palace of the British Resident, where a more substantial breakfast than that afforded by royalty was provided and partaken of.

In the afternoon we drove round the King's park, called Dil Koosha (Heart's Delight), the Kew, or rather Kensington, of Lucknow. It is a high grass jungle, surrounded by a wall, and intermixed with a few trees. The house is a Cockney-looking building, with nothing to recommend it. The park, however, is full of game of all kinds, from the boar and stag to the hare and quail. Our party dined with the Resident, 50 persons sitting down to table.

Dec. 12th.—The King came in state to breakfast with the Commander-in-Chief, at the Residence. On his retiring I went to lionize about Lucknow. I visited one of the royal palaces, and the tomb of the present King's father, Gazee-ood-Deen Hyder, where prayers unceasing are said by ten holy men, day and night, for the repose of his deceased Majesty's soul. When I entered they were sitting round near the door, rocking their bodies to and fro, and muttering their prayers in a monotonous growl.

We were next conducted to the King's aviary and menagerie: in the enclosure of the latter we were entertained with a ram-fight, which is not a very interesting spectacle, though the combatants are regularly trained for the arena, and meet each other in the lists with true chivalrous fury.

In the afternoon our party, occupying three carriages and four belonging to the Resident, drove to Constantia, a magnificent, but strangely constructed building, a few miles from Lucknow. It was erected after the will and testament of an eccentric old General Martin, a Frenchman, who died at Lucknow immensely rich, and left money to raise this edifice over his tomb. The sepulchre itself is deep underground, in a small vault constantly lighted by tapers. A white marble slab, at the head of which is the bust of the General, bears his name, with the following inscription: "Came to India a common soldier in the year 17—, and died a major-general in 18—." Four grenadiers (unfortunately for effect, *in coloured plaster*) stand at the corners of the tomb, resting on their arms reversed.

Dec. 13th.—The Commander-in-Chief having received an invitation from his Majesty to witness some spectacles intended for his amusement, we proceeded at an early hour to the palace, where the King met us. He conducted us a short distance out of the town, where we found an arena prepared for what were announced as "field sports," but which were in fact equally uninteresting and cruel, and totally warring against John Bull's ideas of fair play. First, five or six antelopes were brought out of cages, so stiff and weak from confinement that they could barely stand, and abandoned to the mercy of chetahs and lynxes, which pulled them down without their making any effort to escape. The hawking was little better, the birds turned out having been too long encaged to show any sport. An hyena was next turned loose, and pursued and brought to bay by an heterogeneous pack of about 20 large dogs; and when I arrived near enough to see the fight distinctly, I found that the unfortunate animal was muzzled, and was, therefore, unresistingly mangled for nearly ten minutes. The next victim was a bear, who, having had most of his teeth extracted, was bullied with impunity by a troop of yelping curs, none of them venturing near enough to get within Bruin's embrace.

Having been fully sated with this barbarous sport, we returned to our tents, dressed, and proceeded to the royal palace, to breakfast with the King. On my way there I saw his Majesty's equipage à l'Anglaise waiting at one of the entrances. It was a kind of lord-mayor's coach, with eight long-tailed horses in hand. The coachman, a fierce-looking Mussulman, with a curling beard and mustachios, cut rather a strange figure in a livery of the latest London fashion.

The breakfast was, as before, a bad attempt at English style. I was much amused by the manifest uneasiness and fatigue of the native gentlemen present, who, unaccustomed to the use of chairs, and cramped by a sederunt of two hours, were trying every species of attitude to modify the discomfort of the posture. Some of them also were, no doubt, longing for the pleasing excitement of their hookahs, a luxury which is not allowed in the presence of majesty. The two young Mussulmans on either side of me made several courteous and polite attempts to draw me into conversation during the few and far-between intervals granted us by the nauch-women, and they listened with more than French urbanity to my bad Hindostanee. There is an innate gentlemanliness in the manners and address of the Mussulman, which, taken as a national characteristic, exceeds even that of more civilised countries. He has a dignified composure of countenance, gracefulness of action, and tact in the use of that delicate instrument, flattery, peculiar to himself.

After breakfast digestion was promoted by standing in the sun to see two rams knock their heads together.

In the afternoon we drove to see the Imaun-Barree, a magnificent palace, the most remarkable part of which is the immense hall containing the tomb of Asof-ood Doulah, the great-grandfather of the present Nawaub. Over his remains prayers are still said, and will, I suppose, continue to be said, until the money voted for that good purpose be expended. The hall is built of stone, beautifully carved, and of the most noble proportions. The ceiling, composed of the most stupendous stones, is gently and gracefully arched, and totally unsupported by pillars. The length is 120 feet by 60. It is supposed to be the largest room without supporting columns in the world. A short distance from the court of the Imaun-Barree is the Romee Durwassa, the "Beautiful Gate" of Lucknow.

In the evening our party had the distinguished honour of dining with the King: and although the company could not have amounted to more than 60 persons, there was no room in the palace large enough to contain us all. We were consequently divided into two parties. The smaller division, of which I was one, dined in a large veranda, looking into a capacious quadrangle surrounded with elegantly columned cloisters. In the centre was a spacious tank of water, with sparkling fountains, ornamented with marble statues, and illuminated by many-coloured lamps. The prospect bore a pleasing and fairy-like effect; the faint manner in which the distant colonnades and statues were lighted up reminding me in some degree of the effect produced in the background of Martin's famous picture of Belshazzar's Feast.

Eight or ten Mussulmans, of rank sufficient to entitle them to sit at the king's table, were of our party. Some of them ate beef and vegetables with great appetite. I did not see any of them drink wine; although one of them, whose jolly countenance bore the fruits of good living and confirmed his words, said that he drank it in his own house, though he could not so indulge at the king's table.*

After dinner we were conducted through the numerous small rooms and tortuous passages of an oriental palace, to another veranda, to witness a grand display of fireworks,—an amusement in which the eastern nations greatly excel, and for which an Indian climate is so favourable.

The scene that here met our eyes was beautiful in the extreme, and truly oriental. It appeared almost a realization of some of those splendid fictions in the 'Arabian Nights.' The night, though dark, was calm: the balcony

* By the bye, I looked in vain among the cruets on the table for the "King of Oude's Sauce," which delicacy I hear is boldly placarded for sale in the window of some noted pickler in London.

where we stood overhung the river, which flowed deep beneath, and was thickly studded with many-shaped boats. In one of these, in the middle of the stream, a group of nautch-girls and musicians were dancing and singing. The whole was made visible to us by blue lights, so placed under the veranda as to throw their cold mysterious light over the scene, without annoying the eyes of the spectators. The fireworks, which were extremely well managed, and of great variety, were arranged along the opposite bank of the river, and in the vessels on its surface. At intervals fire-balloons were sent up, which, as they majestically floated over the city, showed us alternately in the distance some elegant palace, temple, or mosque, whose white and gilt minarets were for an instant brightly illuminated, and then left in their original darkness.

Dec. 14th.—The Commander-in-Chief reviewed the 14th regiment of native infantry, a remarkably fine corps, nearly 900 strong, on parade.

In the cool of the day we drove to the country-house of the British Resident, where he generally resides in preference to the palace in the town. The farm and dairy reminded me much of "sweet home," the more so that many of the cows were English; but I looked in vain for the rosy-faced-and-elbowed dairymaids of Derbyshire, whose functions were ill sustained by mustachioed and half-naked natives.

His Majesty dined at the residence this evening, and was entertained much in the same manner as he treated us, viz. with nautches and fireworks. Our pyrotechnic display, I think, even surpassed his own, though the scene was not so picturesque. The king was clad in a tunic of cashmere shawl, well suited to the coolness of the evening. He wore a red and gold turban, ornamented with a superb diamond aigrette, the whole surmounted by an elegant tuft of pendent feathers tipped with brilliants. Eight or ten necklaces of diamonds, emeralds, and pearls, hung on his breast, and his arms and wrists were loaded with bracelets. On his Majesty and suite taking leave, the

English portion of the assembly descended from the stilts of ceremony, and commenced quadrilling.

His Majesty, before he retired, informed the Commander-in-Chief that he had given orders for the wild-beast fights to be prepared for his edification on the morrow; and as these sports are celebrated for the grand scale on which they are conducted at Lucknow, we were all very anxious to witness them. Early in the morning, therefore, the whole party, including ladies, eager for the novel spectacle, mounted elephants, and repaired to the private gate of the royal palace, where the King met the Commander-in-Chief, and conducted him and his company to a palace in the park, in one of the courts of which the arena for the combats was prepared. In the centre was erected a gigantic cage of strong bamboos, about 50 feet high, and of like diameter, and roofed with rope network. Sundry smaller cells, communicating by sliding doors with the main theatre, were tenanted by every species of the wildest inhabitants of the forest. In the large cage, crowded together, and presenting a formidable front of broad, shaggy foreheads well armed with horns, stood a group of buffaloes sternly awaiting the conflict, with their rear scientifically appuyé against the bamboos. The trap-doors being lifted, two tigers, and the same number of bears and leopards, rushed into the centre. The buffaloes instantly commenced hostilities, and made complete shuttlecocks of the bears, who, however, finally escaped by climbing up the bamboos beyond the reach of their horned antagonists. The tigers, one of which was a beautiful animal, fared scarcely better; indeed, the odds were much against them, there being five buffaloes. They appeared, however, to be no match for these powerful creatures, even single-handed, and showed little disposition to be the assaulters. The larger tiger was much gored in the head, and in return took a mouthful of his enemy's dewlap, but was finally (as the fancy would describe it) "bored to the ropes and floored." The leopards seemed throughout the conflict sedulously to avoid a breach of the peace.

A rhinoceros was next let loose in the open court-yard, and the attendants attempted to induce him to pick a quarrel with a tiger who was chained to a ring. The rhinoceros appeared, however, to consider a fettered foe as quite beneath his enmity; and having once approached the tiger, and quietly surveyed him, as he writhed and growled, expecting the attack, turned suddenly round and trotted awkwardly off to the yard gate, where he capsized a palankeen which was carrying away a lady fatigued with the sight of these unfeminine sports.

A buffalo and a tiger were the next combatants: they attacked furiously, the tiger springing at the first onset on the other's head, and tearing his neck severely; but he was quickly dismounted, and thrown with such violence as nearly to break his back, and quite to disable him from renewing the combat.

A small elephant was next impelled to attack a leopard. The battle was short and decisive; the former falling on his knees, and thrusting his blunted tusks nearly through his antagonist.

On our return from the beast-fight, a breakfast awaited us at the royal palace; and the white table-cloth being removed, quails, trained for the purpose, were placed upon the green cloth and fought most gamely, after the manner of the English cockpit. This is an amusement much in fashion among the natives of rank, and they bet large sums on their birds, as they lounge luxuriously round, smoking their hookahs.

Elephant-fights were announced as the concluding scene of this day of strife. The spectators took their seats in a long veranda. The narrow stream of the river Goomty runs close under the palace walls, and on the opposite bank a large, open, sandy space presented a convenient theatre for the operations of these gigantic athletes. The elephants educated for the arena are large, powerful males, wrought up to a state of fury by constant feeding with exciting spices. On the spacious plain before us we counted several of these animals parading singly and sulkily to and fro, their mahouts seated on their backs, which were covered with a strong network for the driver to cling by in the conflict. In attendance upon every elephant were two or three men, armed with long spears, a weapon of which this animal has the greatest dread.

We soon discovered two of the combatants slowly advancing towards each other from opposite sides of the plain. As they approached, their speed gradually increased, and they at length met with a grand shock, entwining their trunks, and pushing, until one, finding himself overmatched, fairly turned tail, and received his adversary's charge in the rear. This was so violent, that the mahout of the flying elephant was dislodged from his seat: he fortunately fell wide of the pursuer, and escaped with a few bruises.

Five or six couple were fought, but showed little sport; the sagacious animals instantly discovering when they were over-matched. I had long been ambitious of witnessing the far-famed wild-beast fights of Lucknow, and having enjoyed an opportunity of seeing them, which few have had, it would hardly be fair to say that I was disappointed.

Before the party left the palace his Majesty took a great fancy to a hookah belonging to one of the staff. It was formed on an entirely new principle, and the king was so smitten with the novel invention, that he signified his royal wish to purchase it, and immediately carried it off, to display its charms to the 350 fair inmates of his zenana.

In the evening a Piedmontese conjuror, in the pay of the nawaub, entertained us much by his ingenious tricks. He must be a useful fellow to amuse the vacant mind of an Eastern despot.

Dec. 16th.—Early in the morning I galloped with the Commander-in-Chief to see a country residence of his Majesty, about five miles from Lucknow. It is a pretty place with fine gardens, but in bad repair. The Commandant of the Royal Body-guard, a fine, stout, handsome fellow (quite the Murat, le beau Sabreur, of Lucknow), accompanied us. He was splendidly dressed and mounted, conversed freely and gaily with us; told us his pay was 12,000 rupees, or as many hundred pounds, a-year, badly paid; boasted of his influence at court, and even hinted at his bonnes fortunes.

In the evening the Head-quarters party left Lucknow, the premier escorting the Commander-in-Chief to the gate of the city. We rejoined our camp, which was pitched about five miles from the town, after having passed six days, replete with amusement and novelty, at the metropolis of Oude.

The king very civilly sent two chetahs, or hunting leopards, to travel onwards with the Commander-in-Chief. We may expect some sport with them, as the country through which we are about to march abounds with antelopes.

On the 20th we encamped near Naubutgunge, on the banks of the Ganges, 54 miles from Lucknow, and a frontier village of the Oude dominions. In the night the thievish subjects of Oude, who had accompanied the camp on a pillaging speculation, made every effort to obtain some keepsake from us before we crossed the frontier; but having been warned of their propensities, every one was on the watch. In spite of sentries and servants, however, one of our party found his trunk broken open in the morning, and some of the contents abstracted. I was within an ace of spearing my faithful old serdar-bearer (head valet, or groom of the chambers!), whom I at first mistook for a robber, as he was groping about my tent in the dark.

Dec. 21st.—Therm. 68, a reduction of 12 degrees in heat since yesterday. Early in the morning the camp crossed the Ganges, and, once more entering the territories of the Honourable Company, was pitched near the hamlet of Nannemow. The difference of the two governments is strikingly manifested in the contrast presented by the rich cultivation of our side the river, and the barren waste on the bank we have just quitted. Our quartermaster-general could scarcely find an untilled spot whereon to pitch the camp.

Having heard that there were partridges in the jungle hard by, Colonel F. and I walked out with our guns in the afternoon. Whilst beating a very thick grass covert, I met with an accident which, though it proved only ridiculous, bordered very near upon the serious. I had flushed a partridge, and was just taking aim, when the ground under me suddenly gave way, and I felt myself rapidly descending into the bowels of the earth. I had scarcely time to speculate upon a 60-feet fall, and a watery grave, ere I arrived at the bottom of the dry old well (which it proved to be) on my feet, unhurt, and with my gun in my hand, full cocked. I first looked around my narrow prisonhouse, to ascertain that it had no four-footed occupant likely to resent my unceremonious intrusion; and having emancipated my feet from about 8 inches of mud, I hailed my servants, who soon discovered my situation, and, by the help of their cummerbunds, or waist-clothes, extricated me from my somewhat premature inhumation. The well was, fortunately, only 10 feet deep, but I found another, soon after, equally well concealed, which was at the least four times that depth.

On the 23rd we reached Merun-ke-Serai, near the ancient city of Kanoge, which is three days' march from Futtyghur, the next station of troops. The Nawaub Moontezim ood Doulah, commonly called Hakim Mendes, arrived in camp to accompany the Commander-in-Chief on his march to the latter place. The hakim is ex-minister of Oude. He is a handsome old man, of exceeding courtly address, and has retired from the troubles of government to a luxurious exile in the Company's territories. In the evening we wandered over the vast ruins of Kanoge. This ancient city, supposed to be the Calinapaxa of Pliny, is said, by Ferishta, to have been the capital of India in the time of the father of Porus, who was conquered by Alexander the Great. To give some idea of its grandeur and extent in the sixth century, it is described to have had 30,000 shops for the sale of betel-nut, or paun, and 60,000 bands of musicians paying tax to government.

We were pestered by sellers of coins, who pretended to have dug them out of the ruins, but who had probably manufactured them for the occasion. One old fellow, to induce me to purchase, showed me some certificates of character which he had obtained from English travellers, but which, being written in English, he could not read himself. Almost the first which he put into my hand ran thus: "The bearer is a d—d old rascal; kick him out of camp."

On Christmas-day Head-quarters camp halted, the roads being too wet for the march of the camels. These animals are exceedingly awkward on slippery ground, and are liable to dreadful accidents from their feet sliding apart laterally. The rain has fallen in such quantities for the last two days, that the camp is converted into one great swamp.

Dec. 27th.—Therm. 58°. Arrived at Futtyghur. Breakfasted with the Hakim Mendes. His house is magnificently furnished in the European style, with a profusion of pier-glasses, mirrors, French organs, and fancy clocks, of the most costly description: with these, in the accustomed bad taste of natives, he has mixed a host of wretched coloured prints in splendid frames.

The next day the Commander-in-Chief reviewed the third local horse, an irregular corps, dressed in the Mussulman costume. The superior officers are English. The men are fine, wild, picturesque fellows.

29th.—Head-quarters proceeded on the march towards Agra, a city about 112 miles from Futtyghur.

On the last day of the year 1827 we marched to the village of Boingong. Just before we reached our ground the shutersuwars (camel-couriers), who always moved on our flanks in search of game, reported a herd of antelopes about half a mile out of the line of march; and the chetahs being at hand, we went in pursuit of them. The mode of conducting this sport I may as well describe. The leopards are each accommodated with a flat-topped cart, without sides, drawn by two bullocks, and each animal has two attendants. They are loosely bound by a collar and rope to the back of the vehicle, and are also held by the keeper by a strap round the loins. A leathern hood covers their eyes. The antelopes being excessively timid and wild, the best way to enjoy the sport is to sit on the cart alongside the driver; for the vehicle being built like the hackeries of the peasants, to the sight of which the deer are accustomed, it is not difficult, by skilful management, to approach within 200 yards of the game. On this occasion we had three chetahs in the field, and we proceeded towards the spot where the herd had been seen, in a line, with an interval of about 100 yards between each cart. On emerging from a cotton-field we came in sight of four antelopes, and my driver contrived to get within 100 yards of them ere they took alarm. The chetah was quickly unhooded, and loosed from his bonds; and, as soon as he viewed the deer, dropped quietly off the cart, on the *opposite* side to that on which they stood, and approached them at a slow, crouching canter, masking himself by every bush and inequality of ground which lay in his way. As soon, however, as they began to show alarm, he quickened his pace, and was in the midst of the herd in a few bounds.

He singled out a doe, and ran it close for about 200 yards, when he reached it with a blow of his paw, rolled it over, and in an instant was sucking the life-blood from its throat.

A second chetah was slipped at the same time, but after making four or five desperate bounds, by which he nearly reached his prey, suddenly gave up the pursuit, and came growling sulkily back to his cart.

As soon as the deer is pulled down, a keeper runs up, hoods the chetah, cuts the victim's throat, and, receiving some of the blood in a wooden ladle, thrusts it under the leopard's nose. The antelope is then dragged away, and

Chetah on Hackery

London Pub^d by John Murray

Death of the [illegible] London [illegible]

placed in a receptacle under the hackery,* whilst the chetah is rewarded with a leg for his pains.

The hunting leopard is a long, slight, flat-sided animal, with a very neat, small head; and, unlike the rest of the feline species, its tail is flat instead of round. In the first plate I have endeavoured to represent the sporting party manœuvring to *gain the wind* of the game: the death of the antelope is portrayed in the second.

CHAPTER II.

Tomb of Etameid Doulah — The Tâj-Mahal — Infatuation of a Fakir — Fort of Agra — Secundra — Futtypore Sicree — Acbar's audience-chamber — Faithfull's Redoubt — Interview with the Rajah — Bhurtpore — Indian dramatic exhibition — Antelope-snaring — Muttra — George Thomas — Allyghur — Belaspore — A day's sporting — Putpergunge — Delhi: the Jumna Musjed — Musjed of Rushin al Doulat — Visit to the Mogul — The Dewanee Khas — Interview with the Great Mogul — Visit to Rajah Kullian Sing — The Hindoo and the Mussulman — Bulwant Sing — The Nautch — Koutub Minar — Tomb of Humaion — Breakfast among tombs — Koutub Sahib — Mirza-Selim — Gigantic observatory — Native horses — Extraordinary leap — Shumshah Deene — Alfina — Paniput — Kurnal — Shamlee — Sirdhana — Meerut — Daranugger — News of a tiger — Sketch of Sancho — Tiger-hunting.

JAN. 1st, 1828, therm. 68°. The reveillé drubbed open my eyes to the first daybreak of the new year. This is the second new year's day I have passed under canvas. The first was ushered in by a salvo of 16 24-pounders, just put in battery against Bhurtpore, and fired, well shotted, at the usurper's filigree palace.

This evening, as morris-dancers, mistletoe, and other Christmas concomitants, were not attainable, we were obliged to be contented with mince-pies and a nautch at Mynporee, at which place our camp was pitched. It is a ruinous and miserable town, surrounded with a dilapidated (a *bull*, I fear) mud wall.

* Indian cart.

Two days after I overtook on the march a poor woman weeping bitterly, and found, on inquiry, that her infant child had been carried off by a wolf in the night, as she lay asleep on the outskirts of the camp. Judging it fruitless to attempt to "patch grief with proverbs" in so lamentable a case, I applied the panacean balm of a rupee, which at least gave a momentary alleviation to her anguish.

On the 7th, between Ferozabad and Etameinpore, I had some capital sport, shooting the bird called the rock-pigeon. They are found in immense flocks, and more resemble the grouse than any other English bird. They are very scarce, and extremely wild.

On the 8th of January we marched into Agra, formerly the favourite residence of the Great Mogul; even in these days a fine city, situated on the Jumna river.

Before we crossed the river by the bridge of boats we visited the beautiful garden called the Râm Baug, and the magnificent tomb of Etameid Doulah, the vizier of Emperor Jehangire, and father of the famous Empress Nourjehan, who built the tomb. It is a spacious vaulted edifice of white marble, beautifully inlaid with divers-coloured stones; and, though upwards of 200 years old, is in fine preservation, even the gilding in the interior of the dome being still bright.

In the evening we visited the far-famed Tâj, a mausoleum erected by the great emperor Shah Jehan over the remains of his favourite and beautiful wife, Arjemund Banu, or, as she was surnamed, Muntâza Zemâni (the most exalted of the age). No description can convey an idea of the beauty and elegance of this monument of uxorious fondness. It is, I think, the only object in India that I had heard previously eulogised, in which I was not disappointed on actual inspection. Nothing can exceed the beauty and truth to nature of the borders of leaves and flowers inlaid in the white marble: the colours have all the delicacy of nuance, and more of brilliancy than could be given by the finest painting. Cornelian, jasper, lapis-lazuli, and a host of the agate tribe, present a fine variety of tints for the flowers, and the leaves are for the most part formed of bloodstone. So minute is the anatomy of the patterns, that a rose, about the size of a shilling, contains in its mosaic no less than 60 pieces. In many places the more valuable pebbles have been fraudulently extracted—an act of sacrilegious brigandage imputed to the Jauts, who had possession of Agra for some time, and carried off to their capital, Bhurtpore, many of the extravagant bequests left by Shah Jehan to his favourite city. Amongst other plunder, they bore away, Samson-like, the brazen gates of the citadel, of immense value, which are supposed to be still buried in Bhurtpore, as we failed to discover them on our warlike visit to that fortress in 1826.

The dome of the Tâj is about 250 feet high, and is, as well as the four minarets at the angles of the terrace, entirely built of the most snowy marble. It was a work of 20 years and 14 days, and cost the Shah the sum of 750,000*l*., although it is said the King compelled his conquered foes to send marble and stone to the spot unpaid for. Had Shah Jehan lived long enough, he intended to erect a similar sepulchre for himself on the opposite bank of the river, and to connect the two buildings by a bridge. Thus, supposing the bridge to have cost three lacs of rupees, the expense of returning this worthy couple to their primitive dust would have amounted to the round sum of 1,500,000*l*.

They show a small marble recess, in which the rhyming portion of the visitors of the Tâj record their extempore effusions in praise of the elegance of the building, the gallantry of the builder, and the beauty of its fair tenant; whilst others simply inform the world that they have visited this celebrated mausoleum by scrawling at full length an uncouth name and date on its marble walls and pillars—a characteristic practice of English travellers. Amid the vast preponderance of trash there scribbled, there are, however, some lines of a superior order. I will subjoin four couplets, which I recollect, perhaps imperfectly:—

Oh! thou—whose great imperial mind could raise
This splendid trophy to a woman's praise!
If love or grief inspired the bold design,
No mortal's joy or sorrow equals thine.—
Sleep on secure—this monument shall stand
When Desolation's wings sweep o'er the land,
By death again in one wide ruin hurl'd,
The last triumphant wonder of the world!

On our return to camp I found there a fine specimen of those holy mendicants called fakirs; although, by the bye, I apply the epithet of mendicant undeservedly to him (as I also do most probably the term *holy*), as he would not take from me the money I offered. He was a pitiable object, although he had a handsome and—in spite of his downcast eyes—rather a roguish countenance. One arm was raised aloft, and, having been in that position for 12 years, the power of lowering it was lost: it was withered to one-fourth of the size of its fellow, and the nails were nearly two inches long. He was about to undertake a further penance of standing on one leg for 12 more years; after which he had some thoughts of measuring his length to Cape Comorin! Poor misguided enthusiast!

"In hope to merit heaven by making earth a hell."

In the afternoon the Commander-in-Chief reviewed the artillery cantoned here, and the whole Head-quarters party were hospitably entertained in the evening by Mr. Sanders, the Honourable Company's collector of revenue, who has a pretty place near Agra.

The next day, after a review and a levee, we started on a visit to the fort of Agra. It is built of a reddish stone brought from Futtypore Sicree, 22 miles from hence. Its lofty embrasured walls, handsome gateway, and a ditch 40 feet deep, present a formidable appearance, though, in fact, they would not stand long before heavy artillery. It was built by the great Acbar, grandfather of Shah Jehan, and called by him Acbarabad. The Motee Musjed, or Pearl Mosque, situated in the centre of the fort, is, indeed, quite a jewel of chaste and tasteful architecture and sculpture. Before we quitted the fort we were led into a small chamber, scarcely 12 feet square, in which Shah Jehan, imprisoned by his rebel son Aurungzebe, lingered through 7 years of confinement, and died. He was buried in the Tâj, by the side of his beloved Sultana.

The next day we galloped over to Secundra, the burial-place of Acbar, about five miles from Agra. The gateway is very grand, though it is falling fast to decay. The white marble tomb itself, on the summit of the interior edifice, displays perhaps the finest specimen of sculpture in India.

Jan. 10*th.* *Agra.*—Review of five regiments of infantry in brigade. It was impossible to avoid remarking the superiority of the Sepoy over the European corps in steadiness and regularity of movement; a declaration on my part which will doubtless surprise some of my martinet friends at home. It must, however, be remembered that an Englishman in India is—unless actuated by some strong excitement which, defying the climate, calls forth his native energies—only half himself: whilst the Sepoy, naturally alert, attentive, and intelligent, has no such disadvantages to contend with. This morning was the coldest I have yet experienced in India, the thermometer descending to 36°. After the review we spurred on 10 miles to the camp, which had moved from Agra; and the next day we encamped under the walls of Futtypore Sicree, on our way to Bhurtpore. This town is a picturesque old place, surrounded by a ruinous turreted wall embracing an extent of five miles; of which, however, the present habitable part of the town occupies not a tenth part. These lofty fortifications appear to have been necessary in isolated towns to protect the inhabitants from the sudden and frequent predatory incursions of Mahrattas, Pindarees, Mawattees, and other military vagabonds, who lived by ravaging their neighbours.

On entering the outer gateway we proceeded for nearly

half a mile through what appeared to have once been a spacious street of fine buildings, but which now presented nothing more than two rows of confused ruins. Below the citadel gate we dismounted, and, after ascending a most disheartening flight of steps, found ourselves under the most lofty gateway in India. By the promise of a beautiful prospect we were induced to surmount this also; and after climbing six stories, our labours were rewarded by a most extensive view, embracing Agra and the Tâj on one side, and Bhurtpore on the other.

We next visited the great mosque, built by Acbar, A.D. 1570. This monarch had a great regard for Futtypore Sicree; his long-cherished ambition of having children being here gratified by the birth of two sons. In the quadrangle of the mosque stands a beautiful marble tomb, raised to the memory of a holy saint, of great learning and sanctity, and the friend and Mentor of the above-named Sultan. By some scandalous annalists he has been considered the real father of Acbar's reputed sons. Be that as it may, he died in the odour of sanctity, and his mausoleum is as pure and chaste as the whitest of marble and the most delicate sculpture can make it.

The audience-chamber of Acbar was the next *lion*, and a curiously-contrived and most uncomfortable-looking invention it is. The room, which is not above 20 feet square, is of stone, with a gallery of the same material running round it, from which four narrow bridges, without railings (not unlike that over which all Mussulmans are to skate—albeit unused to the practice—into Paradise), communicate with a kind of pulpit in the centre, where the Great Mogul was wont to squat within earshot of his surrounding courtiers.

Jan. 13th.—The camp marched 8 miles, and was pitched just on the skirt of the (by us) well-known and often traversed jungle which surrounds Bhurtpore.

In the evening rode with his Excellency to the old redoubt, nicknamed by us "Faithfull's," from its commander. This building, at the time of the siege of Bhurtpore, was fortified by us, constituted one of the chain of posts investing the fortress, and was garrisoned by Colonel F., with 2 companies of sepoys.

We found the old fakir still in possession of the little mud stronghold. During the siege, this man, being suspected of correspondence with the enemy, was sent by the Colonel to Head-quarters. The holy man objected to walk, and demanded a palankeen, which, as well as a horse, was refused. On his still persisting in his unwillingness to march, Colonel F. sent for a baggage-camel, and, strapping his reverence across its back, trotted him four miles into camp, in spite of his then earnest entreaties to be allowed the comparative luxury of walking.

Returned to camp by a short cut through the forest, of which every tree and pool of water recalled to my memory some incident or accident of the siege.

The next morning, a meeting having been agreed upon between the young Rajah of Bhurtpore (the same whom we had the honour of restoring to his musnud, or rather *guddee*) and the Commander-in-Chief, our whole party assembled on elephants, and the rencontre took place near the above-named redoubt. The Rajah entered his Excellency's houdah, and the cavalcade proceeded through the forest by the road formed by our abattis between the posts of investment. The young King's escort was better accoutred and mounted than any native troops we had yet seen, and his suwarree cut altogether a much more showy figure than might have been expected only two years after Bhurtpore had been released from our prize-agents' clutches.

On our arrival at the tents of the British Resident, Major Lockett, with whom our party breakfasted, the Rajah took leave, in order to prepare for the reception of the Commander-in-Chief, who returned his Majesty's visit in the afternoon. There was fine food for recollections on our road to the fort: almost every mound, tree, or ruined tomb, had its incident; and in passing through the town I fancied now and then that I recognised faces that I had seen during our former visit there. The town we found somewhat improved; but here and there a delicate dimple in the façade of some large building betrayed the handiwork of our 18-pounders, and an unroofed house confessed the desolating visit of a 13-inch shell. The inhabitants, who certainly had as much cause to hate as to love us, thronged the streets at our approach, and greeted us with the greatest civility. Indeed there was almost cordiality in their usual vociferated salutation of "Râm râm." Those of our party who had not been at the siege were much struck by the fine stature and martial appearance of the men. In truth their persons and habits differ most distinctly from those of the delicately-formed, languid, and apathetic Bengalee; and nothing can be more becoming than their padded green frock and trouser, red cummerbund, and rakishly-put-on scarlet turban.

The ditch of the citadel looked as formidable as ever, and is still full of water; but the stupendous cavaliers and bastions, both of the citadel and town, are wofully shaken and crumbled by the mines which our government judged expedient to apply to these monuments of human industry.

The young Rajah gave a dinner in the evening to the Commander-in-Chief, and entertained us with nautches and mimics. This latter amusement, which appears to be the only approach to dramatic exhibition among the Indians, is, generally speaking, a tissue of noisy, vulgar ribaldry; but it is sometimes amusing, even to Europeans. I remember one occasion on which the Begum Sumroo entertained our party with a similar patomime, when we were much diverted. It was just after the capture of Bhurtpore. The dramatis personæ of the scene enacted were an English prize-agent, and a poor peasant of Bhurtpore. The former wore an immense cocked-hat and sword, the latter was stark naked, with the exception of a most scanty dootee, or waistcloth. The prize-agent stops him, and demands his jewels and money. The half-starved wretch protests his poverty, and appeals to his own miserable appearance as the proof. The Englishman, upon this, makes him a furious speech, well garnished with G—d d—ns, seizes on the trembling Bhurtporean, and, determined not to leave him without having extracted something from him, takes out a pair of scissors, cuts off his long shaggy hair close to his skull, crams it into his pocket, and exit, swearing.

The next day we had a very bad day's shooting in the royal rumnah, or preserve, during which we witnessed an ingenious method of snaring the antelope. A strong buck is trained to fight, and, being furnished with a series of thong-nooses on his horns and neck, is loosed whenever a herd is in sight. Whilst the hunters lie hid, the trained antelope approaches the herd: the most chivalrous buck of the party comes out to meet the intruder on the sanctity of his harem: they fight, and the stranger, having entangled his horns, is soon secured by the chasseurs.

In the evening we took out some hawks in boats on the jheel, or lake, which supplies the town and fort-ditch with water, and killed with them a great quantity of water-fowl.

Jan. 11th.—Marched through Bhurtpore, 13 miles, to the village of Russoulpore. On this spot, two years ago, the army halted the day preceding its arrival before the fortress, our advanced parties having driven out of the village a picquet of the enemy's horse. The next day we reached Muttra, and Head-quarters occupied the same encamping ground that it covered in 1826.

Muttra is a considerable military station, and a place of great sanctity among the Hindoos. The next morning the Commander-in-Chief reviewed the brigade of three regiments of infantry, two regiments of cavalry, and some artillery. This day being the anniversary of the capture of Bhurtpore, his Excellency gave a dinner to all those of the station who were present on the occasion, about 35 persons. The party was conducted with much spirit, and the slain were thrice slain with great effect towards the *small* hours.

A very interesting beggar besought charity at the door of my tent the following day. He said he had been a sepoy in the service of the famous George Thomas, and had been cut up by the cavalry of Scindia, the Mahratta chief. They certainly had used their swords upon the poor fellow to some purpose. His left hand was cut off at the wrist, and two joints of all the fingers of the other: at the back of his head there was a deep fissure, from the crown to the ear; and a profound trench across his cheek confessed the temper of the blade, and of the cavalier who inflicted it. He had also two shots through the legs, but was nevertheless, *at least*, as well as could be expected. He had a healthy countenance and stout limbs. The history of his former master, George Thomas, presents a fine example of the eventful and chequered life of an ambitious, daring, but low-born man. As far as I can collect, he came out to India before the mast, in those times so advantageous to a bold adventurer, when every petty province was racked by both external wars and civil commotions; served several native chiefs, and eventually set up for himself. He made himself master of the province of Hurriana, Hissar being his capital, and was finally crushed by Perron, the French general of the Mahratta. His strength and dexterity were so great, that it is said he could strike off a bullock's head with one blow of his sword.

Jan. 21st.—Started on our route towards Delhi, which is about ten marches from Muttra.

23rd.—Encamped at Allyghur, a small military station. Visited the fort, which is undergoing repairs in the European style of fortification. It is a small place, but of great strength, as was sufficiently attested by the loss sustained by Lord Lake in its storm and capture in 1803. It was then in possession of the Mahrattas, and defended by the French General Perron. This adventurous people had at that time, assisted by the discipline and countenance of France, seized Delhi, and several strong places on our frontiers. The only vulnerable point of Allyghur, surrounded as it was by a ditch as wide and deep as a second-rate river in England, was the causeway of the gate. Perron's advice to cut it through being neglected by the garrison, it was carried, after considerable loss on our part, by a coup-de-main, the governor taken, and 200 men killed.

On one of the faces of the work the ditch is so wide, that a bevy of wild ducks, swimming in the middle, were out of shot from either scarp or counter-scarp.

After four days' marching, during which we had excellent partridge, hare, and wild-fowl shooting, we reached on the 29th Belaspore, the jaghire of Colonel Skinner, the commander of that distinguished corps of irregular cavalry styled "Skinner's Horse."

His house is handsome and spacious; and in the centre of a flourishing garden (to such an extent does he carry his ideas of luxury) the comfortable old soldier has erected to himself an elegant and snug-looking mausoleum. It will be well for him if he has made equally provident arrangements for the good of his soul, as he has for the comfort of his body, both before and after death. Visited his indigo factory, and the little fort erected by himself for the protection of his property. He can mount some 20 guns on its bastions. The hospitable owner, not content with entertaining the Commander-in-Chief's party with dinner and native amusements, gave a grand feast to all the camp, servants and followers included.

The next day four of us, having sent on our elephants and guns to the covert-side, galloped to a famous sporting jungle about 8 miles from Belaspore. We shot all day; but our bag was inconsiderable, for, being unaccustomed to fire from the backs of elephants (which to a tyro is very difficult), we scarcely killed one in 10 shots. Ten brace of black partridges, 4 brace of hares, and 1 boar, was the extent of our sport. The boar was a very fine one, but he was unhappily much disfigured by the discipline he underwent from my elephant. He was wounded mortally, but, the other elephants being afraid of him, mine was urged to approach, rushed towards him, and, standing over the furious beast, commenced a violent shuffling motion, which almost dislocated me from my seat. On looking over the side of the houdah I saw the poor boar flying to and fro in mid air between the fore and hind legs of my elephant, who, after keeping him thus "in chancery" (as they would term this process in the ring) for about half a minute, gave the coup-de-grace by a coup-de-pied in the ribs. This I afterwards found to be a common practice of elephants. Mahouts have often some difficulty in preventing them from performing the same gibleting operation on even small game.

After the chasse we mounted our horses, and galloped across country 17 miles to the camp, which had continued its march.

31*st*,—a frost,—therm. 6 A.M. 29°! Camp moved to the neighbourhood of Putpergunge, 3 miles from Delhi. On this spot, hallowed by the blood of many of our countrymen, was fought, 25 years ago, the battle of Delhi. Lord Lake, after the capture of Allyghur, marched here, and, with an army of 4500 men, overthrew the forces of Scindia under the French General Perron, amounting to 13,000 infantry and 6000 horse. Sixty-eight pieces of cannon were taken from the enemy. After this victory the British general entered the city, from the towers of which his achievements had been witnessed, and restored the unfortunate and sight-bereaved Shah Alaum to the throne of his ancestors. The battles of Delhi and Laswaree by General Lake, and those of Assaye and Argaum by Sir Arthur Wellesley, put an end to the Mahratta war, and annihilated French power in India.

This evening Mirza Selim, youngest son of the Emperor of Delhi, came forth from the city to greet the approach of the Commander-in-Chief. He is a stout young man, with a handsome and dignified countenance, worthy of his great progenitors.

Feb. 1*st*.—The camp crossed the Jumna, and was pitched near the Cashmere gate of Delhi.

Breakfasted and dined with Sir Edward Colebrooke, the British Resident. His palace is an extensive building, with a fine garden: the latter, through which we passed in our palankeens in the evening, was brilliantly illuminated by coloured lamps suspended amongst the trees.

The next day we passed in lionizing Delhi. The Jumna Musjed, or chief mosque, though in delicacy of finish it falls short of the Motee Musjed of Agra, exceeds it greatly in the grandeur of its proportions. The great quadrangle, as we passed through it, was crowded with the prostrate forms of hundreds of the faithful at their devotions. This stupendous pile was built by the great Emperor Aurungzebe; and at its shrine that royal hypocrite, dressed in the rags of a self-denying fakir, offered up public prayers for the success of his armies, employed in persecuting and murdering his three unfortunate brothers and their families, after he had imprisoned his aged father Shah Jehan at Agra.

In the course of our rambles through the city a small mosque* was pointed out to us as the spot where the famous Persian conqueror of Hindostan, Nadir Shah, sat after he had taken Delhi, A.D. 1739; and from whence, irritated by a shot being fired at him from a neighbouring house, he gave the signal, by drawing his scimitar, for a general massacre of the inhabitants, in which upwards of 100,000 persons were cut off. The plunder of the city (which has no doubt often excited the envy of subsequent besiegers and conquerors in India) has been estimated at about 80 millions of our money; very tolerable forage for one campaign! The throne of the Mogul Emperors, of solid gold and jewels, was alone worth 12 millions. Nadir's successor, Abdalla, paid Delhi a visit, equally destructive to the Mogul, though not so productive to himself, about 20 years later. Nearly 100,000 inhabitants were again sacrificed, and the city was burnt to the ground.

Feb. 3*rd*, 8 A.M.—The Commander-in-Chief, accompanied by the Resident and the staff, proceeded to pay a state visit to the Great Mogul. Mirza Selim conducted us to the

* The Musjed of Rushin al Doulat.

palace, which is within the walls of the fort. On entering the precincts of the royal abode we filed through sundry narrow and dirty alleys, until we arrived at an arched gate, too low to admit our elephants. We were therefore obliged to dismount and proceed on foot. Lord Combermere, however, balked the evident intention of the prince to make him walk, by getting into his palankeen. We shortly arrived at the archway leading into the quadrangle, in which the Dewânee Khâs, or hall of audience, is situated, where the Commander-in-Chief was required to dismiss his palankeen.

On passing the Lal Purdah, or great red curtain which veils the entrance, the whole of our party, English and native, made a low salaam, in honour of the august majesty of which we were as yet not in sight. This optical fact, however, was no doubt attributed by the Mogul courtiers that attended us, not to the mere distance of space between the spot where we stood and the audience-chamber, but to the dazzling effect produced upon our eyes by the intense rays emanating from the throne of the "king of kings"—the sun of their worship! The obeisance duly effected, we advanced, not directly across the court to the edifice containing the throne, but by a respectful, circuitous, oblique, *crab-like* evolution.

At the entrance of the corridor leading to the presence the Resident and his assistants were required to take off shoes and hats; but according to previous agreement Lord Combermere and his suite retained both boots and hats during the whole ceremony.

The Dewânee Khâs is a beautiful open edifice, supported on white marble columns, the whole elegantly inlaid and gilt. The roof is said to have been vaulted with silver in the more prosperous days of the Delhi empire, but it was spoiled by those common devastators of India, the Mahrattas. Around the cornice still remains the (now, at least) inapplicable inscription, "If there be a Paradise upon earth, it is this, it is this." The throne, occupying the centre of the building, is raised about 3 feet from the floor, and shaded by a canopy of gold tissue and seed-pearl. There are no steps to the front of the throne, the entrance being in the rear. Seated cross-legged upon it, and supported by surrounding cushions, we found the present representative of the Great Mogul. He is a fine-looking old man, his countenance dignified, and his white beard descending upon his breast. On his right hand stood his youngest and favourite son, Selim, and on the left the heir-apparent, a mean-looking personage, and shabbily attired in comparison with his younger brother; although endowed, it is said, with superior talents and acquirements. It was impossible to contemplate without feelings of respect, mingled with compassion, the descendant of Baber, Acbar, Shah Jehan, and Aurungzebe, reduced, as he is now, to the mere shadow of a monarch; especially when one reflected that, had it not been for European intrigues and interference, this man, instead of being the dependent pensioner of a handful of merchants, might perhaps still, like his ancestors, have been wielding the sceptre of the richest and most extensive dominions in the world. Whilst employed in these cogitations, a provoking wag whispered in my ear, "Do you trace any resemblance to the Mogul on the cover of a pack of cards?" and I with great difficulty *hemmed* away a violent burst of laughter in the presence of "the Asylum of the Universe."

The old monarch, mindful of his dignity, scarcely deigned to notice, even by a look, the Commander-in-Chief as he approached to present his "nuzzar" of 50 gold mohurs.* He did not even condescend to raise his eyes towards the rest of the party, as we advanced one by one, salaamed, and offered our three gold mohurs. His air, however, was not haughty, but he affected a sleepy, dignified indifference, as he scraped the money from our hands, and handed it to his treasurer. The staff presented likewise a nuzzar of two gold mohurs to the heir-apparent.

On receiving Lord Combermere's offering, the King placed

* A gold mohur is worth 16 rupees. The rupee was always estimated at half-a-crown when I *received* it, and at two shillings when I *paid* it!

a turban, similar to his own, upon his head, and his lordship was conducted, retiring with his face sedulously turned towards the throne, to an outer apartment, to be invested with a khillât, or dress of honour. In about 5 minutes he returned to the presence, attired in a spangled muslin robe and tunic; salaamed, and presented another nuzzar. The staff were then led across the quadrangle by the "grooms of the robes" to the "green room," where a quarter of an hour was sufficiently disagreeably employed by us in arraying ourselves, with the aid of the grooms, in silver muslin robes, and sirpeaches or fillets, of the same material, tastily bound round our cocked-hats. Never did I behold a group so ludicrous as we presented when our toilette was accomplished; we wanted nothing but a "Jack i' the Green" to qualify us for a May-day exhibition of the most exaggerated order. In my gravest moments the recollection of this scene provokes an irresistible fit of laughter. As soon as we had been decked out in this satisfactory guise, we were marched back again through the Lâl Purdah and crowds of spectators, and re-conducted to the Dewânee Khâs, where we again separately approached his Majesty to receive from him a tiara of gold and false stones, which he placed with his own hands on our hats. As we got not even "the estimation of a hair" without paying for it, we again presented a gold mohur each. The Honourable Company, of course, "paid for all," and our gold mohurs were handed to us by the Resident. It was a fine pay-day for the impoverished old Sultan, whose "pay and allowances" are only 12 lacs of rupees, or 120,000*l.*, a-year. His ancestor the Emperor Acbar's revenue was somewhat better; including presents, and estates of officers of the crown falling in, it amounted to about 52 millions sterling.

As we retired from the presence, the heralds, with stentorian voices, proclaimed the titles of honour which had been conferred by the Emperor on his Excellency the Commander-in-Chief. Among other high-sounding appendages to his name, he received the following:—Ghezeffer al Douleh, or Champion of the State; Sipeh Salah, Commander-in-Chief; Saif al Moolook, Sword of the Empire; Khan Jehan, Lord of the World; Khan Behâder; and Rustum Jung, which latter might be translated the Hercules of Battles. In addition to these titular honours, his lordship was presented with a palankeen of state, and the nowbut, or royal kettle-drum, which, if I mistake not, infers the power of life and death. The audience being concluded, we retired, still practising the chassée en arrière, and all gave the Great Mogul a parting salaam ere we passed the Lâl Purdah. The ceremony, though interesting and novel, was irksome and fatiguing. But it is hard to grudge the poor old fallen king this little meed of mockery, or to deny to the descendant of Tamurlane the shadow,* whilst we possess the substance, of monarchy in India. Reduced, however, as he is in power and importance, I doubt whether the present insignificance of the Mogul be not preferable to the dangerous pre-eminence of some of his more puissant predecessors, who, surrounded by rebellious kinsmen and traitorous courtiers, seem only to have been raised to the utmost pinnacle of human grandeur, in order that their fall might be more sudden and overwhelming. In this very palace, scarcely 40 years ago, were the most inhuman cruelties that barbarity could inflict, or human nature suffer, perpetrated upon the imperial possessor by his Rohilla conqueror, Goolaum Kaudir Khan. The unfortunate Shah Alum, the father of the present king, Acbar Shah, was deprived of his eyes; and the last objects his sight closed upon were his children and relations massacred and starving to death around him. These retributive barbarities were visited by the Rohilla on the ill-starred Sultan for the share he had taken in the unprovoked invasion of Rohilcund by the combined forces of Oude, Delhi, and the Company. It was by this unwarrantable league that the interests of Oude and the English became blended. The latter, as usual, got the lion's share of the booty in the ac-

* The white-bearded old man who 30 years ago sat on the Musnud of Delhi is no other than the Mogul of 1857—the adopted chief of the mutineer sepoys.—1857.

quisition of the rich province of Rohilcund, which was formally ceded to the Company by Asof ul Doula, Nawaub of Lucknow, in 1801.

In the afternoon I accompanied the Commander-in-Chief to return the visit of a Hindoo potentate, Rajah Kullian Sing of Krishenghur. At the door of his house, in one of the main streets of Delhi, he came out to meet and embrace his distinguished visitor, and then conducted us up a dark narrow stair to his reception-room. His abode and its equipments certainly gave no very grand idea of his riches or good management: nevertheless, he contrived to get up a nautch for our entertainment.

Kullian Sing is the handsomest Indian I have seen. His complexion is remarkably fair, his eyes almost too large and soft for a man, and his features of the most perfect regularity—an epithet that cannot be applied to his mode of life, which has been one of the most extravagant debauchery. By his wildness he has drawn bills upon his constitution which ought not to have been payable until the age of 70. He is now 30, and well-nigh in second childhood. He seemed to derive an almost infantine amusement from the different medals and ornaments of Lord Combermere's dress, and betrayed the greatest admiration of, and cupidity for, his gold watch, which he did not scruple to ask for.

In these visits of ceremony the distinguishing characteristics of the two great sects are plainly furnished forth. The Hindoo, however high in rank, is commonly fawning and obsequious in manner, and his eyes wander round the durbar circle with a kind of half-frightened curiosity; whilst the Mussulman, whose motto (whatever his inclination may be) is "Nil admirari," sits in quiet, calm, and dignified self-possession.

Just as we were rising to take leave of the Rajah, a purdah behind the throne became gently agitated; and through its tattered lattice-work, pervious by age, I detected the brilliant eyes of some of the terrestrial houries of his zenana, who could not resist the temptation of a parting peep at the strangers. We were happily not long exposed to the "galling and destructive fire" (as the despatches have it) of this masked battery of eyes; but made our retreat—nearly as perilous a one as that of the "ten thousand"—down the dark, crazy, narrow, labyrinthine staircase, into the street; and started on our elephants to pay another visit.

Bulwant Sing, a handsome young *gaillard* of 20, cousin to the boy-Rajah of Bhurtpore, received the Commander-in-Chief in his tents; and the visit was, as usual, enlivened by nautching and music. One fellow played upon a very novel instrument, composed of a graduated series of common English earthenware *slop-basins*, which he struck with 2 plectra of bamboo—a primitive, yet not unharmonious attempt at musical glasses.

One of the nautch-girls, Alfina by name, like Calypso among her maidens, greatly excelled her fellows in stature, beauty, and grace.

I have so often had occasion to mention this purely Indian amusement, the nautch, that, though perhaps rather a hackneyed subject, I will describe it.

Each set of dancing-girls is usually furnished with an old crone of a woman, who takes care of their finery, their interests (and their *morals*, perhaps); and a band of 2 or 3 musicians, generally consisting of a kind of violin, a species of mongrel guitar, and a tom-tom, or small drum, played with the fingers: sometimes a little pair of cymbals are added. The musicians also join occasionally their voices with those of the women—which are dreadfully shrill and ear-piercing—in this "concord of sweet sounds." At the close of each stanza of the song the girl floats forward towards the audience by a sort of "sidling, bridling," and, I may add, "ogling" approach, moving her arms gently round her head, the drapery of which they are constantly and gracefully employed in arranging and displacing; now mercifully concealing with the tissue veil *one* brilliant or languid eye (as the case may be)—sometimes effecting a total eclipse; or allowing the whole head to be seen, in order to display the *Sevigné* of pearl on her forehead (for this elegant ornament, now dignified by a place upon the fairer fronts of my countrywomen, is strictly oriental), the massive and numerous earrings which disfigure the feature they are intended to adorn, or the heathenish and unaccountable *nosering*, the use of which (for it is certainly no ornament) it is hard to discern—unless these dangerous sirens are furnished with them, like pigs, to keep them out of mischief!

The lithe, snake-like suppleness of their arms, excites, at first, great surprise in the European spectator; but not more so, I suspect, than the horizontal evolutions of the nether limbs of our opera nautch-women would astonish the weak mind of a suddenly imported Mussulman.

On entering the room the dancing-girls and their followers salaam respectfully to the company, and then, amid a confused jingling of bracelets and anklets, and an all-pervading odour of attar, squat quietly down in a semicircle, until called upon to display.

For the applauding "Wa! wa! Ka khoob!" ("Brava! Beautiful!") of the spectator, they return a smile and a low salaam. Natives of rank sometimes give more solid proofs of their approbation, by ordering the two hands of the charmer to be filled with gold or silver coins.

The dress of the Indian dancing-girl is infinitely more decent than that of our French or Italian figurantes, the long silken trousers descending quite over the feet. The upper portion of the costume, however, I am bound to say, is not always quite so impervious to sight as a boddice of more opaque texture than muslin might render it.

European ladies not unfrequently attend these spectacles; and, when the dancers are warned beforehand, they only witness a graceful and sufficiently stupid display; but, if thrown off their guard by applause, there is some danger of their carrying the suppleness of the body and limbs quite beyond the disgraceful, and even bordering on the disgusting. The situation of a gentleman in this case is irksome and uncomfortable; and he sits in constant and not unfounded dread lest these fair libérales in morality should commit some, perhaps unintentional, solecism against decency.

Delhi, Feb. 4th.—Started early in the morning to see the famous monument called Koutub Minar, supposed to have been erected in the 13th century. The distance is about 12 miles from the city, and the roads leading to it are all good and highly interesting, running close to several curious tombs, and other ruins well worth visiting. The column of Koutub is supposed to be the highest in the world. It would ere this have fallen into complete ruin, had not the Honourable Company (with the same praiseworthy respect for valuable Indian antiquities which they have evinced in their expensive repairs of the Tâj) taken this beautiful and wonderful piece of architecture under their protection, and restored the flight of about 300 steps which leads to the summit.

From the top the eye of the traveller embraces on all sides one sea of stupendous ruins, the Jumna gliding like a huge silver serpent through the midst. The mausoleums of Humaion and Sufter Jung appear almost the only perfect edifices among the general wreck of ancient Delhi. A little farther back in the landscape tower the stupendous walls and bastions of the old Patan fortress; and in the distance the eye, fatigued with the map-like extent of melancholy ruins, is relieved by the white and gilded mosques and minarets of the more modern city—called by its builder Shahjehanabad,—and the refreshing verdure of the forests surrounding it.

On the road to the Koutub I visited the tomb of Humaion, an Emperor of Delhi, whose burial-place is as magnificent as his life was unfortunate. He was the father of the great Acbar. This building was in after times used as a general receptacle for the murdered princes of the Imperial family.

I also paid a flying visit to the ashes of Sufter Jung, enshrined in a very handsome and picturesque mausoleum of red stone and marble. This worthy rose from the rank of a common suwar to be Nawaub Vizier of Lucknow, under Ahmet Shah of Delhi. The rage for splendid burial-places seems to be general among Mussulmans. No doubt many a prince has hoarded immense sums to be expended upon a receptacle for his bones, for which he has been obliged to stint himself, or, what is worse, to pillage his vassals for his expenses during his lifetime.

As Englishmen seldom venture in search of the picturesque without a provident eye to the wallet, our breakfast had been sent on before to the Koutub; and after earning an appetite by our antiquarian rambles, we went in search of it. The means of sustaining life we found in the resting-place of the dead: no tent being brought, the careful servants had spread a table in a spacious vaulted tomb, near the Minar, the last home of some old Bluebeard, whose name I could not discover, and whose remains occupied a small oblong sarcophagus in the centre of the vast chamber. Mr. Trevilyan, the assistant to the Resident, having sent forward some nautch-people, they came in after breakfast; and the prima donna, Alfina, who unites in her own person the rôles of a Pasta and a Taglioni, sang, in the style of an improvvisatrice, some extempore stanzas in honour of Lord Combermere, whose exploits before Bhurtpore, she said, had won her heart.

I could not help thinking how astonished the old occupant of the grave would be, if he could have raised his head from the pillow where it had rested long before India was subjected to Europeans, and seen on one side of him a long row of white faces drinking tea and smoking hookahs, and on the other a band of dancing-girls screaming and attitudinizing over his mouldering remains.

From the terrace surrounding our tomb we had a commanding view of the stupendous Minar. Were the Parisians to engraft their Colonne de Vendôme like the joint of a telescope upon our monument of London, the combined building would fall short, I should imagine, of this gigantic production of man's industry! The repairing of the Koutub must have been rather a ticklish undertaking; as the engineer, Captain Smith, who accomplished this good work, was obliged to remove some of the enormous stones near the foundation.

There is an archway of a gate close under the column which, I am convinced, for the grandeur of proportions and minuteness of finish has not its equal in the world. Though it is 60 feet high, the ornaments are carved with the delicacy of seal-engraving, and the edge is perfectly sharp, in spite of the monsoons of centuries.

A pillar of metal some 20 feet high, and covered with Greek-like and now unintelligible characters, stands in the centre of a quadrangle, and bears the mark of a shot fired at it by some wanton invading chief, who also applied fire to its base, in the vain hope of overthrowing it.

I could almost fancy myself among the (but for the associations, scarcely more interesting) ruins of Rome, which are more within the sphere of the roving English tourist than those of Delhi: for at this moment I see several groups of my countrymen and women wandering among the prostrate columns; and at a little distance a large tent with well-furnished table,—and (as I live!) 3 or 4 English gallants playing at "hop, step, and jump," before the door.

According to Dow, the historian, ancient Delhi was founded by Delu, Emperor of Hindostan, 400 years before Christ. Why did *he* select, and why did his successors *not* desert, so rocky and barren a site for the metropolis of India?

After passing a morning full of interest at Koutub Sahib, I rode home alone, 12 miles, over a plain studded with remains of gone-by grandeur. How many centuries of chequered prosperity and desolation have passed over this spot, so replete with historical recollections! At one moment my imagination painted the splendour and magnificence of Delhi in the glorious reigns of Baber, Acbar, and Aurungzebe; at another, the picture was reversed, and Delhi, plundered and deluged in blood by Tartar, Afghan, and Mogul invaders, racked by civil wars, and reduced to purchase peace of a Mahratta banditti, recurred to my memory.

In the evening Mirza Selim gave a dinner to Lord Combermere at the residence, and at the expense of the Resident. The prince presided, but did not eat. After dinner his Highness expressed a wish to see the Englishwomen dance; but as there was some delay in getting up a quadrille (the intricate evolutions of which, I think, would have puzzled him), he fancied the ladies were shy of performing before him, and therefore retired early to his palace. I thought his ideas of public propriety seemed a little shocked by the ladies and men sitting together on the sofas, and walking about arm-in-arm.

Delhi, Feb. 5th.—Rode with Mr. Trevilyan, who is an excellent cicerone, to see some interesting ruins in the neighbourhood. The first place we reached was the gigantic astronomical observatory, supposed to be a work of the Hindoo Rajah, Jey Sing, in the 17th century. There is a dial in very good repair, the gnomon of which is 60 feet high, of solid stone masonry. These enormous instruments appear as though they had been manufactured by the Titans, in order to take a reconnaissance of the heavens before they commenced their siege of Olympus!

We rode by the ancient fortress of Delhi,—the lofty walls and gateways of which have crumbled but little beneath the weight of 700 years,—and proceeded, after sundry mishaps from the fighting propensities of our horses, to the great tank, by plunging into which some fellows, bred to the profession, gain a precarious livelihood. By the bye, these Indian horses are great *anti-tête-à-têtists*: whilst their riders are unsuspectingly engaged in conversation, they get their noses together, and suddenly warn you of their misunderstanding, by a loud squeel and a most ill-timed rear; and if one cavalier vacate his seat, the loose horse renders the situation of the still mounted man scarcely less enviable than that of his sprawling companion, by attacking him most viciously. Arabs are generally better tempered; but the native Indian horses from Kutch, Kattiawah, and the Lacka jungles, are proverbially savage. In the cavalry regiments there are always some noted "haram zadehs," or mauvais sujets, that "show fight" the moment a fellow charger comes within 20 yards of them; and instances are known of these vicious brutes (in humble emulation of Diomed's carnivorous mares) worrying their riders with their teeth, after having thrown them. When in the ranks, however, they are, like pugnacious characters in human society, tamed by education, discipline, and custom into better behaviour.

But to our "jumper." The tank above mentioned is surrounded on all sides by ancient buildings of picturesque architecture, and various heights, from 20 to 60 feet above the surface of the water, which is deep and dark, and, as the sun can only reach it during 2 or 3 hours in the day, at this season extremely cold. Entering at an arched gateway, we were conducted to the top of a flight of steps leading down to the water's edge. As soon as we had stationed ourselves there, a figure, flauntingly attired in pink muslin, presented itself at the angle of a house opposite, about 30 feet high; and, on my holding up a rupee, immediately sprung from the roof, foot foremost, and plunged into the cold tank. Several other men and one little boy jumped from the same height, the latter cutting through the water with as little disturbance to its surface, and the same sharp, sudden sound, as a penny causes when dropped edgeways into a cistern. Though I have at Eton often dared the plunge of "Lion's Leap," "Bargeman's Bridge," and "Deadman's Hole," the last leap I saw here quite took away my breath. The performer paused some time before he committed himself to the air, but he could not withstand the appeal of a rupee. He sprung from the dome of a mosque, over a lower building and a tree growing out of the masonry, down 60 or 70 feet, into the dark abyss. The water closed over his head, and had resumed the smoothness of its surface ere he reappeared. He swam to the ghaut, however, without apparent distress.*

This evening the Commander-in-Chief, the Resident, and

* A view of this ancient Bowlee is to be found in the first volume of Daniell's 'Oriental Scenery.'

the whole Head-quarters party, including ladies, dined with the young Nawaub Shumshah Deene, son and successor to the jaghire of the late Nawaub Ahmet Bux, who, for his services to the Company, was rewarded with a territory of 5 lacs of rupees (50,000*l.*) a year. The young noble, who is, I believe, yet in his teens, has a tall and graceful figure, set off in the true Delhi dandyism by the tightly-girded shawl-cummerbund, which, while it compresses the waist, gives expansion to the chest and shoulders. Like the rest of the Mussulman exquisites, he wore the long, heavy curl behind the ear, sweeping gracefully from under the turban, the front part of the head being shaved close. He has a handsome aristocratic countenance, and his fair complexion bespeaks the pureness of his northern blood.

During the repast no less than six sets of nautch-women were singing *at once*, all different airs, and all vying with each other in the shrillness of their screams and the extravagance of their gestures. These, with the assistance of their accompaniment of tom-toms, vinahs, &c., made a "tintamarre" that would have awakened the Seven Sleepers. Signora Alfina was of the party, and her triumph was complete when her compeers were ordered to sit down, and herself permitted to sing a solo and dance a pas seul. Shrill as she was (as the "pipe singing i' the nose"), her single voice was more endurable than the full cry of the whole pack. Shumshah Deene's three younger brothers were present by desire of Lord Combermere, who brought about a reconciliation amongst them, they being at issue regarding the partition of their father's moneyed property. The youngest, about 7 years old, is a beautiful boy, and nearly as fair as an English child.

The next day his Excellency reviewed the Delhi brigade of 3 regiments of infantry. After the review we mounted fresh horses, and rode to the camp, which we found at Alleepore, 12 miles from the city. Kurnâl is the next military station we are bound to. The Rajah of Bullumghur, and Ibrahim Beg, the younger brother of Nawaub Shumshah Deene, pitched their tents near the Head-quarters camp, for the purpose of accompanying Lord C. on the march.

Feb. 10*th*.—Marched to, and encamped near, the town of Paniput, famous as the scene of numerous battles, the most important of which were the great action between Baber, the Mogul invader (afterwards Emperor), and Ibrahim II. of Delhi, in which the latter was slain, with from 20,000 to 50,000 Patâns; and the grand fight between Shah Abdalla, the Afghan, and the Mahrattas, who were beat with great slaughter. The plain on which they fought is extremely fertile, being, no doubt, enriched by the bones of the slain.

In the evening I rode round the walls of the town, which are lofty, but ruinous. A high cavalier in the centre commands a most extensive view: indeed, in clear weather, the Himalaya mountains are distinctly visible from it.

The next day we encamped near a fine old Serai, with a handsome gateway, built, as recorded in a Persian inscription over the arch, by one Khan Feroze, in the reign of Shah Jehan.

Feb. 12*th*; therm., 12 o'clock, 66°.—Arrived at Kurnâl. At this station there are 2 regiments of native cavalry, 2 corps of native infantry, and some artillery. Near this place was fought the great battle between Nadir the Persian and the Emperor Mahommed Shah of Delhi, when the Emperor was defeated, and the invader advanced and took his capital.

We saw here some very pretty practice by the artillery, with round-shot, grape, shells, and shrapnells. A mine, containing 500 pounds of powder, was prepared under a miniature bastion, and exploded with very good effect by the shells. The same evening we crossed the Jumna.

Feb. 17*th*.—Camp pitched at Shamlee. The town is of considerable extent, and there is a paltry little fortress, in which formerly, as I was told, three companies of Sepoys stood a week's siege by 50,000 Mahrattas. The determined little garrison was luckily relieved by the approach of Lord Lake's army, just as their provisions were exhausted.

Feb. 19*th*, therm. 78°.—Incipient symptoms of the hot season. Marched to Sirdhana, the residence of the Begum Sumroo, who has a jaghire of 10 or 12 lacs a-year, with a reversion to the Honourable Company. On the road we visited the Catholic chapel (for the old lady professes that creed) which she is building. It is a tiny imitation of St. Peter's at Rome. The altar is, however, much handsomer than anything of the kind in Europe, being of white marble, inlaid with divers-coloured pebbles, after the pattern of the Tâj. The superstitious old princess is likely never to visit the spot where she has spent so much money, on account of a prophecy which went to say that she would die there. Lord C. and the staff dined with the Begum, and at 11 o'clock we retired to our tents, our ears tingling with the noise of singing-girls and mimics.

Feb. 20*th*.—Arrived at Meerut, the largest, most healthy, and gayest station in this part of India. The Commander-in-Chief tarried here 8 days, during which time every species of hospitality and attention was lavished upon our party. But it is useless to cite any individual spot in our dominions as distinguished for hospitality; this virtue is common to all our countrymen in India; and it is fortunate that it is so in a country where, in 1000 miles, there is not one house of public entertainment. Travellers and strangers are always received by the residents with open doors, if not with open arms; and under the numerous roof-trees where, in my various rambles through India, I have eaten the salt of hospitality, I have never been able to detect anything less kind than a hearty welcome.

We had a beautiful review of the Meerut brigade, consisting of 2 regiments of cavalry, 4 of infantry, and about 30 guns. Meerut is named very early in the history of India, as being a fortress of great strength. It was taken by Timour the Mogul Tartar, in A.D. 1399.

Feb. 28*th*.—Resumed our march; and, on the 1st March, encamped near the ghaut of Daranugger, on the banks of the Ganges. The whole country round about is thickly covered with grass jungle, and it was difficult to find a clear spot of ground of sufficient extent for our camp.

The 1*st of March* will always be a "dies notanda" in my sporting annals, as the day on which I first witnessed the noble sport of tiger-shooting. The Nimrods of our party had, ever since we entered upon the Dooab,* been zealously employed in preparing fire-arms and casting bullets, in anticipation of a chase among the favourite haunts of wild beasts, the banks of the Jumna and Ganges.

Some of the more experienced sportsmen, as soon as they saw the nature of the jungle in which we were encamped, presaged that there were tigers in the neighbourhood. Accordingly, whilst we were at breakfast, the servant informed us that there were some *gongwalas*, or villagers, in waiting, who had some *khubber* (news about tigers) to give us. We all jumped up and rushed out, and found a group of 5 or 6 half-naked fellows, headed by a stout young man, with a good sword by his side, and "bearded like" 15 "pards," who announced himself as a jemadar. As usual in like cases, all the natives began to speak at once, in a Velluti-like tone, and with vehement gesticulations. The young jemadar, however, soon silenced them with a "Chup, teeree!" &c., and then gave us to understand that a young buffalo had been carried off the day before, about a mile from the spot, and that their herds had long suffered from the depredations of a party of 3 tigers, who had been often seen by the cowherds.

At 4 P.M. (so late an hour that few of us expected any sport) Lord Combermere and nine others of our party mounted elephants, and, taking 20 pad-elephants to beat the covert, and carry the guides and the game, proceeded towards the swamp pointed out as the lurking-place of the buffalo-devouring monsters.

Sancho, the jemadar-hurkarah † of the Quartermaster-General's department, insisted upon leading the cavalcade, mounted on his pony. This strange old character—who

* Tract of country between the Ganges and Jumna.

† Chief courier.

obtained his nom-de-guerre from the strong similitude he bears to his illustrious prototype, both in the short, round, bandy proportions of his person, and the quaint shrewdness of his remarks—served under Lord Lake in the Mahratta war, and has ever since distinguished himself as the most active and intelligent of the intelligence department. Almost the last act of Lord Combermere, before he left India, was to obtain for the faithful Sancho a snug Barataria, in the shape of a little jaghire, a possession which had long been the object of his ambition. This noted individual now spurred on before our party, mounted on his piebald palfrey (or *belfry*, as his namesake would have called it), with his right arm bared, and his scimitar flourishing in the air.

The jungle was in no places very high, there being but few trees, and a fine thick covert of grass and rushes. Everything was favourable for the sport. Few of us, however, expecting to find a tiger, another man and myself dismounted from our elephants to get a shot at a florikan, a bird of the bustard tribe, which we killed. It afterwards proved that there were 2 tigers within 100 paces of the spot where we were walking.

We beat for half an hour steadily in line, and I was just beginning to yawn in despair, when my elephant suddenly raised his trunk and trumpeted several times, which, my mahout informed me, was a sure sign that there was a tiger somewhere "between the wind and our nobility." The formidable line of 30 elephants, therefore, brought up their left shoulders, and beat slowly on to windward.

We had gone about 300 yards in this direction, and had entered a swampy part of the jungle, when suddenly the long-wished-for tally-ho! saluted our ears, and a shot from Captain M—— confirmed the sporting *Eureeka!* The tiger answered the shot with a loud roar, and boldly charged the line of elephants. Then occurred the most ridiculous, but most provoking scene possible. Every elephant, except Lord Combermere's (which was a known stanch one), turned tail and went off at score, in spite of all the blows and imprecations heartily bestowed upon them by the Mahouts. One, less expeditious in his retreat than the others, was overtaken by the tiger, and severely torn in the hind leg; whilst another, even more alarmed than the rest, we could distinguish flying over the plain, till he quite sunk below the horizon; and, for all proof to the contrary, he may be going to this very moment!

The tiger in the mean while advanced to attack his Lordship's elephant, but, being wounded in the loins by Captain M.'s shot, failed in his spring, and shrunk back among the rushes. My elephant was one of the first of the runaways to return to action; and when I ran up alongside Lord Combermere (whose heroic animal had stood like a rock) he was quite hors du combat, having fired all his broadside. I handed him a gun, and we poured a volley of four barrels upon the tiger, who, attempting again to charge, fell from weakness. Several shots more were expended upon him before he dropped dead; upon which we gave a good hearty "Whoo! whoop!" and stowed him upon a pad-elephant. As Lord Combermere had for some minutes alone sustained the attack of the tiger—a three-quarters grown male—the *spolia opima* were duly awarded him.

Having loaded and re-formed line, we again advanced, and after beating for half an hour I saw the grass gently moved about 100 yards in front of me; and soon after a large tiger reared his head and shoulders above the jungle, as if to reconnoitre us. I tally-ho'd! and the whole line rushed forward. On arriving at the spot two tigers broke covert and cantered quietly across an open space of ground. Several shots were fired, one of which slightly touched the largest of them, who immediately turned round, and, roaring furiously, and lashing his sides with his tail, came bounding towards us; but, apparently alarmed by the formidable front of elephants, he suddenly stopped short, and turned into the jungle again, followed by us at full speed. At this pace the action of an elephant is so extremely rough, that, though a volley of shots was fired, the tiger performed his attack and retreat without being again struck. Those who had the fastest elephants had now the best of the sport, and, when he turned to fight (which he soon did), only three of us were up. As soon as he faced about he attempted to spring on Captain M.'s elephant, but was stopped by a shot in the chest. Two or three more shots brought him to his knees, and the noble beast fell dead in a last attempt to charge. He was a full-grown male, and a very fine animal. Near the spot where we found him were discovered the well-picked remains of a buffalo.'

One of the sportsmen had, in the mean time, kept the smaller tiger in view, and we soon followed to the spot to which he had been marked. It was a thick marshy covert of broad flag-reeds, called Hogla, and we had beat through it twice, and were beginning to think of giving it up, as the light was waning, when Captain P.'s elephant, which was lagging in the rear, suddenly uttered a shrill scream, and came rushing out of the swamp with the tiger hanging by its teeth to the upper part of its tail! Captain P.'s situation was perplexing enough, his elephant making the most violent efforts to shake off his backbiting foe, and himself unable to use his gun for fear of shooting the unfortunate Coolie, who, frightened out of his wits, was standing behind the howdah, with his feet in the crupper, within six inches of the tiger's head.

We soon flew to his aid, and quickly shot the tiger, who, however, did not quit his gripe until he had received 8 balls; when he dropped off the poor elephant's mangled tail, quite dead. The elephant only survived 10 days, but it was shrewdly suspected that his more mortal wounds were inflicted by some of the sportsmen who were over-zealous to rid him of his troublesome hanger-on. Had the unlucky animal lived in those days "when use of speech was not confined merely to brutes of human kind," he would, no doubt, have exclaimed in his misery, "Heaven preserve me from my friends! I can defend myself from my enemies."

Thus, in about 2 hours, and within sight of camp, we found and slew 3 tigers, a piece of good fortune rarely to be

Tigers attack on the Elephants.

London, Pub.d by John Murray 1850

met with in these modern times, when the spread of cultivation, and the zeal of English sportsmen, have almost exterminated the breed of these animals.

During the hunt the jungle was on fire in several places, and, the wind being high, the flames at one time gained so fast upon us that the line was obliged to retreat. I saw here a confirmation of the fact, that in high grass jungles fires run to windward if there be a fresh breeze. This is easily accounted for: the wind bends the long silky dry grass over that which is already ignited, the flames catch the pendant tops, and thus, as long as there is material, the infection spreads.

When we returned to camp, and had deposited our game in the main street, hundreds of spectators arrived and assembled round us. The claws and whiskers of tigers being looked upon as efficient charms by the natives, some of these desiderata were quickly snatched away before we could prevent the depredation.

Four other sportsmen of our party returned to camp this evening, having been out for 4 days in a different direction. They only killed one tiger, but he was an immense beast, and was shot on the head of Colonel F.'s elephant, which he wounded severely. This is considered the acme of tiger shooting; so I know not how P.'s affair would rank in a comparative ratio!

CHAPTER III.

Nujeebabad — The Dhag-tree — Tiger-hunt — Asofghur — The Ganges — Hurdwar — A north-wester — Booreah — The Seikhs — Bussee — Indian pilgrims — Ruins of Sirhind — Rajah of Patialah — Arms of the Seikhs — Dancing-girls — Visit the Rajah — Seikh war-quoits — Loudiana — Runjeet Singh — Embassy from Runjeet Singh — The kite-dance — Retrograde march — Rajpoorah — Umballah — Mustaphabad — A family group — Booreah — Hurdwar fair — Bathing in the Ganges — Indian robber — Mode of bargaining — Native hunters.

March 2nd.—CROSSED the Ganges, and encamped near the village of Daranugger, in Rohilcund.

On the *5th* we reached Nujeebabad, and the camp was pitched in a beautiful amphitheatre of mango-groves, with a distant view of the Himalaya mountains. Here we got information from some shikkarees (native hunters), of two tigers having been seen in a forest about 6 miles distant in the direction of the hills. A party of 7 will start from our camp to-morrow morning to beat up their quarters.

March 6th.—Whilst the camp marched 13 miles to the hamlet of Asofghur, the 7 sportsmen above mentioned galloped off early in the morning to a tent which had been sent forward, with some provisions, to the spot in the jungle where it was judged convenient to begin the chase. After breakfast we mounted our elephants, and proceeded to the sporting-ground. The features of the country were widely different from those of the scene of our last day's sport. We found ourselves in a luxuriant forest abounding in a species of tree which I had not seen before, namely, the dhâg; bearing a fine wide dark-coloured leaf, and a beautiful tulip-shaped crimson flower. Occasionally we came upon extensive open savannahs of grass jungle or rushy swamps. Vast numbers of wild boars, hog-deer, and other smaller game, started up before us; but we had determined beforehand not to fire at anything until we found a tiger, as these animals, when disturbed by a distant shot, are in the habit of sneaking away, and escaping into the woods, whither it is impossible to follow them. After diligently toiling for some hours, and patiently abstaining from less noble game, I suddenly came directly upon a fine tiger, in an almost impenetrable thicket of bushes. I shot him in the back, at the distance of half a dozen paces, but it only served to make him run faster. On breaking covert he directed his course right through a drove of buffaloes, which stood still and gazed at him, whilst the herdsman quietly smoked his goorhee-goorhee, and sleepily pointed out the direction he had taken. He took refuge in a thick rush-swamp, and Captain Archer shot him after he had severely torn the trunk of his elephant.

Later in the day we found another very fine tiger, but,

although he was viewed several times, he made good his retreat, favoured by the thickness of the covert and the numerous trees which retarded the progress of the elephants. A hog-deer and a little wild pig fell to my gun. The former is a large and rather clumsy animal, with a bristly hide, and is supposed to constitute the chief food of the tiger.

During the day we several times approached within 12 miles of the lower range of mountains of Kumaon. Their bold and well-wooded heights, and the dim blue outline of the more distant Himalayas, were most refreshing to eyes that for so long a period had been accustomed to repose on the flat unvaried plains of Hindostan.

After the chase we had a long and fatiguing march to camp at Asofghur. In the evening the jungle was on fire so near the camp, that we were in some alarm lest it should communicate with the tents of the servants and horses.

The next morning, refreshed by "tired Nature's sweet restorer" from the fatigues of the preceding day, we *sprung* into our *howdahs* (as a novelist would say), and with 20 elephants repaired to the jungle. We had not far to go, for Asofghur, which must be the depôt royal of malaria and jungle fever, is hemmed in on all sides by forests intersected by spacious swampy plains covered with the rankest and most luxuriant grass and rushes. The appearance of the country and the very smell of the air were enough to give a fit of the ague to any one but a truly ardent sportsman. The active employment of the attention, and the constant excitement of the spirits, must act as great preservatives of the constitution of an English sportsman in India; for though I cannot myself boast of "a frame of adamant," I have been constantly on my elephant from "morn till dewy eve," in the hottest weather, and the most pestiferous jungles, and never felt my health affected by it. There can be no doubt, however, that the constitution is eventually broken up by constant exposure to the sun in tropical climates.

This day we were not fated to carry home a tiger; the jungle being so thick and spacious that we could never bring them to bay, though we ascertained beyond doubt that there were several of these animals on foot. Just at the borders of a deep bog we discovered the carcases of two oxen, which, from the liquid state of the blood, had evidently not been killed many hours. The impression of the tiger's claws on the haunches was deeply marked, and the gullets of both the animals were torn out. One of the bullocks was a very fine powerful animal, and the ground was ploughed up for many yards round the spot where the fatal struggle took place. The murderers had been most probably disturbed from their meal by the firing of our party, some of whom, unfortunately, could not resist the temptation held out by the hundreds of hog-deer, &c., which fled before our line. We carried home to the camp,—which we found on the right bank of the Ganges again at the village of Baugpore,—10 hog-deer, a brace of florikans, and about 20 brace of black partridge.

March 6th.—Head-quarters marched 14 miles through a beautiful and picturesque country, along the banks of the Ganges, to Hurdwar. Here the sacred river emancipates itself (or *her*self properly; although Thomson does make the goddess river "roll *his* sacred wave") from the intricate sinuosities of its native mountains, and, rushing through a narrow pass, hemmed in on one side by the abrupt termination of the Dehra Doon Hills, and on the other by the Chandi Pahar,* pours its worshipped stream upon the plains of Hindostan, fertilizing above 1000 miles of country ere it throws itself, by 100 mouths, into the Bay of Bengal.

Hurdwar is an inconsiderable town, and is chiefly noticeable as the scene of the great annual fair, at which thousands, nay, I believe millions, of all the northern nations meet together; the Hindoos to worship and bathe in the holy river, where it issues pure and uncontaminated from the mountains; and Persians, Tartars, Paharrees (moun-

* Silver mountain.

Scene near Hurdwar.

London. Pub^d by John Murray 1838

taineers), and Cashmerians, to drive their several trades in horses, camels, shawls, &c. This fair does not take place until next month.

We found the camp spread out in all its silver symmetry in a pretty crescent of woody hills, the lofty summits of which almost entirely shaded it from the morning sun. I enjoyed a delightful ramble over the hill in the evening, and a beautiful view from the summit. Numerous Hindoo muts * and tombs showed their white pinnacles above the rich mango-groves and bamboo-thickets; and farther down the river some fine buildings, the residences of opulent Hindoos, were ranged, with spacious gardens, along its banks.

The next day the camp halted at Hurdwar. The tents were dreadfully hot; but I passed the day, in quality of aide-de-camp in waiting, with the Commander-in-Chief, in a bungalow half way up the mountain, where we had the benefit of a refreshing breeze. The rest of the party having heard of a tiger went out; but returned disappointed, after having been nearly carried away in crossing the river.

March 10*th*.—The camp resumed its march towards Loudiana—the north-western frontier station of British India —and was pitched near a jungle-hamlet called Dowlutpore. In the morning the weather was dreadfully sultry and oppressive; not a breath of air moved a leaf of the smothering vegetation around us; the parched earth cracked with intense heat; and the animals hung their heads and panted in distress. Suddenly a dark cloud came rushing over the horizon from the north-west, the bamboos on the hills began to bend and creak before the coming storm, brilliant flashes of lightning cleft the black cloud in every direction, thunder rolled in almost interminable echoes among the mountains, the rain descended in torrents, and in an instant the thermometer fell from 88° to 68°.

Two days after, we arrived at Saharunpore, now a small civil station, but formerly a considerable military cantonment. A pretty Hindoo fortress, remodelled by our engi-

* Temples.

neers, and intended as a frontier stronghold, is apparently efficient, for its extent.

The Company has a botanical garden at this place, for rearing plants from the neighbouring mountains. I would have travelled 50 miles to gaze upon the first violet that I had seen for 3 years. The grounds are laid out in the English style; and as I wandered through the serpentine walks, bordered with many flowers and shrubs of English growth, I almost forgot that I was in India; an illusion, however, which was speedily dispelled by the apparition of my faithful elephant waiting for me at the gate.

On the 14th we crossed the Jumna, and the camp was pitched in a most luxuriant grove of huge mango-trees, near the town of Booreah. It is a small place, though the surrounding ruins give evidence of better days. The Ranee, or Queen-Suzeraine of this petty state, sent presents to the Commander-in-Chief, to greet his arrival in her territory. Among other objects, she offered an infant elephant, of about 15 months old. The little fellow was full of fun, and frisked about like a young kid; but he found few of the party inclined to join his game at romps, as, although he was not much higher than a table, his play was rather rough.

From Booreah we enjoyed a fine view of the snowy peaks of Himalaya; and we longed to be suddenly transported from these broiling plains to the cool regions which appeared so near us.

Two days after, we entered the territories of the Patialah Chief, a Rajah of the Seikh tribe, whose dominions extend over a wide tract of country between the Jumna and Sutledge rivers. He is the most powerful of this sect after Runjeet Singh of Lahore, who rules the Punjâb, a district between the Indus and the Sutledge. The Patialah Rajah holds his court at the modern town of the same name; Sirhind, the ancient capital of the province, having fallen to ruin. A political agent of the Honourable Company resides constantly at the seat of government.

The Seikhs owe their existence as a nation to the warlike

inculcations of their great leader, Goru Govind, who flourished about A.D. 1670, and who transformed them from a peaceable race to a martial tribe, by prompting them to take vengeance for the tyranny and cruelties exercised over them by the Mahommedans.

We found our camp pitched near Sidowra, a large village, well fortified with a brick wall and tall towers of the same material, pierced with three or four tiers of loopholes for musketry. The Zemindar of Sidowra managed to muster a little state to receive the Commander-in-Chief, and came to meet us a short distance from his walls. Both himself and his followers were large, stout men, tall, and of handsome and martial countenance garnished with most redundant beards—an ornament of first-rate importance among the Seikhs, to the total exclusion of the razor. The men were chiefly dressed in tunics of quilted cotton or silk, with a peculiar-shaped red turban, and cummerbund or sash of the same colour. Their legs were bare below the knee, and they were all armed with a spear or sword, and black shields of buffalo-hide studded with brass.

The neighbourhood of Sidowra is bleak and barren, and the country thinly dotted over with small fortified villages. It seems that the petty Seikh chiefs are but bad neighbours, and are constantly quarrelling among themselves. During these feuds it is not uncommon for one party to storm their adversary's village fortress, and force him to terms; the English Resident having the irksome and thankless office of mediator to perform between the conflicting chieftains.

At Bussee, where we arrived on the 19th, we visited the little fortress; it consists of a large square, with lofty towers at the angles, the whole beautifully built of a very small hard brick. The garrison consisted of some 20 or 30 remarkably fine men; few of them under 6 feet. Two or three of them were quite Achilleses of strength and beauty. We inspected every corner of their stronghold, and ascended one of the towers; and I thought our prying visit seemed to excite the jealousy of the inmates; for they kept aloof from our party, and eyed us with no very friendly glances. One fellow, who accompanied us to the top of the bastion, wore a peculiarly long sword, which one of us requested to see. The wearer, however, who appeared to be in no very complying humour, drew it half out, closing it again with violence, and stepped back, frowning and muttering sulkily. We, however, pressed our suit, assuring him of our pacific intentions, and he soon drew out the blade, which was as sharp as a razor, and would have served to deprive him of his huge black beard, which he deserved to lose for his uncourteous conduct.

To-day, and, indeed, every day since we left Saharunpore, the road was crowded with men, women, and children, proceeding eastward for the great fair at Hurdwar. Many of the women were remarkably handsome, and wore becoming dresses of red and blue gauze, sprigged with divers colours. The Hindoos carried vessels across their shoulders, intended to convey away some of the precious water of the holy Ganges; and these pilgrims, as they passed us, invariably uttered an exclamation which sounded like "Bom! bom! Mahadeo!"

Near our camp we found a numerous colony of fakirs established for the night, who were as frightful a set of objects as paint, ashes, dirt, and deformity could make them. As these religious devotees are more famed for sanctity and strictness of penance than for the more humble virtue of honesty, our sentries were warned to be particularly alert at night, lest these worthies should levy a tithe upon our goods and chattels during the dark hours.

March 22*nd*, therm. 91°, 2 P.M.—Encamped near the ruins of Sirhind, once a flourishing capital, now a confused mass of crumbling masonry. About 2 miles from Sirhind the Rajah of Patialah came out to meet Lord Combermere. The cavalry portion of his escort were very fine martial-looking troops, but his infantry, dressed in imitation of the Company's sepoys, were the most absurd-looking rabble possible. The commandant of the foot-guards wore a short red cloth jacket, red tight pantaloons, and Hessian boots;

he rode a prancing charger, and seemed to hold a very precarious tenure in his saddle; but whether he was naturally a bad horseman (all the Seikhs are good ones), or had taken his model from some of our infantry field-officers, it is hard to determine. A band of drums and fifes strutted in front of the cavalcade, playing the "grenadiers' march" in most excruciating discord; the big drummer wearing a glazed round hat, like a French postilion's, as a distinction.

The rajah came in the afternoon in grand state to our camp, to visit the Commander-in-Chief. He is a remarkably fine man, with high, noble features, a quiet, benevolent expression of countenance, and a long beard flowing over his breast: but it was not until he had dismounted from his elephant, and raised himself from the stooping posture he was obliged to assume on entering the door of the Durbar tent, that we remarked his amazing stature. He is at least 6 feet 4 inches, large boned, muscular, and erect; and, as he stepped forward to embrace Lord Combermere, it appeared that, with the slightest increase of energy in his hug, he might have crushed him to pieces. His person was totally unadorned by jewels (though his son and nephew, boys of twelve and eight, were covered with precious stones). A large circular shield of buffalo's hide, studded with gold, hung on his broad shoulders, and a long sword and dagger were stuck through his waist-shawl. Many of his warrior attendants, whose rank entitled them to sit at the Durbar, were nearly as tall as their chief, and all armed to the teeth.

The Seikhs have a great variety of weapons. I observed, among his escort, the musket, matchlock, sword, spears of sundry forms, dagger, and battle-axe: but the arm that is exclusively peculiar to this sect is the quoit: it is made of beautiful thin steel, sometimes inlaid with gold; in using it, the warrior twirls it swiftly round the forefinger, and launches it with such deadly aim, as, according to their own account, to be sure of their man at 80 paces.

In the evening I rode on my elephant over the extensive

ruins of the city. Its destruction has indeed been most complete; there is scarcely one stone left upon another. The situation of the present habitable part of the town is desolate and melancholy beyond conception, forming a little nucleus of peopled huts in the centre of miles of dreary ruins.

It is presumed by certain historical speculators, that the battle between Alexander the Great and Porus, the Indian chief, took place somewhere in the neighbourhood of Sirhind. The present Rajah of Patialah is no bad representative of the gigantic Porus, and, indeed, he is distinguished by that title among the English.

The Rajah sent a party of nautch-girls to entertain us after dinner. They were fine-looking women, but in dancing and singing fell far short of their more accomplished sisters of Delhi and Lucknow. One of them was beautifully dressed, having a border of gold lace, nearly half a foot deep, round her white muslin scarf and petticoat. She wore a quantity of gold bangles and necklaces, and five rows of earrings in her ears, which were quite bent down with the weight of pearls and gold.

Head-quarters camp halted the next day, and in the morning the Rajah sent a deputation to inquire after Lord Combermere's health, with an accompanying present of 40 trays of dried fruits, and 60 gurrahs (earthen vessels holding a gallon) of sugar-candy and sweetmeats. This latter delicacy, which the natives delight in, was divided among the numerous servants of the camp. It is a rude species of *toffy* (as we called it at school), made of sugar, flour, and ghee (clarified butter).

The Commander-in-Chief proceeded in the afternoon to return the Rajah of Patialah's visit. Porus received us at the shemianah, or canopied entrance of his tents; and, after the customary embrace, conducted Lord Combermere through two ante-tents to the grand audience pavilion. All were carpeted with rich crimson velvet, and chairs were placed in a semicircle, silver ones being set apart for the two chiefs. The customary dancing and singing went forward during the visit; but as the Seikhs never use tobacco or paun, the hookah and paundân of ceremony were not presented. These little auxiliaries are, in Indian courts, introduced at the heel of an audience, to much the same effect as the bow of dismission practised by European great men to wind up an interview.

One of the Rajah's nautch-girls was, though thin and worn from her wasting profession, extremely pretty; and her eyes, which were very fine, and managed with exceeding art, must have had frequent tutoring in the little mirror-ring always worn by these damsels on the thumb. Unlike the generality of native women, her teeth were remarkably white and regular. For this latter beauty the Seikhs are famous, and they owe it, most probably, to their disuse of tobacco and paun; the quick-lime, an ingredient of the last-named favourite stimulant of Mussulman and Hindoo, soon blackening and destroying the teeth. The first effect of the paun is to give a deep red dye to the mouth and lips, which becoming tincture is quickly succeeded by as deep a black. Its taste is by no means disagreeable, though it is a great provocative of thirst.

The gigantic Rajah was dressed as simply as before, except that the four bosses of his round black buckler were thickly studded with diamonds. The presents he laid before the Commander-in-Chief were strictly characteristic of the warlike sect to which he belongs: a complete suit of chain armour, with casque and gauntlets of steel inlaid with gold; a sword and shield, bow and arrows, spear, matchlock, and dagger.

Returning to camp I met a Suwar, who, in addition to his other weapons, wore half a dozen war-quoits; some round his arm, and others on the top-knot (peculiar to the Seikhs) of his turban. He readily complied with my request that he would show me the use of them; and dismounting from his horse, threw them one by one in the manner I have above described, in a horizontal direction, about half man's height from the ground. They flew with great force about 60 yards, but he did not appear to have a very accurate control over their direction; nor did I feel quite secure whilst he was whirling these razor-like playthings round the first joint of his forefinger.

Quoit-thrower.

March 24*th*, therm. 89°. Left Sirhind, and on the 26th reached Loudiana, which has been styled the "John o' Groat's House" of India. This town is situated on the western side of an ancient bed of the Sutledge river, which, having changed its course, now runs about 3 miles from the town. The Sutledge is supposed to be the Hyphasis of the ancients, on the banks of which Alexander the Great wept bitter tears because his mutinous army refused to advance into the rich provinces of India. At Loudiana, the Honourable Company have a frontier garrison, completely isolated by the surrounding territories of Patialah and Lahore. It forms a convenient vidette-post to watch the proceedings of Runjeet Singh, the ambitious chief of the latter province. The fort is of small extent, but tolerably strong. The town is considerable and flourishing, owing to the successful establishment of shawl manufactures. Though the immediate vicinity of Loudiana is sandy and sterile, the country at a short distance hence is noted for its fine crops of grain. At this moment (to mark the difference in town and country markets), gram (a vetch used in lieu of oats for horses in India) is selling here at 160 seer, or 320 lbs., for a rupee, whilst at Calcutta it varies from 15 to 30 seers to the rupee.

In the afternoon the Commander-in-Chief reviewed the

two regiments of infantry cantoned here, and dined with Captain Wade, the Company's Political Agent. A splendid nautch was got up after dinner. I counted 46 dancing-women assembled in the room at one moment.

The next day Lord Combermere received an embassy from Runjeet Singh of Lahore. The minister and several officers were presented, and were profuse in assurances of their master's esteem for his Excellency, but said not a word indicative of an invitation to his Court. The shrewd Chieftain is prudently jealous of English espionage; though he received without apparent distaste, a year or two ago, an English officer sent to his court by Lord Amherst.

The cavalry escort of the Lahorean Ambassador was well mounted and armed, and dressed in a handsome uniform of yellow and green silk. The officers, who were presented to Lord Combermere, were fine, independent, "swash-buckler," dare-devil looking fellows, of rude and uncourtly mien and manners, and coarse physiognomy.

Runjeet Singh, who is a great horse-fancier, sent, as presents to his Excellency, two fiery black chargers, richly caparisoned, and a handsome collection of the different national weapons.

Our evening entertainments consisted of a dinner, given by the officers of the station; and a nautch, after the speechifying usual on like occasions had been exhausted. Two very pretty sisters performed an exceedingly graceful dance, called the kite-dance. The air is slow and expressive, and the dancers imitate in their gestures the movements of a person flying a kite,—an amusement common in India. The attitudes incident to this performance are most favourable to Indian grace and suppleness, and the heavenward direction of the eyes displays these features—as doubtless my fair countrywomen know—to the very best advantage.

March 28th, therm. 87°.—The camp broke up from Loudiana; and we retraced our steps two or three marches, to Kunee-kee-Serai. Here the Head-quarters took a northerly direction, through the valley of Pinjore, to Simla, in the

Surmour mountains; where it is the intention of the Commander-in-Chief to pass the hot weather.

My friend Colonel Dawkins and myself, having obtained leave of absence, intend to return to Hurdwar, to be present at the great fair; and to march to Simla, through the beautiful valley of the Deyrah Doon,—situated to the northward of the first range of hills,—where we expect some tiger-shooting. We look forward to a very hot trip; but Hurdwar fair is not an every-day event.

March 30th, therm. 91°.—This morning my friend and self took leave of Head-quarters, and commenced our retrograde march. As our direction was nearly parallel with that of the Commander-in-Chief, we galloped across the country to dine with his Excellency in the afternoon, and returned by night to our little encampment, having taken leave of our friends, who hinted at fevers and cholera as the probable consequences of our trip to the fair.

Our equipment consists of 1 double-poled tent, 1 single-poled, and a routee or sleeping-tent, with a pâl for the servants, 10 in number; 5 horses, 4 ponies, camels for baggage, and 4 elephants to carry the tents, houdahs, and shooting equipage, and to beat for game in the jungles. We had a guard of sepoys, and a few men of "Skinner's Horse" pour battre la campagne.

Mar. 31st.—Reached Rajpoorah, and pitched our tents near the dwelling of an ancient fakir, outside the walls of the village. A large serai in the neighbourhood is employed by government as a prison, or depôt of convicts, who are sentenced to work on the roads.

Walked through the surrounding cotton-fields in the afternoon with my gun, not for sport, but bonâ fide for the table: I therefore never shot worse. Whilst returning home with a light bag and heavy heart, I fortunately killed a wild duck, which made a very good second course to our first tête-à-tête dinner.

The next day brought us to Umballa, a town of some consequence. We took up our day's residence, glad of the shelter of a good roof, at the Fort-house, the mansion of the

Political Agent at the Court of Patialah, Captain Murray (a brother of Lieutenant-General Sir G. Murray). The house, which is in fact nothing more than the citadel of the ancient little fortress, is situated in the centre of the enceinte, which is laid out in gardens, orangeries, &c., and forms a very comfortable abode, altogether shut out by lofty walls from the gaze of the vulgar.

After dinner the old greyheaded warder came in and said that his absent master had ordered him to give us a nautch; so we drank our claret and smoked our hookahs to the tune of 'Tâsa ba tâsa,' and other fashionable Eastern airs. The women seemed at least as much amused with us as we were with them, Umballa being seldom visited by Europeans, and the worthy Resident the only white inhabitant.

We left our horses here and some useless servants, together with the heavier parts of the baggage—the impedimenta of our establishment—taking on a buggy and 2 or 3 strong ponies, and reinforcing our escort with a serjeant and 12 of "Skinner's Horse," and 2 shuter-suwars, or camel-couriers. These will form a respectable guard, and a not unnecessary protection to our property at the fair.

Two days after, we reached Mustaphabad, a small town in the midst of rich cultivation, and defended by a good brick wall. Our little camp was pitched in a fine mango-grove, impervious to the scorching rays of the sun. The tope was in full bloom, and afforded us an umbrageous and odoriferous canopy.

On the march we overtook a string of at least 500 camels, laden with grain, and bound to the fair. We made half the march in the buggy, and were sorely jolted over the rough *track* which is dignified by the name of *road*.

Among the numerous and various parties journeying, with religious or mercantile intent, towards Hurdwar, I remarked a family group this morning both novel and interesting. It consisted of a fine, stout, broad-shouldered Seikh, his pretty wife, and 3 children, the eldest of which could not have been more than 3 years old. The woman carried the youngest in her arms, whilst the other two jogged cosily along in a couple of wicker baskets suspended to a bamboo borne on the father's shoulder.

Family of Seikhs.

In the cool of the afternoon we strolled out for an hour in the gram-fields and shot several brace of quails, which, at this season, are like little flying pats of butter! I have heard it averred that these feathered delicacies are sometimes so fat in the grain-season, that, when shot, they burst, from their own weight, as they fall on the parched ground.

This night was dreadfully hot, and our distress was aggravated by an unexpected invasion of our old Bengal persecutors, the musquitos, of whom we had for many months entirely lost sight.

April 4th.—Marched 15 miles, and encamped at Booreah, in the same beautiful mango-grove which the Head-quarters camp occupied on the 14th ultimo.

The country through which we passed is thickly covered with a low stunted myrtle-like plant, called corinda; and the atmosphere was loaded to headache pitch with the odour of its flowers, in appearance and scent much like jessamine.

In the evening, as soon as the sun had finished his day's sport of grilling and killing us poor Hyperboreans (therm. 2 o'cl. 97°), we sallied out to a marsh that I had discovered on our former visit to Booreah, in search of a *second course*; and in little more than an hour we bagged two couple of wild ducks and eight couple of snipes. The snipe-shooting in India, in some provinces, even eclipses that of Ireland, and the quantity and variety of wild fowl are such as would almost glut the sporting insatiability of Colonel Hawker.

The next day we passed under the roof of Dr. Royle, superintendent of the Botanical Garden at Seharunpore, and the day after we drove and rode a forced march of 20 miles to the village of Emly. Therm. in tent, sheltered by thick foliage, 96°.

The evening being too sultry for a walk, we rode on our ponies in search of game, and played terrible havoc with a covey of pea-fowl, which we stumbled upon in a ruined Bâgheecha, or fruit-garden.

April 8th.—Arrived at Hurdwar, after a march of 20 miles; and found our tents pitched in a straggling wood, bordering the road-side between that town and Kunkul. The opposite side of the road was occupied by a merry party of English ladies and gentlemen, whose several encampments were picturesquely disposed among the trees, wherever the two great requisites, space and shade, were to be found.

As soon as we had reached our tents, and given strict recommendations of vigilance to our guards, we mounted an elephant, and proceeded with Colonel Stevenson, an able cicerone, to see the humours of the fair. The horse-bazaar was the first object of our attention, and it seemed the best-stocked department of Hurdwar trade. There was a wide field for choice; from the tall, showy, fiery horse of Katiawah, Cutch, and the Lacka jungles, to the square-cut, sturdy, ambling ponies of Cabul and Cashmere, and the rough Shetland-like ghoonts of the mountains.

A committee from the Company's stud is always in attendance at the fair, to purchase troop horses and mares for breeding.

The moment we appeared in the horse-market, a score of the cattle-owners surrounded us. In the first ranks appeared the well-dressed, shawl-wrapped Persian or Arab, who, with earnest, yet deliberate and dignified solicitation, offered to conduct us to their stables, where we might have our choice of 20 horses of first-rate blood and undeniable pedigree. Behind them stood a wild rabble of inferior mongers, who, with eager countenances, closed hands, and noisy importunity, invited the Sahibs to inspect some anthropophagus of a northern horse, whom the owner libelled with the ill-deserved epithet of "Bhoot Gurreeb," "very quiet;" or some ill-favoured, ragged little ghoont, described as "Khoob-chelna-wala,"—*Anglicè*, "a devil to go." We accompanied the first-named worthies to their serai, but were rather disappointed in their "high-bred cattle." On our expressing a wish to see one of the Persian chargers out, the merchant made a sign to a little, wiry, debauched-looking groom, to loose the animal from the head and heel-ropes which secured him. This being done, a small sharp bridle was thrust into his mouth, the little Flibbertigibbet sprung upon his bare back, crammed his heels into his flanks, and started at once at full speed, pulling his steed up quite upon his haunches, with his nose within ten inches of a high wall; then turning sharp round, he came, at the same speed, and with the same sudden halt, to within a couple of feet of our party. We did not conclude any bargains, as we could not bring the merchants down to our prices, though they followed us some distance, gradually descending in their demands.

We next took our station in the main street of the bazaar, which was crowded to suffocation with buyers and sellers of cloths, fruits, grain, sweetmeats, toys, and gewgaws, of every description. Many of the little mat booths drove a busy and successful trade in a sort of double wicker basket, used by the pilgrims who resort to bathe in the holy river to carry earthen jars filled with the sacred water to their homes. The moment our elephant stopped he was wedged in on all sides by a dense assemblage; and never did my ears drink in such an astounding concatenation of noises. The neighing of horses, braying of mules, ringing of bells, growling of camels, the eternal tom-toms of the fakirs, together with the guitaring, thrumming, "and every other kind of strumming," carried on without a moment's intermission throughout the 24 hours, formed a discord of sounds which defies description.

As I looked over the roofs of the booths upon the town, the mountains beyond, the hundreds of temples, tombs, and ruins, the numerous and many-shaped little camps, the long array of elephants, camels, horses, &c., spread over the well-wooded plain, and the thousands of picturesquely-dressed people, I suddenly contrasted the scene before me with the last fairs I had witnessed, which happened to be those of Portsdown, and Donnybrook of head-breaking notoriety, both first-rate specimens of their respective countries. In fun and frolic our British fairs of course bear the bell; for the Hindoos only assemble at Hurdwar to pray, and the Moslems to traffic; besides, the Asiatics are not, like John and Pat, gregarious and uproarious in their amusements, but enjoy themselves selfishly and individually, each after his own fashion. As for knocking each other down, whether for "love" or anger, it is a strictly unoriental process; disputants rarely come to blows, contenting themselves with abusing each other's fathers, mothers, and relations, dead or alive. The only heads likely to be broken at Hurdwar are drum-heads, which must be "soft with blows" unintermittingly inflicted on them from sunrise to sunrise.

But in the picturesque properties of the scene, how greatly does this Indian assemblage transcend our own! Instead of red, rectangular buildings, square doors, square windows, formal lines of booths, and, what is worse than all, the dark, dingy dress of the figures—with perhaps the rare exception of two or three red cloaks and redder faces among the country lasses,—we have here domes, minarets, fanciful architecture, and a costume, above all, flaunting in colours, set off with weapons, and formed, from the easy flow of its drapery, to adorn beauty and disguise deformity. —As if on purpose to refute me, there are passing at this moment the most disgusting troop of fanatic fakirs, who, with neglected hair and beards, distorted limbs, long talon-like nails, and hideously smeared visages and bodies, look more like wild beasts than human beings. But even these are picturesque! Every hut, equipage, utensil, and beast of India is picturesque, as has been shown by that clever and spirited artist, Chinnery: Eastern manners, customs, attitudes, are picturesque: the language even, replete as it is with figure and metaphor, may be said to be picturesque.

Pursuing our route (with great difficulty, owing to the press) through the town, we soon reached a flight of a few steps leading down to the river. These our sure-footed monture descended in safety, and we entered the Ganges, which, being here very wide, and divided by an islet into two branches, was not above 4 feet deep.

Ascending the stream as far as the Great Ghaut,* and taking up our station directly opposite, we had a distinct view of the bathing ceremony. The Ghaut appeared to consist of about 60 steps, about 100 feet in width; and was closely crowded by hundreds of men, women, and children, some descending, others attempting to ascend in their dripping garments. The verandas of the buildings round about were filled with hideous fakirs, some of whom also occupied little bamboo platforms, erected in the middle of the Ganges. Many of them were stark naked, and one old fellow, perched upon his michaun, close to our elephant, came quite up to my idea of the Satyr of the ancients, in the goatishness of his physiognomy, and the hirsuteness of his limbs.

About 500, of all sexes and ages, promiscuously grouped,

* River Stairs.

were dipping at the same moment. The men, particularly the older ones, and the fakirs, were chiefly employed in praying whilst in the water; the women, on the contrary, were for the most part laughing and chattering, not having the fear of the goddess Gunga before their eyes; and, in the extacy of the moment, and in their desire to admit the sacred element to immediate and unveiled contact with their persons, the fair pilgrims did not quite sustain their usually modest and decorous management of their drapery in the river-bath.

In general, however, it is but fair to say, the women carry their modesty of *manner*, not to mention morals, to an almost ridiculous extent. Should you meet a group of paysannes on the road, they generally stop, turn their backs, and draw their fillet or headcloth over their faces,—a very provoking and curiosity-exciting practice.

By the time we reached our tents the sun had almost addled my brain, and so great was the heat that we did not venture out again until sunset. Therm. in my tent 97°; in Colonel Dawkins's, which was not so well sheltered, 107°. At 6 P.M. I took another stroll through the fair, and found that I had seen everything worth seeing in the morning. The motley concourse of so many sects and nations, and the opportunity presented to the spectator of collecting at one glimpse the characteristic peculiarities of each, are sufficient of themselves to repay a journey like ours of 150 miles in the hot weather: but, on the other hand, the intense heat increased by the assembled millions, the noise, the dust, and the monopoly of all the flies in India (which Hurdwar at this epoch possesses), together with a thousand other nuisances, are the serious drawbacks to which the fair-goer is exposed, to counterbalance the novelty of the scene, and the power of saying hereafter, "I was there."

Hurdwar, April 9th.—This morning Colonel Stevenson's scouts, who had been alert in their inquiries regarding tigers, brought intelligence of two having been seen in a jungle near a village 6 miles from hence. After breakfast, therefore, a party of five started in gigs, and drove to the village, where we mounted our elephants, and entered the forest. We found immense quantities of game, wild hogs, hog-deer, spotted deer, and the niel-ghie (literally, blue cow). I also saw here, for the first time, the jungle-fowl, or wild poultry, in appearance something between the game-cock and bantam. We, however, strictly abstained from firing, reserving our whole battery for the nobler game, the tiger. It was perhaps fortunate we did not find one in the thick part of the forest, the trees being so close set, and so interwoven with thorns and parasite plants, that the elephants were often obliged to clear themselves a passage by their own pioneering exertions. It is curious, on these occasions, to see the enormous trees these animals will overthrow. On a word from the Mahout, they place their foreheads against the obnoxious plant, twisting their trunks round it, and gradually bending it towards the ground until they can place a foot upon it—this done, down comes the tree with crashing stem and upturned roots. The elephant must be well educated to accomplish this duty in a *gentlemanlike* manner, that is, without roaring sulkily, or shaking his master by too violent exertions.

On clearing the wood we entered an open space of marshy grass, not 3 feet high: a large herd of cattle were feeding there, and the herdsman was sitting, singing, under a bush—when, just as the former began to move before us, up sprung the very tiger to whom our visit was intended, and cantered off across a bare plain, dotted with small patches of bush-jungle. He took to the open country in a style which would have more become a fox than a tiger, who is expected by his pursuers to fight, and not to run; and, as he was flushed on the flank of the line, only one bullet was fired at him ere he cleared the thick grass. He was unhurt, and we pursued him at full speed. Twice he threw us out by stopping short in small strips of jungle, and then heading back after we had passed; and he had given us a very fast burst of about 2 miles, when Colonel Arnold, who led the field, at last reached him by a capital shot, his elephant being in full career.

Elephant charging Tiger. London, Pub^d by John Murray [illegible]

As soon as he felt himself wounded, the tiger crept into a close thicket of trees and bushes, and crouched. The two leading sportsmen overran the spot where he lay, and as I came up I saw him through an aperture rising to attempt a charge. My mahout had just before, in the heat of the chase, dropped his ankoos,* which I had refused to allow him to recover; and the elephant, being notoriously savage, and further irritated by the goading he had undergone, became, consequently, unmanageable:—he appeared to see the tiger as soon as myself, and I had only time to fire one shot, when he suddenly rushed with the greatest fury into the thicket, and falling upon his knees, nailed the tiger with his tusks to the ground. Such was the violence of the shock, that my servant, who sat behind in the kawas,† was thrown out, and one of my guns went overboard. The struggles of my elephant to crush his still resisting foe, who had fixed one paw on his eye, were so energetic, that I was obliged to hold on with all my strength, to keep myself in the howdah. The second barrel, too, of the gun, which I still retained in my hand, went off in the scuffle, the ball passing close to the mahout's ear, whose situation, poor fellow, was anything but enviable. As soon as my elephant was prevailed upon to leave the killing part of the business to the sportsmen, they gave the roughly-used tiger the coup-de-grace. It was a very fine female, with the most beautiful skin I ever saw.

My brute got a severe scratch over the eye, and his ears were a good deal clawed. It grieves me to convict so sage an animal as the elephant of that purely human vice, inconsistency; yet the case is flagrant; for—if the reader recollects—the last time I was out, he ran away at the charge of the tiger—an act which might, however, be attributed to the influence of bad example shown him by his brethren. The mahout escaped, most fortunately, without injury. This practice of charging is, in an elephant, almost as bad a fault as the other extreme; the more so, that these animals usually follow up the kneeling position by rolling over

* Iron goad to drive the elephant. † Hind seat in the howdah.

upon their side, in order to crush their foe by their weight; in which case, the sportsman is exposed to the triple casualties of a bad fall, being shot by his own guns, and getting within the clutches of the tiger. The courage of a well-trained elephant is passive; and I have heard an experienced sportsman say that this kind of furious attack, and the more common precipitate flight, proceed from the same source, fear. This I believe to be true; more particularly since the "Immortal William" (doubtless thinking of anything but elephants) says, "to be furious is to be frighted out of fear."

In spite of the almost intolerable rays of the sun, the intenseness of which made my brain swim, we continued to beat for the male tiger, whom we knew to be in the surrounding jungle, and from whom we augured a more determined resistance than that which we experienced from the retiring qualities of his better half. We toiled in vain. I shot, however, a fine spotted deer, and a few more were bagged before we reached our gigs.

The party dined together with great hilarity at the tents of a gentleman of the civil service, who had been out with us, where we learnt that an Italian traveller, who called himself Count Vidua, had arrived at Hurdwar, and that Colonel Stevenson had promised to show him a tiger-hunt.

I retired to my tent this evening pretty well knocked up; and during the night had an adventure, which might have terminated with more loss to myself had I slept sounder. My bed, a low charpoy,* was in one corner of the tent, close to a door, and I woke several times from a feverish doze, fancying I heard something moving in my tent; but could discover nothing, though a cheraug, or little Indian lamp, was burning on the table. I therefore again wooed the balmy power, and slept. At length, just as "the iron tongue of midnight had told twelve" (for I had looked at my watch five minutes before, and replaced it under my pillow), I was awakened by a rustling sound

* Literally, "four feet."

under my head; and, half opening my eyes, without changing my position, I saw a hideous black face within a foot of mine, and the owner of this damnable index of a cut-throat, or, at least, cut-purse disposition, kneeling on the carpet, with one hand under my pillow, and the other grasping—not a dagger!—but the door-post. Still without moving my body, and with half-closed eyes, I gently stole my right hand to a boar-spear, which at night was always placed between my bed and the wall; and as soon as I had clutched it, made a rapid and violent movement, in order to wrench it from its place, and try the virtue of its point upon the intruder's body—but I wrenched in vain. Fortunately for the robber, my bearer, in placing the weapon in its usual recess, had forced the point into the top of the tent, and the butt into the ground so firmly, that I failed to extract it at the first effort; and my visitor, alarmed by the movement, started upon his feet and rushed through the door. I had time to see that he was perfectly naked, with the exception of a black blanket twisted round his loins, and that he had already stowed away in his cloth my candlesticks and my dressing-case, which latter contained letters, keys, money, and other valuables. I had also leisure, in that brief space, to judge, from the size of the arm extended to my bed, that the bearer was more formed for activity than strength; and by his grizzled beard, that he was rather old than young. I, *therefore*, sprung from my bed, and, darting through the purdar of the inner door, seized him by the cummerbund just as he was passing the outer entrance.* The cloth, however, being loose, gave way, and ere I could confirm my grasp, he snatched it from my hand, tearing away my thumb-nail down to the quick. In his anxiety to escape he stumbled through the outer purdar, and the much-esteemed dressing-case fell out of his loosened zone. I was so close at his heels, that he could not recover it; and, jumping over the tent-ropes—which, doubtless, the rogue calculated would trip me up—he ran towards

* The tents in India have double flies; the outer khanaut, or wall, forming a verandah, of some 4 feet wide, round the interior pavilion.

the road. I was in such a fury, that, forgetting my bare feet, I gave chase, vociferating lustily, "Choor, choor!" (thief, thief!) but was soon brought up by some sharp stones, just in time to see my rascal, by the faint light of the moon through the thick foliage overhead, jump upon a horse standing unheld near the road, and dash down the path at full speed, his black blanket flying in the wind. What would I have given for my double-barrelled Joe at that moment! As he and his steed went clattering along the rocky forest road, I thought of the black huntsman of the Hartz, or the Erl-king! Returning to my tent, I solaced myself by abusing my servants, who were just rubbing their eyes and stirring themselves, and by threatening the terrified sepoy sentry with a court-martial. My trunks at night were always placed outside the tent, under the sentry's eye; the robber, therefore, must have made his entry on the opposite side, and he must have been an adept in his vocation, as 4 or 5 servants were sleeping between the khanauts. The poor devil did not get much booty for his trouble, having only secured a razor, a pot of pomatum (which will serve to lubricate his person for his next exploit),* and the candlesticks, which, on closer inspection, will satisfactorily prove to him the truth of the axiom, that "all is not gold that glitters," nor even silver. One of my dogs was usually chained to the pole supporting the tent, but having annoyed me the preceding night by his restlessness, I had unfortunately banished him to the stables.

The next morning, on relating my adventure, I was told that I was fortunate in having escaped cold steel; and many comfortable instances were recited of the robbed being stabbed in attempting to secure the robber. The thermometer this day was 97° in my tent, but in that of Colonel Stevenson it was lowered to 88° by the thermantidote, an invention not unlike a winnowing machine, by which air, cooled by tattees of kus-kus grass is thrown into a tent or room.

* Indian thieves oil their bodies to render their seizure difficult.

April 12*th.* *Hurdwar.*—Before breakfast, went into the cattle-fair with Colonel Stevenson, and bought a handsome though small mule for the mountain journeys. The price was 80 rupees, for which sum a fine camel may be purchased. We took a native bargainer with us, and I was much amused by the manner in which the buyer and seller arranged their bargain. The business of chaffering was carried on through the medium of their hands, concealed under a cloth, certain movements of the fingers having corresponding prices. It was a matter of some minutes; and much shaking of heads, though no verbal altercation, was gone through on both sides before the bargain was concluded.

We next inspected some elephants for sale, and the dealers descanted upon their good points as largely and as knowingly as Tattersall could do on those of a horse—though the perfections of the two animals differ considerably. An elephant is extolled for a large head, large ears, arched back, sloping quarters, deep flank, long trunk well mottled, short legs, and the forearm bowing out well in front. The flat bunch of hair at the extremity of the tail is also a great desideratum.

After breakfast we drove to a village 6 miles off, to beat for a tiger, in hopes of showing one to Count Vidua, the Italian, who accompanied us duly mounted and armed.* Several village shikkarees (hunters) accompanied us, and fearlessly entered the jungle on foot, though they told us that a tiger had been prowling round the village all night. There is, no doubt, a strong mixture of predestinarian faith in the courage of the natives: they bolster up their bravery with their favourite theory of chances; and whatever

* This enterprising traveller has since met with a tragical end; for I doubt not that the extract from the 'Javashche Courant,' in the 'Asiatic Journal' of November, 1831, describing the death of Count Charles Vidua de Gonsavo, applies to our unlucky companion. Whilst examining some boiling springs near Cape Coffin, on the coast of Celebes (an island of the Indian Archipelago), he slipped into one of them, and was so severely burnt, that he did not long survive the accident.

of good or evil does or may happen to them they lay upon the shoulders of their nusseeb (fate).

The guides directed us to a spot where we found the skeletons of two bullocks, which they told us had been carried off three days before ; and we had the mortification of knowing that there were tigers within 100 yards of us, without the power of getting at them.

The swamps were so deep that the sagacious elephants refused to enter them, and we were, unfortunately, not furnished with fireworks and ropes, or other means resorted to by sportsmen to rouse wild beasts from inaccessible lurking places.

Much to our regret, and that of the Count, who hoped to have been able to describe a tiger-hunt in his journal, we returned home tigerless; but had some very good shooting on the way back. I shot a very fine wild boar just under the Count's nose, and several brace of black partridges, which the Italian declared to be the coq de bois. The poor fellow was so completely knocked up when we reached home, that he was obliged to decline joining the dinner-party. Indeed, we had a fatiguing day of it, the elephants themselves being quite jaded.

This day is the last of the fair, and to-morrow the party will break up, all, like the rays of a star, starting different ways.

CHAPTER IV.

Valley of Deyra — Tiger-hunting — Deyra Doon — Mr. Shore — Llandowr — Missouree — Kalunga — Peleon — Synspore — Futtypore — Raj Ghaut — Kearda Doon — Wild elephants — Nahun — Jytuck — Rajah of Nahun — Nahun to Bernetti — Suran — Mountain matrimony — March towards Subbatoo — Boor's Peak — Subbatoo — Sahree — Simla — The Chota Bursat — Embassy from Runjeet Singh.

On the 12th of April Colonel Dawkins and I left Hurdwar, and commenced our march through the valley of Deyra Doon. Our route was most beautiful, and reminded me much of some of the milder and least wild regions of the Alps. The road, which is made with great art, winds down through a woody declivity, sometimes closely hemmed in by abrupt rocky banks, and at others traversing a luxuriantly wooded plain. We found our tents pitched in a thick forest near the small chokee of Karsrah.

On the summit of the hill above our encampment is a small bungalow, built for the accommodation of persons travelling without tents; and similar buildings are established at nearly every stage through the Doon. From this point we enjoyed a magnificent prospect. Below us lay the beautiful valley of Deyra, luxuriant with many-tinted forests, and refreshed by the rippling little rivers which, with as many arms as Briareus, run in a meandering course through the whole length of the vale, from the Ganges to the Jumna. The view is bounded on all sides by mountains. In the north and west, those of Gurhwal and Surmoor rise, series after series, till they are terminated by the snow-capped peaks of Himalayah. In the south the prospect is abruptly closed by the range of woody hills which form the boundary of the Deyra Doon, and cut it off from the plains of Hindostan.

We had provided ourselves with a punkah and tattees of kus-kus at Hurdwar; and by their means, together with the umbrageous canopy overhead, reduced the temperature of our tent to 78°.

During breakfast a hurkarah arrived with a note from a gentleman who passed by this same route yesterday, informing us that, as he was fishing in a mountain-stream near at hand, a tiger came to drink at it within pistol-shot of him, and retired without seeing him,—an uncommon predicament for a disciple of the philosopher Walton. We determined to look for him in the evening, though our chance of success is small in a country so full of ravines, by which the tigers can sneak away to the woods when they hear the crashing approach of the elephants.

At 4 P.M., having caught a wild-looking shikkaree, we established him upon an elephant, and, descending the woody hill, entered the thick grass jungle bordering the beautiful little river which runs through the valley. The hunter promised us good deer-shooting, but denied all knowledge of tigers. We had not, however, been out more than half an hour, when, in a small patch of high silky grass, a very fine one jumped up close under my elephant's trunk, just as I was in the act of taking aim at a peacock, one of a large covey which rose before me. I immediately transferred my aim to the royal quadruped, and in the hurry of the moment gave him the advantage of a load of small shot, instead of the bullet in the other barrel. He uttered a loud roar, rushed through the grass, plunged into a ravine, and I lost sight of him. We beat all the surrounding jungle without finding him, when I suggested trying a small rushy island which was only divided from the main land by a shallow branch of the river, and was directly opposite the point where the ravine debouched upon the stream. We had no sooner entered the islet than D. came upon the tiger, and fired two shots at him. The beast, being, however, upon the retreating system, escaped from the covert, and I saw him cross over to another islet, thickly set with brushwood; it was not more than 50 yards square, and as he entered it I saw by his action that he had been wounded. We, nevertheless, beat in vain for him; and though the elephants showed all the usual signs of the vicinity of a tiger, we never saw him again. My elephant imagined more than once that he had stepped upon the object of our search, and kicked a huge stump of a burnt tree into a thousand pieces in his mistaken fury.

On the road back to the camp I shot a hog-deer and a young spotted deer, the latter of which made very good venison, the other furnishing a plentiful feast for the servants.

The next morning, whilst our tents advanced 8 miles to the village of Luckawala, we started on our elephants to look for our lost tiger of yesterday, who only escaped us by a combination of bad luck and bad management on our part. We were again balked in our expectations, although we traced him, by the assistance of the mahouts, who were uncommonly keen, for nearly a mile on the sand. Returned to Karsrah, quitted our elephants, and drove to the next encamping ground in a gig, the road being now nearly level.

April 14th.—Marched 11 miles to the town of Deyra, whence the name of the valley. The first half of the day's journey led through a thick forest of very lofty trees, many of them strangers to the plains of India. The underwood was formed of richly-flowering plants, among which the corinda sent forth its well-nigh sickening fragrance; and parasites of the most gigantic proportions twined round the trunks and branches of the larger trees, resembling, in their grotesque writhings, the folds of huge boa-constrictors—a similitude so strong in some instances as to be almost startling.

In some places the trees on either side the road met over head, forming a long and dark arcade of impervious foliage, the lofty arches being not uncommonly knit together at the apex by the luxuriant creepers. In one of these natural cloisters we overtook a party of peasants, who were singing in a wild and monotonous cadence; and at some distance their voices, echoed and reverberated by the vaulted forest, sounded not unlike the chanting in a cathedral. In the immediate neighbourhood of the town of Deyra the jungle has been cleared away, and the wheat-crops are remarkably fine.

On arriving at our tents we received a polite invitation from Mr. Shore,* the political agent for this province, to pass the day in his house. He is a remarkably tall and handsome man, has adopted the Mussulman costume, and wears a long beard. He is also distinguished as the scourge of all the brigands and wild beasts that infest his province. In bringing the former to justice he seldom trusts to inferior agents, but, taking one or two determined assistants,

* The son of the present Lord Teignmouth.

mounts his camel or his horse, slings his rifle on his shoulder, and with no better food than rice, and no more efficient night-shelter than a good blanket, makes two or three forced marches to the lurking-place of the robbers; and by the terror of his name, or prowess of person, generally brings his expedition to a speedy and successful termination. His most remarkable exploit was the following:—A numerous and determined banditti, being pursued by the battalion of Ghourkahs cantoned at Deyra, took refuge in a small fortress, I think called Khoonda. Mr. Shore, with Major Young, the commandant of the corps above mentioned, arrived before the walls, but, having no guns capable of effecting a breach, Mr. S. proposed that they should cut down a tree, and, forming a battering-ram, force the gates in this primeval method. The machine was prepared and carried up to the gate in spite of the fire of the garrison. The instrument did its work—down went the gates, and in rushed my hero and Major Y. at the head of their men. I hope, for the perfection of my story, that the legend, which went on to say that each gentleman saved the other's life during the conflict, is true—true it is that the fort was taken, and Mr. Shore wounded.

The verandah and rooms of this active persecutor of the wild animals of the forest are adorned with the grim skulls and stuffed skins of tigers, bears, boors, monkeys, and other characteristic drawing-room furniture: and while we were at breakfast two black bears, with silver collars round their necks, strolled quietly into the room and took possession of the posts of honour on the right and left of our host. These proved to be domestic pets, and ate their breakfasts out of wooden bowls placed on either side of his chair. One of them was unruly, and, after devouring his own meal, attempted to forage some honey from the table, upon which he received a very good threshing with a dog-whip from his master.

Mr. Shore described to us his general method of killing tigers, which militates a good deal against my ideas of good sport. However, it is a good plan in a place where

elephants are scarce, and where the thickness of the forest almost renders these animals useless. When intelligence arrives of a bullock having been killed in the jungles by a tiger (which animal generally defers his meal until evening), Mr. S. orders the carcase to be dragged under some convenient tree, among the branches of which he lays a michaun, or platform of bamboo. Here he takes his station with his guns and ammunition, and patiently awaits the arrival of his victim, who does not fail to return about sunset to his prey, and is shot before he has time to begin his meal. The accompanying plate will afford the reader a pretty correct representation of the above-mentioned sport, and of the scenery through which we are now travelling.

Mr. Shore describes the approach of the tiger, on these occasions, as equally crouching and cautious as though he were in pursuit of living prey. He also gives an amusing account of the several animals which succeed each other—during the doubtless entertaining vigil of the sportsman—in possession of the carcase; until the jackals, the latest occupants, begin to cower and sneak away, which is a hint to the shooter to prepare for the arrival of the arch-bully, the tiger himself, who is sure then to be creeping towards his feast.

At a quarter before 4 P.M. we went out to witness an eclipse of the sun, which was beautifully and distinctly visible through the medium of a looking-glass and a pair of green spectacles. After the eclipse, we had a distinct view of the new-formed invalid station of Llandowr, and Missouree, where Major Young and some others have cool summer residences. They are situated on a lofty ridge of the mountains directly north of Deyra.

In the evening our host walked with us into the town: it is inconsiderable, but much improved by the exertions of Mr. Shore. The cantonments are good, and there is an extensive parade-ground. I visited a very beautiful and very sacred temple, the burial-place of its founder, a holy goru of great learning and piety. Such was the sanctity of the spot, that I was required to leave my shoes at the entrance of the sanctum sanctorum, which I did not hesitate to do, in compliance with the custom of the country, and as a mark of respect paid to religion, of whatever form.

The temple is built of stone ornamented with sundry-coloured chunam (a cement made of cowrie-shells), which, at a little distance, has all the effect of marble. The beneficent founder has also endowed Deyra with a fine stone tank, covering about an acre of ground.

There is something remarkably *snug* and "world-forgetting" in the situation of Deyra and its little community. To a man who could be contented in retirement, possessed of his "domus," and, I suppose I must add, "placens uxor," and fortified by the "vrai désir d'être oublié," Deyra might really be a "Happy Valley." Though it is cooler than the plains, the English inhabitants retire to the mountain stations, so conveniently at hand, during the hotter months; and they have a feasible and direct communication with the "cities of the plain" by the pass of Kerie, due south of Deyra. However, to counterbalance these and other utopian advantages, I am told that the surrounding forests are, during the annual rains, so loaded with malaria, that it is fatal even to travel through them.

April 15th; therm. in our tents at Deyra, 82°.—At 4 A.M. this morning my friend and myself started on an expedition to the two mountain-stations above mentioned, Llandowr and Missouree. Mr. Shore was kind enough to send 2 capital ghoonts (mountain ponies) for us to Rajpore, a village at the foot of the mountains, 7 miles from Deyra. We galloped on our own horses to this place, where we found the rough little brutes with 2 guides awaiting us.

We immediately mounted upon the well-padded saddles and commenced the ascent, being duly cautioned by the men to lay the bridle on the necks of our ponies, and allow them to rest when they pleased. We accordingly yielded the usual prerogative of a horseman to influence the motions and will of his steed, and proceeded.

The distance from the base of the hill to Llandowr, the

most elevated of the two stations, is 8 miles; and the road (which, for the sake of necks and nerves, I rejoice to say is in progress of improvement) sometimes winds down the edge of the rocks, sometimes zigzags up the face of the hill, plunges into the dark depths of a ravine, or creeps over the giddy summit of a naked crag. It is, in its present unfinished state, in most parts not more than 3 feet wide, not unfrequently diminishing to 1 foot, and even 6 inches!

The journey is certainly a nervous one for beginners; for though we have both rambled through the Alps, we have been rather accustomed to trust to our own feet than to ride in mountainous expeditions. The obstinate little ghoonts, too, always select the very outermost edge of the track, so that the rider, glancing his eye over the shoulder of his beast, sees nothing between him and the unfathomable abyss below; unless it be detached atoms of stone or earth, crumbling from the passing tread of the animal, and rolling over the precipice.

We were an hour and a half in reaching a little halfway hamlet, situated, or rather perched, in a small nook of cultivation; and an hour and three-quarters in accomplishing the last half of the upward journey. On a narrow but elevated platform of earth on the right of the road we passed the new-made grave of Sir Charles Farrington, of the 31st regiment, who died of consumption on his way to Llandowr, whither he was repairing, as a last hope, about a fortnight ago. In this romantic spot, surrounded with trees, and overhung with black rocks, a monument is to be erected to his memory.

We reached the little half-built colony without accident, and breakfasted with Major Brutton of the 11th Dragoons, who commands the depôt of European invalids. During the building of the bungalows and hospitals, which are to be roofed in before the setting in of the rains, the Major and the rest of the officers, and invalid men, amounting to 80, are living in tents; and many of the sick are already, from the effects of the delightful climate, recovering.

To us, just emerged from the plain, it appeared disagreeably cold. The therm. stood at 54°, whilst at Deyra it ranged at 80°. Llandowr is 7400 feet above the level of the sea. The establishment of this station, so convenient for the invalids of Meerut, and other great northern cantonments, will be a great saving to government, who were obliged before its creation to send their sick servants to the Cape of Good Hope, or at least to sea.

After inspecting the several buildings, and enjoying the most splendid view of the snowy range, the beautiful Doon, the mountains beyond it, and in the dim distance the wide-spreading plains of Hindostan, we remounted our ghoonts, and set off for Missouree, which is somewhat lower than, and 3 miles distant from, Llandowr. Among the various and beautiful trees and shrubs of these mountainous regions, I was delighted to recognise many old English friends. The oak and the rhododendron are the largest timber trees; and of the latter, which in Europe and America is a mere shrub, the beams of the Llandowr houses are formed. At this period they are covered with a luxuriant crimson flower, and their stems, as well as those of the oak, are thickly clothed with a long and hoary moss. During our descent I also discovered the cherry, pear, barberry, and raspberry, which are unknown in the plains.

Missouree is situated on a table-hill, and is less wooded than Llandowr; but it has greatly the advantage in point of space. We called upon Major Young, who resides here, and he obligingly furnished us with directions for finding tigers in our progress through the Doon towards Simla.

The descent we found infinitely more fatiguing than the ascent, but our nerves grew callous in proportion to our fatigue; though we were obliged to dismount in a few bad places. At Rajpore we found our gig, and drove into Deyra just in time to dress for dinner. It was a good day's work. We rode 26 miles, 19 of mountain equitation; and drove 7 miles.

On our arrival at our tents we found 5 elephants sent to us from the Head-quarters commissariat, as a reinforcement for our tiger-campaign. Having already 4 of these animals, we shall possess a good string of beaters for the marshes of Synspore. This evening, as if on purpose to give employment for our sporting forces, a despatch arrived from one of a fishing party of gentlemen at Synspore, informing us that a Captain Kent had that morning been attacked and severely injured by a tiger. He was brought into Deyra, and his wounds examined, which though severe were not dangerous. The monster's claws had cruelly lacerated his shoulders and breast, and one tooth had penetrated his cheek. His escape was most marvellous. He was imprudently shooting on foot in the thickest of a jungle famed for tigers, and had just fired both barrels at a deer, when the lurking tyrant of the forest sprung upon him from a tuft of grass, and knocked him down. His life was probably saved by his gun. He was carrying it on his shoulder, and the tiger seized it in his mouth, instead of the captain's head. The marks of his tusks were distinctly impressed upon the barrel, and a fragment of a shivered tooth was found afterwards in the gentleman's waistcoat. It is, therefore, probable that his abstaining from further attack was in consequence of his finding an Englishman so much tougher a mouthful than he expected; true it is that he bounded on, satisfied with one round. We propose reaching Synspore the day after to-morrow, to give the captain his revanche.

April 16th.—This evening, Mr. Shore having furnished us with a guide, Dawkins and I rode to see the site (for little else remains of that once impregnable fortress) of Kalunga, which successfully resisted and repelled a British army; and before whose walls the gallant but rash General Gillespie fell, leading on the attack. Kalunga is situated on a lofty woody hill, isolated from the main range of mountains, and commanding the Doon east and west. It was eventually taken, and our pioneers (in retribution for its former resistance, and the death of 2 more officers in the second attack) left not one stone upon another. Two white obelisks in the midst of a corn-field in the valley mark the resting-place of the slain.

The next day we took leave of our entertaining and eccentric host; and, bidding adieu to Deyra, resumed our march. We found our canvas tabernacles erected on a hilly forest-ridge, near the hamlet of Peleon. This ridge is cut up by the violence of the periodical rains into numerous deep and tangled ravines debouching upon the valley: the vale itself is intersected by numerous streams and nullahs; the centre is grassy and swampy, and free from trees, which, however, grow thickly and wildly on the higher ground, and in the ravines. Being now in the midst of the most favourite haunts of wild beasts, our servants received directions to secure themselves and our camels, ponies, and sheep within the circle formed by the tents and the elephants, and to keep large fires blazing all night.

At 2 P.M. we took our little pack of elephants, and, descending to the valley, commenced a battu for a tiger. We hunted in vain for 2 hours along the river-side, and my companion, taking a detachment of beaters, wandered up a grassy ravine, to try his fortune in the forest jungle. We had not been long separated, before I heard one of his elephants trumpeting and snorting most furiously; and, guessing the cause, hurried to the scene of action. I found that my friend had come suddenly upon a fine tiger, which had charged him when he was most awkwardly situated among large trees, and on the steep brow of the ravine, and had then disappeared among the brushwood. Proceeding cautiously up the hollow, we soon found the mangled carcase of a heifer concealed in the dry channel of a little nullah; and, farther on, a perfect Golgotha of bones. We were just congratulating ourselves on having so correctly hit upon the spot, when, looking diligently among the bushes thickly clothing the flanks of the ravine, I distinguished the well-known black stripe and yellow skin through a small aperture in a thicket, within 10 paces of me, and on a ledge of ground higher than my houdah. In this contingency consists the chief danger of ravine-shooting; the animal, by his advantage of position, being enabled to spring even into the houdah, a feat which, on fair ground, he could never accomplish.

Stopping my elephant, I took, as I thought, a good aim, and pulled both triggers; when, instead of the monster which I expected, out rushed a little cub-tiger of about 3 months, and charged me so courageously, that my elephant (a female, which I selected to-day as smaller and easier than my sturdy old "Crooktusk,"* whose violence among trees I rather dreaded) took to her heels, and was in full career towards the deep dry nullah above mentioned, when I made a successful *Parthian* shot with my favourite Joe Manton, and slew my determined little pursuer.

My friend's elephant, equally ill-behaved on this occasion, in her anxiety to escape slid down the steep bank about 40 yards, dragging her hind legs after her in the most ridiculous but *periculous* manner. The mahouts declared that there must be another cub; but as it was growing dusk, we deferred our pursuit until the morrow.

The next morning, whilst our camp advanced to Synspore, we pröceeded in due form to our appointment with the tigress and the remaining cub. Mr. Grey, a young medico from Deyra, joined us by invitation, and we mounted him for the occasion: it was his first tiger-chasse. We proceeded as direct as we could to the scene of yesterday's skirmish. Grey and I were close together, and D. a little on the flank; when, about 100 yards from the spot where the tiger was seen yesterday, G. suddenly exclaimed, "Here she comes!" and I saw the beautiful animal creeping quickly out of a richly-flowering lemon-thicket, about 40 paces from us, and approaching us in a crouching attitude, with her fierce eyes fixed upon us. We fired so simultaneously, that neither heard the other's shot, and the tiger rushed back into the thicket. Fearing her escape, we hurried to the spot, and my old "Crook-tusk," tearing up the bush, discovered her in the centre. I immediately

* This elephant is well known in the Commissariat by his great size, unruly character, and a deformity in one of his tusks.

fired, but the shot was useless, for she was stone-dead,—a fact I might have known before, had I not mistaken the exclamation, "Purra hui!" "She's dead,"—of the mahout, for "Para, para," a "hog-deer!"

On dragging her out of the odoriferous lemon-bush, she proved to be a very fine tigress, her dugs full of milk, and measuring in length 10 feet 5 inches. She had 3 shots in her; one, the fatal ball, in her shoulder, one in the thigh, and another through both houghs. Coming out of the thicket, we fell in with the surviving cub, the last scion of this ill-fated family; and Dawkins, dismounting from his elephant, and arming himself with a kookaree or mountain-dagger, attempted to take the beautiful little creature alive; but it made so furious an attack, that he was obliged to knock it on the head.

Having secured our game upon the elephants, we drove on to our camp at Synspore, Mr. Grey accompanying us. Our encampment occupied a beautiful site on the edge of the forest, with a green lawn in front, gently sloping down to the rushy level through which the little river meandered. For miles in advance the banks of the stream are clothed with thick grass; and the frequent patches of tall, rank rushes and reeds, with the filmy marsh-miasma floating and dancing in aguish wreaths above them, wore greater charms in the eyes of us tiger-hunters, than would have the far-famed gardens of Shalimar, or even those of royal Kensington.

But, in spite of its promising qualities, and the notoriety of the spot as a tiger-haunt, our disappointment was as great as our expectations were overweening. We had no sooner arrived at Synspore than the Jemadar of the village presented himself, and, with a thousand "khodabunds!" and "mharâjs!" besought our aid against a tiger, which, he said, had this season killed 9 bullocks and a horse belonging to his village, and had two days ago wounded a veleitee sahib (English gentleman), doubtless Captain Kent. Making sure of our prey the next day, we determined to give our elephants a good rest (for they were beginning to look thin, and grow footsore), and employed this morning in casting balls and manufacturing squibs and crackers for the swamps on the morrow. In the afternoon our medical companion made a very interesting dissection of the tigress, and traced the course of the fatal shot. It had entered the right shoulder a little above the elbow, and, glancing upwards from the thick bladebone, lodged in the vertebræ of the neck, in the very centre of which we found it wedged, and almost flat. This spinal wound sufficiently accounted for her instantaneous death. Mr. G. dissected the arm of the animal, and it presented, when deprived of the skin, the most beautiful and powerful system of muscles and sinews that it is possible to conceive.

Synspore, April 10th.—Out all day, with a line of 12 elephants, in search of Captain Kent's tiger; but returned without finding even a trace of him, and proportionably disappointed: the more so, that we might have had the best day's deer-shooting possible, but refrained from firing out of respect to our more royal game. The villagers, who accompanied us in great numbers, were as much disappointed as ourselves, and supposed the tiger had retired to the inaccessible parts of the marshes. Into some of these we obliged the mahouts to force our elephants in spite of their sagacious resistance: and more than once we were nearly thrown out of the houdahs, by the violent exertions made by the frightened animals to extricate themselves from the sinking quag. We threw fireworks as far as we could among the reeds, and were even imprudent enough to dismount and try to proceed farther into the swamp on foot; but after getting thoroughly wet, and finding ourselves, when above our ankles in a most retentive bog, in a poor situation for resistance should the tiger attack, we retraced our way back to the elephants, and returned, well tired, to a late dinner. The evening was beautiful; one side of the tent was raised to admit the coolness of the night breeze, which wafted gently to us a delicious tribute of fragrance from the surrounding forest; and as we sat in the bright moonlight, sipping our lâll-sherâb (claret), and inhaling long draughts of complacency from our rose-odoured hookahs, we all agreed that this gipsy-like life in the wilderness, with the requisite ingredients of good health, good spirits, good shooting, beautiful scenery, and (oh romance!) a wild-boar pork-chop and clean table-cloth, is, for a season, enjoyable in the extreme.

The next day, long before "common-kissing Titan" had begun to gild the hills, we were in the field; and without finding the tiger, shot our way to the next encamping-ground at the hamlet of Futtypore. We had a very good day's sport, killing 2 boars, 3 deer, 3 brace of black partridges, 3 brace of hares (which greatly abound in the Doon), and a few snipes. The solitary snipe found in the swamps is a very handsome and large bird. If we had secured the tiger, our game-bag would have presented a pleasing variety. During the day my servant had a curious escape;—he requested permission to dismount from the houdah to drink at the river, and was in the act of stooping to raise the water in his hands to his lips, when I heard him utter a scream, and then a grand splash in the river. I rushed forward through the long grass, fully expecting that a tiger had seized the poor fellow, and found him standing in the stream, feeling his limbs all over, and blubbering from fright. An immense boar, roused from his lair, had charged him in the rear, and, ripping up his voluminous cummerbund, tumbled him headlong into the stream—fortunately without the least injury. The animal continued his career without repeating his attack, and had not gone 20 yards when, to the great delight of the poor bearer, he was brought to the ground by a shot from my friend.

21*st.*: therm. in tent 87°.—Dr. G. left us, and returned to Deyra. Shot our way to Raj Ghaut, a timber depôt and ferry on the Jumna. This great river, the next in rank to the Holy Gunga, emerges at this point from the Himalaya mountains, and is even here, so near its source, wider than the Thames at Windsor.

It issues upon the Doon through a beautiful defile

flanked by richly-wooded hills, and, sweeping across the valley, receiving the tributary waters of the little stream along whose banks we have been travelling, forces its way through the southern range of mountains, and bursts upon the plains; where, after running through the great cities of Delhi, Muttra, and Agra, it finally blends itself with the Ganges at Allahabad. In the vicinity of Raj Ghaut there is very good trout-fishing, both in the Jumna and in the smaller streams.

The following day we crossed the river in a rude boat—the elephants wading and swimming over—and entered the Kearda Doon, a continuation of the Deyra valley, to which it bears in its features a miniature resemblance. Our day's march was 8 coss, or about 12 miles; the roads were execrable, and almost dislocated every joint of the poor buggy. The valley gradually narrowed as we proceeded, and we found our tents at the village of Kearda, romantically situated in a dell completely encompassed by woody heights, on the summit of the nearest of which are the ruins of what appears to have been a petty Goorkah fortress.

A little, ugly, but athletic Shikkaree, who visited our camp, informed us that the surrounding forests abounded in bears, leopards, hyænas, wild elephants, and even tigers; but the coverts are so heavy, and cut up by ravines, that they are not accessible to mounted sportsmen. A small species of pheasant and the jungle-poultry are also found in the hills; the latter were crowing all day on the heights above us.

We took a sporting stroll in the afternoon, and brought home a good bag of partridges and hares: we also roused a very large boar, but he escaped. During the chasse I found myself in a fine grove of mulberry-trees, and regaled myself with the fruit, which was very refreshing on the hottest day I almost ever experienced. The berry is sweet and juicy, but much smaller than it is in Europe. Returning towards camp in the dusk of the evening, I saw a large snake (the only one I ever met with when out shooting), which, as it rolled its scaly length over the brow of a ravine, seemed to be about the thickness of a man's arm. I had but a momentary glimpse of it, and fired, the ball splintering the piece of burnt timber under which it was gliding.

23rd.—Continued our march and found our advanced tents scarcely pitched. The servants, and the Goorkah sepoys who formed our guard, told us that they were much delayed during their night-march by the wild elephants, who made several attacks upon their tame brethren carrying our tents, and were only repulsed by the firing of the sepoys. These huge inhabitants of the woods are rarely seen except in the night, when they commonly descend to the valleys. We may expect some annoyance from them to-night, as the Doon is here scarcely a quarter of a mile in width, and completely hemmed in by overhanging hills; but such is their dread of fire, that it is no difficult matter to repulse these Brobdignag foes, who, if they could succeed in making good their attack, would quickly level our canvas home.

I strolled out among the wooded hills in the cool of the evening (if one can call any part of a day, with Fahrenheit pointing at 93°, cool), and shot a cock and hen jungle-fowl. They flew like pheasants, and had a very game plumage. The tail of the cock is not nearly so much arched as that of the English bird, though it is more curved than that of the pheasant; his crow is more wild and short, and less sonorous, than the voice of our British Chanticleer. I did not feel quite comfortable as I returned down the forest hill on foot in the dusk, and I eyed the dark thickets rather jealously as I passed them. My faithful bearer too looked somewhat *livid*, when I dropped a couple of bullets over the shot into each of my four barrels, and bid him keep close to my elbow. However, nothing alarming occurred; except, perhaps, that we heard the wild elephants trumpeting and crashing in the distant forests as they commenced their descent to the valley to drink at the nullahs.

Our sheep having failed us, the jungle-fowls, with the

orthodox concomitant of bread-sauce (in the wilderness!), proved exceedingly dainty food. At night the jungles around us being on fire in several points presented a most grand and beautiful spectacle; long streams of flame ran rapidly up and athwart the sides of the hills, and the elephants were heard screaming and rushing through the forest to avoid the invading element.

Our wheel-carriages having been sadly tumbled about by the rough tracks of yesterday and to-day, we sent them back, with orders to the hurkara who accompanied them to take them into store at Kurnal.

The following morning we renewed our march towards Nahun. The first 6 miles of the route lay through a very picturesque, well-watered and wooded valley; when we suddenly quitted the vale and began to ascend the mountain to our right, on whose summit glittered the white buildings of the town. The path was exceedingly steep and craggy, and occasionally so narrow that we marvelled how the tent-loaded elephants could have passed. These sure-footed creatures did succeed, however, though with great difficulty, in reaching Nahun, which is, I suppose, nearly 4 miles of precipitous ascent from the river. We found the camels with the baggage about halfway up, the Surwâns declaring they could get them no farther.

On arriving at the picturesque little hill-town we found the public bungalow, built for the accommodation of the few travellers that pass this way, occupied by two officers, and we therefore pitched a tent. Nous voilà fairly in the mountains!

Nahun, which is the chief town of a small Râj, is a very pretty little place, curiously dotted about on several adjoining eminences. In the centre, and much elevated, stands the palace of the Rajah, commanding a most extensive view, bounded on the north by the snowy peaks, and on the south by the plains of India, which, contrasted with the abrupt and rugged outline of the hills, have, in the indistinct distance, precisely the appearance of the ocean.

On hearing of the arrival of two officers of the "Lord

Sahib's" suite, the Rajah very civilly sent us a present of several trays of pomegranates and sweetmeats, and dispatched 40 coolies to bring our baggage up the hill. Two of the least clumsy of the camels were also brought safely to the summit. These animals are manifestly intended, by their conformation of limb, for the straightforward business of the plains: when we had succeeded in getting them to the top, the poor creatures stared about in evident alarm, and appeared quite out of their element. With the presents, the Rajah of Nahun sent us an intimation of his intention to visit us in the afternoon; so we prepared the larger tent for our little durbar.

On the north side of the Nahun mountain we saw for the first time, except indeed at Llandowr, the fir-tree. It is of a very beautiful species, with large spreading branches, like the Scotch fir. The raspberry grows wild and eatable, and the pomegranate in the sunny nooks shows its dark green leaf and beautiful bell-shaped crimson blossom. Within view of our tents, in a north-easterly direction, lies the hill-fort of Jytuck (4854 feet above the level of the sea), which cost the lives of 4 British officers in its capture, during the Gourkah war. The tombs of these officers, marked by a lofty obelisk, are on the bank of a spacious tank in the centre of the town of Nahun.

At 4 P.M. the Rajah paid us his promised visit. He was mounted on a handsome young elephant, and brought a small train of courtiers with him. He appeared not more than 22, rather tall, very handsome, with a fair complexion and light grey eyes. He presented Dawkins, as the Burra Sahib, with a matchlock, and was exceedingly liberal in his offers of assistance in our progress through the mountains.

As is usual with native potentates who have the advantage of the Honourable Company's protection, he complained that he had merely the title of Rajah, with few of the more substantial privileges of that rank, and said that it was his intention to make a journey to Calcutta, to petition for the increase of his Râj, a pilgrimage which we advised him at least to defer. He has, indeed, some reason to bewail the poverty of his kingdom, for it consists chiefly of the thinly peopled and scantily cultivated mountain regions between Deyra and Pinjore.

The Rajah informed us that the road from hence to Subbâtoo, four long marches, though formed with care and tolerably wide, is too steep for loaded camels or elephants. We shall, therefore, send our heavy baggage round by Pinjore—by which route the Head-quarters entered the hills—and carry on with us a light equipment on the shoulders of coolies. In spite of the Rajah's assurances of the impracticability of taking on camels, my friend determined to send on 2 of these animals to carry a couple of very light tents; which arrangement will render us independent of the stage-bungalows.

The young chief appearing anxious that we should visit his killar, or fortress, we promised to see him again to-morrow, which engagement, however, we intend to excuse ourselves from performing; as we find it rather laborious and irksome, with our "light marching" stock of Hindostanee, to support a durbar conversation.

April 25th.—Sojourned at Nahun, to give the Rajah time to muster his coolies from the different villages for the transport of our baggage. We are now, I fancy, about 4000 feet above the sea, nearly 500 feet higher than Snowdon, and yet the thermometer keeps up at 86° in the tent. The heat, however, is not distressing, being modified by the north breeze, which blows refreshingly upon us.

The next morning the mountaineer coolies arrived, and a strange ill-favoured race they are. In their high cheeks, long narrow eyes, broad fronts, and narrow chins, they bear an evident affinity to the Tartar. Their stature is very short, but they are wide-chested and strongly limbed, and show prodigious strength in carrying burdens up the steep mountain-tracks. The Gourkahs, in our wars with them, proved the enemies best worthy of the British arms in India. It is said that these hardy little warriors speak with the greatest contempt of their gigantic long-bearded neighbours the Seikhs. They make first-rate tirailleurs, and at the siege of Bhurtpore one of the Company's Gourkah regiments much distinguished itself. They appeared, on that occasion, somewhat pigmy by the side of our British grenadiers, their average height being barely 5 feet.

We despatched the men with the baggage some hours before we started ourselves. The first 2 miles were an abrupt descent: down this same hill and up the opposite one the British with infinite labour dragged the guns, cased in hollow trunks of timber, to the attack of Jytuck. The road by which we now travelled is a work of the Nahun Rajah, and is remarkably well constructed; and though in several precipitous points it has been found necessary to support it with masonry, it is rarely narrower than 8 feet. I found my ghoont, or mountain-pony, rather too small and weak for the steep roads and long marches; but my mule, which bears not half its appearance of strength, carried me extremely well, and is, fortunately, not stubborn, like most of her tribe. A jibbing mule in a precipitous road *must* gain his point with a prudent master.

Our stage was 11 miles, and we were in sight of the town we had left and the bungalow we were bound to during nearly the whole journey. We were 3 hours in accomplishing it, and, on reaching Bernetti, found all our coolies safely arrived. They were about 50 in number, and the weight these little fellows carried was astonishing. Their usual burthen is one maund and a half, or 120 pounds, and the price of their labour 2 annas, or *4d.*, a day. The Rajah civilly furnished us with a chuprassee, who was very useful in paying and arranging the relays of coolies, and procuring milk and other necessaries for us: he also sent with us a well-stocked bunneer, or victualler, for the accommodation of our servants and followers.

The bungalow of Bernetti is prettily situated on a little level platform in a shady recess, with a good spring of water, and backed up by a woody mountain. The pheasant, black partridge, and chekoar, are said to abound in the ravines, but they are difficult to get at. Our two camels had performed their first day's hill-march very well, but with one or two narrow escapes. The bungalow being occupied by the 2 travellers who preceded us, we pitched our little tents. The thermometer yielded a few degrees in our favour this day, being at 83°.

The next morning we proceeded to Suran, outstripping our precursors, and thus securing the bungalow. This stage is about 12 miles, and some portions of the road are so steep and abrupt that we were obliged to dismount and walk. The first half of our march led through a pine forest; the scenery was beautiful, and we had several favourable peeps of the snowy peaks through the gorges of the hills to the north. During our passage through the forest we were amused by the absurd freaks of a numerous band of monkeys. Our dogs gave chace to them, but they easily avoided them by springing up into the trees, and when I whistled my spaniel away they followed in a crowd close behind him, but leaped up into the pines the moment he turned to the attack.

The bungalow at Suran, which is a considerable village, is a well-constructed building of fir timbers and planks. The vicinage is bleak, rocky, and graced with but little vegetation. About 10 miles south-west of Suran stands the little fortress of Mornee, belonging to the Râj of Nahun. Its situation, on the pinnacle of a rocky mountain, is both strong and picturesque. Fahrenheit, gradually descending, arrived to-day at 73°, a very enjoyable temperature.

In our village a marriage was being solemnized all the morning. The women were perched on the flat roof of a house, and the men squatted on the road below, where they remained drumming and fiddling for some time; and then suddenly, as if by signal, joined the ladies above. These mountaineers act precisely the reverse of their neighbours in the plains in regard to polygamy—the advantages of the institution accruing to the women, instead of to the lords of the creation. One hill-woman is, I am told, in frequent cases the sole wife of 3 or 4 brothers. It is hard to comprehend how the brotherhood manage to agree as to the division of the property; and it must be a matter of some difficulty for the fair polygamist to mete out a due proportion of affection impartially to each of her lords. It is to be inferred, from this unnatural plurality, that these highlanders,—luckless race!—are cursed with a paucity of "the sex whose presence civilizes ours;" a fact which sufficiently accounts for their deplorable state of barbarism.

As I sat before the bungalow in the afternoon, enjoying such a cool bracing breeze as I had not felt for more than 3 years, a curious and beautiful animal, which the natives informed me was a mountain-fox, ran across the rocks in front of the building. Calling for a gun, and favoured by the inequality of the ground, I intercepted his retreat, and shot him. He was nearly twice the size of the fox of Hindostan, measuring 3 feet 11 inches from the nose to tip of brush. The hair was of a light colour, and very long and furry. I preserved the skin, but it was afterwards unfortunately torn to pieces by a mischievous puppy.

28th.—Started at 4 A.M., and occupied 5½ hours in accomplishing a most fatiguing march of 13½ miles. There was so much clambering, that the 3 animals which I rode were completely knocked up. The country we traversed was more barren and rocky than the march of yesterday; but in the ravines, which have generally the advantage of water, the little hedge-rose afforded us its fragrance, and the pomegranate refreshed our sight with its purest of green leaves and crimson blossom, which, however, I would willingly have exchanged for its fruit during our hot journey. The oak and peach-tree also grow sparingly in the little strips of cultivation, which, terraced one above the other, occupy the narrow interstices of soil between the rocks. The produce of the ploughed land, a meagre and abortive crop of barley, does not promise an adequate recompense to the husbandman for the trouble of cultivation, and, above all, of irrigation, which is a matter of difficulty in these arid regions. Amongst the brambled ravines, after sunrise, we heard the call of the black partridge, and above our heads, on the rocky peaks, that of the chekoar.

This bird generally, at these early hours, takes up so commanding a position, that he is pretty safe from the sportsman. I succeeded, however, with some difficulty, in shooting one. It is much like the red-legged partridge of France, though a heavier bird. The back is of a dove-colour; beak, legs, and eyes red; and on the sides of the head and under the wings there are some beautiful feathers of a brownish pink.

We passed to-day over a mountain which commands all the hills for a great distance round about: it is called Boor's Peak, and is 6439 feet above the sea, only about 100 feet lower than the Simplon.

Bhole is the name of the village at which the stage-house is situated. The bungalow is a miserable hut, built of what the Anglo-Himalayans call "wattle and dab;" an expressive term, giving a clearer idea of the component materials of the hill-houses than does the English term "lath and plaster."

The following morning we were early en route, and arrived, after an interesting and not very precipitous march of 13 miles, at Subbâtoo, the first residence of Europeans we have seen since Deyra: we took up our abode at the public bungalow, where we found two other travellers established;—it is a commodious building with five good rooms. The town consists of some 15 or 20 houses and bungalows—built after the fashion of many English villages, round a nearly level green of about 4 acres—cantonments for a Gourkah regiment of 700 men, and an extensive bazaar. There is an ancient Gourkah castle of inconsiderable extent at one extremity of the parade-ground, perched on a mound not much loftier than the barrow at Salt-hill.

The commanding officer of the above-named corps holds also the appointment of political agent to the district. Subbâtoo is the most northern European settlement in India, except Khôtgur, which is situated about 70 miles to the north-east of this place, near the banks of the Sutledge river. The elevation of Subbâtoo is about 4500 feet; and it is consequently much cooler and more healthy than the plains. During the hotter months, however, the English inhabitants found a greater elevation desirable, and the Political Agent established a summer residence at Simla, a name given to two or three miserable shepherd's huts, situated 24 miles north-east of Subbâtoo, beyond the British dominions, and in the territory of a native Ranee, or feudal baroness—for the ruler of a small uncultivated cluster of mountains can scarcely be dignified with the title of queen. The climate of Simla soon became famous; invalids from the plains resorted there, and built houses—instead of breaking up establishments and sailing for the Cape of Good Hope, with little hope of reaching it;—and finally Simla was rendered fashionable by the Governor-General, Lord Amherst, who resided there with his family for several months, and brought back to Calcutta rosy complexions, and some beautiful drawings by Lady Sarah Amherst, to attest the healthful and picturesque properties of the spot.

Simla is distinctly visible with the naked eye from the Subbâtoo parade-ground: in the morning it was enveloped in a white shroud of clouds, but, as soon as they were dissipated by the sun, I distinguished the broad union flag floating over the Commander-in-Chief's residence.

Halted the next day at Subbâtoo, therm. 77°; and the succeeding morning, May-day, marched to Sahree, a stage-house, 13 miles from Subbâtoo, and 11 from Simla. The first 3 miles of our route was a rapid descent, till we reached a beautiful little river rushing through a narrow and precipitous gorge. We forded the stream, which is inconsiderable, except during the rains, when travellers, by making a détour of about a mile, may cross it by a hanging bridge of ropes, an ingenious invention of Mr. Shakespear, late Postmaster-General. After passing the river, the road winds in a zigzag course up the face of a hill, and continues, with few exceptions, a gradual ascent to Sahree. We only passed two hamlets on the road-side, near one of which there are the ruins of a small fort: but on the flanks of the mountains on either hand, several small châlets, and one or two more considerable villages, are visible: round each of these there is a little green spot of cultivation amid the wide, rocky waste of the surrounding hills. Sahree is below the range in which the pine flourishes; but at this distance we can distinguish, by their black colour and serrated summits, that the mountains of Simla are thickly covered with this tree.

At Sahree we breakfasted, and tarried during the heat of the day; and in the afternoon began our ascent to Simla. About 3 miles from the latter place we entered upon the forest range, and the 2 last miles were on the tolerably level summit of the lofty ridge at one extremity of which Simla is situated. Here the vegetable ordinances appear the reverse of what I remarked at Llandowr. The south side of the mountain is clothed from peak to base with pines and larches, whilst the bleak northern flank is equally luxuriantly wooded with oak of several kinds, and the rich, crimson-flowered rhododendron; and so abrupt and uncompromising is this distinction of vegetable castes, that the road running along the spine of the narrow ridge is the only neutral or debatable ground between the two forest sects.

On reaching Simla we pitched our tents for the night, and hurried to change our entire suit of white linen for a costume more suited to the temperature of 61°, which to us appeared almost inclement; indeed it was a dreadful night. I was completely drenched in my bed by the rain, which fell in torrents; and the wind was so violent, and the situation of our tents so exposed, that I lay awake in momentary expectation of being blown away bodily into the valley 500 feet beneath. A goat and a sheep, the remains of our live stock, made a most piteous bleating all night, and were found dead in the morning—a bad compliment to the climate of Simla.

My friend and myself had just been absent a month from head-quarters ere we joined them at Simla. We found Lord Combermere, with his surgeon and an aide-de-camp, established in Captain Kennedy's (the Subbâtoo Political Agent) summer residence; and the rest of the Staff were either accommodated in the already existing houses, or busily employed in building—residing, in the mean time, in tents. The frequent clash of axe and hammer give evidence of the diligence with which they are labouring to provide roofs for themselves before the rains set in—nor have they much time to spare. Many hundreds of mountain-labourers and coolies are employed cutting timber, raising stone, and erecting the several buildings; the materials for which are close at hand in the excellent firs of the forest, and the fine flaky stone which abounds here.

The houses are irregularly scattered over the confined ridge, every level or gently-inclining space being taken advantage of for building; and three or four dwellings are erected on a spur of hills running at right angles from the Simla range towards the north. Communication between the several residences and the bazaar is secured by well-formed roads, which, though narrow, are tolerably safe for *sober* passengers. However, during our sojourn there, more than one neck was put in jeopardy by dark nights and hospitable neighbours.

A bazaar in India is a never-failing appendage to an assemblage of three or four European families, whether in town or camp. It is an excrescence originating from, and existing upon, the wants of the society; an epitome, indeed, of trade and commerce on a larger scale. The bazaar of Simla is, therefore, proportionate to the necessities of its patrons, and forms a neat little village, snugly situated under the shoulder of a lofty, conical mountain called Jâko, which protects it from the north-east wind. There are grain-shops, butchers, drapers, tailors, &c., to meet the exigencies of the place, and a guard-house for the Gourkah escort; and a long pennant, erected on a bamboo, marks the residence of the Kutwâal, or police-officer. The houses of the English residents are neatly and scientifically built of unmortared stone, intersected horizontally, at intervals of 2 feet, by pine-beams dovetailed at the angles. Many have flat roofs covered with a red clay, which requires many days' labour to beat it into a solid cake impervious to rain, and not liable to be cracked by the sun. Others have sloping or gable roofs, formed of fir-planks or of flakes of clay-slate, of which there are plentiful quarries in the vicinity. Outhouses, stables, and huts are commonly erected of the compound material styled "wattle and dab," and thatched with the bark and even with the dried leaves of the pine; which tree, in general utility, only falls short of the cocoa-tree of Bengal. In some few instances I have seen, in these mountains, log-huts formed of unsawed pines, after the fashion of the mountain châlets of Switzerland. Many of the Simla householders have already cultivated small spots of ground for cabbages and potatoes, and other vegetable esculents—the last-named valuable root thriving remarkably well in these climates. Captain Kennedy is liberally disseminating it through his district, and the poor natives, who live almost entirely on the precarious fruits of a not very productive soil, are not a little grateful for this useful addition to their provisions. Others of the residents of Simla have begun to embellish their abodes, and mingle the dulce with the utile, by rescuing some of the numerous and beautiful wild-flowers of these hills from their deleterious shade, and fostering them in the more sunny aspects round their habitations. Flower-seeds also, procured from the plains, have sprung up and flourished. Among the indigenous forest-flowers may be enumerated the violet, primrose, the hedge-rose, single and double, white and pink; the orchis, a great variety of convolvuli, and geraniums of many hues and forms. Ginger grows spontaneously and in great quantities on the sides of the hills. The beautiful and sweet-scented wild rose assumes, in some instances, the form of a creeper: I have seen it entirely enveloping a lofty pine, and, for want of further support, feathering down in thick-flowering clusters from the summit of the tree. The stems of many of the oaks and rhododendrons are profusely clothed with ivy of several beautiful kinds, which are strangers to the plains.

Fruit is to be had in great abundance, but of little

variety. The peach and apricot are cultivated by the natives, and brought for sale (at prices that would astonish Mrs. Grange) to the residents of Simla: they are carried in baskets, strapped on the shoulders, precisely in shape and fashion like those used by the Vaudois peasants. Walnuts are abundant. In the deep glens the pear and apple are found, but they are hard and tasteless; and strawberries are cultivated with great success, as, indeed, they are in the more northern provinces of the plains.

On the whole, from this summary, the hills must, in the article of fruit, yield to the plains—an inferiority which, however, is no doubt partly attributable to the hitherto little interest that has been taken in its cultivation. The delicious mango, the plantain, and orange, are imported to the English at Simla, with the usual monthly stores of wine, poultry, &c. Grapes, of a superior quality to any obtained in Hindostan, are occasionally brought from the mountain provinces beyond the Sutledge; but they seldom reach Simla in very fresh order.

Mutton, of a very inferior species to that of the plains, is the "toujours perdrix" of Simla gastronomy; the sacred character of the cow rendering beef unattainable, except in the imported shape of salt-junk. Captain Kennedy, however, in order to supply variety to his well-stocked and often well-guested table, has established at Subbâtoo a *very pretty piggery*.

However unromantic it may be to place scenery in juxtaposition with the means and appliances of good living, I must now attempt to give some idea of the prospect enjoyed by Simla. I have already mentioned that the eastern extremity of what may be properly called the Simla ridge is abruptly terminated by the conical mountain of Jâko, which is thickly wooded from base to summit, and is elevated about 400 feet above the houses of the bazaar. The western termination of the ridge is also designated by a mountain, of less considerable elevation than Jâko, whose summit is destitute of trees, and crowned by a now nearly effaced ruin.

The dark, deep, precipitous valley immediately below Simla on the south, is, as well as the neighbouring hills, thickly covered with pine-forests. Farther south, the mountains about Subbâtoo—which town may be distinguished in the half-distance of the picture—assume a less rugged outline, and are more bare of wood; and still more distant in the same direction the mountainous district comes to a sudden and abrupt conclusion, the view terminating in the horizon formed by the ocean-like plains of Hindostan, along whose broad, level bosom, on a clear day, may be distinguished the silver meanderings of the Sutledge.

The attributes of the northern prospect from Simla are still more grand; the valleys are more extensive, the mountains of more expanded proportions than those of the south view, assuming more the appearance of ranges, and rising gradually, one above the other, until the panorama is majestically terminated by the snowy crescent of the great Himalaya Belt, fading on either hand into indistinct distance. In fine weather these stupendous icy peaks cut the dark-blue sky with such sharp distinctness of outline, that their real distance of 60 or 70 miles is, to the eye of the gazer, diminished to one-tenth part.

During a residence of nearly two years in Switzerland, the first object that my eyes opened upon every morning was the snow-clad summit of Mont Blanc; and I thought *that* a glorious sight. But the glaciers that now form—next to the Omnipotent Being who created them—my first objects of matutine contemplation, present a battalion of icy pinnacles, amongst which Mont Blanc, with his pitiful 15,000 feet, would scarcely be admitted in the rear rank! But, belle Suisse! let me hasten to do you justice on another point: though Himala may boast of loftier mountains, and throw her Ganges and Jumna into the scale against your offspring, Rhine and Rhône, where are her lakes of Leman and Constance? She has none. In my tours through these hills I never saw a body of water, collected on one spot, that covered an acre of land. This lamentable deficiency (which I suppose scientific travellers are ready to account for) of that most requisite ingredient of scenery, and necessary of life, water, creates a hiatus in the Himalayan scenery, which is not to be supplied. The eye, fatigued with the rugged profile and sombre tint of the mountains, and the brown horror of the pine-forests, yearns for the refreshment and repose which it would enjoy in the contemplation of such a lake as that of Thoun, reflecting in its mirrored surface, dotted with sails, the blue sky above, and, in its soft medium, giving a flattering double of the impending scenery.

The elevation of Simla above the sea is 7800 feet; and, during the month of May, I find the thermometer was never higher than 73°, or lower than 55°, in my *garret.* This apartment, occupied by me during our stay in the hills, was pervious both to heat and cold, being, in fact, of that elevated character which in England is usually devoted to cheeses, or apples and onions, and forming the interval between the ceiling of the dining-room and the wooden pent-roof of the house, which, descending in a slope quite to the floor, only admitted of my standing upright in the centre. Though this canopy of planks was lined with whitewashed canvas, it by no means excluded the rains (the burra bursât) so peremptorily as I, not being an amphibious animal, could have wished; and, during some of the grand storms, the hailstones rattled with such stunning effect upon the drum-like roof, that the echo sung in my ears for a week after. This my exalted dormitory was rendered accessible by a wooden ladder; but, spite of its sundry désagrémens, I thanked my stars—in whose near neighbourhood I was—for my luck in getting any shelter, without the trouble of building, in the present crowded state of Simla. I enjoyed, as stated above, a splendid view from my windows (I beg pardon, window), and the luxury of privacy, except at night, when the rats sustained an eternal carnival, keeping me in much the same state as Whittington during his first week in London. I soon grew tired of bumping my head against the roof in pursuit of these four-footed Pindarees, and at length became callous to their nocturnal orgies, and kept a cat.

The temperature of Simla seems peculiarly adapted to the European constitution.

> " ——— The scorching ray
> Here pierceth not, impregnate with disease."

We have reason to be thankful that we are here far elevated above the atmospheric strata that have hitherto been subjected to the cholera, a disease now raging at Calcutta. This destructive pestilence, two years ago, ascended as high as Subbâtoo, strewing Lord Amherst's line of march with dead bodies. It is hard to say where its incursions may be arrested. The salubrity of this little abode of Hygeia is well attested by the presence of no less than 16 ladies, who gladly embrace the inconveniences attendant upon narrow accommodations and want of equipages (for no carriage has ever been at Simla), for the advantages accruing from the climate to themselves and their children. The cheeks of the latter quickly exchange their mealy, muffin-like hue—the livery of Bengal—for a good healthy ruddy bronze.

Our native servants at first took fright at the cold; and some of them even refused to enter the hills; but others were persuaded, by the promised advantages of additional warm raiment, to accompany us; and though they sometimes looked sufficiently miserable, yet they did not suffer in their health by the unwonted change of climate.

Our mode of life during the six months of our residence at Simla was somewhat monotonous; enlivened, however, occasionally by little excursions, in the form of *picnics*, and diversified, now and then, by the novelties that are always to be found by an inquiring sojourner in a strange country. Of sporting we had very little; for though there are several beautiful species of pheasants in the hills, black partridges in the ravines, and quails in the little patches of cultivation, game is on the whole so scarce as not to repay the great fatigue by which it must be attained. Eagles are very numerous, building their eyries in the rocky and inaccessible peaks; and, during the day, sailing with steady wing along the valleys in search of prey. They are the condor of the Himalayas, though by all accounts inferior in size to him of the Andes. The first week of my stay at Simla I was very active in pursuit of these tigers of the air, and succeeded in shooting a very fine one, measuring, from tip to tip of wing, 8 feet 5 inches. The back and wings were of a deep brown, whilst the breast and thighs were covered with a thick, soft, yellowish down.

There are bears, hyænas, leopards, and jackals in the woods, and several kinds of deer. The kucker, or barking-deer, so called from his voice, which resembles the short single bark of a dog, makes himself heard every night in the neighbourhood of the houses. He is a curious animal, with two long sharp tusks protruding from the upper jaw. The royal tiger is seldom seen so far northward as Simla; but on one occasion, Colonel Finch's shikkaree (a well-known character at Head-quarters), being in search of game in a valley 10 miles distant, came suddenly upon one of these jungle marauders, and, making good his retreat, reported the circumstance to his master. The shikkaree was sent back to the spot with an unfortunate donkey, which animal is a most approved bonne bouche—to be picketed near the place, whilst the man kept watch in a tree, until the tiger should kill his victim; when he was to report the fact, and we were to make a party to meet the monster at his dinner. The life of the poor devoted donkey was, however, saved, and our consciences the burden of his murder. The shikkaree returned from his vidette-post one morning with a very long face, bringing information that one of the mountain hunters had killed the tiger in the act of pulling down a bullock. The fellow shot him in the head with his matchlock, and then, attacking him sword in hand, cut him through the spine. We never heard of another tiger in the hills.

Whilst Head-quarters remained at Simla, which was about 7 months, the leisure hours of many of the officers

Cumbermere Bridge Simla

London, Published by John Murray 1838

were employed in building their houses, and afterwards in enlarging and beautifying them. Lord Combermere amused himself, and benefited the public, by superintending the formation of a fine, broad, level road round the mount Jâko, about 3 miles in length. It was worked entirely by Hill-men, and exceedingly skilfully done; and will, when finished, be a great acquisition to the loungers of Simla. Across a deep ravine, a quarter of a mile from the town, his Lordship erected a neat Sangah, or mountain-bridge of pines; and under it a capacious stone tank was constructed, to obviate the great scarcity of water. During the progress of this miniature Simplon, which occupied the hours before breakfast and those after sunset, the attendant A. D. C. amused himself by watching the formation of the mines for blasting the rocks, cutting down the proscribed pines, making grotesque rustic arbours at intervals on the road, or whistling after the huge blocks of stone, which, moved by levers off the road, toppled, bounded, and crashed through the wooded declivity into the valley below, reminding one of Homer's expressive line, describing the retrograde descent of the stone of Sisyphus. When the longest half of the road was completed, the workmen were presented with two sheep, on which they were to feast, after having offered them as propitiatory sacrifices to their deity.

In these religious rites it appears that it is necessary—in order to manifest the deity's acceptance of the offering—that the victim, on being presented before the altar, should exhibit some signs of external agitation. This to me appeared a hopeless case, as the animals in question held down their heads, and looked as sheepish as might be expected. My simplicity, however, quickly received a lesson from these unsophisticated mountaineers, which led me to conclude that they are not so much blinded by their superstition as to allow it to interfere with the gratification of their appetites.

As the victim did not manifest the smallest degree of confusion when confronted with the little mis-shapen idol, whose countenance—the work of some mountain Canova—

might have been an excuse for terror in a bolder animal, the officiating pontiff obtained by artificial means what he might have despaired of through natural agency.

Approaching the animal with all the solemnity due to the occasion, he took a mouthful of spring water, and squirted it, with the force of a fire-engine, into its ear! The victim could not do less than shake its head: the movement was hailed in triumph by the congregation: at one blow of the high priest's kookery* the head fell to the ground, the blood sprinkled the altar, and almost before the body of the sheep had ceased to palpitate it was roasting before a huge pine fire.

Another equally peculiar trait of the customs of the Himalayan peasants I witnessed a few days afterwards, namely, the putting an infant to sleep by the action of water. The successful issue of this experiment I had quietly made up my mind not to believe in, until convinced by actual ocular proof. The method was as follows. The child—whose age might be a year or two—was laid by its mother, who was employed in bruising grain, on a charpoy placed on a sloping green bank, along the top of which ran a small spring stream. A piece of bark, introduced through the embankment, conducted a slender spout of water, which fell, at the height of about half a foot, on to the crown of the infant's head. It was fast asleep when I witnessed the process! The natives believe that it is a great fortifier of the constitution. It may be that it fortifies the pericranium, and addles the brains of its advocates, for the generality of the mountaineers are decided numskulls.

That frightful disease, the goître, is nearly as common here as it is in Switzerland; and *cretins* are by no means rare, though they do not shock the eyes of the traveller at every turn, as is the case in the villages of the Valais. This is accounted for by the well-known and undisguised

* The *kookery* is a long, heavy, crooked knife peculiar to the Gourkahs. It performs the several duties of the warrior's sword, the woodman's axe, and the butcher's knife.

practice of the natives, of destroying their deformed children as soon as they are born. In most mountainous countries I think it may be remarked, that those whose minds are from infancy deranged are equally distorted in person.

The periodical rains called the chota bursât (little rains) set in on the 10th of June, with a violent storm, and the thermometer immediately sunk from 80° to 58°. The approach of the tempest was one of the most glorious sights I ever witnessed. The morning was bright and hot, the sky presenting one unbroken canopy of blue; when suddenly a black bank of clouds invaded and quickly enveloped the snowy peaks in the north, and then rapidly approached us up the deep gorges of the mountain; accompanied by a deafening noise of thunder and wind, and the most vivid flashes of lightning, which seemed to issue even from the clouds *below* us. This agitated mass of dark vapours resembled a vast *storming party*, as it rapidly, and in succession, took possession of, and overran, the different hills before us, and then came rushing onwards to the spot where we stood.

On the storm ceasing, Simla was left an insulated clear spot in a wide ocean of clouds; huge, heavy masses of them lying, torpid, in the valleys around and below us, and appearing as though they were fatigued by the impetus that had brought them from the snowy range to Simla, about 70 miles, in the space of half an hour.

From the 15th to the 30th of June we enjoyed the usual fair interregnum between the little and great bursât; the mean state of the thermometer at 2 P.M. being 73°.

After this interval the rainy season set in in real earnest. It seemed as though St. Swithin had come to the hills for his health! for we had scarcely one day without a shower from this date until the middle of August. However, in justice to the climate, it is fair to state that there were very few days on which we were entirely confined to the house.

Vegetating as we were, so quietly and for so many months, in the mountains, far from the bustling pleasures of the flaunting town, it is natural that we should be on the eager look-out for novelties of any kind. We were, therefore, one day—more especially the naturalists of the party—put on the qui vive of expectation by the arrival of a native of the more northern mountains, who reported that he had lately caught an unicorn, and that it was only 3 marches off. Of course all were anxious to see the rare and hitherto-believed fabulous animal; and some went so far as to declare their intention of purchasing it, at whatever price, and sending it, with a fine male lion, to the king of England, as an appropriate present. Two days after, the unicorn's arrival was reported, and eagerly hastening, pencil and paper in hand, to the spot, where a crowd was assembled, I discovered—a fine fat sheep—no more! He was, indeed, literally an unicorn, for his horns were curiously grown together into one, an almost imperceptible line marking the division. It grew curving backwards over the animal's head, and would have entered the spine had the point not been sawed off. The soidisant unicorn would, no doubt, have made very respectable mutton, though he would have proved but a tame supporter of the arms of England.

Sept. 15*th.*—Having 6 weeks more to enjoy the hills, Lord Combermere resolved to devote a month to a tour in the more unfrequented parts of the country, and to visit one of the grand passes in the Snowy Belt.

Two parties being formed, it was agreed that Colonel Dawkins, Baron Osten (16th Lancers), and myself, should start on the 24th, for the pass of Shattoul; and Lord Combermere, Captain Kennedy, and 3 others, will soon after migrate towards the Borenda pass.

During the remainder of our stay at Simla my journal records little else but an uninteresting routine of rambles among the valleys, occasional trips to Subbâtoo, and a few picnic expeditions to a mountain 12 miles north of Simla.

On one occasion, however, the quiet inhabitants were drawn out of their houses by the appearance of a numerous and picturesque group of cavaliers, winding up the mountain-road towards the town. They proved to be an embassy from Runjeet Singh of Lahore to the Commander-in-Chief; bringing presents of a dozen very neatly-worked hand punkahs, or fans, made of ivory and sandal-wood, with filigree gold handles. The rest of the Maha-Rajah's offering was more weighty than valuable, consisting of no less than 35 maunds of almonds and dried fruits.

On another occasion the English of Simla were put into a general ferment by an occurrence which—as we are only supposed to hold our supremacy in India by "the force of opinion"—is, fortunately, almost without a parallel in our annals. Two Mussulman-sepoys, belonging to a corps of irregular horse in the service of the Company, conceiving themselves (as it afterwards proved, without cause) to have been insulted by an English officer of artillery who was living at Simla in bad health, determined on vengeance; and dogging him to an unfrequented part of the road, assaulted him in the most brutal manner, striking him several times on the head and face with the heels of their shoes (the greatest indignity that a native can inflict or suffer), and otherwise seriously maltreating him. It is impossible to say to what extremities they might not have proceeded in their rage, had they not been interrupted by a lady, who, hearing of the affair from one of her servants (the man passing the scene of action without an attempt at interference), hastily and heroically repaired to the spot with her attendants, and rescued the officer when he was quite exhausted by the ill-treatment he had received. Though the young Englishman was of rather small stature and in bad health, the sepoys on their appearance before the court-martial presented a pretty severe illustration of the power of a pair of English fists, even against odds of two to one. A closed eye of one of the prisoners, and a dislodged tooth of the other, confessed the efficiency of the young bombardier's battery. One of the sepoys was a tall, lathy fellow; the other a most ferocious-looking ruffian, short, but square-shouldered and muscular.

The Bhisty, who reported the conflict to his mistress, was an important witness; he was a man of uncommon muscular strength—as most of his arduous trade are,—and looked as if he could have killed and eat both the defendants without difficulty. When asked by the Judge-Advocate, why he did not assist the Sahib? he said, with the characteristic apathy of a Hindoo, "I am a poor man; I was carrying my mussuck;* it never entered into my head. The sentence of the court was 800 lashes and dismission from the service, which was duly inflicted. The long rascal yelled under the "cat;" the short ruffian bore his punishment bravely.

CHAPTER V.

Khôtghur — Fargoo — Parellee — Tour in the Surmour mountains — Khotekie — Koopa mountain — Jubul — Deora — Saree — Rooroo — Mountain tour — Chergong — Dogolee — Roole — Birch region — The Shattoul Pass — Retreat from the pass — Krassoo — Kushaine — Khôtghur — Nackandeh — Mutteanah — Simla — Subbâtoo — Bahr.

Sept. 24th.—IN the afternoon I started, with Colonel Dawkins and the Baron Osten, on our tour to the Snowy Mountains, with the further intention of crossing the pass, and returning towards Simla by the valley of the Sutledge.

Our travelling equipage consisted of 2 small but convenient and warm tents, with a pâl for our servants and batterie de cuisine ambulante; 3 ponies, 2 mules, and a jâmpaun for the transport of our persons; and a small stock of sheep, milch-goats, claret (for nothing can be done in India without lâl sherâb), port, spirits, and spices. With these appliances we hoped to be able to *rough it* pretty comfortably.

Our first day's stage was on the Khôtghur road, and we took up our quarters at the travellers' bungalow at Fargoo, an edifice by no means remarkable, unless it be for a rather

* Sheepskin water-bag.

From a Sketch by G. C. Mundy

Etched by T. Landseer

Travelling in the Hymalaia Mountains

London. Pub.d by John Murray

uncommonly smoky chimney. The elements did not smile upon the commencement of our journey, a dense fog enveloping us soon after we left Simla, and continuing to enshroud us the whole evening. Fargoo is about 12 miles from Simla and a mile beyond Mahasoo, the spot which, from its convenient properties of shade, space, good water, and beautiful scenery, was dedicated by the fashionables of Simla to picnic purposes. Indeed, no place could be better calculated for a fête champêtre. The tents on these occasions were usually pitched on the declivity of a hanging wood of pines, oaks, and hollies, thickly interwoven with an underwood of currant-trees, raspberries, straw berries, and jasmine; which, "with woodbines wreathing and roses breathing," formed a fragrant and almost impenetrable fence round three sides of the spot cleared for the camp; whilst a smooth gently-shelving lawn in front, and an unwooded vista terminating in an abrupt precipice, led the eye of the spectator, with scarcely an intervening object, to a grand prospect of the Snowy Range. The chief *lion* of Mahasoo is a wood of the most enormous pines, some of them measuring from 120 to 130 feet in height, 20 feet in circumference, and growing as straight as an arrow. The timber of these trees is said to be remarkably sound. Such a forest in England would soon put to shame the mast-trade of Archangel.

The situation of Fargoo is about 10,000 feet above the sea, and it is therefore much colder than Simla; the thermometer to-day being at 58°.

The next day our route took us off the beaten road of Khôtghur. The morning being rainy, we sent off our baggage early, and started ourselves about mid-day. The first 5 miles of our march led us down one continual descent to the bottom of a valley, where we crossed a little river called the Ghirree. Thence we skirted the stream—sometimes close to its banks, sometimes elevated many hundred feet above its bed—all the way to Parellee, where there is a stage-house. We passed on our left 2 hill-fortresses, one of which, Theog, appears, from its situation among the clouds, perfectly impregnable. The weather became clear in the course of the morning, and we enjoyed magnificent scenery the whole of our journey. At this season the sides of the cultivated hills are much ornamented by a beautiful crimson grain, called bâttoo, which is now nearly ripe, and forms the chief article of food among the natives. In the valley we passed the castle of the Ranah of the province, a title equivalent to the Rajah of Hindostan. It is a strange, uncomfortable-looking building, but well situated near the river. The latter is here a shallow, rapid, and rocky stream of most translucent water. The few specimens we saw of the male inhabitants were handsome and stout made, and appeared of remarkably cheerful and contented dispositions, saluting us smilingly as we passed. The women, on the contrary, were "dumpy," and, for the most part, *grumpy*. There was a good pattern of a hill-house at Parellee, which I examined: it was built of stone and wood, with a wooden pent-roof; the lower story was entirely devoted to the accommodation of cattle, whilst the first, or habitable story, was made accessible by a rude ladder formed of a notched beam. I took a hasty sketch of it.

We have descended some thousand feet in this day's march, the thermometer being 77°, nearly 20 degrees higher than at Fargoo. The scenery about our tents is tame in comparison with that of Simla. The afternoon being sultry and close, we descended to the river and enjoyed a delicious bath, an imprudent measure which two of the three had afterwards cause to repent—"hinc fons et origo malorum." The water was biting cold, and so rapid that it required all our strength to stand upright in the stream.

I think it right, thus early in my mountain tour, to give my reader the probably welcome information that I am totally unskilled in botany and geology, by which fortunate default in my education he will escape the usual inflictions of scientific travellers—such as being delayed half an hour to dissect a daisy, or being planted the best part of a forenoon before a block of stone to decide whether it be gra-

Palace of the Chief of Khotakee

London Pub.d by John Murray, 1838

nite or marble, primitive or secondary rock, till the bored peruser becomes almost petrified himself.*

26*th*.—Left Parellee about 7 A. M., and marched to the town or village of Khote-kie, about 14 miles. The road ran the whole way just above the little brawling Ghirree, and the scenery reminded me much of that part of Wales near Llangollen. The hills are almost entirely devoid of trees and covered with a verdant clothing of grass and grain-crops. The chief produce appears to be the red corn and buckwheat on the hill-sides, and rice in the valleys low enough for irrigation. The houses are from two to three stories high, and are picturesque objects in the landscape. We crossed the river over a very romantic sangah, or bridge of pines, at least 100 feet above the bed: it afforded an interesting subject for a flying sketch. Ere we descended upon Khote-kie we traversed a wood of firs resembling the Weymouth pine; on emerging from which we came abruptly upon the village. There are two remarkable masses of buildings—the castle of the Ranee of the province and the residence of the Zemindar, both situated on lofty promontories of rock, just extensive enough to contain the houses and their offices. Round the foot of the precipice on which the former edifice is perched, the little river winds its course.

We took up our abode in the stage-bungalow, near which is the comfortable residence of a Subadar, or native commissioned officer, of Captain Kennedy's regiment of hill-rangers, who was promoted to that rank by Lord Combermere for his bravery at Bhurtpore. The wooden eaves of his house are carved and ornamented much after the fashion

* Little did I foresee that this unlucky sentence would be construed into a serious attempt to exalt my own trifling lucubrations at the expense of science. Yet has an otherwise indulgent critic, in his review of my first edition, ascribed to me some such monstrous aim. Let me, therefore, hasten to plead "not guilty" to so grave a charge; and to confess in sober sadness—since it is no joking matter!—that there was not a furlong of my Himalayan rambles unproductive of hearty lamentations at my want of power to fully appreciate those opportunities which would have been so invaluable to the scientific tourist.

of the better buildings in the mountain-hamlets of Switzerland. The gallant inhabitant paid us a visit immediately on our arrival, presenting us his sword, as is usual with native officers, in lieu of a "nuzzur." In these cases the superior touches the sword with his right hand and makes a salaam. The Subadar was particularly civil, and provided us with an abundance of milk, butter, eggs, walnuts, &c.; more particularly with several pairs of shoes, the manufacture of some mountain Crispin, whose prices would sadly undersell Hoby: he asked one rupee for four pair. I take advantage of my Irish birth in describing the *upper-leather* of these shoes as made of worsted net, and the sole of tough hide sewed with thongs.

In the evening the Subadar showed us his favourite charger, of which he is, and has a right to be, proud. The manner in which he became possessed of the horse is perhaps worth recording. During the siege of Bhurtpore, and after our parallels had been pushed to within 300 yards of the counterscarp, a white horse was observed to be picketed close under an outwork of the fort, and in a situation so exposed to the fire of both besiegers and besieged, that no one on either side seemed willing to run the risk incident upon an attempt to appropriate him. The poor neutral nag was therefore in a fair way of being shot or starved to death. Our hero—then jemadar, or sepoy serjeant, and, doubtless, too poor to be well mounted—cast the eye of covetousness upon the snowy charger; and one morning, determined "to do or die," jumped over the gabions, and, running across the glacis, reached the horse, cut him adrift, and, under a heavy fire of musketry from the walls, trotted him in triumph into the trenches, himself unscathed, and his prize receiving only one bullet through the nose, which scarcely blemished him. The right of conquest is so well established in British India, that there is no fear of the gallant Subadar being disturbed in his acquisition.

Our native friend caused some specimens of iron, manufactured in the neighbourhood, to be brought for our inspection: it is procured from a micaceous stone thickly encrusted with small garnets, in which the hills in the vicinity abound.

The following day we left Khote-kie; the attentive Subadar, on his white charger, convoying us as far as a bridge built by him across a furious torrent, and of which he is nearly as vain as he is of his horse. The first four miles of our day's march was one continued steep ascent to the summit of a hill well clothed with firs, among which we heard the pheasants crowing.* At the top of the mountain we were met and accosted by a dirty, shabbily-attired native, who announced himself as the Ranah, or chieftain of the soil on which we stood. This impotent potentate presented a nuzzur, and then commenced a long oration, setting forth the poverty of his dominions and the riches and power of "Company Sahib." If my guide spoke true, he had, indeed, some cause to grumble over his domains; for it appeared that he possessed but two villages, the most productive of which only brought him a half-yearly addition to his treasury of 20 rupees, 8 of which, according to my informer, were claimable by the Company, as conquerors of the soil. Of late, however, government have charitably refrained from urging a claim which robs a poor man of half his revenue, and "little profits" them.

The mountains here are less wooded and precipitous, and have more arable land, than those of Simla; and they are studded, from their extremest summits to their very base, with picturesque villages and the respectable habitations of Zemindars and petty Ranahs. About 7 miles from Khote-kie we began the ascent of the Koopa mountain, from the top of which we again caught a glimpse of the snowy peaks, of which we had entirely lost sight during the last 3 days. The road, which might without great difficulty have been conducted round the flank of the hill, leads by a series of steep and exceedingly slippery zigzags right over the crest; from whence we had 4 miles of disagreeably abrupt descent to the village of Deora, the metropolis of the province of

* The road is seen in the right distance of my sketch.

Jubul. The last of the Company's bungalows in this direction is situated here.

On an insulated rock in the bottom of the valley, along which the mountain-river rushes, stands the strange-looking palace of the Jubul Ranah, one of the most considerable of the highland barons. It is an immense mass of building, the upper stories formed chiefly of wood. The sides of the mountain in rear of the castle are beautifully alternated with pine-woods and veins of cultivation, up to the very summit; the rich crimson tint of the bâttoo-crops contrasting well with the dark hue of the forests, and the lighter verdure of the grass-lands.

On our arrival at the stage-house the Ranah sent to announce his intention of paying us a visit—a compliment which all petty chiefs pay to us on hearing that we are of the Commander-in-Chief's family. Jubul is famous for the beauty of its inhabitants; and the Ranah and his minister, who came in the evening according to promise, both do justice to its fame. The chief himself is about 25 years of age, nearly as fair as a European, with very handsome features, but his eyes so immeasurably large, that they give a vague and foolish expression to his countenance, an expression which is by no means belied by his intellect. The vizier is a fine, stout young man, with a beard in better preservation than his tunic. He has greatly the advantage in intelligence over his master, who, during the interview, was evidently under the influence of opium, and towards whom he was obliged to act in much the same capacity as the flapper of Laputa.

Lord Combermere passed through this place about a week after our party; when the Ranah of course paid his respects. Hearing that there was an English hakim in his Lordship's suite, the chieftain took an opportunity, during the audience, to beseech the doctor to prescribe some specific that would procure him an heir for his dominions, which he despaired of having, in spite of the multiplicity of his wives. I know not what satisfaction he obtained. Deora is, as its name would imply, a place of some sanctity. There is a very pretty modern temple, much ornamented with carved wood-work; and the ruins of one of more extensive dimensions.

Sept. 28*th*.—Proceeded on our march at the usual hour. The road we traversed to-day is in no places too steep for riding, though it is not more than 4 or 6 feet wide. It runs along the side of one unbroken range of green grass hills, at the foot of which rushes a little stream, called the Ranse, bordered thickly with alder-trees. We skirted this brook all the way to Saree, where we found our little camp pitched on a bare barren moor. Here the Ranse throws itself into a more considerable stream, the Pahbur, which, in its turn, is tributary to the great Jumna. This day's march was on the whole much less interesting than any of the preceding —the scenery was tamer, trees more scarce. The only plant peculiar to these regions is a species of alder—*Indicè* Siou. It attains a much greater bulk than in England. I think one that I measured was about 18 feet in circumference.

By the difference of temperature, and the peculiar flowers and plants, which characterise very distinctly the different elevations, I should judge that Saree is much lower than Simla. We found the tents very hot; thermometer standing at 82°. In these mountains princes are as common as yeomen in England. We quitted the Jubul territories this morning, and are now in the mooluck of a Ranee. The old woman civilly sent her heir-apparent to welcome us, and offer assistance. He brought us a present of a kid, and some jars of remarkably fine honey—a rare luxury in India. The queen's residence, which she dignifies with the title of Killar or fort, is situated far below us, on a scarped rock on the banks of the Pahbur; and is, in fact, nothing more than a congregation of wooden huts. The river is famous for its fish, which grow as large as 15 and 20 pounds. We had some difficulty at this place in procuring coolies to carry our tents and baggage, but at length succeeded through the intervention of the Ranee.

The next morning we marched about 8 miles to the village of Rooroo. Our route lay along the side of a verdant hill, just above the right bank of the Pahbur, and without much variety in its elevation. The river, which is remarkably rapid, and about 40 yards wide, meanders fantastically, sometimes in a single stream, at others in many little rills, through a Khâder, or valley, between two ranges of hills. The banks are at this season covered at intervals with very fair crops of rice and other grain. The village of Rooroo is more considerable than the generality of mountain-hamlets, and the quantity of level land in the vicinity affords greater scope for cultivation. A large building in the town was pointed out as the palace of the Barageh Ranah. He visited us in the afternoon, and gave us much useful information regarding our route, affording us small hopes of being able to take our horses more than two marches farther. One of the Ranah's attendants brought us a plentiful basket of fish and fruits. He also produced a musk-ball, which I persuaded him to exchange with me for a small penknife. Its scent was so powerful, that I could hardly bear it among my clothes in the boxes.

Our next day's journey was about 11 miles, and very tedious from the sameness of the scenery and the intense heat. The road continued partly along the Khâder of the river, and was in parts cut through the rocky mountain overhanging its bed. There are one or two very nervous passages in it, where the path, scarcely two feet wide including the coping-stone, turns abruptly round jutting buttresses of rock several hundred feet above the stream, which foams and boils at the foot of the perpendicular precipice. The fort of Buttoulee, belonging to the Rajah of Bussahir, a very extensive district, stands on the left bank of the Pahbur, and is—as is usual with the mountain-strongholds—situated on a lofty rock, standing out in lonely grandeur from the main range.

We passed two or three very considerable villages on our way, one of which, Bourah, is very picturesque and romantic in its situation. The method of preserving hay about here is curious, and appears to answer very well. It is loosely twisted into long, thick ropes, which, being fastened together at one end, are thrown over the fork of a tree, the extremities hanging down, and the apex being thatched with straw. Our camp was pitched just under the village of Chergong, on the banks of a small stream, which, running from the north, falls into the Pahbur half a mile hence. The thermometer 84°. Here we take leave of the latter river, and of the good road (which continues along its banks towards the more eastern pass of Borenda), and, striking off in a more northerly direction, we are to expect nothing more than mountain tracks for the four marches between Chergong and the Shattoul Pass. A dâk hurkarah reached us to-day with a letter from Captain Kennedy, advising us not to attempt to carry forward our ponies beyond Chergong—a piece of good advice completely thrown away, as we had predetermined to make the experiment. The plan of carrying a letter in these countries is novel enough. The letter is tied in a split stick—resembling the rods used in courts of justice for the conveyance of notes over the heads of the multitude—and the postman runs along bearing it aloft; thus at once declaring his office, and preserving the despatch from being soiled.

Oct. 1*st.*—Left Chergong early, and, turning our faces in a northern course, rode, walked, and clambered to the village of Dogolee, a short but very fatiguing march. The path—for there was no road, led alternately through rice-fields and along the rocky flank of the mountain on the left bank of the little torrent above mentioned. Many points were extremely difficult for the passage of horses, but sufficiently easy for the highlanders who carried the tents and baggage. After sundry narrow escapes, the Baron's pony fell over the side, and became in consequence so timid, that it was not safe to bring him on: he was, therefore, sent back, with orders to wait at Khôtghur, a large town in Bussahir, until our arrival there. Both the mules got falls, but fortunately in a spot where there was no precipice. The narrow defile through which we pursued our way presents very different features to the comparatively tame scenery of our two last marches: the banks of the stream are beautifully fringed with magnificent alders and other trees of gigantic size; and the precipitous mountains flanking the valley on either hand are bristling with fir-forests, from the midst of which the jutting peaks of black rocks rear their heads.

About half a mile from Dogolee we crossed the river by a rickety temporary bridge of rough pines and turf, thrown across two rocks, which confine the stream in a narrow channel. The ponies accomplished the passage with great difficulty and risk; but the regular sangah having been carried away by the overflow of the river in the rains, there was no better means of passing the torrent.

From the river we had a most fatiguing ascent of a mile and a half, which, as our ponies and mules were all knocked up, we were obliged to perform on foot; a necessity not a little unwelcome to the Baron and myself, who for the two last days have been labouring under an indisposition, arising from our imprudence in bathing in the iced streams of the glaciers, and from the constant sudden changes of temperature to which we have been exposed. We found our tents pitched on a piece of ploughed ground near the hamlet of Dogolee. Though we are now within 30 miles of the pass, the snowy peaks are entirely hidden from our view; yet these same glaciers are visible from Meerut, a distance of some 20 marches.

Oct. 2nd.—At 7 A.M. our trio started from Dogolee, and, owing to the many "moving accidents by flood and field" encountered on the journey, we did not reach our camp—a distance of about 10 miles—until half-past 12 o'clock. The first part of our route serpentined along the bottom of this most beautiful defile, still skirting the little brook, which is an offspring of the glacier of Shattoul. We were overshadowed by enormous trees resembling elms, but with stems varying from 18 to 25 feet in circumference. Here we also met with—for the first time in India—the horse-chestnut; the Spanish chestnut, sycamore, and filbert; the latter bearing a similar gigantic superiority as the elm over its namesake in England. Peaches and apricots are as common here as blackberries in Europe. About half way we were obliged, by the extreme narrowness and rockiness of the defile, and the impenetrable thickness of the jungle, to ascend the flank of the mountain, high above the left bank of the torrent; and here difficulties began to grow upon us. In many points the half-formed rocky path, not more than a foot wide, and only calculated for the passage of bipeds, was so steep, slippery, and abrupt in its turnings, that we began to despair of getting on our quadrupeds in safety. We were, however, encouraged to persevere by the comfortable assurance that to recede was at least as difficult; more especially as the syces, if sent back, would probably, when not excited to exertion by the presence of their masters, relax in their care and attention to the animals in the dangerous passes. Another consideration also weighed with us, which was, that, if we should succeed in getting across the pass to the valley of Rampore, we should find it very inconvenient to make six marches in that sultry vale without horses. On we went, as stubborn—in our purpose—as the poor devoted mules that followed us; ourselves on foot, whilst the most determined of our servants led the nags with long halters. Many hairbreadth escapes did we brave, and extricate ourselves from; till at length we arrived at a sudden break, an "imminent deadly breach" in the path, which I, at first sight, pronounced to be a ne plus ultra. At an acute angle of the track, with a nearly perpendicular precipice above and below, stood a mass of rock directly across the road, which, immediately beyond this obstacle, sunk about 3 feet, turning sharp round the overhanging angle. My mule crept over it like a cat, without once hesitating; Dawkins's mule came next, and accomplished the pass after a long and obstinate refusal; next followed my friend's pony, one imported from the plains, and, though bold and active, not much skilled in mountain-clambering. The place where we stood would have turned the heads of even us foot-passengers, had not the precipice below us been thickly veiled with trees and shrubs, which prevented the eye of the spectator from plunging at once to the bottom of the giddy abyss, where we heard the torrent rushing along its rocky channel. The gallant chestnut, on being led to the pass, cleared the rock at a flying leap, alighting on the very brink of the path; the deceitful earth gave way, the pony tottered, struggled vehemently for an instant, and then rolled headlong over the precipice. He was fortunately arrested in his downward career by a stout tree, about 20 feet below the road, where we found him uninjured, but so weak from alarm, that we could hardly get him on his legs again. Our kookeries*—which we always wore—now came into play, and with great labour we cut a passage up to the path through the underwood; during the accomplishment of which pioneering the horse had time to recover his strength. We now endeavoured to lead him up again to the road by the abbatis which we had formed. I had already reached the track, holding his head, and D. urging him in the rear, when he placed his fore feet on a large loose piece of rock forming the coping-stone. I saw it shake beneath the poor pony's weight as he struggled for a firm footing:—another spring would have landed him in safety—but the treacherous crag deserted its post, and "fell it?—it fell!" and once more over went the chestnut, nearly carrying his master with him. We heard the poor animal, together with his rough companion, the detached rock, crashing through the trees, and presently the latter plunge into the torrent 300 feet below us.

Almost despairing of a second rescue, we clambered down to the pony's assistance, and found him in a situation even more precarious than before. A friendly tree had again interposed between him and destruction. He lay on his back, supported by a sycamore, whose huge roots seemed to possess but a frail hold on the very verge of a scarped rock. We saw that the first movement the animal made must inevitably precipitate him over a cliff of about 30 feet perpendicular height. He *did* move, and immediately dis-

* Gourkah knives.

appeared; and we heard him rolling among the loose rocks beneath. We discovered him lying in a hollow, which had been luckily rendered soft by a plentiful deposit of decayed vegetation, about 50 feet below the road. On reconnoitring the spot, we found a comparatively easy, though circuitous ascent to the path, by which we succeeded in getting the chestnut up without further mishaps; and so little injured was he by his by no means "facilis descensus," that he began to nibble the grass the instant his resurrection was completed.

On returning to assist my ghoont in his passage of the strait, we found his case still more desperate, by reason of the gap which the other had made in his fall. This we repaired, as well as we could, with branches, laying a white handkerchief over them to prevent the pony from jumping on them; and the little rough brute slid down the block of granite in perfect safety.

During this day's journey we twice crossed the river. At the first passage we crossed by a sangah loosely formed of pines, between which the wide intervals showed the impetuous torrent beneath to the dizzy passenger. By this insecure bridge it was impossible to transport the ponies; and, after some trouble, we found a place in the stream tolerably free from rocks, through which they were led by our mountain servants. This was done at some risk, for so furious was the stream, that in some places we saw large masses of stone rolled along by the force of the current. At the second passage we were fated to encounter another mishap. The torrent was at this spot almost one continued cascade, so that the only possible means of crossing was by a sangah framed of the same frail materials as the former, with a few flag-stones spread over it for foot-passengers. To render it more difficult, the rock which formed the opposite buttress was several feet lower than that on the side upon which we approached this flying-bridge. The sketch, which I made during the passage of the animals, will give some idea of the spot. The sangah was not more than 3 feet wide, and, though it was thickly strewed with boughs, I saw several dangerous interstices between the beams. Though we had all been Alpine travellers, we found it rather a nervous performance. The two ponies and one of the mules accomplished it in safety, though I trembled for them, as I saw the insecure bridge bending under their weight. The other mule had just reached the middle, when one of his legs went through between the pines, and, after a brief and fruitless struggle, over he went headlong into the boiling torrent, 30 feet beneath. He luckily fell into a deep gulf free from rocks; and, after being carried down about 20 yards, recovered his legs and scrambled to the bank, a good deal shaken, but with whole limbs.

From this "Pont du Diable" we had a most heart-breaking ascent of about two miles. D., who was in good health, and an active pedestrian, confessed himself nearly knocked up when he reached the tents; and the Baron and myself, whose indisposition, caused by the ice-bath, had daily increased, were more dead than alive when we arrived. The head of the former was swelled to nearly twice its natural size, accompanied with excruciating pain; and I, in addition to cholera symptoms, was covered with a rash, which was much aggravated by the myriads of sand-flies abounding here.

We found our camp pitched at the respectable village of Roole, the situation of which is wild and romantic in the extreme. It is so shut in with lofty pine-covered mountains that the snowy peaks of the Shattoul Pass are invisible. After the practical proof we had enjoyed of the difficulty, nay cruelty, of persevering in the attempt to take forward our horses, and the discouraging accounts of the roads we received from the villagers, we determined to send them back, with a few men to pioneer them through the most difficult passes. Our eyes have become by degrees opened to the fact that we are travelling in rather too much *style* for such a wild, unfrequented part of the world. We ought to have relinquished all idea of bringing horses farther than Chergong; and the inconveniences attendant upon so large a suite of tents more than counterbalance the comforts. We have four in all, and these, with our baggage, require 82 (!) men for their transport. It is almost impossible to levy such a regiment at a day's notice in a country so thinly peopled; and, to render our present case more desperate, the only two villages within reach of us are at issue, and, during their feuds, will not enlist together in the same service.

The next day we were obliged to halt at Roole to collect coolies, which we at length managed by bribing a good many of our last stagers to proceed with us. These mountaineers are unwilling to enter into a longer service than two days, as they are now engaged at one of their numerous harvests. The thermometer at 2 P.M. stood at 76°, and at night sunk to 45°. It was bitter cold, and the insomnious hours of the invalids were aggravated by the unceasing attacks of the sand-flies, whose bites were exceedingly venomous, and the more annoying that the enemy who inflicted them was invisible—the satisfaction of returning evil for evil being thus denied to the attacked.

In the evening our hurkarah returned according to order, and reported the safe arrival of the quadrupeds at Dogolee, on their way to Khôtghur. The whole of the clothing of both syces and horses was, however, lost in the passage of the torrent.

Oct. 4th.—Early this morning the Jemadar of the village paraded his 82 coolies, and we immediately forwarded a detachment with the tents. Baron Osten was so extremely unwell that it was impossible for him to proceed; we therefore persuaded him to take the jampaun and return to Chergong, where we calculated he would find Lord Combermere's medical attendant. At 12 o'clock we separated, the Baron proceeding southwards, and my friend and self towards the north. My enjoyment of this romantic day's march was a good deal diminished by my present unfitness for pedestrian exertions; but I managed to crawl through a most toilsome journey of 3½ hours. Passing through the village of Roole, we were civilly and smilingly accosted by a good-looking girl, who offered us a draught of fresh goat's milk; in this act of hospitality presenting a strong contrast to the women of Hindostan, who, on meeting a European, usually cover their faces and turn their backs upon him. I made her understand that I had taken a fancy to a pair of massive anklets which she wore, and left my servant to bargain for them. The mountain belle parted with her only piece of finery for 3 rupees. The bangles were made of a metal resembling lead, but harder, and must, from their weight, have made the wearer "souffrir pour être belle"—albeit the ankles which supported them were, if the truth must be spoken, by no means so delicate as those of the nautch-girls of Delhi. On weighing these tasty baubles I found them to exceed 30 ounces. Some of the females of these regions are profusely ornamented with beautifully-worked earrings and chains of gold, and both men and women wear usually a little silver medallion containing a charm. In some parts of the mountains the inhabitants are famous for their manufacture of chains and filigree work in gold; the former ornaments pretty closely resemble those of Trichinopoli, but the metal, by its weight, softness, and colour, appears to be purer than that used by the southern manufacturers.

After leaving the village of Roole we ascended a steep, grassy hill, adorned here and there with fine groups of cedars, and soon entered a great forest. It differed essentially from the woods which we had passed through in the lower regions; and there was a chilly blackness in the trees peculiar to these elevations. In addition to the oak, cedar, and rhododendron, we here first fell in with the cypress and yew; the berries of the latter, my guide told me, were good to eat, which I took his word for. The tree grows very differently from that of England: instead of the wrinkled stunted stem and gnarled branches common to the British yew, it grows as straight and taper and much taller than a poplar.

Our progress through this mountain-forest was very slow and fatiguing; but we soon overtook our tents, which had had 3 hours' start of us. Whenever I halted for breath, the guides seized the opportunity to enjoy a refreshing smoke; they could not muster a pipe between them, but managed very well without it. Two holes connected with each other were made in the earth—one to contain the tobacco, the other to admit a short hollow reed, which material abounds in the woods; a flint, steel, and dried fungus completed the simple hookah apparatus.

Our route continued about three miles through this forest, and then ascended a bare hill, at the top of which we entered the Birch region. This highly-beneficial plant—Thwackum's universal panacea, which beats Latin and Greek into, and spirit and emulation out of, the rising generation of England—does not in this country deign to flourish in a less exalted situation than about 13,000 feet above the sea—a fact that would at once account to the illustrious pedagogue above mentioned for the slow march of education in the plains of Hindostan.

The first glimpse that I caught of its silver bark and graceful pensile branches transported me, in spite of the petty obstacles of time and space, to those "distant spires and antique towers" under whose classic shadow I ought (according to the self-deceiving theory of some of Mater Etona's stepsons) to have passed the happiest days of my life. Seating myself upon a block of granite, I abandoned myself to a retrospective reverie, in which I traced a very natural parallel between my quondam laborious attempts upon Parnassus—the poetic Himalaya—and my present panting, faultering, yet resolute aspirations (et omne quod exit in *spirations*) after the too substantial Himalaya of Nature, a parallel destined to be supported throughout; for as mental insufficiency cropped my flight in the one case, so did physical inability crush my efforts in the other, as will be seen in the sequel. My vision was, however, suddenly dissolved by the report of a gun fired by my companion at an eagle "towering in his pride of place;" and, in the twinkling of harlequin's wand, my excursive imagination flitted back from Windsor Hill and Salt Hill to those which, a few years ago, I never expected would be trodden by foot of mine.

From the Birch mountain our march was, owing to the extreme narrowness and roughness of the path, slow and irksome. The planting of each footstep was a matter of serious speculation, and one false step would have given us a tragical illustration of the "pas qui coute."

Our tents were pitched—when they arrived, which was some time after us—on an isolated green space, on the side of a brown hill dotted over with huge detached masses of granite. Near the camp we passed a spot where, by some grand convulsion of nature, a vast rocky peak had been driven from its exalted station, and tumbled, in a cataract of enormous stones and uprooted trees, down the flank of the mountain; reminding me of the Rossberg, or écroulement of the mountain near Sweitz in Switzerland.

The prospect from the tents was sublime and awful, but, from the absence of timber, much less beautiful than the two preceding marches. The only vegetation around us which even assumes the respectability of a shrub is the juniper, with a few sorry bushes of the red and black currant. Large masses of snow, having survived the summer, lie in the ravines and valleys around and below us; and to the north, at the distance of 10 miles, the two lofty pinnacles of ice, flanking the Shattoul Pass, rear their heads above an intervening mountain. Some 2000 feet beneath us we descry the great oak forest through which we passed this morning; and, luxuriant as it is in its internal recesses, the outer skirts are blasted and blackened by the chill hurricanes from the north. The night was extremely cold, though Fahrenheit did not descend below freezing point. My companion and myself found considerable comfort in a good jorum of mulled port well spiced, and a brasero of hot embers placed in the tent: and our followers, Hindoo, Mussulman, and Mountaineer—to use the figurative language of the East—put the scruples of religion into the pocket of emergency, and were most thankful for a cold-expelling dram of pure brandy-sheråb.

Oct. 5th, 7 A.M.—Started for the pass—so unwell that my limbs almost refused their office—with a prospect of a climb of 10 miles: I was, however, agreeably disappointed in my calculations of the difficulties of this day's march. For a person in good walking condition the route was both easy and safe, in comparison to some former marches; but I accomplished it with great difficulty, my mountain hurkarah dragging me by the hand; notwithstanding which assistance, I was obliged to sit down every 50 paces.

The extreme tenuity of the atmosphere common to these elevated regions, by rendering respiration difficult, increased my weakness, though, by its reviving freshness, it no doubt enabled me to resist a very strong inclination to faint, which seized me more than once.

After walking about 6 miles we arrived at the top of a hill which had hitherto interposed itself between us and the pass, and a wide amphitheatre of snow-capped peaks suddenly burst upon our view. The scene was certainly grand and magnificent in the extreme, and we viewed it under the most flattering auspices. The weather was perfect, not a breath of air or a rack of cloud was felt or seen; the sky was almost indigo in intensity of blue; and the same bright sun, whose piercing ray we had so often shrunk from in the plains, now tempered, by its genial influence, the exceeding keenness of the air. I must, however, confess disappointment at the first opening of the pass to my sight; a feeling which I also saw reflected in the countenance of my friend. Though the spot where we stood was scarcely 1000 feet lower than the summit of Mont Blanc, and many thousand feet higher than the usually-arrogated elevation of eternal snow in colder latitudes, a thick carpet of long grass and rushes intermingled with stawberry-plants and other flowering shrubs lay under our feet; and there was tolerably level space enough around us for the encampment of an army.

There was no object in the prospect so astounding as the "mer de glace" of Chamouni, or so gloriously horrific as the glacier of Grindelwald. The rocky peaks of Shattoul, covered with snow from summit to base, rise about 1000 feet above the heath upon which our tents were pitched; the pass itself bearing somewhat the shape of a demi-pique saddle.

A large share of the imposing effect of the scene is lost by the very easy and gradual manner in which it is approached; so much of the grandeur consequent upon mere altitude being absorbed in the several ranges of mountains which the traveller ascends like steps, seriatim ėt gradatim, before he gets within eyeshot of the main object of his tour. From the immediate vicinity of Mont Blanc, on the contrary, the subordinate mountains seem to shrink away in abashed insignificance, and this monarch of the Alps bursts suddenly upon the eye of the tourist, with 7000 or 8000 feet of almost unbroken snow—more than one half of its elevation above the ocean.

Our original intention had been to cross the pass into the valley of the Sutledge, to travel through that vale as far as Khôtghur, and thence to return to Simla. As my indisposition, however, and my consequent inability to proceed on foot, did not abate, my companion refused to advance. Had we persisted in advancing we should very probably have lost half our baggage, as our mountain coolies seemed strongly inclined to desert us, and there was no possibility of recruiting their ranks—Roole, which we left two days ago, being the last village we should see for five marches. A highland messenger, too, who crossed the pass to-day, bearing a letter from Mr. Gerard (who is making a scientific tour in the Thibet mountains) to one of Lord Combermere's party, gave us the important information that the cholera was raging in the above-named valley, which intelligence greatly assisted us in making up our minds to retreat.

We witnessed the native's descent, which he accomplished with most alarming velocity; sometimes making three or four successive jumps with the assistance of his pole, and at others placing himself in a sitting posture on the snow, and sliding down 20 or 40 feet. He was warmly clad in the usual costume of black blanket, with a small snug turban of the same material, crowned with scarlet cloth. This latter article of clothing, my companion and myself have adopted on account of its warmth, lightness, and elasticity.

In the afternoon Colonel Dawkins mounted to the ridge of the pass, and looked into the valley beyond. He described the prospect as dreary and wild in the extreme; the Sutledge river was, from the height of its rocky banks, and its great distance below his station, scarcely visible; in the distance towered yet another grand range of snow-clad mountains, some of whose peaks claim the supremacy in altitude over all the mountains of the globe; the highest of the Dewalgiri range being above 26,000 feet. The Shattoul Pass is above 15,560 feet, and the inaccessible peak which elevates itself above its right flank has been computed at 17,035 feet. Thus the Pass of Shattoul is, as near as may be, co-lofty with Mont Blanc, which boasts an elevation of 15,630 feet. I found myself totally incapable of attempting the short, but, as my companion described it, very arduous ascent to the summit—thinking it best to husband my remaining strength for my pedestrian retreat to Chergong, where I hope to find Dr. Murray, who accompanies Lord Combermere on his tour to the Borenda Pass. I was most fortunately furnished with a little stock of a very rare and delicious root called sallup-misseree, a great allayer of all internal revolutions in the animal system: it is something like arrowroot in consistence and appearance when prepared, but has a naturally sweet and aromatic flavour. From this pleasant medicine I found great relief.

As it is well known that the point in the thermometer at which water boils is affected by different altitudes, and that by this simple test elevations of mountains may be computed, we were curious to try the experiment whilst we were at a height above the sea which it is more than probable we shall never reach again. With all the gravity, therefore, of a Humboldt or a De Saussure, and to the great edification of the gaping natives, who no doubt took us for a couple of scientific emissaries from the Royal Society, instead of two of Sterne's "idle travellers," we prepared an assortment of portable materials for making a fire; which, with a Fahrenheit's thermometer, my friend carried with him to the top of the pass. About a dozen mountaineers accompanied him, and to my surprise two of the Hindoo servants asked leave to be of the party. I sat on the outside of the tent, with my telescope, to watch their progress, and was well pleased to see my brother Englishman assert his superiority in activity and "wind," by being the first to reach the summit—the party of natives trailing off by degrees, and some of them sneaking back to camp. In about 2¼ hours the Colonel-*Sahib* returned, his person profusely decorated with garlands of a large blue flower common in these regions, with which the natives had insisted upon investing him, in honour of his exploit. At 2 P.M. he found the thermometer at 32°; and on immersing it in boiling water the mercury only rose to 185½°—26½° below the point at which it boils at London. My Bengalee bearer, who ascended about half way, returned full of importance, and vaingloriously described to his less enterprising companion the wonders of the *burruf*,* and the dangers he had braved.

We passed the night under the pass; and a bitter cold one it was—the thermometer descending to 21°. The poor natives of the plains must have suffered much, though they had plenty of clothing and blankets, and a good tent to shelter them.

Oct. 6th.—Two hours after sunrise (therm. 32°), broke up our encampment, and, taking leave of the Shattoul Pass, the ultima Thule of my Indian peregrinations, commenced our retreat. Our plan was to retrace our steps as far as Rooroo, and thence branch off over the mountains to Khôtghur.

We slept this night on the same hill-side occupied by our camp on the 4th instant (therm. 8 P.M. 49° in the tent), and the next day reached Roole. I found the descent

* Ice.

comparatively easy in my present broken-down state, though I had two or three trifling falls from the excessive weakness of my knees. We took this day's march very easily, breakfasting in the oak forest, and continuing our descent to Roole in the afternoon, where we occupied our former encamping-ground. Many of the inhabitants came to meet us, and brought us baskets full of apricots and peaches. The roofs of the houses are completely covered with these fruits, spread out to dry in the sun; they serve for food both for man and beast in the winter months, so common are they in these regions.

Oct. 8th.—This morning an hurkarah reached us at Roole, bringing the intelligence of Lord Combermere's arrival at Chergong, and a jampaun and eight bearers for me. We therefore made a forced march to give them a meeting, passing Dogolee and the spots rendered famous by the disasters of the mule and pony, and arriving at Chergong at 1 P.M. Here we found ourselves again in a temperature of 82°. His Excellency's party, consisting of five gentlemen, was encamped near the village; and our ci-devant companion, Baron Osten, was nearly reinstated in health by the able prescriptions of Dr. Murray. The two parties, arrivers and returners, dined together very hilariously, and the latter did their best to alarm the former by their description of the cold, dangers, difficulties, &c., of the journey to the snowy peaks.

The next morning his Lordship's party resumed their progress towards the Borenda Pass, and our trio—the Baron having rejoined us—marched in the opposite direction, and encamped at Rooroo. Captain Kennedy, on hearing that we were retracing our steps from the pass, sent a messenger after our ponies, who brought them back to Chergong to meet us. I passed with the greatest unconcern the narrow points in the road which had rather affected my nerves on a former occasion—the two last marches to and from the Shattoul having rendered me callous to hair-breadth paths.

The harvest was going on merrily on the road-side as we

passed, and the sharpening of the sickles almost made me fancy myself in England—an illusion scarcely destroyed by a custom, not unlike that which occurs before harvest-home in England, that I witnessed soon after. As I was walking through a field of barley, a group of young female reapers approached, and, forming up in line across my path, threw their sickles at my feet in smiling silence. It was not difficult to interpret this mute language; and had I been inclined to avoid my smirking petitioners, I should have found it impossible to turn the well-appuyé flank of their line; so I threw them a few small coins, and, stepping over their stockade of reaping-hooks, marched on.

The women of these mountainous and unsophisticated regions have not, or do not affect, the same timidity towards Europeans as those of the plains display. On the contrary, these Highland belles—though by the bye few of them deserve that epithet—stare and laugh at, and talk to a white face willingly enough; and more than once, in passing through their villages, I have had civil proffers of milk, fruit, &c.

The poor wretches are treated as disposable property by their natural protectors. A good instance of this was afforded to Lord Combermere's party: a very pretty girl being brought to the camp at Deora, and offered for sale at the moderate price of 150 rupees—more than which sum I have seen given for a Scotch terrier at Calcutta!

Oct. 10th.—Left Rooroo, and continued our course about 3 miles along the road towards Saree, when we suddenly diverged to the right, and leaving, our old track, ascended a steep hill by a rough and ill-defined path. After a march of 2 hours we reached the village of Krassoo, and encamped a little beyond it in a stubble-field neatly walled in with stone. The hamlet is of considerable extent, and some of the better houses present beautiful specimens of the mountain masonry. The beauty of the inhabitants was also remarkable: a man of some consequence in the village, who offered himself as our guide, was particularly handsome and fair. By the species of vegetation around Krassoo, I should judge it to be about the same elevation as Simla. The thermometer in the tent, 2 P. M., 83°.

The following day we made a march of 2 hours, and formed our camp near Kushaine. There is a road the whole way, which, though narrow, is sufficiently good. The latter half of the journey was very beautiful, and reminded me much of the scenery about Matlock and Buxton. We encamped in a fine grove of cedars on the summit of a lofty mound. Some 300 feet below us lies the large village of Kushaine, its slate roofs glittering with an almost intolerable glare; and just above our heads, on a bare bleak eminence, stands the little fort of Tikkur, belonging, as indeed does all the neighbouring territory, to the Rajah of Rampore, a town which gives its name to the valley beyond the pass. The little stronghold is garrisoned by 30 of the rajah's sepoys.

The hills about here are of a more gentle acclivity than those nearer the pass, and, where wood does not grow, they are thickly cultivated. The handsome chief of Krassoo accompanied us to-day, and proved an intelligent cicerone. His countenance reminded me much of some of the great painters' representations of our Saviour—the same open forehead, gracefully waving hair and beard, gently arched brows, and straight, well-formed nose. His expression, too, was one of mingled meekness and intelligence. He was adorned with handsome gold earrings and silver bangles, and wore a chased kookeree in his girdle. When he took leave the next morning I was rather surprised to find, by his begging for a buckshees, or present of money, that he had not accompanied us for the mere pleasure of our society.

Oct. 12th.—Commenced this day's journey by passing close under the fort of Tikkur, whence we ascended a bleak, treeless mountain, which took us 1½ hour to surmount. On reaching the summit we continued for about 2 miles along the ridge, enjoying most extensive and magnificent prospects on either side; more particularly to the north, where an immense sea of hills lay below us, backed up by the snowy range, amongst whose peaks rose pre-eminent the crags of Shattoul. The mountain upon which we were travelling must by the cold—for the hoar frost lay upon the ground—and by the trees and shrubs, the holly, sycamore, and strawberry, be about the same elevation as Roole. The descent was extremely rapid and abrupt, but the road was formed of such adhesive materials, that it was impossible to slip in walking down. We soon reached the fir-region; and after pursuing a zigzag descent through a fine wood, crossed a small stream and recommenced ascending; passed through the village of Rara, and finally found our camp pitched on the side of a verdant hill, thinly wooded with clumps of young pines. The day's march was a very long one, employing us nearly 4 hours in its performance, and the very severe and sudden changes of temperature which we experienced greatly retarded my convalescence. Some parts of it, however, were extremely interesting, and most refreshing to the eye after our late marches through close narrow valleys. The thermometer stood to-day, at 2 P.M., at 69°—seven degrees cooler than yesterday.

The following day we had an equally long, but still more beautiful journey. We passed a ruined fort on the summit of a mountain of the Whartoo range, which is 9000 feet high; leaving on our left the main mountain of the same name, which has also a fortress on its summit, 10,673 feet above the sea; as near as possible the height of Mount Etna. The greater part of our route lay through a luxuriant forest of the most enormous trees, and we enjoyed, throughout, a most splendid view of the Snowy Belt. From Whartoo we made a rapid descent to Khôtghur, the whole march occupying 3½ hours; and we took up our abode in the house of Captain Newton, who holds a political appointment at this little outwork of the Company's territories, and is second in command of the First Nusseeree battalion of Hill Rangers. This gentleman and his sister live very comfortably and contentedly in this lonely spot, far from the haunts of their compatriots, enjoying at least the blessing of a most delightful climate. We were received most kindly by this secluded couple, and entertained during two days. Khôtghur is 6900 feet above the sea, and is beautifully situated on the side of a gently sloping mountain, well wooded, and yet having space enough for cultivation; the river Sutledge, even here a fine stream, runs at the foot of the hill, and the rugged and barren mountains on the opposite bank are in the district of Cooloo, subject to Maha-Rajah Runjeet Singh of Lahore. Every considerable eminence is fortified. I counted, with the naked eye, nine of these little mountain strongholds. In the afternoon we had a grand storm of hail and rain, which fell in the shape of snow on the more elevated mountains around us. Thermometer, 2 P.M., 76°.

Oct. 15th.—Early in the morning quitted Khôtghur, and, travelling on the Subbâtoo high road, reached the stage bungalow at Nackandeh to breakfast. Our route lay through perhaps the finest forest scenery that we had yet met with; the ascent was steep and continual, for we mounted 3000 feet in a very few miles. We found a great change in the climate as we approached the summit: the shady places were thickly covered with snow from the storm of yesterday, and during the whole day the thermometer in the verandah of the stage-house did not rise above 50°. The ridge of Nackandeh is one of the rays, if I may so express it, of the great star of mountains which all concentrate at the Whartoo Peak; whose fort-crowned summit commands every eminence for many miles round. From hence is perhaps the most glorious prospect in all the hills. The forest, extending from the base to the utmost peak, is famed for the stupendous size of its pines, which have been accounted from 130 to 160 feet in height. In this thick covert every species of game, from the bear to the pheasant, is to be found; though the great labour and fatigue entailed upon the sportsman among the forest acclivities would discourage any one but a Swiss chamois-hunter.

We had not been long in the bungalow ere we received

the visit of the Kumarsen Ranah, chief of all the beautiful surrounding country; which, doubtless, he would be very glad to exchange for one quarter of the number of good broad ugly acres of arable land. He sat with us for some time, and smoked a cigar, which we offered him, very willingly. He is a little Jewish-looking youth, and speaks, as he says, "a leetel Anglish"—his main pursuit being sporting. Of his acquirements in our vernacular he only gave us these specimens, "Good morning, Sir,"—"Very fine *bull-doag*," pointing to a spaniel,—and "Good evening."

The next day we had a long and fatiguing march of 4 hours, to Mutteanah, and took up our residence in the bungalow, which is situated on the summit of a bleak hill of great elevation. In the vicinity there are fewer villages, and consequently less cultivation, than we had found in the more northern provinces. The day was bitter cold—thermometer, 52°.

I saw here the most extraordinary effect of mirage that I ever met with. That optical delusion, styled by the Arabs suhrâb, or "water of the desert," is common in the plains of India; but I did not suppose that mountain scenery was susceptible of it. A deep precipitous valley below us, at the bottom of which I had seen one or two miserable villages in the morning, bore in the evening a complete resemblance to a beautiful lake; the vapour, which played the part of water, ascending nearly half-way up the sides of the vale, and on its bright surface trees and rocks being distinctly reflected. I had not been long contemplating the phenomenon before a sudden storm came on, and dropped a curtain of clouds over the scene.

Oct. 17th.—On our march to-day towards Fargoo (the bungalow where we made our first halt on setting out from Simla), we travelled close by the elevated fort of Theog, of which I made mention on our second day's march, as appearing, from its situation among the clouds, perfectly impregnable. Having now turned its position, we find that we might almost take it with our own little party;

and this may be received as the general character of these, at first sight, inaccessible strongholds among the hills. Between the stage-house at Mutteanah and Fargoo is about 14 miles.

On our arrival at the latter place I found a relay of bearers kindly sent me by a friend at Simla; I therefore pushed on, and arrived there at 4 P.M. The jampaun-bearers, who were quite fresh, ran away with me at a capital pace, sometimes turning the precipitous corners so sharp, that I more than once expected a tumble. The fellows are so sure-footed, however, that no accident through their neglect is on record.

Our tour among the mountains had just occupied 24 days, and during that time Simla had been deserted by the majority of the Head-quarters party, who had started for the plains. This delightful spot, therefore, looked as forlorn as tenantless houses could make it. I remained there two days to recruit my strength, and then, with a heavy heart, began my descent toward the plains.

I cannot doubt but that Simla will rise in importance every year, as it becomes better known. Its delightful climate is sure to recommend it for invalids; and its beautiful scenery, healthful temperature, and, above all, the "procul negotiis" relaxation which they will there enjoy, will induce the Governors-General and Commanders-in-Chief to resort there, during the hot months, in their official tours through the upper provinces.

Oct. 20*th.*—I reached Subbâtoo, and Lord Combermere arrived there on the 24th.

25*th.*—The two parties of tourists dined with Captain Kennedy, the hospitable Political Agent—"a merrier man I never spent an hour's talk withal"—and not a little fun was elicited from the several narratives of the adventures of the journey.

At 5 P.M. we mustered our forces, and, taking leave of our worthy host, continued our descent towards the plains. The Commander-in-Chief bivouacked for the night on a hill 3 miles above the village of Bahr, and I continued my march, by a bright moonlight, to that village, where my tent was pitched.

My night journey was beautiful, and I enjoyed it extremely, although I felt a manifest increase in the temperature every hundred feet that I descended. The road led sometimes through deep wooded glens and ravines, into whose dark recesses the silver beams of the moon could not penetrate; and at others, down the face of declivities, which this planet, so glorious in India, lighted up with almost the clearness of day.

CHAPTER VI.

Plains of Hindostan — Munny-Mâjra — Syphabad — Patialah — Seikh Principalities — Pewur — Khytul — Seikh States — Jheend — Narnound — Canal of Feroze Shah — Hansi — Skinner's horse — Head-quarters camp — March towards Delhi — Mohim — Mundeena — Rhotuk — Seeta-Ram-ka-Serai — Delhi — The Chandee Chowk — The Mogul — March towards Meerut — Boor-Barore — The Begum Sumroo — March towards Moradabad — Ghurmuktesur, on the Ganges.

THE next morning we made a march of 17 miles, and fairly turned our backs on the Himalaya mountains. In the valley of Pinjore, and near the town of that name, we passed some delightful gardens belonging to the Rajah of Patialah, who often visits them in the hot season, as being, from their situation to the northward of the first range of hills, much cooler than his residence in his capital. During the rainy season this beautiful vale—a very Tempe in outward show—is so unhealthy that it is considered almost certain death to travel through it. At this place we found our Arab horses, which had been brought to meet us; nor were we sorry to discard our little, rough, ambling ghoonts in their favour. At 8 P.M. we found ourselves once more on the wide-spreading plains of Hindostan, and soon after discovered the canvas city of Head-quarters *ambulant*, erected in its accustomed symmetry of streets and bazaars, in the rear of a fine grove of trees, near the town of Munny-Mâjra. My ideas of space had been so narrowed by a 7 months' residence among the mountains, that my double-poled tent seemed a palace after the tiny tabernacles of Simla; and the contrast was further sustained by the surprising difference of stature between the Patagonian Seikhs, in whose country we now are, and the pigmy natives of Surmour. My Arabs, too, appeared like dray-horses, compared with the ponies and mules which had formed my stud for so many months; and the delight of being able to take a good swinging gallop, without the constant companionship of a precipice (which in my Simla rides haunted my "impia cervix" almost as incessantly as the "destrictus ensis" of Damocles), was so great as nearly to counterbalance what we had lost in climate and scenery.

The heat, although we have got so far through October, is certainly distressing in the extreme—thermometer 89°—and is more oppressive from the sudden change. At Simla 6 days ago the glass stood at 56°, and a very few days before that we were under the influence of zero.

We had not been many hours in camp before we were equipped in full panoply, to receive the visit of two Rajahs; he of Munny-Mâjra, and another of an adjoining district. The former brought a very ragamuffin escort with him, at the head of which was General Love, his Majesty's Commander-in-Chief. This hero's birth and parentage are, unhappily for his biographer, shrouded in obscurity; but the first public character in which he appeared was that of a half-caste drummer-boy in the Honourable Company's service. This appointment the "ambitious Love" disdained; he deserted the Company's standard, and was next heard of in his present exalted situation. If report speaks true, he has made greater acquisitions in honour than in emolument, his salary amounting to 10 rupees per mensem, ill paid.

The two next marches were uninteresting enough; and the third morning found us en route between Nulroo and Patialah, the present capital of the Sirhind territories. The prospectus of our serpentine and digressive journey towards Allahabad—which we are not expected to reach before the middle of February—holds out to me great hopes of amusement and interest: more particularly in our intended visit to the court of Scindia, the Mahratta, and the numerous petty principalities of Bundelcund.

Near the town of Syphabad, where there are some fine gardens belonging to the Rajah, we quitted our horses, and the whole Staff (as was the custom whenever the Commander-in-Chief approached a native capital) mounted elephants, and proceeded to meet the chief of Patialah, who came forth from his city with a grand retinue to welcome his Excellency. I have already had occasion to describe the gigantic stature and martial appearance of this counterpart of Prince Porus; but I believe I have not yet done justice to his kingly and private character, in which he is distinguished as one of the very few Indian potentates who have any real regard for the interests of their subjects, and as a kind and affectionate father and master in his zenana. The British chief having undergone the ursine embrace of the Seikh monarch, the whole cavalcade proceeded towards the town. Since we last saw Kurrum Singh, he had freshly accoutred his guards and attendants, his suwarree making a very splendid figure. Several troops of well-mounted matchlock cavalry lined the road as we approached the walls. There were four especial squadrons whose uniforms were exceedingly handsome and showy. The men of the first were attired in purple silk tunics, with orange turbans, scarfs, and sashes of the same material; the second, in white, with turbans and sashes of dark-blue cloth, twisted with silver cord. The third squadron flaunted in an entire suit of silk couleur de rose; and the fourth and most military-looking party were dressed in green, with yellow silk trousers and turbans of green cloth and gold twist. The infantry escort, in evident imitation of the Honourable Company's Sepoys, wore red coats and white pantaloons, with a purple turban—by no means a happy combination. Immediately in front of our cavalcade marched the Rajah's band, which, with the jingling of the elephant's bells, and the bellowing of the hurkaras and chobdars of the two dignitaries, vociferating in rival halloos the titles of their respective chiefs, struck with stunning discord upon the ears of those who, for the last 7 months, had been accustomed to the tuneful but seldom awakened echoes of Simla. On reaching the camp, which was situated a few hundred yards from the walls, Lord Combermere received a salute from the guns of the town, and the Rajah took leave with the promise of another visit in the evening. His Majesty sounded Captain Murray, the British resident, on his meditated scheme of giving a dinner to his Lordship; but his peculiar method of administering a feed, though novel, was not adopted. As Seikh prejudices would not admit of his killing beef for our entertainment; and as, even in more civilized nations than Sirhind, the idea that an Englishman cannot dine without that article of food is pretty generally run away with, the Rajah proposed to give Lord Combermere's khansamah 2000 rupees to furnish forth the feast in our own camp.

He, however, did less than justice to his Lordship's well-known respect for the religious prejudices of the natives, if he believed that in private we devoured the object of their worship; and he would doubtless be much edified if he knew that during our long residence in the hills no cow had ever been reduced to a state of beef-hood for the satisfaction of our appetites. In the afternoon the Rajah paid his visit of ceremony, and was received at the entrance of the durbar-tent with presented arms. He brought with him several sets of dancing-girls, among whom I easily recognised the pretty Kaboutree (the dove!), who, on a former occasion at Sirhind, exerted her talents for our amusement. The conference lasted about an hour, when, attar having been circulated, his Highness retired.

Early the next morning the Commander-in-Chief, accompanied by the whole Etat Major, proceeded to return the royal visit. The portion of the town of Patialah through which we passed on our road to the palace was more remarkable for the clean whitewashed state of the houses than for any splendour of architecture; nor can the royal abode itself boast much external magnificence. The durbar was held in an open vestibule, supported on carved stone pillars, and occupying one side of a spacious quadrangle. Our chairs were placed, en demilune, on a platform carpeted with crimson velvet, and the staff and courtiers of the two chiefs sat promiscuously together. On a floor about a foot lower than the dais, and shaded by a striped silk canopy, the nautchlôg exhibited their powers; and in their rear, in the centre of the court, a handsome marble fountain threw *rose-coloured* water into the air.

The minister, as is usual with viziers, sat immediately behind the Rajah, with his grey beard brimful of experience close to his royal master's ear; and leaning against the pillars in front of his Majesty stood the court-jester, a shrewd, impudent-looking fellow—whose office is "as full of labour as the wise man's art,"—and two favourite dwarfs. Here we have at a Hindoo court two species of hangers-on who with our Saxon kings were almost as indispensable as any other important government official. The jester has here no bad place of it: in addition to the office of time-killer to his Majesty, enjoying those of master of the revels and superintendent of the women;—a plurality of appointments which must give great umbrage to the less fortunate placemen of the Patialah court. The dwarfs, unlike most of their genus, are neat little abridgments of the animal, man; having straight, slight, and symmetrical figures, and well-proportioned heads and features, with long hair curling down their necks. They are brothers, aged 30 and 24; but their proportions are those of boys of 5 and 8 years old. Their dresses were uniform, scarlet tunics, yellow silk sashes and trousers, and skullcaps of embroidered crimson velvet; and each bore a painted rod of office in his hand. They appeared sharp, active, meddling little fellows—like "Puck," or "Flibbertigibbet."

The amiable giant of a Rajah seems very proud of his Lilliputian favourites; indeed he appears to be a good-natured, kind-hearted man, and took much notice of some children of a staff-officer who were present, loading them with toys.

The durbar concluded with the presentation of some trays of armour to Lord Combermere, and we adjourned to see the royal stud paraded. The horses were generally large powerful animals from the jungles of Lacka (famous for its breed), and all the light-coloured ones were frightfully stained on their sides, tails, and limbs, with a brickdust pigment. As they were brought round, an attendant, bearing an enormous chabouk, or whip of rope 20 feet long, which he managed with uncommon dexterity, flanked them up to make them show off. Many of them walked upon their hind legs, and lay down by word of command, like the well-tutored horses of Astley's theatre. They were for the most part very fat, but much battered about the legs; which is not surprising, as the Rajah, though 6 feet 4 or 5 inches, and more than proportionably stout, is (as "Mrs. Ramsbottom" would say) a perfect *Ramrod* in the chase, and rides unmercifully hard.

On our taking leave, the Rajah having requested Dr. Murray to vaccinate his children—a process of which the natives are generally very distrustful—he conducted him to the private apartments, and, with the greatest appearance of anxiety and interest, witnessed the operation, which was performed on his three boys—the native hakims also looking on. We afterwards heard that, the virus being old, the vaccine did not take: an unfortunate event for the honour of British medical skill. The hakims informed Dr. Murray that the lusus naturæ, the hermaphrodite, is very common in this province. They are outcasts from society, and herd together in an out-of-the-way village. One or two of them are, however, employed about the court in the usual capacity of eunuchs.

After dining in camp we again mounted elephants, and attended a grand fête given by the Rajah. Passing through the brilliantly illuminated town, we proceeded to the quadrangle of the palace, which for the evening's entertainment was covered in with a canopy of white cloth, and splendidly lighted up. Nautching en vogue as usual. The sets were numerous, amounting perhaps to 100 women; and the beauty of their dresses was more remarkable than that of their persons. After viewing the waterworks in the inner square, we proceeded to see some fireworks in the outer court; these were very fine, and put all our elephants and escort to the rout. After thus amusing ourselves for an hour we took an affectionate farewell of old Porus, and our departure. The heat of yesterday and to-day has been excessive—thermometer 92°. What would we give for a half-hour's visit of a Simla zephyr? but we may cry "Aura, Veni!" in vain.

Oct. 31st.—Camp broke up from Patialah, and marched 14 miles to the village of Koralee—the face of the country still uninteresting, and devoid of large trees, but well cultivated.

Nov. 1st.—A heavy shower of rain brought the thermometer down to 79°, relieving us of 13 degrees of heat,—an amelioration hailed by us as the precursor of the cool season.

This day's march brought us into the territories of the Khytul Rajah, which are divided by a small stream from the Patialah dominions. The effects of the efficient government of the latter province are plainly visible in the great superiority in cultivation possessed by it over the Khytul country, whose Rajah, a mere boy, is ruled entirely by his mother, who is, in her turn, swayed by a host of paramours and parasites.

Two marches brought us to Pewur, through a country which, with the exception of sufficient cultivation round the villages for the bare existence of the inhabitants, presents one vast sheet of wild jungle, abounding in game. Two mounted Shikkarees of the Rajah brought a couple of wild hogs into camp which they had killed, and three others arrived from Colonel Skinner, to assist us to find a lion between this place and Hansi. Of these animals there were formerly great numbers in the surrounding wilderness: but

Lion and Elephant.

London ... 1858

from the zeal of English sportsmen, and the price put upon their heads by Government, the royal race of the forest—like other Indian dynasties—is either totally extinct, or has been driven farther back into the desert. By *crack* sportsmen the lion is reputed to afford better sport than the tiger: his attack is more open and certain; a peculiarity arising either from the noble nature of the jungle king, or from the country which he haunts being less favourable for a retreat than the thick swampy morasses frequented by the tiger. Colonel Skinner relates many interesting anecdotes of lion-hunts, with the exploits and narrow escapes of the horsemen of his corps, who always accompanied the line of elephants into the jungle on these occasions. Major Fraser of the same regiment is, however, the lion-queller par excellence.

A gentleman of our party had, perhaps, as perilous an adventure with one of these animals as any one of the former; he having enjoyed the singular distinction of lying for some moments in the very clutches of the royal quadruped. Though I have heard himself recount the incident more than once, and have myself sketched the scene, yet I am not sure that I relate it correctly. The main feature, however, of the anecdote, affording so striking an illustration of the sagacity of the elephant, may be strictly depended upon.

A lion had charged my hero's elephant, and he, having wounded him, was in the act of leaning forward in order to fire another shot, when the front of the howdah suddenly gave way, and he was precipitated over the head of the elephant into the very jaws of the furious beast. The lion, though severely hurt, immediately seized him, and would doubtless shortly have put a fatal termination to the conflict, had not the elephant, urged by the mahout, stepped forward though greatly alarmed, and, grasping in her trunk the top of a young tree, bent it down across the loins of the lion, and thus forced the tortured animal to quit his hold! My friend's life was thus preserved, but his arm was broken in two places, and he was severely clawed on the breast and shoulders. The lion was afterwards slain by the other sportsmen who came up.

The village of Pewur towers boldly up from the midst of the jungle; and is situated on a small river, the banks of which are ornamented by several neat ghauts. Like the generality of towns in this part of the country, the houses are built of good brick; but, like the rest, the abodes of the present generation are stuck cheek by jowl with the ruins of their ancestors' habitations, no one troubling himself to clear away the rubbish of the fallen buildings, and few caring to finish an edifice commenced by their deceased predecessors. By this accumulation of material, however, an ancient village in course of time gains one advantage; namely, a site elevated above the surrounding flat country. I shot my way over to Pewur this morning, and got a good bag of partridges, hares, and wild fowl.

Nov. 5th.—A short march of 8 miles to the town of Khytul, which gives its name to the Rajah of the province. This prince came a mile or two out of the town to meet the Commander-in-Chief, and escorted him into camp. He is a fat, uninteresting, heavy-looking boy of 12 years, but is said to possess more brain than his appearance indicates. The town is irregularly built, but of very good brick; and from the kilns are produced large quantities of sal-ammoniac. The palace is a striking lofty building, and, as we approached, we had a very flattering view of it through a break in a fine grove of trees overhanging a spacious sheet of water. The Rajah is a relation of him of Patialah, and his revenue only amounts to 5 lacs of rupees, whilst that of his more powerful cousin is at least 5 times as great. The boy, however, being of the elder branch, and by inheritance a Goru or holy teacher, his gigantic relative cannot sit in his presence without special permission.

In the evening, the young king having signified his intention of visiting Lord Combermere, I was despatched, with the Persian interpreter, on an elephant, to marshal him into camp. We met him at the city gates, and he raised himself 100 per cent. in my estimation by presenting us with a handsome matchlock and a couple of bows.

Nov. 6th.—The shikkarees having brought intelligence of two tigers in the jungle about 14 miles off, four of us started very early in search of them. The swamp where they had been seen proved the Slough of Despond to us, for we found nothing of them but their footmarks, those of a young female and a full-grown male—for the experienced natives can distinguish the prints. After a hot day's work we returned to Khytul, where Head-quarters had halted.

The day following we reached the hamlet of Kussaun, where the bush-jungle was so thick and extensive that we could scarcely find a spot to pitch the camp: and the morning after, we made a march of 14 miles to Shamdore. The morning was extremely cold, and the mid-day equally hot—therm. 82°, 2 P.M. In this province the cultivators adopt the following plan for scaring birds from their grain-crops. Several platforms are raised in every large field, upon each of which a man stands, armed with a sling, formed (much like those used by mischievous boys at Eton to break windows and bargemen's heads) of two pieces of thong or cord, with a leathern receptacle for the missile, a pellet of hardened clay. This is thrown to the distance of several hundred yards, and each shot is followed by a loud crack—like that of a French postilion's whip—managed by the slinger when he lets fly the string of his weapon.

9th.—Encamped near the town of Jheend, the metropolis of the province of that name. The Rajah, as usual, met, welcomed, embraced, and ushered into camp the Commander-in-Chief. He is a handsome, wild-looking young man of 22, and is said to divide his inclinations and his time pretty equally between his zenana and his stable. Of the former addiction we have, of course, no means of judging; but amongst his suwarree, which was otherwise shabby and paltry, I observed more fine horses than I had yet seen in the Seikh country. The young prince is, like the Rajah of Patialah, a great lover of the chase, and a desperate rider. He received the best portion of his stud from the Maharajah

Runjeet Singh of Lahore, who honours him with his countenance and friendship. This latter was some time since put to a severe trial by the ungrateful youth, who, on his return from a visit to Lahore, violated the most sacred laws of hospitality by carrying off a beautiful female favourite of his patron; an outrage which has, however, been forgiven, if not forgotten, by the magnanimous chieftain.

Lord Combermere received the visit of the Jheend Rajah in the morning, and in the afternoon returned it at the palace, where the usual entertainments were prepared for us. Captain Murray informs me that the royal youth has nearly deserted the town of Jheend, and is never seen at his palace; and that he has two young and beauteous wives immured within its towers, whom he has never once visited since the morning of their weddings. It is ridiculous enough that the neglected young virgin-brides have both, at different times, sent their vakeels to the English Political Agent to complain of their husband's want of common attention; and he has promised to remind the oblivious young prince that he is possessed of a couple of pretty young brides, to whom he has omitted to dedicate even the brief honeymoon of Hymen in high life—nay, whose very existence he seems to have forgotten.

Captain Murray told me a good anecdote illustrative of his hairbrained wildness which occurred on the day of his first marriage. The bride elect was the daughter of the Chief of Shahabad, at which place the ceremony took place —the Rajah of Patialah, as guardian to the youth, and many chieftains of note, attending. The Political Agent was likewise bidden, and went. When the cavalcade of elephants was ready to proceed to the house of the bride, the *impatient* bridegroom, who had previously been duly attired in his wedding raiment of white and gold muslin, was nowhere to be found. The Patialah potentate was in dismay, and sent his attendants in different directions in search of him. Murray and some others at length discovered the defaulter in a wood, a little way from the road, striving to leap a fiery charger over a tremendous yawning bowlee, or well: the horse was refusing, and the mad wag "cramming him at it"—as the knowing ones call it—in vain. Having politely reminded him of the *primary* object of the meeting, they conducted him to his elephant, covering his head and face with the customary wedding veil of gold tissue. This he wore with the most exemplary patience for some minutes, until at length, tired of being muffled up, he made a sudden exclamation, equivalent to "Hang me, if I will be smothered any longer!" and, "having both said and sworn it," he struck his fingers through the gauze, rent it open, and thrust out his face through the aperture. At such utter and open disrespect for the solemn ordinances of this august ceremony the Patialah chief was greatly shocked; and at the conclusion of the rites, the "merry monarch" was summoned before a grand divan of the high contracting powers, where he was severely reprimanded by each member in succession.

Nov. 10th; therm. 82°.—This day we marched 15 miles to the village of Narnound, and the day following to the great fortress and station of Hansi. The Jheend Rajah, glad of an excuse to quit his capital and to gratify his truant disposition, joined the camp, which was also augmented by the arrival of the Nawaub Ameen-ood Deene, second son of the late Nawaub Achmet Bux, and brother of Ibrahim Beg, who travelled with us on a former occasion.

These young Mussulmans are fine, spirited, intelligent youths of 14 and 15. I formed a great sporting alliance with them, and they joined us very frequently in our expeditions with the chetahs and falcons. Our route from Jheend to Hansi skirted the grand canal of Feroze Shah, excavated by that munificent monarch to conduct water from the Delhi canal through the sterile district of Hurreanah. During the subsequent anarchy and desolation of the Mogul states this source of fertility went to ruin, and with it the cultivation and prosperity of the province. It was afterwards restored through the beneficence of the Honourable Company, by the hands of Captain Rodney

Blane, son of the distinguished physician of that name. On each of its banks there is now a wide tract of well-tilled ground.

The fortress of Hansi, from the abrupt and uncommanded elevation on which it stands, presents an appearance of great strength; and is, very early in the history of India, made honourable mention of for its impregnability: it is now the Head-quarters of Skinner's Irregular Horse, about 500 of whom are present; and the station of a regiment of native infantry. The town lies at the foot of the hill on which the citadel stands, and is defended by a good wall: the cantonments are also spread out upon the plain. Our camp was erected about half a mile from the fort, near the residence of Colonel Skinner. This brave officer, whom I have before had occasion to mention, when we paid him a visit at his jaghire, Belaspore, served with much distinction in the wars of Lord Lake and Lord Hastings; and for his conduct at the siege of Bhurtpore received the order of Companion of the Bath. In his youth he was the partizan of more than one native power; and in his recollections of 40 years of chequered service he possesses a fund of interesting incident and anecdote, upon which the old soldier is not unfrequently induced to draw for the amusement of his friends. In this Cossack-like life he was joined by a near relation—since dead—who was as valiant a warrior as himself; but he was a man of wild and ungoverned passions, and the last scene of his life was Othello exaggerated! Having suspected his wife, a native lady, of infidelity to his bed, he surrendered himself to the bloody suggestions of the green-eyed monster; murdered her and her two female attendants, and concluded the tragedy by blowing out his own brains. His passion for the sex, and extravagance in expense, knew no bounds; of which addictions the following anecdote, related to me this day, affords no bad instance.

Being present at a grand entertainment given by some native prince at Delhi, he became desperately enamoured of a young and beautiful nautch-girl, a slave of the prince's wife: and at the close of the fête he seized her by force and carried her off to Hansi. Being pursued by some troops from Delhi, he shut himself up in his house, which was soon surrounded by a force that rendered resistance hopeless; when, rather than yield up his charmer, he offered to purchase her for her weight in silver. The bargain was struck, the scales produced, and, the maiden being weighed against rupees, the ravisher retained his prize.

In the afternoon a review of Skinner's Horse took place, and it was a most interesting spectacle. Their costume is very picturesque; consisting of a long tunic of red cloth ornamented with black fur, quilted cotton pantaloons, long boots, and a neat snug soldier-like casque of polished steel, with a spike on the crown, and scales under the chin. The horse-furniture is red and yellow: the weapons, the matchlock, spear, and sword. They have adopted many of the manœuvres of our regular cavalry; but their peculiar evolution, and which is the most striking to an European eye, is the Mahratta charge. In this movement the whole corps advances in line, two deep, at a canter or trot, which, like John Gilpin's, becomes "a gallop soon;" and as they approach their object, the files open out, and every man, uttering a wild shrill scream, comes thundering on with his sword waving above his head. In spite of the apparent disjointed irregularity of the charge, and the amazing speed of their approach, at the word "halt" every horse is brought upon his haunches within ten paces of the reviewing General. The Mahratta charge is certainly well calculated to strike terror into a foe already wavering, but its real physical effect upon stanch troops must be far inferior to the close combined charge of *our* cavalry.

After the review we proceeded to a spot set apart for the practice of the matchlock. On our way thither we were preceded by a band of chosen spearmen, who played their elegant exercise before us with long lances tipped, like foils, with a button. The combatants kept in constant motion, caracoling and circling about, and dealing pretty heavy blows upon any one who happened to wheel within reach. Sometimes one fellow retreated at full speed, trailing his long spear after him with the point on the ground, and skilfully warding off the thrusts aimed at himself or his horse by his pursuer: then, when he thought his assailant was off his guard, he would make a sudden wheel and assume the offensive; and, in the midst of a cloud of dust, the too confident pursuer was thrust from his saddle and rolled on the ground. There were two champions, remarkably fine-looking fellows, who, from their great skill at the weapon, and their complete suit of beautiful chain armour, moved with impunity through the tilting throng. Now and then, some of the officers of the corps, quitting their station round their chief, spurred their fiery steeds into the mêlée, to show off their skill in arms and horsemanship; and young Skinner, son of the Colonel, and Adjutant of the regiment, a fine stout young man, was constantly aux mains with the best spearmen, displaying great command of his horse and weapon. On one or two occasions, when the combatants waxed warm—for the temper of your Mussulman is somewhat fiery—and their blows began to smack strongly of their feelings, the sturdy old commander himself, forgetting for a while his "increasing belly and decreasing arm," would take a spear from an attendant, and, putting his favourite dekkanee into a rocking-horse canter, "mix in the game of mimic slaughter." I think I see him now, with his goodnatured twinkling eyes and white teeth shining through his dark countenance, smilingly approaching the irritated combatants, and challenging one of them to measure spears with himself. In his youth he was a first-rate lancer, and even now there are few in his regiment who can touch him. Of this fact, however, we had no sterling opportunity of judging; for no subaltern, in India or elsewhere, would commit so gross an error in policy as to display his own skill at the expense of his Colonel's! The uniform of Colonel Skinner and his officers is very handsome and showy. The tunic is similar, except in the fineness of the materials, to those of the soldiers. They wear over the shoulders a broad embroidered belt confined round the waist with a rich shawl, and their helmets are adorned with a short plume of black and white feathers tipped with drops of gold fringe, in addition to the steel aigrette which the privates wear in front of the headpiece. A somewhat similar plume dances between the ears of the horse, who is further ornamented with rich embossed trappings, and a series of necklaces, some formed of blue beads, others of tigers' claws set in gold or silver, and others again of silken cords supporting little amulets, or charms against the evil eye. Over the saddle is thrown a richly-embroidered velvet jeenpose, or shabraque; and before and behind the stirrup leather hang clustres of fine chowries, formed of the tail of the yâk, or Thibet cow. Before we reached the ground prepared for the matchlock practice it grew so dusk that the marksmen could not display their science to advantage.

In the evening Lord Combermere and all the staff, general and personal, together with the officers of the station, dined with Colonel Skinner. A good many English ladies were present, and after the repast there was dancing to suit all tastes, namely, a grand nautch in the tent where we dined, and quadrilles in the drawing-room of the house. The latter appeared to be the most inviting spectacle to the men of the corps, who assembled in crowds in the verandahs to witness the performance. I asked one of the nautch-girls, who was peering through the window, what she thought of the English ladies' dancing; and the nutbrown disciple of Terpsichore replied, that "they nautched very well, only they jumped too high."

During dinner a party of Khalâmuts, or bards, sang several songs, accompanying themselves on a species of guitar and violin—one of which instruments was formed of a hollow gourd.* These musicians, who were the private servants of the Colonel, and the best of their *jât*, accompanied the Commander-in-Chief for several weeks on his

* India boasts a variety of stringed instruments, the least jarring of which is, I think, the vina or beena.

journey. At first I hated the very sight, much more the sound, of them; next tolerated, and finally liked, their simple music. The airs are usually soft, melancholy, and monotonous, particularly those to which the love-sick ditties of the Persian poets are set. But others, setting forth the exploits and virtues of "*Jimmes* Sahib,"* or the glories of the "Company kee Nishân,"† are couched in gayer and more heroic strains. Before the musicians left us I had become quite a fanatico for Indian minstrelsy, and gave my "wah! wah!" of applause to a favourite gazzul‡ of Hafiz, or sprightly kuhirwa air, with at least as much judgment and discernment as is displayed by one-half of the pit-frequenting cognoscenti in their distribution of "bravos!" to the productions of Rossini and Paesiello.

The following day, whilst the Commander-in-Chief drove over to Hissar to inspect the Honourable Company's Stud Establishment, I repaired to the Hansi parade-ground to witness some feats of arms by Skinner's men. Four prizes were given to those who excelled in the use of the matchlock; and much skill was shown by the competitors. The following is the method of conducting this exercise. A bottle is placed on the ground or suspended from a gibbet, and the column of mounted marksmen is formed up at right angles with the spectators. At a signal from the officer one of the party gallops forth at full speed, with his matchlock supported across his bridle-arm, darting past the object at the distance of 15 or 20 yards. Just as he passes, the rein drops from his hand, the matchlock is raised, makes a short horizontal sweep, the ball is sped, and the bottle flies, or *should* fly, into a thousand atoms; a loud shout of applause proclaiming the cavalier's success. Captain Skinner smote two bottles in his two first careers. Some of the most emulous of our party also tried their hands at the sport: but as an empty bottle has few attractions for an

* Colonel *James* Skinner, whose surname the natives have also mutilated into *Secunder*.

† The standard of the Honourable Company.

‡ Love-song.

Englishman, none of them went within a mile of it, and some execrable equitation was displayed for the edification of the Mussulmans.

Though the matchlock is, to an unaccustomed hand, unwieldy and ill-balanced, yet the barrel is remarkably true, and the very weight of the weapon makes the aim more steady. The bore being small and very long, the ball is thrown to a distance greatly exceeding that of a musket: as an instance of which, I remember at Bhurtpore an officer being wounded by a matchlock shot at a distance of 800 yards from the walls.

As soon as the games were concluded, and the "Irregulars" were well out of sight, I took a couple of clandestine shots myself; but as I had never before handled a matchlock, and my horse would not stand fire, I had cause to congratulate myself that my modesty had induced me to make my début in private. I afterwards galloped to the colonel's house, where, amongst other curiosities, he showed me a bullock of astonishing size. He measured just 16 hands high behind the hump, which rose above the back about 3 hands more. The beast was stout in proportion to his stature, and in beautifully sleek condition. I was informed that he could carry 10 maunds of water, or 8 hundredweight.

Nov. 13th.—Head-quarters advanced to the village of Moondahil, 14 miles,—an accident happening on the line of march, such as is fortunately of rare occurrence. An elephant carrying a tent, being irritated by the wanton blows of his mahout, turned his rage upon an unhappy inoffensive peasant who was drinking at a tank, and, seizing him in his trunk, dashed him on the ground, and trampled him to pieces. In the afternoon, depositions of several witnesses were taken on the subject, which did not tend to criminate the mahout, although one fellow swore stoutly that he heard wrathful words pass between the parties, and saw the mahout urge his elephant to play the assassin. The body of the deceased, a very fine athletic old man, was crushed even to mummyism—his chest, ribs, and collar-bones pounded into one confused mass. He was a man of some consequence in the village; and after his corpse had been laid out, the women assembled in a circle round it, pouring forth lamentations for his death. One of them, a tall thin Pythian-like figure, with her grey locks dishevelled and floating on the wind, stepped within the ring and delivered a wailing declamation in short extempore sentences, at the conclusion of each of which the others joined in a chorus of Haiee! haiee!—Alas! alas! The ceremony was wild and affecting; and as I retired from the scene, their mournful ululations, coming on the breeze from a distance, reminded me of the "wakes" which I had heard, in times past, floating tristfully over the waters of Loch Rea, in Ireland.

The next day brought us to the town of Mohim. It is one of the most ancient places in India; and though now a mere heap of ruins, with 100 or 200 inhabitants, was formerly an extensive and wealthy city. It was one of the first large towns which the Mussulmans took possession of in their invasion of the country; and the conquerors settled there in great numbers. It is said that many of the principal inhabitants of Delhi are descended from the ancient buniahs, or merchants, of Mohim.

The most remarkable relique of Mohammedan magnificence is a stupendous bowlee, or well, situated near the town walls, or probably formerly within their enceinte. The shaft is extremely wide, and about 130 feet deep: but this is the least remarkable part of it. For the use of the bhistees there is a fine open flight of stone steps, 20 feet wide, which by an easy descent enters the shaft just above the water. A square subterranean tower, three stories deep, and open at the top, is sunk alongside the well, and at each of the stories there is a capacious arched window broken through into the shaft; so that hundreds of persons may draw water at the same moment. The grand flight of steps leads through the lower story, which forms a kind of waiting-room for the bhistees. It is probably known to my readers that the wells in India are not accommodated with so unpicturesque an utensil as a public bucket; and that those who come to draw water bring their own little brass vessel and cord—a custom which, to the eye of a draftsman, is richly productive in grace and variety of attitude and effect. I know no more elegant object in nature than the Hindoo girl returning from the well; her light graceful raiments veiling, yet not concealing or impeding the movements of her upright and supple figure, and slender, though well-rounded limbs; with the classic-shaped vase artfully poised on her head, and seldom requiring the support of the naked bangled arm, which is, perhaps, as often raised from coquetry as from necessity.

Then you may see the tall, graceful sepoy—divested of his disfiguring uniform soiled by a dusty march, and with no other covering than the long flowing dhooty,—displaying his broad chest and well-compressed waist, as he swaggers towards the bowlee to take his morning bath. Plucking the little wooden comb from his top-knot, he shakes his long black hair down upon his shoulders, and, dropping his well-polished lota * into the well, pours the refreshing element over his head. If he happens to be a Brahmin, ere he leaves the well he carefully washes the mystic zennar, or sacred thread of his caste.

The next figure, brawny and bow-legged, and clad in a dhooty of red *curwa* with a white skullcap, is the plodding, hard-working bhistee. He drops his leathern jack into the water, fills and shoulders his weighty mussuck, and, "with difficulty and labour hard moves on" towards the camp, where he is eagerly expected by both man and beast.

The above-described bowlee, with its ghaut and tower, must occupy nearly as much space as the chapel at Eton College. It is a monument of public utility, worthy the munificence of a Roman emperor.

When the bright orb of day,—the Guebre's god—the

* Vessel of brass, of which every native of India, Hindoo or Mussulman, male or female, is possessed.

Anglo-Indian's scourge,—had sunk in the west, I wandered with my gun through the stunted bush-jungle around Mohim; and, although I took a wide sweep, I was constantly surrounded with remnants of serais, mosques, and temples; and tombs where the Hindoo and his conqueror repose side by side—their different monuments confounded by the lapse of ages in one common ruin.

The next day the camp moved to the hamlet of Mundeena. A low thick jungle of stunted bushes covers the surface of the country as far as the eye can range. I shot my way from camp to camp, mounted on my elephant, and brought in a good bag of hares, quails, and pea-fowl. Great herds of that gigantic species of deer, the niel-ghie, were roused by my firing, but after they had once seen the elephant I could never get within 300 yards of them. Therm. in camp, 2 P.M., 82°.

The following morning we marched to the ancient, and, consequently, ruinous town of Rhotuk. The wide circuit of its dilapidated fortifications, and the still elegant domes of many time-worn tombs, tell melancholy tales of gone-by grandeur. On reaching our camp we found a deputation from the Nawaub Fyse, Khan of Delhi, to the Commander-in-Chief, with a letter of compliments, and (what was of greater consequence to us sportsmen) a train of four hunting leopards and several falcons. In the evening, whilst strolling with my gun and spaniel through some old jungle-covered ruins in search of game, I stumbled suddenly into the presence of an enormous raw-boned hyæna, who was greedily gnawing a carcase as raw-boned as himself. He gave me one ghastly grin, and, as he cantered clumsily off, I gave him in return, at the distance of 15 paces, the contents of two barrels of shot, which only served to hasten his retreat. On looking round for my dog, undeservedly named after the hero Rustum,* I found he had decamped, and left his master to fight his own battles. On my return to my tent he was waiting for

* The Hercules of the Persian poets.

me at the door, his tail expressing deeper contrition than all the countenances in the world could have done.

Three long marches brought us, on the 19*th of Nov.*, to the ancient Serai of Seeta Ram—6 miles from the present walls of Delhi. In the days of its prosperity the ground upon which our camp is pitched was probably the Hampstead or Putney of the great capital; as the country round about is covered with the ruins of gardens and buildings, which were doubtless the rus-in-urbe residences of the ci-devant cits of ancient Delhi. Jheels of water and swamps have formed themselves in the hollowed foundations of the crumbled edifices, from under the friendly shelter of which I shot several wild fowl and snipes, their present tenants. A hundred years hence some of my descendants may, perhaps, be enjoying the same sport in Berkeley Square.

Nov. 20*th*, therm. 81°.—A march of 6 miles, through one continued avenue of ruined tombs, gardens, serais, and palaces, brought us to the walls of Delhi: they were built by the English government, and, though they are strengthened by handsome solid bastions and an embattled coping, are more formidable in appearance than in reality. We passed through the city to the residency, where we were once more welcomed by the hospitable, talented, and eccentric Resident. In the afternoon I rode with Lord Combermere round the walls, and returned to dinner at the residency, where about 90 sat down to table. The repast was followed by a ball, and the verandas and gardens, redolent with orange-blossoms, were illuminated with a profusion of coloured lamps.

Head-quarters halted the following day at Delhi. In the morning his Excellency reviewed a regiment of native infantry on the cantonment parade-ground, distant from Delhi about 2½ miles, and separated from the town by a lofty ridge of arid barren rocks. The review was attended by several natives of distinction, one of whom came to the ground in a regular English coach, with four horses and postilions.

In the cool of the evening I strolled into the great street, called Chandee Chowk, which may be well styled the Boulevard of Delhi: it is the most spacious and least dirty street I have ever seen in an Asiatic town. A fine canal of clear water—the munificent bequest of some Afghan worthy with a long name—shaded by an avenue of trees, runs down the centre; and yet the indolent and apathetic inhabitants, equally blind to their own and the passengers' comfort, will not take the trouble to allay by its waters the clouds of dust which float from morning till night in the atmosphere of this constantly well-thronged street. This canal, upon which the Delhians alone depended for a supply of wholesome water, was, during the decline of the Mogul empire, neglected and choked up, remaining so for more than a century; when the Company, wishing to bestow some monument of beneficence on the country which fate had placed in their hands, determined upon the restoration of this important aqueduct, with its lateral branches. It was accomplished at an enormous expense, and by the unremitting labour of nearly three years, and was completed in 1820. The joyous gratitude of the natives must alone have been sufficient reward to the English government—not to mention the benefits accruing to their treasury from the fertilizing effects of the canal upon the provinces through which it passed. A most touching account is given of the tumultuous rejoicings with which the long-coveted waters were greeted as they approached the city. The grateful inhabitants thronged out to meet them, and threw garlands and sweetmeats into the stream in token of welcome, loudly lauding the government that had put them in possession of such a blessing. The canal is, I believe, 180 miles in length.

The Chandee Chowk presented a lively and bustling appearance, people of all nations passing to and fro in busy pursuit of their several avocations; and the hardware, cloth, and pawn shops, driving a noisy, chaffering, yet thriving trade. In the midst of these industrious traffickers you might occasionally distinguish a group of lazy, lounging, debauched-looking Mussulmans, dressed in the most extravagant colours, with yellow slippers, their muslin skullcaps stuck jauntily over one ear, and their long hair frizzed out over the other, like a black mop. If you watched their motions, you might detect knowing looks passing between them and the hundreds of ladies of no very equivocal profession, who sit in the verandas or behind the trellised chicks of the windows smoking their little hookahs, and displaying to the passengers their thinly-clad persons, well-antimonied eyes, and henna-tipped fingers. Now and then the suwarree of some bloated nobleman would rush past—kicking up a dust equivalent to his pretensions—or the closely curtained car of some fair "light of the harem," drawn by a pair of handsome white oxen with gilded horns, trotted by, the bullock-bells ringing merrily. If you looked sharp, you might detect a little pink finger, or a brilliant dark eye peering through the small aperture upon the unwonted scene, and making one long—from the innate contrariety of man's disposition—to see more of the, doubtless, beautiful owner.

The Commander-in-Chief and the Staff dined with the British Resident, and after dinner the party adjourned to another apartment to hear the songs, and see the glissades, for it can scarcely be called dancing, of nearly 100 nautch-girls. There were present many of the first-rate dancers of Delhi, and some of their dresses, shawls, and jewels were really splendid.

The pretty, though rather dusky Alfina, whom I have previously had occasion to eulogize, shone pre-eminent in stature, grace, and voice: in this latter, however, *I* discovered nothing peculiar, except its exceeding shrillness. These attributes the siren has turned to some account; for it is said that she has stripped some of the dashing young nawaubs of Delhi of half their fortunes; and that, during a campaign of 3 months at Jheend, she levied 30,000 rupees on the mad young Rajah.

Nov. 22nd.—The Commander-in-Chief, having learned that the attention would be pleasing to the old monarch, determined on paying the "Great Mogul" a private visit. He received us in the Dewânee Khâs, and was pleased to take more notice of us than he conceived it consistent with his dignity to do on the occasion of our public audience, 9 months ago. As I described that ceremony at some length, I shall content myself with saying that this latter visit was merely a P.P.C. call; no nuzzars were offered on our parts, nor were we, as before, bedizened and bedevilled with spangled muslin khilauts, fillets, and tiaras. The audience was short; indifferent subjects, such as health and weather, were discussed, as they might be at a morning visit at my Lady Anyone's in Grosvenor-square; and when we salaamed a farewell to the venerable descendant of Timur, who cast upon our retiring forms the listless, melancholy gaze of dotage, I felt my heart swell with involuntary respect and pity for the fallen state of the poor old imperial pensioner, who, to counterbalance the loss of the wealth and power of his ancestors, possesses one sole advantage, namely, a tolerable chance of dying a natural death.

Almost the earliest recollections of my infant days were associated with the riches, splendour, heroism, and *barbarity* of the Great Mogul.—'Timur the Tartar' was the first play I ever saw, and my remembrance of every scene and incident is as vivid as though the years had been abridged to minutes. How little did I then foresee, as I sat in the box at Sadler's Wells, so entirely absorbed in the interest of the piece as to call down the anger of the audience by my screams of delight—how little did I then foresee that I should one day stand in the presence of my hero's descendant, and on the very spot where the dreaded Timur held his warrior court!

In the dusk of the evening, after dining at the residency, we got into our palankeens, and, rolling myself up in my quilted silk *labâder*, I was soon jogged into a doze, from which, ere I reached camp, I was only twice awakened, at the passages of the rivers Jumna and Hinden.

The next morning the reveillé and the usual tapping of

the tent-pegs by the impatient *classies*,* unkennelled me by daybreak, and I had a pleasant gallop over a well-cultivated country to the village of Bekunpore, taking, on the road, a last look at the lofty mosques of the once haughty, now humbled Delhi. The plain over which I passed swarmed with deer, antelope, hares, and foxes. In the afternoon we had some excellent coursing with English greyhounds. The hares of India are small, but very stanch, and have one more chance of escape than their brethren in Europe, namely, by running to ground. The foxes are also diminutive and very beautiful. Before a pack of hounds they do not live long, as they are not strong enough to run straight—but they afford excellent sport with the greyhounds, turning much sharper than the hare.

The following day, on the road to Boor-Barore, we passed the picturesque ruins of an ancient and extensive serai; objects which are much more frequently met with in he Mussulman States than in those provinces which have remained subject to Hindoo rule. Few monuments of the munificence or taste of the latter people are now to be seen, though it is difficult to say whether they ever existed, or whether they have not been defaced and destroyed by the Mohammedan conquerors of the soil.

Nov. 25th.—Head-quarters arrived at Meerut, which I have already named as the most considerable British station in the northern provinces: and the Commander-in-Chief had scarcely reached the camp, ere he received invitations to dine with her Highness the Begum Sumroo, and to a ball given by the General of Division, Sir J. Nicolls. I have already made mention of the Begum, on the occasion of our visit to her at her Jaghire of Sirdhana: but I believe I have not yet described her; and as her Highness is, beyond dispute, one of the most extraordinary characters in India, I cannot let her pass without a sketch.

Her Meerut residence is at a short distance from the cantonments. As we entered her gates, his Excellency was

* Tent-pitchers.

received with presented arms by a heterogeneous body-guard drawn up along the approach, and on the steps of the portico, by the old lady herself. In person she is very short, and rather embonpoint: her complexion is unusually fair, her features large and prominent, and their expression roguish and astute. Her costume consisted of a short full petticoat, displaying a good deal of her keemcab trousers, from under which peeped a very tiny pair of embroidered slippers. Of her hands, arms, and feet the octogenarian beauty is still justly proud. She wore on her head a plain snug turban of Cashmere, over which a shawl was thrown, enveloping her cheeks, throat, and shoulders; and from the midst of its folds her little grey eyes peered forth with a lynx-like acuteness. During the repast, which was served in the European style, the old lady smoked a very splendid hookah, a similar one being offered to his Excellency. The party consisted of about 60 persons, and the Begum, who considers herself now on an equality with the lords of the creation, was the only lady at table. Indeed, if the absence of all the softer qualities, and the possession of the most fiery courage, stubbornness of purpose, and almost unexampled cruelty can give her a claim to be numbered among the hardier sex, her right to virility will scarcely be disputed. The history of her life, if properly known, would (according to Colonel Skinner, and others who have had opportunities of hearing of and witnessing her exploits) form a series of scenes, such as, perhaps, no other female could have gone through.

The above-mentioned officer has often, during his service with the Mahrattas, seen her, then a beautiful young woman, leading on her troops to the attack in person, and displaying, in the midst of carnage, the greatest intrepidity and presence of mind. The Begum has been twice married, and both her husbands were Europeans. Her appellation of "Sumroo" is a corruption of the French word Sombre, the nom de guerre of her first lord, Remaud, who *bought* her when a young and handsome dancing-girl, married, and converted her to the Roman Catholic religion. Her second husband, named Le Vassu, was an independent, roving adventurer—a sort of land pirate; became powerful in his own right, if right it can be called, and possessed a considerable army. It is of this man that the following anecdote is related, which is "wondrous strange—if it be true:" it was the closing scene of his life, and the first in which our heroine played any very distinguished part. I have said that her husband had become possessed of wealth, power, and a numerous army; of these his ambitious wife coveted the undivided possession, and she thus accomplished her purpose.

A mutinous disposition, on the subject of pay, having manifested itself among Le Vassu's body-guard, the Begum, then about 25, exaggerated the danger to her husband, and got intelligence conveyed to him that the rebels had formed a plan to seize and confine him, and to dishonour his wife. They consequently arranged to escape together from the fury of the soldiery, and at night started secretly from their palace in palankeens, with only a few devoted guards and attendants. The whole of the following scene was projected by the ambitious and bloody-minded lady. Towards morning the attendants, in great alarm, announced that they were pursued; and our heroine, in well-feigned despair, vowed that, if their escort was overcome and the palankeens stopped, she would stab herself to the heart. The devoted husband, as she expected, swore he would not survive her. Soon after the pretended rebels came up, and, after a short skirmish, drove back the attendants and forced the bearers to put down the palankeens. At this instant Le Vassu heard a scream, and his wife's female slave rushed up to him bearing a shawl drenched in blood, and exclaiming that her mistress had stabbed herself to death. The husband, true to his vow, instantly seized a pistol and blew out his own brains. No sooner did the wily lady hear the welcome report than she started from her palankeen, and, for the first time exposing herself to the gaze of men, claimed homage from the soldiery. This her beauty and promises of speedy payment of arrears soon obtained for her; and she assumed, in due form, the reins of government.

Well knowing, however, that so inconsiderable a state as hers could not exist long in those troublesome times without some formidable ally, she prudently threw herself under the protection of the Company, who confirmed her in the possession, with the condition that it should revert to the English government after her death. The old lady seems disposed to make the most of her life-lease. Her revenue is, I believe, 100,000*l.* sterling, and she has amassed considerable treasures. I never heard how her other husband was disposed of, but we will, in charity, suppose that he died a natural death. His tomb is at Agra.

During her long life many acts of inhuman cruelty towards her dependants have transpired, one of which is thus narrated:—The Begum, having discovered a slave-girl in an intrigue, condemned her to be buried alive. This cruel sentence was carried into execution; and the fate of the beautiful victim having excited strong feelings of compassion, the old tigress, to preclude all chance of a rescue, ordered her carpet to be spread over the vault, and smoked her hookah and slept on the spot, thus making assurance doubly sure. It may be from this anecdote that the something similar act of barbarity of Madame Montreville, in the 'Surgeon's Daughter,' 'Chronicles of the Canongate,' is taken.

The Begum Sumroo, at the epoch of the last siege of Bhurtpore, followed our army and pitched her tents in the neighbourhood of the Head-quarters camp. The martial old Amazon was most eager to share our glory (and prize-money), and harassed the Commander-in-Chief with daily importunity that she might be permitted to support the British army with her handful of vagabond retainers—a reinforcement which was politely declined.

Her Highness afterwards protested a great friendship for his Lordship, sent him her portrait, and insisted upon a return of the compliment. The picture, a work of a native artist who resides at Meerut, and has made respectable progress in the art, was an exceeding good likeness; and my fingers always itched to transform her hookah snake into a broom, with which adjunct the old dame would have made no bad representative of Mother Shipton.

At the dinner the Begum seemed in excellent humour, and bandied jokes and compliments with his Excellency through the medium of an interpreter; but towards the conclusion of the repast she seemed quite worn out; a faint, sickly smile alone indicating that she understood what was said to her.

The feast being ended, an European officer in her service walked round the table and invested each of the guests with a long massive necklace of tinsel.

The two following days Head-quarters halted at Meerut; our mornings being employed in reviews, and our evenings in dinners and balls, provided for the entertainment of the Commander-in-Chief by the inhabitants of this gay colony.

Nov. 28th.—Head-quarters again en route, and its course directed toward the Rohilcund stations of Moradabad and Bareilly. Three easy marches brought us to the ghaut of Ghurmuktesur, an euphonous title given to the ferry which at this point crosses the Ganges. Though the spot which we occupied is at this season nearly half a mile from the water's edge, during the rains the great river rolls its swollen flood over the ground where there is at this moment an encampment of nearly 5000 souls. Both banks of the stream are bordered for some miles in width with a thick jungle of grass and bush, abounding in tigers, and the favourite resort of the sportsmen of Meerut during the months of April and May; but at this time of the year, the high grass, luxuriant from the late rains, not yet having undergone its annual burning, the attempt to find the game is almost hopeless; as, on the approach of the elephants, the tiger steals away under the thick impervious covert, in which he has paths invisible from above.

This morning the thermometer stood at 42° in my tent at 6 A.M., and at 80° at 2 P.M.—a striking difference of temperature to occur in the space of 8 hours, and in weather uniformly fair and unclouded. It might be supposed that such sudden variations of the atmosphere would be extremely prejudicial to the health of those exposed to them. I am, however, convinced that there are few climates more congenial to the European constitution than that enjoyed in the upper provinces of India during the months of November, December, and January. Were it not for the regular annual recurrence of this bracing and invigorating season, the parching sirocco of the "hot winds" and the miasmatic exhalations of "the rains" would, no doubt, quickly rid India of its European possessors.

At Ghurmuktesur, Mr. or rather Major ——, who had marched with the camp from Delhi, took leave of us, and in him we have lost a most entertaining and instructive companion. His history and appearance equally declare him to be a *character*. He is a man of considerable talents and acquirements, and holds a high post under Government in the civil service of the Honourable Company. In this capacity his pen is said to have proved as trenchant as his sword is known to be in his second character of Major in a regiment of irregular cavalry. His countenance is remarkably handsome and intelligent, and much set off by his black beard and mustachios. At the siege of Bhurtpore—where the Major distinguished himself and was wounded—this ornament was of much more luxuriant growth, flowing down upon his breast; but subsequent to that period, a depilatory mandate from the Supreme Government was fulminated against himself and other civilians, who, with less reason, indulged in this military decoration, and he was constrained (in the spirit of these half-batta times) to reduce the exuberant proportions of his beard; his fostering another crop looks very like *bearding* the Government.

Major —— is a great sportsman, and of the noblest order. He spurns the idea of securely butchering the tyrants of the desert from the turreted back of an elephant, and encounters the lion and tiger on horseback with spear and sword. He describes this species of sport, particularly with the king of brutes, as the only hunting worthy of a man. Indeed, there is a combination of courage, strength, and dexterity required which few sportsmen are able to bring into the field.

The Major employs sometimes an hour or more in destroying his game, riding swiftly round in a circle, alternately approaching and retreating, and gradually narrowing the ring, until at length his furious antagonist becomes so confused and fatigued by his own exertions as to enable him to gallop past and deliver his spear. In these encounters he prefers the large country horse to the Arab, as being generally better on his haunches and more powerful.

He is known to have, on one occasion, encountered on foot and slain a lion; but as he is not one of those who perform doughty deeds merely for the pleasure of recounting them, I could never cheat him out of a description of his combat with the king of the desert. Athough he is so fond of, and excellent in, these manly exercises, Mr. ——'s diet is ultra-Hindoo, as he seldom eats meat, and never touches wine.

CHAPTER VII.

Rohilcund — Amroah — Moradabad — Passage of the Ram-Gunga — Rampore — Futtygunge — Bareilly — Dougan's Horse — Burra-Muttana — Jellahabad — Falconry — Left bank of Ganges — Futtyghur — The Hakim Mendes — Sixth Local Horse — Anecdotes of the battle of Setabuldree.

Dec. 1*st.*—The camp crossed the Ganges—the horses, camels, and equipages performing the passage in boats, and the elephants swimming the stream. The ferry presented a glorious scene of bustle and confusion, the horses fighting like tigers in the boats, and even kicking each other into the water; camels roaring and blubbering, and resisting every effort, soothing or forcible, of their serwâns to induce them to embark; and when some of these ungainly though useful brutes were persuaded to emulate the fabled bear, they not unfrequently blundered in on one side the boat, and out on the other into the river; where they stood answering with helpless bellowings the execrations of the serwâns and maungees, who, equally helpless, quickly resorted to mutual recrimination, followed by a brisk fusillade of abuse, of which the fathers, mothers, and even collateral kindred of the principals, were sure to come in for their full share.

The trajet of the elephant, that "wisest of beasts," is the most easily effected. The sage animal, on arriving at the river-side, is divested of his burthen, which is sent across in the boats; on a hint from the mohaut he steps into the stream and wades or swims through the element in which he delights, and on the other bank again patiently receives his load. In swimming, the elephant's trunk is alone seen above water. The mohaut directs his course kneeling or standing on his back.

Soon after our arrival in camp a party of 9 started with a line of 16 elephants to try for a tiger; but our endeavours were completely frustrated by the extreme thickness of the covert. We did not get sight of a tiger the whole day, although on several occasions the elephants showed by their uneasiness that we were close upon one, and we found their footmarks on the sand of every rivulet. We had, however, very tolerable sport with deer, wild-hogs, and black game.

Two days after, we encamped under the walls of the Mussulman town of Amroah, which, though now in ruins, bears the appearance of having been formerly a large and populous city. The country in the immediate neighbourhood is spread out in wide tracts of cultivation, and extensive groves of fine trees; amongst which are scattered here and there the picturesque remnants of mosques and tombs, memorials of the once warlike and powerful Patâns. As we rode past the walls, amongst the numerous groups of the idle inhabitants, who assembled to gaze at the English cavalcade, I scarcely saw a single Hindoo. The gay raiment of the Mahommedan, with its various and flaunting colours, appears to great advantage over the plain white garb of the less showy disciple of Brahma, more particularly in groups. The walls of Amroah and the road-side were dotted with little parties of these graceful blackguards, who stood, sat, and lounged in attitudes as natural to their supple forms and elegant drapery, as they are incompatible with the stiff joints and stiffer costume of English figures. Each group appeared as if it had been previously drilled by some posture-maker for a "tableau." An experienced eye may readily distinguish individuals of the two sects Mussulman and Hindoo, by a certain rakish, "devil may care" air in the former, strongly contrasting with the placid and orderly demeanour of the latter tribe. In some instances, however, where the dress and manners may have gradually assimilated, there is still preserved one characteristic mark —the vest of the Islamite is uniformly open on the left breast, and that of the Hindoo on the right.

From Amroah two marches, through a pretty country abundantly provided with shady groves, brought us to the town of Moradabad. It is a considerable place, and the streets and bazaars are better scavenged than most native towns are. The population is almost exclusively Mahommedan. The English cantonment, in which a native infantry regiment is quartered, is prettily situated amid luxuriant trees, round an open parade-ground. The chief duty of the troops is the guard of the goal, wherein there are incarcerated no fewer than 1800 native convicts. These are condemned to work, in chains, on the roads: but I fancy their labours do not extend much beyond the gravel walks of the magistrate's garden, for the roads through which we have jolted for the last 3 days seem perfect strangers to the spade and pickaxe.

In the evening I strolled to see a house near the town, which, many years ago, as I was informed, proved the city of refuge to the Europeans of this station. Mr. Leicester was collector of revenue at Moradabad, and at this isolated spot was only supported by 5 companies of sepoys; when one night the cantonments were surprised by a sudden attack of some thousand Mahratta cavalry, headed by the famous Holkar in person. Mr. L. threw himself, with his sepoys, into this fortified house, which was fortunately provided with a deep ditch and a wall flanked with miniature bastions, and had just time to secure himself in his little stronghold when it was beset by the enemy. The garrison succeeded in keeping the besiegers at bay, until Holkar, hearing of the near approach of Lord Lake, who was in pursuit of him, was obliged to draw off his troops from the blockade.

The following morning Head-quarters, pursuing its flying tour, passed the river Ram-Gunga, and encamped 6 miles from its left bank. This little stream proved quite a Berisina to our camp-followers; though the scene of confusion on its banks was rather mirth-provoking than horror-striking. The only boat had been rendered useless by a camel having put its foot through the bottom: kuranshees and hackeries,* full of women and baggage, were sticking fast in the quicksands; and many of them, capsized in the river, poured forth their contents, living or inanimate, into the water: whilst the ladies themselves—unused to play the naiad—picked their way, with well-uplifted pyjamas,† to terra firma, reviling in no very choice terms the awkwardness of their garreewâns (charioteers), which had exposed their well-curtained charms to the vulgar gaze, and their silken dresses and tender limbs to the chilling stream—and on a December morning.

I remained behind on my elephant to witness "the fun," and had the satisfaction of seeing my property, carried on the backs of camels—well styled the "ships of the desert,"—accomplish the passage, high and dry; whilst sundry cart-loads of office records and other impedimenta were immersed in the deep.

The portion of Rohilcund through which we are now journeying is watered by many streams, and much adorned

* Native vehicles. † Trowsers.

by beautiful topes of mangoes and other trees. These groves, so refreshing to the sun-worn traveller, have been for the most part bequeathed to posterity by rich natives; amongst whom it is, or was before our reign, the custom to leave behind them some monument of public utility, such as a tank, well, or grove;—an inculcation of their religion which, if it does not tend to benefit their own souls, is at least highly advantageous to the bodies of their descendants. The topes are usually planted in regular series of avenues, along the umbrageous alleys of which the camps of travellers in the hot season are erected.

The next day we crossed the small river Kosila, and on the left bank encountered the Nawaub of Rampore, who came in state to welcome the Commander-in-Chief to his dominions. On meeting, this prince entered Lord Combermere's houdah, and, instead of the usual embraces, shook hands à l'Anglaise. He affects Anglicism in many other points, an assumption by no means rare among Mussulman potentates; but the commixture of British and native manners seems as unnatural as the blending of oil and water: the ill-sustained attempt at John Bullish cordiality soon sinks out of sight, and the frothy pomp of the Mahommedan floats again to the surface. His dress was a singular mixture of splendour and bad taste, consisting of a black velvet surtout, richly embroidered in gold—such as one might imagine Talleyrand to have worn at the Congress of Vienna—upon which he had stuck several rows of the Honourable Company's livery buttons, displaying the rampant lion upholding the crown. This chef d'œuvre was, as he assured us, perpetrated by an English tailor at Calcutta. His head was adorned by a unique-looking head-piece, in form something between a cap of maintenance and the pinnacle of a Chinese pagoda. Several carriages of British fashion and manufacture followed in the cavalcade; the most remarkable of which was a barouche drawn by a pair of young elephants beautifully caparisoned. His *cab* would have put to shame all its fellows in Hyde Park; it was of the most approved architecture, and the hood was of black velvet, enriched with deep gold embroidery.

The Nawaub of Rampore is a stout, vulgar-looking man, of middle stature, and deeply marked with the smallpox: he is an ardent sportsman, and is accounted the best ball-shot in India. He bears the character of a drunkard and spendthrift; and owing to misrule and neglect of business, his kingdom, which if well managed should produce 20 lacs per annum, scarcely affords him a revenue of one-fourth of that amount.

In the evening Lord Combermere paid the usual compliment of returning the visit, when the ordinary ceremonies and entertainments were put in vogue. The audience-hall, where we were received, is of Eastern architecture, but splendidly, though heterogeneously, furnished with mirrors, chandeliers, &c., from England. The presents offered at the close of the sederunt to his Excellency were strictly characteristic of the Nawaub's sporting reputation: a pair of powder-flasks formed of the tusks of the female elephant, richly carved; a sylvan picnic chair, made entirely of stags' antlers; an enormous elephant's tooth, about 8 feet in length; and a stupendous pair of buffalo's horns.

We only passed 24 hours at Rampore, and on the third day our camp was pitched near the village of Futtygunge, on the very plain where some five-and-thirty years ago a British army under General Abercrombie gained a hard-earned victory over the Rohillas. It is related that at the commencement of this battle the scales of Jove long hung doubtful; the enemy's cavalry even got into our rear, and cut to pieces 6 companies of infantry. Within eyeshot of the action we had some 30,000 native allies, in the troops of the Nawaub of Lucknow: but the Rohillas being looked upon as the most determined fighters in India, these crafty, cold-blooded auxiliaries did not hold it convenient to interfere in the affray until one of the principals had achieved a decided superiority. Accordingly, they held aloof, until the British, though sorely knocked about, had proved themselves the better men; and then, like the fabled fox, they rushed in, and bore off the chief part of the spoil. As a counterpoise to this base act, however, they did the British the distinguished honour to change the name of the village which beheld their exploits from Beetora to Futtygunge, the "place of victory."

In the evening I strolled out to visit the monument raised by government in memory of those who fell. It is of obelisk form, and stands on a small mound, the only elevation in this vast plain, on which point of vantage the enemy's guns were ranged and afterwards taken. The names of 14 British officers are recorded on the "storied stone;" among whom were 3 commanding officers of regiments: a son of one of these now commands Lord Combermere's infantry escort. I met him returning from his father's grave. With what intense interest must he have contemplated the spot on which his sire, a most intrepid soldier, distinguished himself, and perished! This officer is described as having possessed uncommon personal strength: when surrounded by overwhelming numbers, he slew several of the enemy, until his treacherous sword shivered in his hand, and he fell covered with wounds.

Within a stone's throw of this plain and simple monument rises the carved and minareted tomb of two illustrious Rohilla chiefs who fell in the action, bravely leading their cavalry to the charge. Our cavalry behaved infamously on the occasion: on the first onset of the enemy, Ramsay, who commanded them, turned his horse and fled with his troopers at his heels, leaving the flank of our line en l'air. To this base desertion may be attributed the great carnage which took place in our right wing; and here the dashing Rohilla chiefs ended their career in the midst of our broken ranks. Part of our runaway cavalry was rallied and brought back to the field by two subaltern officers: the recreant commander awaited not the judgment which would have overtaken him, but fled to America.

The editor of the 'Naval and Military Magazine' mentions that this same officer was afterwards employed by Napoleon in the Commissariat department.

The next day Head-quarters arrived at Bareilly, a considerable town, and a civil and military station. On the road we were met by the Governor-General's Agent, Mr. Hawkins, who escorted the Commander-in-Chief into camp. The town appears to be tolerably populous, and the bazaars present the prosperous confusion and busy bustle of successful traffic. Bareilly is chiefly noted for the manufacture of house furniture, particularly chairs and tables, which, though painted and gilded very handsomely, are remarkably cheap. Chairs, highly ornamented, are sold for 35 rupees, or 3*l.* 10*s.* a dozen.

In the afternoon we had a very pretty review of "Dougan's corps of Irregular Horse." The young and handsome commander, who had exchanged the scarlet and gold-stiffened mummy-case of the A.D.C. for the graceful, easy-flowing Mussulman vest, was prevented by severe illness from attending: nor did the youthful soldier, who had just attained the acme of his ambition—the command of a cavalry corps—ever spring into his saddle again. On visiting my friend, whose sickness was alleviated and his love of life augmented by the presence of a blooming bride, I found the grim livery of death already impressed upon his handsome features. He spoke cheeringly and confidently of his recovery; and in a few weeks he was in the grave—whither two others of my brother aides-de-camp had already preceded him.

The regiment collectively did not perform so well as Skinner's Horse: individually, however, the men were equally expert in the spear and matchlock exercise, and in feats of horsemanship. The Adjutant, Captain Anderson, played for some time in front of the regiment with one of the native officers, a very expert spearman, and struck his man the three first blows, displaying the utmost equestrian skill and knowledge of his weapon. He rode with the strength of an Englishman, and the grace of an Indian. His Mussulman antagonist, as I was informed, was on one occasion brought into the arena of the Meerut riding-school, to try his powers with the best lance of his Majesty's 16th Lancers; when the latter was obliged to confess that the Asiatic had him quite at his mercy, through the superior length and handiness of his spear; and, he might have added, I suspect, the more perfect manège of his horse. This latter point of superiority is doubtless brought about by the severe though light bit, and the still lighter hand, with which the natives break and ride their horses. Unlike the ponderous English cavalry bit, it does not oppress and deaden the mouth when the rein is slackened; and the tenderest touch of it throws the steed much more immediately upon his haunches than could be accomplished by the massive piece of mechanism with which our horses are gagged. The soft, deep saddle, too, and short stirrups of the Indian are much more adapted to equestrian exploits than the narrow, slippery saddle and long seat of the English cavalier.

The most difficult of the feats that I saw this day practised was the following. A tent-peg is driven by a mallet some 8 or 10 inches into the earth, so firmly that the strength of 2 men would not suffice to draw it out. The horseman, holding his spear reversed in the rest, rides at full speed past the object, drives his weapon into the tough wood, drags it out of the earth, and brandishes it aloft, amid the cheering plaudits of the spectators. We have seen the cavalier successful; let us now follow the *bungler's* career: he places his spear in the rest, and comes thundering down direct upon the object; his horse swerves, he makes his coup, the peg stands scatheless, the ferule of the spear plunges deep in the earth, whilst the reverse end strikes the ill-starred rider a violent blow on the back of the head, and brings him to the ground, amid shouts of laughter from the crowd. I should premise that this feat is performed with the butt of the spear, which is furnished with a strong, sharp, steel ferule. The greatest adept at the exercise only succeeded twice in 5 courses.

When the regiment marched past the General, it was

preceded, in place of a band, by a company of mounted singers, who chanted verses in a monotonous but not unmusical key, accompanied solely by kettledrums.

On the present occasion they sung to the praise of the Commander-in-Chief,—no doubt delicately adverting to his Bhurtpore exploits—but the usual subjects of their strains are triumphant recapitulations of the warlike achievements of the regiment, and exhortations to future acts of glory—much after the fashion of Tyrtæus, the great elegiac poet, who, by his spirit-stirring war-songs, spurred on the Lacedemonians to conquest.

In the evening Mr. Hawkins entertained the Head-quarters party with a grand dinner, at which was displayed a magnificent service of plate, the same presented, at the epoch of Lord Amherst's embassy, by his Majesty of England to the Emperor of China; but which that cautious, self-sufficient potentate declined accepting. It was sold at auction, and purchased by the present princely proprietor. Although profuse and prodigal in some points, Mr. H. has not, if report speaks true, altogether neglected to provide for his declining years: yet, in spite of the handsome sum which rumour announces as the amount of his thrift, he does not, I believe, meditate a return to his native land. Indeed, it has always been a matter of marvel to me, how any man, after passing the best years of his existence in India,—accustoming himself to its splendid establishments and inert luxuries, and playing the despot among a crowd of fawning, cringing dependants,—can complacently settle down to a younger brother's mediocrity in England, and school his disordered spleen to the constant aggression which it must put up with from the independent, liberty-and-equality bluntness of English servants and the English lower orders in general,—not to mention the probable dissolution, or at least relaxation, of the ties which attached him to home, and the formation of new ones in the land of his pilgrimage.

The next morning we rode to see Mr. Hawkins's country-seat, called Cashmere, about 5 miles from his town residence. It is a pretty place, surrounded by grounds which might easily be made very park-like: but the beauty of the whole is marred by the turf having been ploughed up, for the sake of a paltry crop of grain, under the very windows of the palace,—for such it may be styled. We did not view this Trianon of Bareilly under the most favourable auspices; for we started in one of those well-nigh choking fogs which are common to the cold-weather mornings, and had returned to camp long before the sun had driven his misty antagonist from the face of nature. But this is only one of the many rambles in search of the picturesque that I have made in India during the cool season, in which my horse's "dew-besprent" ears formed the utmost distance of the prospect.

Having passed two pleasant days at Bareilly, we resumed our march towards Futtyghur on the 13th. On the 14th and 15th we encamped at *another* Futtygunge, and at a village called Burra-Muttanah. The former place is, perhaps, the spot where, in the reign of Mr. Hastings, the Rohilla satrap Hafiz Rhamut lost his life and his country, in a game at soldiers with the combined forces of Oude and the Company. It is left for *me* to celebrate the latter place by the following encounter. On our journey this morning, an enormous wild boar crossed the line of march directly before the Commander-in-chief's horse, and struck into some fields of cotton and other high crops. Snatching one of the hurkarahs' halberts—a very inefficient weapon by the bye—and followed by the two cavalry orderlies, I spurred after him, and was close at his heels when he dashed into a thick cate of sugar-canes, inaccessible to horsemen.

Some idle camp followers, being attracted to the spot, entered the cate to expel the animal by their shrill outcries, whilst I posted myself, en vidette—like the Don waiting for the attack of the lion—at the farther corner. I was in the act of speaking to one of the orderlies, when a sudden crash through the canes, and a savage grunt close to me, was followed by as sudden a rear from my horse, who entertained quite a Mahommedan antipathy to swine, dead or alive. The hog passed under his lifted fore legs, and in a trice I found myself sprawling on the earth with my little Arab rolling by my side, whilst my successful foe, satisfied with having made me "vider les arçons," pursued his career, mercifully abstaining from bringing the combat "à l'outrance," and leaving me to shake the dust from my person, and my spear at my retreating antagonist, with a muttered threat of retribution. Accordingly I had not been 3 hours in camp before, Meleager-like, I assembled three or four good spears to join in my crusade against the far-famed boar. We beat diligently but fruitlessly for some hours; and I had time to digest the venom of my spleen during a ride of 12 miles. The crafty hog had, no doubt, saved his bacon by a forced march from the scene of his success.

The following morning we passed under the walls of Jellahabad, a ruinous fortress of inconsiderable dimensions; but surrounded by a lofty mud parapet, formidable bastions, and a deep fosse. It was built—as I was informed by a melancholy-looking old man, one of the few inhabitants—by Hafiz Khan, about 70 years ago—probably the same Rohilla chief whose death I have lately recounted. Like most other small native forts in the British dominions, the fortifications have been allowed to become the prey of time; the Company's monopoly of power in India precluding the necessity—which formerly existed—of every petty town being furnished with defences against the sudden attacks of the numerous predatory hordes which infested the country. A little beyond Jellahabad we crossed the river Ramgunga, and encamped on its western bank.

Dec. 17th.—Marched to the town of Imrautpore, through a country spread for many surrounding leagues with one sheet of luxuriant cultivation, interspersed with beautiful and ancient mango-groves. In the rainy season this rich and fruitful tract is scarcely habitable or passable; the whole country between the Ganges and Bareilly exhibiting one vast lake of water. These inundations contribute greatly to fertilize the land. During this morning's journey we diverged a good deal from the line of march, accompanied by the Head-quarters falcon establishment, and enjoyed some more than usually good sport. With the long-winged, soaring bheiree, we had a best-speed gallop of 4 miles after a black curlew—a bird giving flights almost equal to the heron—and the bhauses, or short-winged, killed for us a couple of wild geese, some teal, and several partridges. This latter species of hawk does not soar, but darts from the wrist with the speed of lightning, and seldom fails to strike its quarry within 200 yards—generally in a much shorter distance. We had also some amusing sport with another kind of falcon, of which, I believe, I have not made mention. It is a very small bird, perhaps barely so large as a thrush, and its prey is proportioned to its strength. It is flown at quails, sparrows, and others of the feathered tribe of the like calibre. The mode of starting it is different from that used with any other hawk. The falconer holds the little, well-drilled savage within the grasp of his hand, the head and tail protruding at either opening, and the plumage carefully smoothed down. When he arrives within 20 or 30 yards of the quarry the sportsman throws his hawk much as he would a cricket-ball, in the direction of it. The little creature gains his wings in an instant, and strikes the game after the manner of the bhause.

There is a queer tribe of gregarious little birds, common in India, which afford very laughable sport with the above-described hawk. They are usually found in a chattering fluttering congress of ten or a dozen, at the foot of some baubul-tree; where the little busy-bodies are so absorbed in the subject under immediate agitation, that the falconer may approach within 6 paces of their noisy court of parliament, ere they entertain a thought of proroguing it. In the heat of the debate, down comes the little hawk (like some Cromwell) into the midst of the astonishe assembly, and begins to lay about him right and left; when, strange to say, the whole tribe set upon him, unguibus et rostris, and with a virulence of tongue as

o 2

manifestly vituperative, to a discerning ear, as if it were couched in words. In the dust of the contest the sportsman runs up, and all the party take wing, except some two or three unfortunates, who, having caught a tartar, lie fluttering in the clutches of the feathered tyrant.

The camp was pitched the next day on the left bank of the Ganges, opposite to the town of Futtyghur, which is situated about a mile from the other bank, and, with its numerous respectable buildings embosomed in fine groves, presents a very handsome appearance.

The march of intellect, which seems to occupy so much of the interest of the English newspapers at this period, is evidently rapidly extending itself to these distant regions; as is, I think, happily illustrated by the following note which I have just received from a native of rank at Futtyghur. Few of his compatriots have hitherto reached that climax of civilization, an invitatory billet to dinner:—

"Nawaub Moontezim ood Doulah requests the honour of Captain M.'s company to dinner on, &c., to meet his Excellency the Commander-in-Chief."

The gentleman in question can, however, afford better proof than this trifling note of ceremony of his intellectual attainments, being accounted one of the most enlightened and liberal-minded natives in India.

Dec. 19th.—Early this morning the holy Ganges once more received upon her glittering bosom the 5000 members of the Head-quarters camp. On reaching the opposite bank we mounted our horses and sped into the town of Futtyghur, where a pressing invitation to breakfast from the Nawaub Moontezim ood Doulah, alias Hakim Mendes, greeted our party. On the threshold of his palace—which it is just a year since we crossed on our journey northwards—the Commander-in-Chief was received by the venerable noble with that dignified and gentlemanly courtesy for which well-born Mussulmans in general, and the Nawaub in particular, are distinguished. His house I have already described as handsome in its architecture and proportions; but furnished in an inconsistent and heterogeneous fashion. The table was well served, and, on the removal of the cloth, numerous costly nick-nacks of French manufacture, such as ooo-coo clocks, musical-boxes, &c.—for which the natives entertain a great passion—were displayed for the amusement of the company.

The memoirs of our host would, I imagine, present a pretty fair delineation of the life of eastern courtiers in general; except, indeed, that, by some lucky combination of circumstances, or by the progress of intellect—which has taught men to respect the *seat* of intellect—the Hakim has been enabled, in his disgrace, to keep his head upon his shoulders. By his distinguished talents he raised himself to the Vizierate of Oude under Sadut Ali, which office he long held; but, as the tenure of ministers in the favour of their patrons is often ephemeral and insecure, he was supplanted in the king's good will by a knave, and condemned to an honourable banishment as governor of some frontier province. In this appointment his abilities poured an increase of revenue into the royal treasury; whilst, at the same time, his own cassette waxed heavier; and, when he finally took up his residence at Futtyghur, he was accounted a man of immense wealth. Of this he has devoted a considerable portion to sundry public benefactions, among which may be noted a handsome bridge, built for the English government at his own expense.

Of the extent to which the Nawaub carries courtesy and good-breeding, the following anecdote affords fair proof. On the occasion of the marriage of a young relation he gave a grand entertainment, to which the English of Futtyghur were invited. In the midst of the festival a string of costly pearls—doubtless as big as plovers' eggs!— worn by him as a necklace, broke, and the precious beads rolled on the floor among the crowd; an accident of which the Hakim did not take the slightest notice until the breaking up of the assembly, remarking, that it was not worth while to disturb the harmony and hilarity of the party for so trifling a cause.

Having here slightly sketched the bright side of the Nawaub's portrait, I leave to his future biographers the exposure of the reverse. In person the Hakim Mendes is tall and thin, and slightly bowed by age; his complexion fair and pale, his features small, and their expression that of cunning veiled and neutralized by exceeding blandness.

At the conclusion of the breakfast the Nawaub conducted us to a veranda opening upon a grass-plot, where his stud of horses was paraded, consisting of a showy assemblage from England, Persia, Arabia, Caubul, the Deccan, &c.

Dec. 20th.—A halt—review of the 6th Local Horse, a corps accoutred à la Mussulmane, and mustering about 700 men on parade. After going through some skirmishing manœuvres, the usual practice of the spear, sword, and matchlock was displayed. The most amusing part of the spectacle was the confusion of the crowds of spectators, who were suddenly put to the rout by the whizzing of the bullets, liberally and promiscuously expended by these wild cavaliers, without much solicitude as to their direction. The regiment is commanded by Major Fitzgerald, who obtained the appointment in reward of an act of intrepidity which, about 11 years since, saved the Europeans at Nagpore from a hempen catastrophe, a fate ordained them by the Rajah of Berah, who, with a numerous army headed by fierce Arabs, had surrounded the handful of an English force near that place, with the resolution to exterminate them.

The following account of the action I received from oral authority, and not from authenticated history; should it be incorrect, therefore, in the details, let my informer prepare his broad shoulders for the onus. Indeed, many of the historical anecdotes interspersed throughout this journal were gleaned—after the manner of an indolent, yet inquisitive traveller—more by asking questions than by consulting documents. Having thus turned king's evidence against myself as an author, I will proceed.

The British force did not exceed two regiments of native infantry and four troops of native cavalry, the latter commanded by the then young Lieutenant Fitzgerald. Our men had bravely resisted for some time, but were falling fast from the repeated onsets of the overpowering enemy, and from the discharge of a numerous artillery, to answer which the English had only two guns (and even these shortly fell into the hands of the Mahrattas), when Fitzgerald at length remarked to the commanding officer the utter hopelessness of standing still to be mowed down without the power of retaliation, and offered to try the effect of a charge with his four troops. The commandant refused to hear of it, and, on our hero persisting, declared that, if he carried his rash project into execution, it would be at his own peril in case of failure. In such an emergency, however, a court-martial would present few terrors even to the most buckram martinet: the gallant youth only exclaimed, "I accept the alternative!" and, after a few words of exhortation to his men, charged at the head of them through the centre of the enemy's thousands.

The impetuosity and unexpectedness of the attack produced a momentary panic among the Mahrattas, who, opening out on all sides, left their artillery exposed. Fitzgerald saw his advantage, assaulted and overthrew or put to flight the golundaze,* and, dismounting about 40 of his men, turned the guns against the enemy. But for this exploit, their little party must have been quickly cut to pieces: for the Arabs, recovering from the shock, and becoming aware of their assailants' weakness, resumed the offensive, and had nearly surrounded the three troops, who were fighting desperately with their young commander at their head, when the latter suddenly ordered his men to disperse, and to re-form behind the guns, which were still in possession of the fourth troop. This they accomplished, the enemy pressing so close on their heels as to cut down their rearmost horsemen; and a tremendous fire was immediately opened, which checked the career of their pursuers, destroying those who pressed hardest on them, and spreading havoc among their crowded ranks. By these means the English

* Gunners.

retained their defensive position till nightfall; and in the morning, a lucky discord, by no means uncommon in Eastern armies, having arisen in the enemy's ranks, the two parties were thinking more of cutting each other's throats than those of the English.

Another interesting incident was related to me of a Lieutenant ——, Fitzgerald's junior officer. He was described as a very powerful young man, and an expert and dashing swordsman; and in the affray many of the adverse cavaliers had bit the dust under his puissant blade. Among the rest he dismissed to the shades below an ancient grey-bearded warrior, who was fighting, "ενι προμαχοισι," with his son, a young Arab, by his side. The English officer pursued his career in search of fresh conquests; but the youth had seen his father fall, and, bent on pious vengeance, followed his destroyer over the whole field. At length he came up with him, just as he was retiring, the last among his troop, behind the guns. They met for an instant; the Arab's sword, urged on by revenge, pierced the Englishman's side, and he fell from his horse; whilst the appeased son, uttering a shout of triumph, flew back to seek his sire's body.

This evening I attended a grand dinner given by the Nawaub to the Commander-in-Chief. The ladies of our camp and those of the Station were present, and the party sat down about 40 in number. The repast was served strictly in English style; whilst for those guests who had imbibed a taste for eastern gastronomy there was a profusion of curries the most rêcherchés; pillaus of marrow, redolent with spices, and tinged with saffron; and kawâbs that might have created an appetite "under the ribs of death."

CHAPTER VIII.

The Dooab — Falconry — Etawar — Budeapore — Scindia's territories — The Mahrattas — Bhind — Gohud — Gwalior — Scindia's camp — A sporting digression — Hog-hunting — The Tent Club — An anecdote — Martial games — A Mahratta feast — Mahratta entertainments — Antree.

THE next morning Head-quarters was again en route towards Etawar, a town on the Jumna river, distant five marches from Futtyghur. The fertile province between the two great rivers is called the Dooab, a term synonymous with the Mesopotamia of the Greeks. Our first day's march, 14 miles, brought us to the village of Jehangunge. The Nawaub sent his hunting leopards and a lynx to accompany us through a country abounding in antelopes; and our hawks were in high feather for the plentiful provision of game which we were rightly led to expect in this beautiful district. Of the latter sport we had this morning several good specimens; but, as I have already described the flights of the bheiree, bhause, and little hand-hawk, it only remains for me to sketch the peculiarities of the lugger, a bird of the long-winged order, whose exploits I witnessed for the first time to-day.

A hare, scared from its form, crossed the line of march at full speed, and, the falconers being at hand, a couple of the last-named birds were flown at her. The lugger, being a light hawk, has not sufficient power to stop the hare by one swoop, but, keeping just above her, the two confederates alternately stoop and strike her, in such quick succession, and with such force, that the timid animal, being frequently rolled over by the blow, becomes so alarmed and exhausted, that she soon lies helpless, and is taken by the attendants. In this instance the hare was brought-to after running about 300 yards. The blow of the lugger, which is inflicted by the heel-talon, must be very severe, as the back of the animal was deeply scored in several places, and stripped of its fur.

The wide-extending, lightly-fenced, and level champaign through which we are now marching, is particularly favourable to falconry; but the great numbers of old, forsaken wells, which are invisible to the rider until he is close upon them, render the sport dangerous, particularly to the really stanch falconer, whose eyes are too eagerly employed in following his bird among the clouds to see and avoid the dangers that lie in wait for him on the earth.

Between Futtyghur and Etawar my journal presents little more than a sporting diary; a chronicle of damage done by our chetahs among the antelope race; an obituary of herons, curlews, and others of the feathered tribe, that fell to the hawks. These I shall pretermit, as presenting little of novelty or variety; and invite my reader, without further ceremony, to spend Christmas-day with me at Etawar, a place, by the by, as little calculated for hilarious purposes as can well be imagined. This season of religious exultation and domestic merrymaking in England is in India so little marked by any external demonstrations, that I am free to confess that mid-day was treading on the heels of morning ere I was reminded that the sacred anniversary had nearly half passed over me, by the distant sound of the well-known Christmas hymn, played by the native drummers and fifers of the escort, who were marching up the street of the camp, and, in return for their rub-a-dub version of the beautiful canticle, petitioning at each tent-door for Christmas *buckshees*, * or Christmas-*boxes*. And here I afford my discerning reader—if he chance to be a speculator on analogies of languages—a wide scope for his ingenuity. How much more satisfactory, because how infinitely more erudite, laboured, and far-fetched, than

* A gift. It is strange enough that Bishop Heber (whose interesting journal I did not peruse until after my return to England) has also remarked and recorded the analogy between these two words. I shall take shelter, from the charge of plagiarism, under the well-known apology of Mr. Puff.

the commonplace method of deducing the word, is the derivation here presented! Let him, therefore, pursue his philological labours through the intricate yet evident relations which connect the two expressions: with the consolatory assurance, that his solution cannot be much more absurd than the theories of some of his precursors, who have been at such pains to father some little innocent English words upon Chaldee roots. Whilst he employs himself in tracing the importation of the eastern word into Britain to the epoch of the Crusades, or to the confusion of tongues at Babel, if he pleases, I shall proceed to the humdrum task of describing Etawar.

The town is large and flourishing, and there still remain the ruins of an extensive fortress. The river Jumna runs within a couple of miles of its walls: the country in the vicinity is ploughed up in all directions into profound ravines by the violence of the rains; so that it is almost impossible for the English inhabitants to indulge in equestrian rambles—their chief recreation in India—except on the roads, which are much raised, and deeply trenched on either hand. The cantonments of Etawar contain five companies of native infantry, which may be considered a sort of vidette force on the frontiers of the Mahratta.

Dec. 26th.—Crossed the Jumna by a bridge of boats prepared for us, and encamped 10 miles from its western bank, near the village of Budeapore. The first part of the road led through a labyrinth of steep and narrow ravines, which greatly retarded the progress of the baggage; and on two occasions the whole line of march was brought to a stand-still by the breaking down of a baggage-cart and the caprices of a restive camel. On clearing this intricate defile, we came upon the beautifully wooded and highly cultivated tract of country occupying the narrow interval between the rivers Jumna and Chumbul; the grain produce of which is consumed by the troops of Scindia. The camp was, owing to the delay of the matériel among the ravines, obliged to halt the next day; and we amused ourselves in hawking the peafowl which abound in the Arrhye Cates. The bhause is used in this sport, and the young peachicks, at which they are usually flown, are, on the table, no bad representatives of the pheasant.

The following morning Head-quarters crossed by a bridge of boats, constructed for the occasion, the picturesque river Chumbul, which divides the British and Mahratta territories; and by sunrise we found ourselves in the dominions of Scindia. It was with feelings of much-excited interest, and well-sharpened curiosity, that I prepared myself to make acquaintance with this extraordinary race of people, who have played so great a part in the modern history of India; this horde of military mushrooms,—which, like the destructive tare, took root in an obscure corner of the vast field of Hindostan, gradually extended its shoots, and finally spread its baleful sway over the greater part of the immense Continent. The rise and progress of the Mahratta power appear like a judgment from Heaven, inflicted upon the tyrannies and enormities of the established despots of the country. In the words of a late lamented soldier and statesman, "the Mahratta government has, from its foundation, been the most destructive that ever existed in India. It never relinquished the predatory spirit of its founder Sivagee. That spirit grew with its power; and when its empire extended from the Ganges to the Cavary, this nation was little better than an imperial horde of thieves. All other Hindoo States took pride in the improvement of the country, and in the construction of pagodas, tanks, canals, and other public works. The Mahrattas have done nothing of this kind—their work has been chiefly desolation —they did not seek their revenue in the improvement of the country, but in the exaction of the established chout from their neighbours and in predatory excursions to levy more."

The strongest acknowledgment of the talents and character of Sivagee was paid to him by the great Aurungzebe, in whose reign he died, and to whose schemes of universal conquest he had opposed an obstinate and unceasing barrier. On hearing of the Mahratta founder's death, the Emperor exclaimed, "That man must, indeed, be a great general, who had the magnanimity to raise a new kingdom whilst I have been labouring to destroy all the ancient sovereignties of India; my armies have been employed against him for 19 years, and nevertheless his state has always been increasing." After Aurungzebe's death, the Mahrattas, profiting by the civil struggles of his sons for the succession, greatly extended their power, and even ravaged Delhi itself.

After being a thorn in the side of every native state, that turbulent race became a worm in the budding power of the Company. But that which the crafty generalship and countless resources of Aurungzebe had failed to achieve against the unassisted Mahrattas, was at length accomplished by the valour of the English; and the Mahratta armies, supported by the talents and discipline of the French, were, after a long and obstinate struggle, crushed by the instrumentality of that genius which was destined at a later period to humble the pride of their European allies, even on their own soil.

The death-blow to the Mahrattas' independence as a nation was struck when they received a British subsidiary force at their courts. The faith of a Mahratta is about equivalent to the Punica fides of yore. No treaty is with them inviolate. These sacred compacts are known, proh pudor! to have been broken by more civilized nations; but some sophistry is always attempted in excuse by the rupturer. The Mahratta, on the contrary, openly glories in his ill faith, conceiving any scheme to overreach an enemy excusable, and even praiseworthy.

The constitution of this singular government, in its days of prosperity, has been aptly compared to the Germanic empire. It was composed of two great principalities under Scindia and Holkar,—the progenitors of the present incumbents—the component parts preserving their connexion under the Peishwar, as one common supreme head. The territories of Scindia are considerably more extensive than those of his confederate.

Proceed we.—On the western bank of the Chumbul we encountered Major Fielding,—Assistant Resident at the Court of Scindia,—who was accompanied by several chiefs of note, amongst others the Commander-in-Chief of the cavalry and the Minister for Foreign Affairs. They brought with them an escort of 1000 horse; and a more ragamuffin crew, dignified with the name of soldiers, I never beheld. That their equipments are mean and ill kept, and their doublets "not over new," is, however, not a matter of astonishment; since it is well known that the troops frequently go for years without receiving a fraction of pay.

Every second or third year they mutiny; and Scindia pays them up, after deducting about two-thirds of their allowance for the expense of keeping their accounts, paper, ink, scribes, &c.,—a strong exemplification of Mahratta discipline and Mahratta good faith. At first sight it appears strange that soldiers should continue in a service in which they do not get their dues. They, nevertheless, prefer it infinitely to ours, and for obvious reasons. English discipline is severe; theirs is lax in the extreme: our sepoys, though they receive handsome and regularly paid wages, get nothing beyond the fixed stipend; whereas the Mahratta troops, in default of pay, may seize by force whatever they covet from the defenceless ryot, without fear of retribution. Major Fielding informs us that our visit to the country has proved an angel's visit to the army, who seized upon this opportunity to make one of their periodical exactions of their dues, and positively refused in a body to turn out on the important occasion of the British Commander-in-Chief's arrival at the court, until their arrears were paid up. The Maha Rajah was thus constrained to draw from his unwilling treasury no less than five lacs of rupees for this purpose.

The personal appearance of the Mahrattas is mean and unprepossessing. They have neither the fair stature and noble bearing of the Mussulman, nor the delicacy of feature and elegance of figure of the southern Hindoo; and they appear to greater disadvantage in our eyes, that we have just left the territories of two of the finest races of people in India, the Seikhs and the Rohillas. Their acknowledged character as brave and skilful soldiers, however, amply makes amends for their personal deficiencies.

The chief weapon of the Mahratta is the spear, which is formed of the male bamboo, and from 12 to 18 feet long. He is also skilful in the use of the matchlock. The troops are for the most part mounted on mares, which, although, like the cossack's horse, lanky and ill-fed, are, like him, capable of going through a great deal of work.

Pursuing our march, we crossed another small river, and found the camp pitched on an extensive sand-bank, enclosed by two arms of the stream and surrounded by deep ravines. The red and white striped tents of the Mahratta party were spread out on the farther banks; and in a few minutes after our arrival their wild-looking steeds were picqueted around them, their long lances standing in upright clumps in the ground, and every man, with a diligence worthy of a German hussar, preparing forage for his horse or himself. In the afternoon the two ministers of Scindia visited his Excellency, and presented to him about 40 chiefs of the country—a rough, uncourtly crew, "wearing a swashing and a martial outside," and armed to the teeth with divers-shaped daggers, shields, and immeasurable swords. As they severally approached to present their nuzzar, they swaggered up with a rakehelly nonchalance of manner, most of which was perhaps assumed for the occasion: one fellow, when asked by an officer of the Staff if he understood Persian, surlily answered, "We are soldiers, like yourselves, and understand little else but fighting."

Two marches brought us to a ruined fortress of some strength called Bhind; and two more to the fortified town of Gohud, where the Commander-in-Chief's approach was greeted by an ill-fired salute from the rusty guns of the town wall and the bastions of the citadel. It is held by a

Killardar for Scindia.* The outer curtain, which is of mud faced with stone, encloses a vast enceinte, and between it and the lofty commanding citadel there are two other walls. The whole place has a melancholy air of ruin and desolation, though there are some few good modern houses, particularly that of the governor. The country round about is barren and stony, and in the immediate neighbourhood of the town there are several rocky elevations covered with stunted wood. The contrast between this desert and the richly cultivated plains of the fertile Dooab is commensurate with that which exists between the two governments presiding over them. During the Mahratta war, Gohud, strong as it appears, fell an easy prey to our armies: a fact which was ascribed to the insufficiency of the garrison to defend so large an extent of wall. We lost two officers in the storm.

Jan. 1*st.*; therm. 6 A.M. 46°. The first sun of 1829 broke with difficulty through a black bank of clouds, which seemed to rest heavily on the eastern horizon; and we had scarcely cleared the camp ere we were overtaken by a violent shower of hail and rain. Satisfied with having presented us with a gratuitous bath, by way of new year's gift, the congregation of vapours suddenly dissolved itself, and in an hour the firmament presented one canopy of untainted blue. As we passed under the walls of Gohud the Commander-in-Chief received a P.P.C. salute from the citadel, and of so dribbling and unconnected a nature, that we felt satisfied that most of the old rusty guns, "unaccustomed to public speaking," had burst in the operation.

We found the camp near the fortified village of Behaderpore. This stronghold is of small extent, but very lofty, and one of its flanks overhangs a rapid stream, which has so undermined its foundations, that the recurrence of a few more rainy seasons must inevitably bring it down.

Whilst wandering near the village in the evening I

* The territory of Gohud and the fort of Gwalior were given up to Scindia by the Company in 1805.

discovered among the thickets an old tomb, evidently not of eastern form; and, on examining it, found by an inscription that it had been erected to the memory of a compatriot, a Captain Hicks, who met his death in 1781; but whether he fell in battle, or died ingloriously, was not recorded.

The next march brought us to the hamlet of Jenaira, 5 miles from Gwalior, where Scindia's court is at present held. Our camp was situated in the Rumnah, or royal preserved park, which swarms with antelopes, deer, and other game. The sportsmen of the party were already, in anticipation, spreading havoc among them, when two shikkarees came into camp and represented that it was the Maha Rajah's wish that the preserve should be respected; a proclamation which was immediately enforced by a camp order. It afterwards proved that this uncourteous game-decree had originated in a mistake. The surrounding country, as far as the eye can range, is dotted over with small hills, which, unconnected by any chain of heights, start abruptly and independently out of the level plain. In our front, 5 miles distant, and situated on one of these isolated eminences, 300 or 400 feet above the plain, stands the formidable fortress of Gwalior, uncommanded by any other elevation within gunshot. The flanks of the rock appear to be escarped on all sides; the summit perfectly flat and crowded with lofty buildings, whose minareted outline is now strongly and beautifully relieved against the red sky of sunset.

In the evening the Commander-in-Chief held a durbar for the reception of the Prince Hindoo Rao, the nearest male relative of the Bye Sahib, or Queen Regent of the empire, during the minority of the Maha Rajah. His approach was first announced by breathless hurkaras armed with spears, and soon confirmed by the distant jingling of bells, and the dissonant strains of trumpets and shawms; and finally by the glittering of the long lances of his escort, consisting of 1000 cavaliers and 30 chieftains of rank. His Highness's mode of travelling was quite new to us, and smacked more of the hardy warrior than the luxurious eastern magnate.

In place of the usual silver-plated houdah, half-filled with soft cushions, his monstrous and beautiful elephant was provided with a kind of double saddle elevated high above his back, and ornamented with costly housings. The prince rode astride on the front part of the saddle, with his feet in silver stirrups, and guided the animal with a long silver aucoos, whilst the rearmost seat was occupied in like manner by a favourite attendant, clad in complete armour.

In front of the durbar tent Hindoo Rao descended from his elephant into a state palankeen, in which he was carried to the Shemiana or entrance canopy.

Here, contrary to the etiquette of other native courts, he waited until all the Surdars had been presented to his lordship, after which he was himself introduced by the commandant of cavalry. The whole party then entered the great tent, and sat around.

Hindoo Rao is a short, stout man, with a countenance indicative of courage and even ferocity. His manner towards the British Chief was cool, haughty, and provokingly indifferent. Among his own people I was not surprised to hear that he bears the character of a vain, overbearing prince, and, to his immediate dependants, a cruel, tyrannical master. His attire presented an affected mixture of magnificence and slovenliness: he wore a red muslin turban put on puppyishly over one ear, and fastened, after the usual Mahratta fashion, under the chin with a silk scarf of green and silver. Round his waist was a sash of yellow silk, through which was thrust a long straight sword with a yellow velvet scabbard, and an equally long sword-knot of green silk fringed with silver. Massive gold bracelets and amulets were clasped round his arms, and a necklace of about forty strings of yellow beads adorned his thick muscular throat. Yet under all these showy paraphernalia—instead of the glittering keemcab dress worn by the rest of the chiefs—appeared a plain, coarse white cotton tunic; which, with an evidently affected contempt for the cold, was left unfastened at the neck, exposing the whole of his broad brown breast to the sight.

After the customary circulation of attar and paun, Hindoo Rao took his departure, without much abatement of his sulkiness. His spleen had been, perhaps, a good deal stirred up by his lordship's refusal to accede to the wishes expressed by the Regent, that he and his suite should appear barefooted in the august presence of the schoolboy Rajah. This point of etiquette was waived after some altercation, and we are to go to Court, like soldiers, booted and spurred.

Jan. 3rd.—At sunrise we all mounted our elephants, and, the prince having joined the procession, we started for the British Residency. Our group of elephants, escort, and guard, were during the whole march completely surrounded and hemmed in by the swarms of horsemen forming the suite of His Highness. They marched totally without order, and might be seen in straggling parties caracolling and circling their well-broke horses, as far as the eye could reach. The plain looked like a Birnam wood of spears! It was impossible to avoid feeling at that moment how completely we were at the mercy of a people who only a few years back were considered the most lawless and unprincipled marauders in India; and who must up to this period cordially hate the sight of those white faces and red coats which put an end to their devastating piracies, and reduced them to a state of comparative dependence.

A heavy fog unfortunately came on as we passed under one extremity of the frowning fortress; and we were only enabled to catch glimpses of its perpendicular flanks at intervals. The rock on which it stands appears to be in length about 1½ mile, and varying from half to a quarter of a mile across. Its appearance, as it loomed through the mist, was not unaptly likened to the hull of a huge man-of-war.

The town, for it has gradually grown into one, though it still retains the name of "Scindia's Camp," is spread around the base of the rock-fortress, and seems to cling to its gaunt parent's feet, as if for protection. Our camp was pitched near the British Residency, about 4 miles from Gwalior; the house is badly situated among bleak, barren hills, with a forbidding prospect of arid plains studded with rocks; but its interior is extensive and comfortable; and comfortable, indeed, ought the residence to be of that English minister, who, with half a dozen of his compatriots, is exiled to a spot so little favoured of Heaven, and amongst a people so barbarous and unrefined.

At half-past two his Excellency, accompanied by the whole Staff, in costume of state, proceeded to pay a visit of ceremony to the young Maha Rajah. We were all mounted on elephants, and preceded by the cavalry escort. The road, for 4 miles, was lined by the Mahratta troops at extended order; and they were, for the most part, well mounted and armed. The men appear to have no particular uniform, but the most usual dress is a jacket of thickly-quilted cotton, which is proof against sword-cuts, though it is penetrable by the spear or bullet. Some few of the officers saluted the Commander-in-Chief, but the horsemen scowled sulkily at us as the cavalcade passed, and showed no mark of courtesy or respect. About halfway between our camp and the fort the Resident caused our party to halt; as that spot had been diplomatically calculated to be the exact distance which the Maha Rajah, in consideration of Lord Combermere's rank as Commander-in-Chief and Member of Council, should advance to meet us. His Majesty—doubtless purposely—kept us waiting for half an hour; and when at length he did make his appearance, there was so much preliminary conversation, so much court by-play between the British Resident and the Mahratta M.C., who were, perhaps, employed in exacting and refusing, de part et d'autre, some paltry point of etiquette, that the sun, disgusted with the farce, went down without witnessing the presentation.

Mahratta Chief and Horseman. Gwalior in the distance

London. Published by John Murray. 1858

The scene was, however, even to us who had seen so much of eastern courts, novel and interesting; the ceremony striking, and the locale very favourable for display. The interview between the two chiefs took place on a pretty extensive plain, half surrounded by a crescent of heights, the view being suddenly terminated by the craggy and sombre fortress of Gwalior. This plain was completely covered by the cavalcade of the Mahratta sovereign, whose glittering spears and floating pennons we could distinguish even as far as the foot of the rock; and each elevation of ground was thickly thronged with spectators. Every invention of barbaric pomp was lavished on the elephants and equipages of the Rajah's immediate suite. The elephant of the Hindoo Rao, in particular, was the most beautiful animal I ever saw, and caparisoned in the most costly style; the whole of his head and trunk was painted in the richest colours; he wore a deep frontlet of solid silver network, and each of his huge tusks was fitted into a sheath of silver richly embossed; massive silver chains encircled his legs (which were about circumferent with a forty-years' oak-tree); large and sonorous bells of the same metal depended from his sides; his ears were decorated with silver earrings about 6 feet long; and his housings, the fringe of which reached nearly to the ground, were of velvet embroidered in gold and silver. And here I should remark that the Mahratta elephants — at least those which are merely used for the Suwarree—have a style of gait and carriage peculiar to themselves, and are as superior in appearance to ours, as the English thorough-bred racer is to the earth-stopper's hack. The Company's elephants, probably from having been rode too young, and oppressed with burthens, shuffle along with short steps, their necks bent, and their heads hanging with the melancholy air of an Oxford-street hackney coach-horse. The Mahratta elephant strides majestically along, his head elevated far above his shoulder, and his tusks standing out horizontally. The chiefs pride themselves greatly upon these animals, and take pleasure in teaching them a variety of tricks. As the procession passed one of the courtiers who was riding or driving his own beautiful little elephant, he made it kneel down and salaam with its trunk, and then follow the cavalcade, still on its knees, for about 100 yards.

As soon as Scindia had arrived within 100 paces of our party, he drew up his elephant; and after the master of the ceremonies had passed and re-passed (and trespassed upon our patience) about twenty times between the two great powers, a space was cleared from the curious Mahratta mobility, who seemed to be endowed with the same propensity for staring and gaping as other mobs. The two parties descended simultaneously from their houdahs, and confronted each other, more like bitter enemies preparing to come to blows, than as friends meeting in amity and concord. The old Commandant—with his triangular knave-of-spades face—then came forward, and, with the Resident, led the officers of the Staff up by twos, to be presented to the Maha Rajah, who, no doubt well schooled beforehand, coolly and indifferently returned our salaams. Maha Rajah Mookub Rao Scindia, the descendant of the Peishwa's slipper-bearer, is about 12 years old; and, for a Mahratta, a well-grown, good-looking boy, though of unusually dark complexion. He wore a dress of quilted crimson silk, with pyjamas of gold keemcab, and a plain crimson turban ornamented with a diamond aigrette; pearls, emeralds, and diamonds being profusely disposed over his whole person. As soon as the English Staff had undergone presentation, the Mahratta courtiers were, to the number of 40, introduced in like manner to the British Chief; some of them were very richly accoutred, and others, on the contrary, most shabbily and even squalidly attired. There was one ragged lord, in particular, whom, by his greasy cotton jacket and unreaped chin, I had mistaken for one of the low-born multitude; and under that impression, when he crushed his way and his fat person, not "perfumed like a milliner," before me, and thrust his long sword over his shoulder into my face, I struck his toledo up, and pushed him back with my elbow. He looked ten thousand daggers, and twisted his long mustachios most savagely; and I was not aware that I had underrated his dignity until I saw my friend ushered up in his turn among the nobles to receive the embraces of his Excellency. The accollade fraternelle between his Lordship and the boy-King next took place; after which ceremony we all remounted our elephants, and, having given his majesty a quarter of an hour's start, in order to allow of his reaching the palace before us, we followed him to the "Mahratta Camp." The amphitheatre of hills around us was crowded with moving masses of spectators, whose persons all bowed to the ground as the little despot passed. A body of about 30 camel-artillery* separated the two cavalcades, and kept up a tremendous fire à discretion.

On passing a narrow defile in the chain of hills we suddenly came in view of "the Mahratta Camp," stretched below us in a tolerably fertile and well-wooded valley, and bearing about as much the appearance of a camp, as do the Pavilion and Steyne of Brighton. In place of tents, handsome snow-white minarets, temples, and palaces peep from among the neem-trees in every direction; and we very soon found ourselves in a street as long, and nearly as well provided with shops, as the Chandee Chowk of Delhi. At the entrance of the royal palace—a fine white building with red purdars to the windows—Lord Combermere received a salute from the cavalry and infantry body-guard, who were drawn up on either side the court, accoutred and clothed in imitation of the Company's army. The "present arms" of the infantry, however, was not quite in strict accordance with "Torrens;" for at the third motion every man raised his right hand to his cap. The horse-guards are beautifully mounted; in their ranks, as I was informed, there are a

* The gun revolves on a swivel fixed on the pummel of the saddle: and the bombardier, sitting astride behind it, loads and fires with wonderful quickness. During the latter operation the poor camel's head seems to be in imminent jeopardy. The animals move along at a swinging trot, following each other with long outstretched necks, like a flock of wild-geese: at a word they halt, fire a broadside, and jog off again at the rate of 15 miles an hour.

considerable number of troopers who were formerly in the Honourable Company's service, and who broke up in a body from the 4th cavalry in a fit of discontent.

Dismounting from our elephants, and entering the palace, we were piloted through numerous dark alleys, and stumbled up sundry blind staircases, ere we reached the hall of audience, which was, in fact, nothing more than a long veranda. The floor was carpeted with white cotton, so thickly quilted that we sank up to our ankles as we walked; and to this stuffing we were subsequently much beholden, as there was not such a quadruped as a chair in the Mahratta camp; and during the audience, which lasted a full hour, we were obliged to sit cross-legged, like Turks or tailors, on saddle-cloths spread on the floor, the characteristic seat of the warlike Mahratta, to whom the unsheltered and unfurnished bivouac is a natural home. In sitting, the great point to be observed was the keeping the soles of the feet out of sight, an article of etiquette which the native chiefs easily accomplished by sitting on their heels, with their knees resting on the ground; but this posture, I found, after several fruitless (I was going to say bootless) experiments, totally incompatible with our armed heels. We therefore squatted, each after his own fashion: nor do I think any novelty of attitude was struck out which was likely to be adopted by the natives, who did not disguise their amusement at the unpliable rigidity of British limbs, the uneasy contortions of which they were in a good situation to witness, as *we* were all drawn up on one side of the narrow passage, whilst they were marshalled in a parallel line immediately confronting us. At the end of the hour—one of the longest I had ever passed—attar and paun were handed round, and we rose to depart with legs so cramped and benumbed, that we quitted the presence more like a troop of hobbling Chelsea pensioners than sound and active adolescents.

We reached camp in time for a 9 o'clock dinner at the Residency.

The next morning I accompanied the Commander-in-

Chief on a visit to the fort of Gwalior; the Mahrattas granting the desired permission without any apparent jealousy of our inspection. There is only one entrance to this stronghold, by a gateway and stair practised in the abrupt face of the rock, on the north-west side: the steps, which are of so gentle an ascent that our elephants followed us up without difficulty, are protected on the outer side by a high and thick stone wall, and are swept by several traversing guns pointing down them.

On the inner side, the rock has been in many points excavated for water-tanks; or to form the rude retreats of sundry pious anchorites, who, smitten with an ascetic disgust for the vanities of the world, and a still greater distaste for manual labour, retire to meditate in rags on the immortality and transmigration of the soul: and in the mean time retard as much as possible the mortality of the body, by living on the fat of the land, which is poured into their dens by their superstitious and less crafty neighbours. Other portions of the precipitous face of the rock are ornamented with sculptured editions of gods and devils. The surface of the hill is nearly flat; its outline presenting numerous natural angles favourable to fortification; and the whole circumference is defended by formidable stone walls and bastions.

The northern extremity is totally impregnable; and on that point stands the citadel, a fine collection of half-ruined buildings, though not *snug* enough for English ideas of fortification. Seven or eight spacious tanks, cut at vast labour in the rock, supply the place with a quantity of water sufficient for a long siege; though a very numerous garrison—not fewer than 15,000 men—would be required for its defence. In spite of its boasted impregnability, Gwalior was not proof against English enterprise. It succumbed in 1780 to Major Popham, who gained it by a successful stratagem, with little loss and without the aid of guns. Its fall is thus described:—Two noted robbers, who had been in the constant habit of plundering the fort, and escaping undiscovered through some unknown outlet in the fortification, offered, for a handsome reward, to lead Popham and his men to the accessible point. Rope-ladders being secretly prepared, and the sepoys provided with shoes adapted to climbing, in the middle of a dark night the robbers guided the little party to a point in the southern face where a wooded ravine runs for some distance into the fortified rock. Captain Bruce—a brother of the African traveller—who led the advance, gained the spot in silence with 20 picked men; the guides climbed up by crevices in the stones, with which they were well acquainted, fixed the ladders on the wall, and the Englishman and his merry men were soon at the top. The gallant Captain, with his little party, had scarcely reached the summit when they encountered a piquet of the enemy, going the rounds; these they attacked with the bayonet and dispersed; but the alarm was given to the citadel, and so little were the enemy aware of the smallness of the force which had gained the ramparts, that they delayed their attack for some time, in order that they might collect their strength to repulse the little handful of assailants. In the mean time, Popham, with a whole regiment, had ascended by escalade, and were now at Bruce's side. They immediately seized some important points of the fortress ere their guards were sufficiently reinforced; and the Killardar, completely taken by surprise, and paralyzed by the suddenness and impetuosity of the attack, quickly surrendered the citadel.

An old grey-headed officer, who had served in the fort at the time of its fall, pointed out the escaladed spot. From above it appears almost inaccessible. It still bears the honourable appellation of Feringee Pahar, or the "Englishman's Hill." In the zenith of the Mogul empire Gwalior was used as the State prison. In its dreary dungeons the emperors confined unsuccessful rebels, and usurpers incarcerated deposed princes: here they lingered until death, natural or violent, put a period to their miseries. The most fashionable method of getting rid of objectionable captives was by administering to them an infusion of poppies, which gradually benumbed the faculties of the mind, and slowly but surely undermined the constitution of the body. In these dungeons, and by these means, Aurungzebe imprisoned and disposed of his brothers Dara and Morad, his son Mohummed, and various other delinquent relatives. The date of the founding of Gwalior is uncertain, but Rajahs of that place are made honourable mention of in Indian history as far back as A.D. 1008.

On leaving the fort we received a "present arms" from the garrison, which is officered by Armenians, who cut rather strange figures in their sepoys' clothes and little round hats.

After breakfast, having heard of three wild hogs in the neighbouring sugar-canes, we assembled some beaters, mounted our horses, and went in pursuit of them. We had several good gallops, but the cunning animals would not be forced to take the plain, and easily eluded the sportsmen by running from one cate to another.

The boars of the northern provinces are greatly inferior in size and courage to those of Bengal. In the latter district these brutes will not bear much driving, but turn round and come to the charge at the slightest provocation. The same halloo from the rider, which would only add wings to the flight of the lank northern hog, would be resented as an insult by the brawny Bengal boar, who is often in better condition for fighting than for fleeing. I have heard of more than one of these irascible brutes being brought to the attack by no greater affront than the sportsman waving his hat towards him; and I have seen a sulky old tusker take post—like a knight-errant of yore—in a narrow path, between two hoglas,* where his flank could not be turned, and repulse half a dozen experienced spearsmen who came up to the attack in succession.

To the hog-hunting of Bengal the palm of sporting supremacy must certainly be adjudged. Few who have had opportunities of enjoying both in perfection will balance

* Covert of gigantic reeds.

between the tiger and the boar. In the pursuit of the former shikkar, the sportsman—though there are certainly some casual risks to heighten the interest, and add to the excitement—feels himself in his pride of place, 10 feet above the ground, comparatively secure; and, should any accident befall him, it is generally traceable to the misconduct of the elephant or the timidity of the mahout, whose situation, poor devil! with a furious tiger before him, and a bad shot behind him, is anything but enviable.

In the boar-hunt, on the contrary, the sportsman depends entirely on his own adroitness. To have any chance of distinguishing himself, he must have the seat and the judgment of a fox-hunter, the eye of a falconer, the arm of a lancer, and above all a horse fleet, active, bold, and well-in-hand. The art of following the headlong progress of a hog through a covert is only to be gained by experience. I have seen young hands ride boldly and furiously all the day, and tire two or three good horses, without once blooding a spear, whilst an adept at the sport has had the first spear at every hog, and hardly put his horse out of a hand-gallop.

In some cases, however, gentle riding is nothing worth. When a good fresh boar, not overcharged with flesh, is driven on to the meidaun,* and tempted to try his speed across it to the opposite jungle, nothing short of the best pace of the best horse will suffice to bring him to bay, or to cut him off from the covert. A hog, bent on retreat, will dash through the thickest fence of prickly-pear as if it were a young quick edge; spring over a 15-feet ditch with the agility of a deer; and should he meet with a precipitous ravine in his path, he tumbles into it, and out of it, as if he had not got a neck to break. These same obstacles lie in the way of the rider, who has to bear it constantly in mind that, unlike the fox-hunter, he carries a sharp-edged weapon in his hand, which, in an awkward grip, he may chance to run into his steed, and which in a fall may prove an ugly companion to himself.

At Calcutta there is—or rather *was*, for the paucity of

* Plain.

game has obliged them to give it up—a hog-hunting society styled the Tent Club; who, not having the fear of fevers and cholera before their eyes, were in the weekly habit of resorting to the jungles within fifty miles of the city in pursuit of this noble sport. Each member was empowered to invite two guests; the club was well provided with tents, elephants, and other sporting paraphernalia; nor was the gastronomic part of the sport neglected. Hodgson's pale ale, claret, and even champaign, have been known to flow freely in those wild deserts, unaccustomed to echo the forester's song, or the complacent bubble of the fragrant hookah. Gaunt boars were vanquished in the morning, their delicate steaks devoured in the evening, and the identical animals thrice slain again, with all the zest of sporting recapitulation. How often has the frail roof of the ruined silk-factory at Buckra rung to the merry laugh of the mercurial S——, trembled with the Stentorian song of the sturdy B——, and the hearty chorus of a dozen jolly fellows, who, on quitting Calcutta, left a load of care behind, and brought a load of fun!

The above-named deserted edifice is situated, far from the busy haunts of men, in the midst of an extensive forest, and was a favourite resort of the Tent Club on these occasions. The ground floor was occupied by the horses of the party; a large room in the upper story was dedicated to refection; whilst three or four smaller apartments formed the dormitories of those who had come unprovided with tents. Some of the pleasantest days of my life were passed in these excursions, and I shall ever look back to them with the most grateful recollections.

To the ardent sportsman and the admirer of Nature these gipsy parties were replete with excitement and interest:—the busy preparation in the morning—inspections of spear-points and horses' girths—instructions and injunctions to syces and bearers—the stirrup-cup of strong coffee—and the simultaneous start of the lightly-clad sportsmen, on their elephants, to the covert side. Then the marshalling of the beating elephants, the wildness of the scene and richness of the foliage, the mounting of impatient steeds, the yells of the coolies, rattling of fireworks; and finally, the crash of the roused boar, and the headlong career of the ardent rider. Next follow the return in triumph to camp, the refreshing bath and well-earned breakfast. The sultry hours are employed by some in superintending the feeding, grooming, and hand-rubbing of their faithful steeds, lounging over the pages of some light novel, repointing spears, or rattling the backgammon dice; and by others—who perhaps the day before were driving the diplomatic quill, or thundering forth the law of the land in the Courts of Calcutta—by others (frown not, ye beetle-browed contemners of frivolous resources!)—even in that recreation in which, unlike most other sciences, the least experienced is often the most successful, namely the game of *pitch-farthing!*

At 3 P.M. the forces are again mustered; 3 hours more are passed in threading the mazy fastnesses, and scouring the wide savannas of the forest. The sun sinks behind the lofty Palmyras; the sylvan feast is spread; the jocund evening flies swiftly by, and is followed by a night rendered sweet by "tired Nature's soft restorer," whose balmy influence is so often wooed in vain by the panting inhabitant of "the City of Palaces."

It was at one of these sporting conventions "under the greenwood tree," that I first put my lance in rest against a real old crusty Bengal boar. Accustomed to ride with impunity up to, and even over, the less pugnacious porker of the northern plains, I followed him close, without consulting the expression of his backward-turned eye, which would have told a more experienced pig-sticker * that he was already meditating his oblique attack: † I could hear the angry champing of his tusks—my beamy spear was within a few feet of his devoted head (which

* An elegantism of nomenclature, commonly applied to an adept at the spear.

† Verris obliquum meditantis ictum.—HOR.

by anticipation I almost saw smok*ing* or smok*ed* on the table with an orange in the mouth)—when he made a sudden wheel : I passed him at full speed; my weapon, delivered with an over-eager hand, bounded innocuous from his arched back: my little Arab made a violent swerving spring; and, looking back, I saw the blood trickling down his hind leg. The boar had given him a wound in the stifle-joint which laid him up for a month. Ere I had recovered my truant weapon, the most distinguished rider of the club was drawing his "encarnadined" spear out of the deep shoulder of the prostrate yet still panting animal. I leave it to the Indian contributors to the Sporting Magazine to furnish descriptions of successful exploits of the hunter against his tusky prey; liking better myself to record the not uncommon victories obtained by the beast over the man. I have only another egotistical hog-hunting incident to relate, the which I take leave to subjoin, craving pardon from my reader for this unwarrantable digression, by which, without consulting his tastes, I have transported him some 600 or 800 miles from the scene of our tour. It was on the day following my brilliant début above narrated that three of us had pushed a fine boar through a thick mulberry-cate into a small patch of rushes, bordering a nullah, where we lost him. Near the spot where he had disappeared, a turf dam about 4 feet wide intersected the almost stagnant brook; and, fancying that I traced the hog's footprint along it, I spurred my horse on it, in order to cross to the opposite bank. I had reached about the middle of the narrow causeway, when the rushes which fringed the tête du pont suddenly opened to the right and left, and disclosed the foam-sprinkled snout and little savage eyes of the already slightly-wounded hog.

To retreat was impossible; and I had just determined on a desperate advance, when the furious brute, bursting from his lurking-place, came thundering along the dam—a word which, with the final addition of "nation!" I had scarcely time to ejaculate ere I found myself and steed floundering in the deep, muddy, and by no means fragrant pool. Half drowned, and with the loss of a stirrup—which, being made after an improved principle, slipped backwards out of the socket in my struggles to keep my seat—I at length regained terra firma, and with my remaining stirrup sped my way to an extensive plain, where I fell in with a scene which will be readily remembered by those who were present. The boar was at bay—but how at bay? he was standing grinding his tusks, and completely blown, his legs trembling with mingled fury and fatigue; and immediately opposite to him, at the distance of half a dozen paces, stood a hapless cavalier, divorced from both horse and spear, with a pallid countenance, and hands outstretched in a deprecating attitude towards his remorseless foe, who was manifestly only delaying his attack until he had recovered sufficient breath for the purpose. The unhorsed knight was, however, not left to the tender mercies of the boar, whose attention was diverted—pleasant diversion!—by a spear through the loins from a second horseman, followed by such a shower of javelins, that the beast, who still kept his legs, though life was ebbing fast, looked more like the fretful porcupine than any other of the pork genus.

But it is high time that I should dismount from my hog-hunting hobby, and, remounting my "enchanted horse," offer my reader a seat on the crupper. 'Tis done; the magic screw is turned, and after a breathless flight through the air we alight once more at Gwalior, just in time to assist at the visit of Maha Rajah Scindia to the British Commander-in-Chief. His juvenile Majesty arrived for that purpose at the Residency, in grand state, at 4 P.M., the whole of the Head-quarters party having sallied out to give him a half-way meeting, and the British escort giving him a rattling "present arms" as he descended from his elephant. The Residency-rooms having been duly qualified for a Mahratta sederunt—by a previous ejection of all chairs and sofas—we enjoyed a cross-legged squat on the carpet for an hour. The prince Hindoo Rao, in order to create a sensation, came in very late; all the chiefs, and even the Rajah himself, rising at his entrance. After making a sweeping salaam, he threw himself down on his saddlecloth, and drawing his sword, dagger, and pistols from his belt, placed them before him on the carpet with an air that would have been in good keeping with a reckless chef de brigands just returned from an unsuccessful expedition. The custom, so prevalent among the Mahrattas, of wearing arms from their earliest infancy, and even on court occasions, is at variance with the usage of the Mussulmans, who, with the exception, perhaps, of a few immediate favourites, are forbidden to carry any weapon in the presence of their sovereign.

Among others of Scindia's suite, a little, pursy, bustling, aldermanish character, in "fair round belly, with good *curry* lined," was presented to his Lordship: his name, Munny Ram, bespoke his profession, as his appearance indicated its prosperity—he was a banker. The funded proprietor of 3,000,000 sterling, the little Schroff lives in apparent security amongst a people whose name a few years back was almost identified with robber and marauder, and in a kingdom where a regular court of justice is not known.*

Mahratta proper names are certainly anything but musical, and grate as harshly upon an ear accustomed to the sonorous titles of Mohammedan courts, as would the Russian Tchitchagoff when in juxta-position with the Italian Montebello. The Maha Rajah's denomination is Mookub Row Scindia, and that of the Commandant of Cavalry—a nom de guerre, indeed!—is Ram Row Polkee.

Jan. 5th.—Head-quarters camp broke up from its site on the north-east side of Gwalior, marched through Scindia's Camp, and was re-erected at the village of Jinseer, on the south-west flank of the fortress. Our route led us through Scindia's park of artillery, which appears to

* Disputes are settled by a temporary assembly of five, called a Puncheyat, from whom there is no appeal, except to the sovereign. The most *liberal* of the litigants generally gains the cause.

be the most efficient arm of his force. It consists at present of about 150 brass guns of various calibres; and the golundâze, or artillery-men, are celebrated for their skill and their desperate devotion to their guns. They distinguish every piece with some pet title, and on holidays deck them out with garlands. This day every one of Scindia's artillery was honoured with a chaplet of marigolds. At the storming of Bhurtpore we had an interesting proof of the almost superstitious valour of the golundâze: as our troops forced their way along the ramparts of the town, every gun in succession was desperately defended, and, ere it fell into our hands, its entire complement of men were strewed dead around its carriage.

We had not been many hours in our new camp before we found ourselves again in cap-à-pie panoply, mounted on our jaded elephants—who must be at least as tired of these visit-making, sight-showing Mahrattas as their riders—and once more *trudging*—for I know of no other word so significant of an elephant's action—towards Scindia's Camp. Nothing would suit His Majesty but giving us a dinner: in pursuance of which fancy we are this evening to be paraded, in "heavy marching order," with our knives and forks, in the grand audience-hall; in order that the "barbarians" may witness how the infidel Feringees swallow their food, and guzzle down their wine. The latter commodity is fortunately to be furnished by the Resident, or we might have a still better chance of being poisoned than we enjoy as it is. If looks could convey that "soon speeding gear," we should already have quaffed quantum suff. from the crusty countenances of our hosts.

On our entrance into the town our cavalcade was met by that of the arch-ruffian Hindoo Rao. The two chiefs dismounted, embraced, remounted, and we proceeded. In our progress through the streets of the brick-and-mortar camp, I observed a large house, which, though evidently of recent structure, was in complete ruin; the walls riddled with cannon-shot, and the offices blackened with fire; and I inquired its history from a respectable-looking courtier, who was on his elephant alongside of me. After looking suspiciously around him (as though any lengthened verbal communion between individuals of the two suites was interdicted), he made me understand, as well as he could, that the owner of the house, a member of the royal family, and enjoying under Scindia a command of 500 Arabs, had revolted for arrears of pay for his troops and himself. His mutinous requisition was refused, and the troops of the Company's Contingent were directed to seize the rebel in his palace. His Arabs fought, as they always do, like devils incarnate; but the house being soon battered to pieces, and rendered untenable, the besieged made a desperate sortie, wounded the commanding officer of the contingent, Major Stubbs, cut their way through all opposition, and finally made good their retreat to Eujaine, a fortress in the extreme south of Scindia's territories.

Thither the English Major, with his forces, followed him, and before we quitted Gwalior the intelligence of the capture of the rebellious prince reached the camp.

Our first visit was to the late Scindia's Ranee. The old lady of course did not expose her charms to the rude gaze of men, but held converse with Lord C. through a purdar at the end of the hall. His Excellency was next invited to attend the prince to his palace; and there we were treated with the luxury of chairs. The walls of his audience-room were adorned with several European prints; amongst others, a fine ruddy-coloured one of Titian's Venus. Two infant relations attended his levee; the youngest, a pretty boy of 5 years old, was already a warrior, and wore a jewelled sword in his belt, that would have been a meet weapon for "mighty Thomas Thumb," and roused the jealousy of the embryo heroes of our English nurseries.

After half an hour's session, pawn and spices richly gilt and plated were distributed; and our party, accompanied by the prince, adjourned to the meidân or plain, to witness some tournaments prepared for our entertainment by the

Mahratta officers. On our arrival at the lists we found two parties of cavaliers, all showily attired, and mounted chiefly on beautiful Deckanee horses, ranged opposite each other on either extremity of a level piece of ground. Each man carried a lance made expressly for practice; much longer than the war-spear, and pointed with a ball of cloth. This weapon is ill calculated for real service, for when the horse is in violent action it quivers so strongly, that it must be impossible to direct its point with any degree of accuracy.

The two adverse troops soon came to action, one retreating and defending themselves, the other pursuing and attacking. The prettiest part of the sport, however, was the single combats. The parties stood confronting each other; presently a warrior dashed forth from one of the groups, and curvetted about the plain, until a knight from the opposite side accepted his challenge, and spurred to the encounter. Some of the chiefs showed considerable skill in the use of their unwieldy weapon, but I would gladly have backed Captain Anderson of "Dougan's Horse," or Captain Skinner, against the most expert amongst their ranks. In the last of these single combats there was an evident loss of temper on the part of a burly old chieftain, who received a tremendous thrust in the ribs, and retaliated on the bestower by some unfair blow. A cry of disapprobation immediately arose, and half a dozen partisans rushed from the ranks on either side; and would doubtless soon have betaken themselves to their swords, had not the old commandant galloped up, and with a stern voice ordered them to their posts.

Quitting the scene of the jousts, we proceeded to our dinner engagement at the royal palace, and after undergoing another durbar—which appeared even longer and more tedious than that heaviest of half-hours which usually precedes a dinner-party in England—we were ushered in grand state into the banqueting-hall, a lofty vaulted apartment, bearing more the appearance of a chapel than a dining-room. A long table was laid down the centre of the hall, and a line of chairs ranged for the guests along one side of it, whilst the other was left open for the operations of the ministers to our appetites, and to expose us more satisfactorily to the curiosity of the spectators. The former were chiefly Hindoos of respectability; and it was the first time that any of us had been waited upon at table by members of that sect. The latter were composed of the Maha-Rajah, his relatives and courtiers, who sat apart from the table, but in such a position as enabled them to enfilade its whole length with their curious eyes. The partial upraising too of a silken purdar, above the door at the top of the hall, betrayed to us that eyes invisible from below, those of the pretty prisoners of the Zenana, were employed in criticising the Feringees' feast.

The Hindoos are mere tyros in gastronomy as compared with their more courtly and fastidious neighbours the Mussulmans: some of their pillaus and cawâbs were, however, sufficiently savoury. The dishes were not placed on the board; but were carried by troops of zealous attendants down the untenanted side of the table; each in rapid succession presenting his smoking burthen, describing its exquisite qualities with the eloquence of an auctioneer, and exhorting the guests in the most moving terms to partake of it. Refusal was out of the question, and in a few minutes my plate became a perfect mountain of confused sweets and savouries — a rudis indigestaque moles!—a complete culinary chaos!

Our entertainers must have thought us a right merry set of fellows; for we were all nearly convulsed, and I was *quite* choked with laughter, excited by the very eager and enthusiastic manner in which some of the table-attendants displayed the good points of their respective viands. One fellow exalted a large fried fish in mid air, holding it up by the tail in his fingers; and wound up his declamatory eulogium by plumping it down on my plate, which was already swimming with a kind of crême fouettée, administered by his precursor. A second uplifted by the leg, and twirled between his finger and thumb, a huge cawâbbed capon, which from its gigantic proportions, and the sprawling, untrussed state of its limbs, exceedingly resembled a young grilled Hindoo.

No dish appeared a second time, each being carried off as it reached the foot of the table: series after series came in, and we might have been dining until this moment, had not his lordship requested their forbearance just as they were ushering in the fiftieth course. I omitted to say that the table appurtenances were furnished by the Resident. Thus ended the first and only feast that I was ever bidden to by the disciples of Brahmah: and if in culinary qualities it fell short of the Mussulman tables which had been spread for us during our tour, it was at least infinitely more productive of food for merriment.

We rose from this amusing though fatiguing banquet, with heads aching from the savoury vapours of the smoking hecatombs heaped by our profuse hosts upon the altar of our appetites, and with sides aching from the cachinnatory convulsions we had undergone, the semi-suppression of which was even more arduous than its unrestrained indulgence would have been.

From the banqueting-hall we were conducted to a veranda, where we were entertained by a splendid display of fireworks. I remarked, not without amusement, that the courtiers eyed us with cautious curiosity after dinner; and seemed rather to avoid entering into conversation; and I immediately concluded that, in accordance with the natives' generally-received idea of the proneness of Europeans to vinous excesses, they imagined, as a matter of course, that we were all more or less under the influence of the merry god.

The pyrotechnic spectacle being concluded by about 11 o'clock, we arose, and, taking a final farewell of the young Scindia, mounted our elephants, and proceeded towards camp, accompanied by the prince Hindoo Rao and a party of the Mahratta nobles. I was just complacently calculating on an uninterrupted retreat to my tent, from which I had been now absent nine hours,—the fagged elephants even showing by their alert motions their sympathy in our homeward aspirations,—when the cavalcade was suddenly arrested (at the entrance of what appeared to us through the dusk to be an extensive plantation of rather formal-looking shrubs) by the artificial forest bursting forth into leaves and fruits of vivid flames; a miracle of vegetation which instantly routed our astonished elephants; who, turning about, made off at a frightful pace through the town—no matter of mirth in a dark night. As soon as my animal was prevailed upon—by half a dozen digs on the head, the tenderest of which would have brained an ox,—to return to the cavalcade, my friend the chief—whose name, a tissue of dissonant consonants, I cannot recollect—offered to show me that prejudice, even in elephants, is vincible by education. At a single word of encouragement, his beautiful animal carried him into the midst of the blazing and crackling forest, and, on a hint from his master, wrenched up by the roots one of the trees which had already shed its golden fruits, and stood in the way of those which were still unexhausted. After this exhibition the prince and his followers took leave, and we reached our camp without further molestation. With what joy did I throw off my heavy, embroidered dress, and commit myself to the refreshing offices of my faithful bearers, after a long day of constant excitement and exposure to the sun. To the ministry of these toilet assistants I was, like many of my countrymen, for the first year of my life in India, resolutely averse: but finding all my efforts to exclude them from my presence unavailing, I at length surrendered at discretion, and gave up all right and title to dress my own person: a cession of privileges which certainly saves the yielder a great deal of unnecessary and uninteresting labour, in a climate where the pulling on of a boot is a work of inordinate exertion, and the tying of a cravat is accomplished in the sweat of the brow.

Jan. 6th.; therm. 6 A.M. 34°. Head-quarters camp broke up from Gwalior; and we saw the last of that gaunt and frowning fortress as we entered the rocky defile of the

Pass of Antree; beyond which, near a village of the same name, our canvas home was erected for the day. After having extracted three days' novelty and amusement from the Mahrattas, I was not sorry to exchange the restless and bustling Tumâsha of Scindia's court for the pleasant morning march, constant variety of scenery, and evening field-sports of our roving camp.

In taking leave of this eccentric people, however, it is but justice to pay them the passing compliment of confessing that my personal acquaintance with them, slight as it was, tended to raise them a hundredfold above the standard of my preconceived opinion. The wandering horde of lawless freebooters who, like a flight of locusts, spread for so many years their desolating influence over the fertile provinces of India, have at length, emulative of the more respectable bee, quietly alighted in one swarm, and gradually settled down into a regular government; contenting themselves with the revenues drawn from their own states, instead of playing the highwayman in the dominions of their neighbours: an amelioration in civil government, as well as in moral policy, for which they are indebted more perhaps to the overawing influence of the British power than to the march of honesty in themselves. Be the cause, however, what it may, the effect is beneficial. In Mahratta ethics, meum and tuum are no longer so confounded and blended as to be scarcely distinguishable one from the other: property is respected, as the rich Munny Ram's unviolated coffers attest; hospitality and good faith towards strangers are in pretty good practice; and heads rest with a tolerably secure tenure on their own native shoulders.

I was not sorry to see the last of his hectoring highness Hindoo Rao; whose swaggering carriage, haughty air, and overbearing character made him no great favourite at Headquarters; and I was more inclined to be gratified than to sympathize with him when the following anecdote, in which one of his most violent passions, that for the sex, was thwarted in the most provoking manner, was related to me.

The prince had purchased at an extravagant price a young slave girl, with the fame of whose extraordinary beauty he had become enamoured. A young roué Mussulman, a half-brother of the royal purchaser, heard of the fair maiden's arrival, and contrived to get the first introduction to her. The elder brother was furious on hearing of this exploit; but the mishap was irremediable, and his only consolation was in revenge. The reprobate sprig of royalty was seized, bound, and most cruelly bastinadoed in the presence of the wronged brother.

CHAPTER IX.

Bundelcund — Dutteah — Amaba — Jhansi — Burwah-Sauger — Ourcha — Paharee Banka — Kaitah — Chirkari — Banda — Zoolficar Ali — An hour's sport — Kallinger — British siege of Kallinger — Shere Khan's siege — Last day in camp — Dâk journey — Allahabad — Embark on the Ganges — Voyage down the Ganges — The budgerow — Mirzapore — Chunar — Benares — Sporting intelligence — Gazypore — Buxar — Dinapore — Deega Farm — Bankipore — Patna — Monghir — Seeta's Well — Janguira — Boglipore — Colgong — Sicrigully — Rajemâl — Suja's palace — Bogwangola — River Pubna — Dullaserry river — Borigunga river — Dacca — Ruins of Dacca — Nawaub Shums-Ood-Doulah — A day's sport.

On the 8th we crossed the river Sind, leaving the territories of Scindia behind us, and entering Bundelcund, a province cut up and subdivided into numerous petty principalities, or baronies, the greater proportion of which are not more productive in revenue than the unpretending estates of some of the richer commoners of England.

The following morning we were welcomed by the Rajah of Dutteah, who escorted the Commander-in-Chief through his capital to the camp, which was pitched without the walls. The city of Dutteah is extensive, commandingly situated, and surrounded by a beautifully-built stone wall. On a lofty, rocky foundation, in the centre of the place, stands an ancient palace of very elegant architecture. The

Rajah chiefly resides in a more modern building lower down in the town. Dutteah is one of those principalities which were confirmed to their hereditary chieftains when the province of Bundelcund was ceded to the Company, under condition of reciprocal support. The revenue of the state is about ten lacs of rupees or 100,000*l.* pounds. It appears surprising that, with so inconsiderable a sum, the chief can support an army, three great fortresses, and a considerable retinue. The Rajah has always been considered a true and faithful ally of the Company; and as a proof of their confidence in his friendship, the government have presented him with a couple of brass guns, a gift which, in the eyes of the natives, implies the most implicit trust. He has defended himself more than once successfully against the inroads of Scindia, whose overpowering force, however, would have, long ere this, swallowed up his little kingdom, had not the all-potent Ægis of British protection been extended in his defence.

Dutteah is altogether the prettiest spot and most habitable place I have yet seen in the plains: gently-undulating hills, plentifully supplied with wood and water, surround the town; and the royal Rumnah is well stocked with game of every species. On one of these eminences, four miles from the walls, there is a curious cluster of temples, built by a now almost extinct sect of Hindoos, called Jeines. Their persuasion bears, I believe, some affinity to that of the Bûddists. Though they are now in the minority, they still uphold their creed as the orthodox Hindooism, and look upon the majority of the Hindoos as ignorant dissenters.

We paid a visit of ceremony to the Rajah in the afternoon; but to have described one visit to a native prince is to have sketched the leading features of all Indian court levees. The Dutteah chieftain is a fine-looking, respectable old man, and a ci-devant great sportsman. For sylvan amusements he is, however, now disqualified by excessive corpulence and lameness from a distorted foot. His minister is a fine specimen of patriarchal beauty, and retains all his faculties at the age of ninety.

After the durbar we went to see the royal gardens, which, like most other native baugs, were replete with straight walks, fountains, orange-trees, and marigolds. The most interesting object was a well, truly magnificent in its architecture and proportions. The shaft presented an octagon of about 20 feet span, surrounded with columned cloisters, and at each angle a stone elephant, with uplifted proboscis, spouted water to a vast height into the air.

The following morning was devoted to a grand battue in the royal preserve. Our elephants were sent forward by daylight, and we rode on horseback to the place of rendezvous. At first we were posted upon the top of two small turreted lodges on either side of the only outlet from the walled Rumnah, and the game was driven towards us through the thick covert by crowds of men, who cheerfully confronted the very good chance of being shot, for the sake of a paltry reward. The loss of two or three subjects, on such occasions, is considered by the natives of rank as a contingency of trifling moment: but I confess I could not bring myself to pull my trigger when the chances were about equal whether a boar or a fellow-creature fell to the shot. Tired of our stations on the gateway, we soon mounted our elephants, and entered the preserve, where we in a very short space killed a dozen hogs. The deer and niel-ghie, of which there were great numbers, for the most part escaped by leaping the walls. Our morning's sport was concluded by nine o'clock. The day was spent by me in a solitary and tolerably productive *poach* in the Rumnah; and in the evening the Rajah entertained us with a display of fireworks.

Jan. 11th.—Marched from Dutteah to Amaba, nine miles, through a country abounding in the wild beauties of wood and rock; but cheerless and melancholy from the total absence of cultivation. The whole of the Raj can hardly be of the like stamp, for the Rajah must be a subtle alchemist if he can extract 100,000*l.* from such materials.

In this part of India—as in the mountains of the north—

Rajahs are almost as rife as country-gentlemen in England. A couple of easy marches suffice to take us through the territories of the richest of them. The traveller has barely lost sight of the fortified towers of one metropolis, ere he finds himself in the suburbs of a neighbouring capital: he has scarcely bowed himself out of the august precincts of one royal court, ere he bolts into the presence of another crowned head.

We are now enjoying an opportunity of seeing this little *rookery* of royalties under the most favourable circumstances. On the occasion of the auspicious visit of a British Member of Council, every chieftain furbishes up his almost rusted sword of state, musters his ragged retainers, and cooks up a portion of pomp commensurate with his means. With a little activity of imagination, a retrospective abridgment of time and space, we might almost fancy ourselves back to the "good old" feudal times of merry England; and that the grim and lordly turrets, under whose shade we almost daily pitch our tents, were the goodly castles of those burly barons who, on the occasion of a visit of a stranger of rank, came forth with a retinue of men-at-arms, squires, and pages, to welcome the noble traveller; and entertained him during his sojourn with jousts, pageants, and minstrelsy.

I was busily employed in drawing the above parallel, as we crossed the frontier of the Dutteah chief, when the sudden appearance of the Rajah of Jhansi, mounted on his *elephant*, and preceded by two *camel*-heralds, burst the analogical bubble that I had been blowing with so much ingenuity. The Chief of Jhansi is a young man of 24, of Jewish but handsome countenance, and of Mahratta extraction. His royal revenue is from 15 to 18 lacs of rupees. At the distance of a few miles his capital bears some resemblance to Windsor: the citadel, a lofty mass of building, and distinguished by one huge round tower, is situated on a rock, at the foot of which lies the town, defended by a good wall, and set round with fine timber.

The Rajah seems to take more pride in the appearance

of his equipages and court than he of Dutteah, for which the difference in years between the two potentates may account. The streets and bazaars of the town are clean and well regulated; and the young Chief enforces, with the greatest strictness, the enactments which he has made for the well-being of his subjects.

We visited him in his palace in the afternoon, and he seemed much gratified by our commendations of the favourable situation and apparent strength of his little fortress. From the top of one of the bastions we had a distinct view of the castellated citadels of two of his brother Rajahs, Dutteah and Ourcha.

Jan. 13th.—A march of 12 miles to the town of Burwah-Sauger. On the road we crossed the pretty river Betwa, which, during the rainy season, must be a considerable stream. The country in the vicinity is barren in the extreme, and almost entirely devoid of game of any kind. Our guns and our hawks are consequently completely thrown out of work. The surface of the earth is stony and sandy, presenting no encouragement to the labours of the cultivator; yet from its flinty bosom spring spontaneously the most luxuriant forests of fine trees, the dark and sombre tints of whose foliage, however, are strongly contrasted with the lighter and more tender colouring of Bengal vegetation. The town of Sauger is snugly enveloped by a screen of verdure, and just above it, on the extremity of a long and high ridge of rocks, stands a picturesque old castle. I walked up to this building after sunset, and on reaching the parapeted terrace was surprised to find, spread beneath its southern wall, a piece of water which has a better title to the name of a lake than any other I have seen in India. It may be about 2 miles across, and in the centre of its fair sheet of water are two woody and rocky islets, which form striking objects in the landscape. The bund, or head of the jheel, is of solid stone masonry, 60 feet wide and nearly a mile in length, and furnished with several ghauts, or flights of steps, to the water's edge. The château and circumjacent town have been frequently made the bone of contention between the chiefs of Dutteah and Jhansi, and Scindia; and its western wall retains to this day the impressions of the cannon-shot of the latter worthy, who attacked the place about forty years ago. In the dusk of a gloomy and rather stormy evening, the hoary old château, with its frowning towers and its accessories of black beetling rocks and deep foliage, presented a peculiarly romantic appearance; reminding me of the scenes of some of Mrs. Radcliffe's interesting horrors.

The following day the camp halted, and the Commander-in-Chief, accompanied by the Staff, started on a visit to the Rajah of Ourcha, who holds his court at a town of the same name, 7 miles from Sauger. Our route lay through a country, the surface of which is undulated here and there with gentle eminences thickly clad with forest-trees, and interspersed with those gigantic natural cairns of fantastically piled rocks peculiar to the province of Bundelcund. These accumulations are usually of a conical form, and the huge round blocks of stone are sometimes heaped up to the height of 100 or 200 feet. Were it not for the unwieldy size of the component portions, the traveller would almost be led to imagine that the mechanical ingenuity of man had been employed in the structure. The rocky masses being of a circular form, wide interstices admitting the light are frequently found halfway down the pile; and the enormous crag which generally forms the apex of the natural pyramid is, in many cases, so nicely poised, that it looks as though a puff of wind would destroy its delicate equilibrium, and the whole edifice would dissolve partnership and roll away into independent masses like a pile of oranges. The most obvious mode of accounting for these phenomena of nature is by the supposition that the blocks of hard rock were formerly imbedded in a stratum of a softer nature, which, yielding before the lapse of ages and the fury of the elements, crumbled down in sandy particles to the base, and left the more durable portions to support themselves as they best could, and take up such positions as the laws of gravity dictated.

Elephants crossing a Nullah. London Pub^d by John Murray 1858

During this march we crossed more than once the rocky bed of the picturesque river Betwa. On such occasions as this, as well as whilst traversing countries the most tangled, broken, and precipitous, that chef-d'œuvre of animal creation, the elephant, most conspicuously displays his superiority. It is wonderful to see him patiently and effectually surmounting obstacles which the horse could not have a chance, and even ubiquitary man himself might despair, of overcoming.*

We now arrived at the town, situated on one of the arms of this Briarean stream: it is of great extent and surrounded by a stone wall. The principal objects in the view are the ancient palace, crowning an elevation in the centre of the town; and a remarkably fine temple, which, after the usual form of the Bundeela muts, is ornamented with lofty spires. When seen through the forest at the distance of 2 miles, it reminded me in some degree of the cathedral of Lichfield.

That Ourcha was formerly a place of consequence is attested by the many interesting ruins which we passed, but its prosperity has waned with the fortunes of its chief, whose present possessions (in spite of his genealogical tree, which derives him in direct line from the ancient Bundeela monarchs of Kallinger) do not bring him a revenue exceeding 50,000*l.* or 60,000*l.* The present ruinous state of the city is further accounted for by the Rajah's long alienation from it. About 30 years ago he was counselled by his seers or his ministers to quit the place, as unpropitious to his ardent aspirations for an heir to his throne, and to remove his court to the fort of Teary, situated at the southern extremity of his dominions. He followed these injunctions; and such is the force of faith, that a bouncing burly prince immediately appeared to verify the predictions of the sages. The Rajah only returned to Ourcha a few

* The penetrating reader will, doubtless, ere this, have discovered the author's penchant for the elephant. He owns "the soft impeachment;" and, although generally abominating the tribe of *Pets*, if ever—as he descends into the vale of old-bachelorism—he should be induced to establish one, it shall be AN ELEPHANT.

months ago. He is a fine, venerable old man, and has just abdicated in favour of his man-mountain of a son. The warriors forming his little body-guard are active, hardy-looking fellows, well mounted and armed, and, like the rest of the inhabitants of Bundelcund, famed for their fighting qualities—qualities which are likely to lie dormant for some time; for, turbulent as the Bundeela chiefs have always been, and strong as the temptations still must be for one armed principality to commit inroads upon another, no two potentates can come to a decided feud without having their heads knocked together by the all-powerful interference of the Honourable Company. It would therefore be a praiseworthy adaptation of good metal if these worthies would turn their now rusting swords into ploughshares for the cultivation of their neglected and not naturally fruitful soil, and at the same time educate their pampered chargers to the more useful labours of the Georgic department.

The following three marches brought us gradually out of the land of rocks and sand into a tract enriched with cultivation and adorned with luxuriant groves. On the second day we passed, on the left of the line of march, a very picturesque and baronial-like castle, perched on a woody ridge, and looking down upon a lake nearly as extensive as that of Burwah-Sauger. These fine pieces of water, peculiar to this province, and such valuable accessories to the scenery of India, are in few cases entirely natural, most of them being supplied with artificial embankments.

Jan. 17th.—The camp was pitched at the village of Paharee Banka. The country in the vicinity is well cultivated, and the tamarind, mango, and other trees grow to a great size. Among the branches of these I discovered large flights of the beautiful bird called the green pigeon, many of which I shot. On the bare arid plains, too, the sportsmen of the party fell in with the rock pigeon, a very beautiful and delicate species, but difficult of access. It has nothing of the pigeon but the feet; and the larger kind, in shape, size, and plumage, bears some resemblance to the grouse. These birds are so exceedingly wild that sportsmen are obliged to resort to stratagem in order to get near them. One method consists in covering the head with a long white cloth after the manner of the native cultivators, and walking behind a bullock trained for the business. I had often worn out my knees and my patience in creeping after these vigilant objects of my sporting wishes, and was this day destined to be successful. I discovered an ill-starred couple playing the turtle apart from the main flock, and by the assistance of an intervening bush and their own all-engrossing employment, contrived to get within 30 paces of them before they rose, when I slew them both at a shot.

On the march this morning, whilst diverging from the road with our hawks, we found a fine bustard on the plain. He took wing as we approached, and a couple of large hawks were flown at him. After reconnoitring their gigantic opponent, however, they seemed afraid to engage, and came back to wrist. The falconers marked the bird, and, proceeding to camp, provided themselves with a series of snares—the same used by them to catch live birds for training their hawks—and returned to the spot. These they spread in a convenient place, a few hundred yards in advance of the bustard's station; and then, describing a wide circle, they came round to the rear of the bird, and, by cautiously and slowly approaching, gradually drove the infatuated victim into the nets, where his long legs were soon entangled, and he became an easy prey. He was an immense bird of the kind, measured 7 feet 6 inches from tip to tip of wings, and weighed 27½ lbs.—twice the weight of a good Norfolk turkey.

The next day being the anniversary of the capture of Bhurtpore, this noblest of feathered game made no bad pièce de résistance for the head of his lordship's table.

On the 19*th* we crossed the river Dussaun; and on the 20*th of January* reached the station of Kaitah, where the Commander-in-Chief reviewed the two regiments of infantry, and one cavalry corps, cantoned there. The situation of the town is sultry, from the air being intercepted by a considerable rocky eminence which half surrounds it, and the rays of the sun being reflected from the same. At 2 P.M. the therm. rose to 90°. Kaitah is an advanced post of the Company, pushed into the heart of the native principalities of Bundelcund, for the usual purposes of supervision and coercion.

We halted one entire day at Kaitah, and on the 22*nd* made a march of 16 miles to the town of Chirkari; another of the miniature royalties of Bundelcund. The Rajah came forth to give the embrace of welcome to the Commander-in-Chief, and accompanied us to the camp. He is very old and infirm; and his grandson, a boy of 12 years old, is his heir apparent. He is a sharp and intelligent lad, and is already, at his tender age, a benedict. The royal revenue of Chirkari amounts to about four lacs of rupees, or 40,000*l*. The old man talked about his want of means to supply us with suitable entertainment at his court, but promised a good day's sport in his rumnah by way of succedaneum. We returned the chief's visit in the afternoon. His palace, situated in the centre of the town, has nothing remarkable about it, but the site of the city itself is extremely picturesque. It is spread round the foot of a lofty rocky hill, on the summit of which the fort is situated. This latter would be almost impregnable by native troops, if the Rajah had not—agreeable to the usual custom of Indian princes—neglected to complete the fortifications begun by his predecessor, which would have probably enclosed in their enceinte two important elevations, now without the walls, and commanding the citadel. The only access to the fortress is by a flight of steps cut in the rock, sufficiently easy of ascent for elephants. In viewing the surrounding country from the bastions of the fortress, the spectator is led, by the rich, luxuriant appearance of the forests, to imagine that the soil is fruitful; but on a nearer acquaintance with these wide-spreading woods he finds that the trees, deriving their sap from an arid and rocky bed, are of dwarfish growth and inferior qualities.

The next morning a large party of sportsmen was early in the field. At the entrance of the rumnah the elephants were left behind, and, conducted by two young natural sons of the Rajah, we soon commenced action. Our guides are fine handsome dashing youths; and were it not for the vigilant guardianship of the Company, there is little doubt but they would (instead of calmly sitting by to see their infant brother ascend the throne) seize the obnoxious stripling immediately on the death of the present incumbent, wring his neck, usurp the throne, and, having thus far proceeded hand in hand, one would cut the other's throat, and lo! the survivor sole proprietor of the Raj! For this style of royal succession they have abundant precedents in the history of every ancient kingdom in India.

Our party had not penetrated many hundred yards into the preserve ere we fell in with large herds of antelopes, spotted deer, and niel-ghie; but we found that, with a numerous troop of laughing and talking Englishmen, it was hopeless to attempt to approach these wild denizens of the forest. I, therefore, soon parted company, and went on a solitary cruise; but it was not a very lucrative one. I fired away all my cartridges in random shots, and when I found myself in the very heart of the preserve, with deer bounding past me in all directions, I had not a ball to expend upon them. I killed a niel-ghau early in the day, but could not find an elephant to carry him home. Add to this, I lost my way, and when at length, directed by the reports of my companions' guns, I steered through the thick bushes in the direction of the sound, I was saluted by such volleys of bullets, aimed at the herds which I was driving towards my friends, that I was quickly obliged to alter my course; gave up all idea of joining convoy, and, after some difficulty, piloted myself back to the elephants by sunset.

The scene of our chase lay in an extensive forest spreading for many leagues over a plain studded with wild groups of black rocks, and backed up by a picturesque range of well-wooded elevations. The whole jungle was redolent with the fragrant blossoms of the baubul; and the juicy bhaire extended its well-loaded branches for the refreshment of the parched hunter.

The niel-ghau, which abounds in these forests, grows to an immense size; in some instances attaining the height of 15 hands. The limbs of this beautiful animal unite the strength of the ox with the activity and elasticity of the deer. The head is very small and fine, furnished with short horns directed backwards and set on a neck of prodigious strength. The colour of the male is a deep slate, whence the epithet of *niel* (blue).

Jan. 24th.—Head-quarters quitted Chirkari, and, after four days' marches of little interest, crossed the pretty river Cane, famous for its pebbles, and re-entered the British dominions. On the eastern bank we met the Nawaub Zoolficar Ali, who escorted His Excellency into the town of Banda, where a small force of the Company's troops is stationed.

The Nawaub, who has a palace near the town, is the younger brother and successor of the Nawaub Shemshere Bahauder (son of Ali Bahauder, the Mahratta conqueror of Bundelcund), with whom, at the cession of the Bundeela provinces to the Company in 1803, the English government entered into a conciliatory engagement, securing to him an estate of 40,000*l.* per annum.

It is related that, at the capture of Banda by the English, the fort, which is situated on the opposite bank of the Cane, only fired *one* shot—as a point of honour—and that that one shot ended its career in the breast of a British officer.

The present Nawaub is a short stout man, of remarkably fair complexion and good-natured countenance; his age is about 29; although from his corpulence—which with natives of rank is generally commensurate with their means of supporting it—and from the usual dignified and *posé* manner of the Mussulman, he appears much older. He is a great admirer and follower of English manners and customs, and his adoption of them corresponds with his Mahomedan education about as aptly as do his English top-boots with the splendid keemcab tunic and cashmere shawl which form his usual costume.

His Anglomania, it is said, costs him annually many thousands of rupees, which glide into the pockets of the knowing ones of the Cawnpore turf; and at the price of which he enjoys the distinction of entering two or three unsuccessful horses every season, and secures to himself from his English friends the enviable title of a d—d good fellow!

He led us, with evident pride, through his stud and racing stables, and, amongst a host of lanky *weeds*, showed us some few promising colts. Among his stallions he has many English horses of note, whose names have been well known even at Newmarket and Doncaster. In his carriage stables he paraded about 15 pair of respectable horses; he has a vast variety of English vehicles; 20 elephants; and a numerous troop of body-guards, well mounted, and accoutred after the fashion of the Company's cavalry. With this extensive establishment, and a whole colony of poor relations living upon him, it is surprising that the good-natured Nawaub can keep his head above water.

28*th*.—Halted at Banda. In the morning a review of a native infantry corps, and in the evening a grand dinner with his highness Zoolficar Ali, at which he made a special petition that the ladies of the party should be present. He received Lord Combermere on the threshold with a French embrace, and then led the way into a well-furnished drawing-room, where, during the half-hour preceding the repast, he stood up and conversed freely and fluently with the men, but did not venture to address the ladies. The Nawaub's evening costume was a shawl coat, buttoned à l'Anglaise, and richly laced down the breast; with an embroidered velvet skullcap in place of a turban; the ill-assorting top-boots still held their place, and his nose was decorated with a pair of English silver spectacles. A profusion of the Scrap-book tribe was spread upon the table, and there were as many sofas to lounge upon, and tabourets to tumble over, as are to be found in the most approved drawing-rooms in England.

Dinner being at length announced by a train of liveried servants, our host—without taking the slightest notice of his lady-guests—led the way into a spacious saloon where a table was spread for about 40 persons. An excellent dinner was laid out in the Calcutta fashion, and there was a good supply of claret and other European wines. Amongst the dishes I was somewhat surprised to recognise a ham, and a very palpable group of sausages—portions of the unclean beast on the board of a follower of the Prophet!

Contrary to the usual custom of our Mussulman hosts, Zoolficar Ali ate, without the least scruple or reserve, of the dishes which were common to us all, and seemed to take it as a compliment when his lordship helped him to some pillau. My station at table was directly opposite to "the chair;" and I could not forbear smiling as I watched his futile attempts to prevent that most awkward of instruments, an English silver fork, from turning in his hand; and I thought that, in his perplexity, he was sore tempted to have recourse to the more primitive agency of his fingers—after the example of poor "Hajji Baba in England." As I was pursuing my rather rude observation, he suddenly caught my eye, and very nearly converted my smile into laughter long and loud, by giving me a steadfast, penetrating look, and saying in a sharp tone, "Glass vaine!" I salaamed, filled my glass, and the orthodox Islamite drank to me in water.

The entertainment was conducted throughout in an orderly and respectable manner; a choice set of dancing girls were allowed to perform before the party during the dessert, and the evening was concluded by a display of fireworks.

The Nawaub's late brother, Shemshere Bahauder, was by no means so respectable a character, or so conscientious an observer of the inculcations of the Koran, as his successor. He was elected honorary member of an English dragoon mess, and there and elsewhere indulged in large libations of the forbidden juice. Constant communication with the English confirmed him as a mauvais sujet; for he cared not what his company was, so that it was European.

Jan. 29*th.*—Despatched my heavy baggage and servants to Allahabad by the direct route, and made arrangements to leave Head-quarters on the 1st prox., after having seen the famous fortress of Kallinger. We left Banda this morning, and the next day the camp was pitched in a wide, cultivated plain, 11 miles from the above-named stronghold. At this distance the vast fortified rock, like an inland Gibraltar, is distinctly visible; and beyond it, in faint perspective, is discerned the great range of lofty table-land, extending from the mountain-fort of Rhotasghur on the Sone river more than half across central India.

In the evening I took my pony and my gun and rambled among the neighbouring ravines, in whose tangled gorges the crowing of the partridges held out a tempting invitation to the sportsman. I had an hour's capital sport, killing a good bag of partridges, quail, and rock-pigeon. At the first report of my gun the plain was alive with niel-ghie and deer, great herds of them scouring away in every direction. With the hope of taking one of these wild creatures by surprise, I kept one barrel loaded with ball, and on my way home my expectations were realized. Whilst walking along the bottom of a ravine, a couple of red deer, roused by my dog—who had been playing the truant at some distance—came at full speed along the brow towards me. I dived into a bush; they passed me at about 30 paces; I let the lady-doe pass; and the buck answered my shot by a convulsive bound, rolling down the flank of the ravine almost to my feet. The ball had severed the spine.

Jan. 31*st.*—By daybreak, as usual, our canvas city was taken up by the roots, carried over 11 miles of space, and replanted under the rock of Kallinger. It was my last march with the Head-quarters camp. About a mile from Kallinger we encountered a numerous cavalcade, which proved to be that of the Rajah Bukt Singh of Adjeeghur, another formidable rock-fortress, 20 miles to the south-eastward. This place fell to the British, after a desperate resistance and a considerable loss on our side, in 1809; and its capture was signalized by a most barbarian act on the part of a relative of the Zemindar. This old man was sent to the zenana to prepare the fair inmates for their removal with their chief, and, the messenger not returning, the house was broken into, when it was discovered that—instigated by a dread of the besiegers' violence—he had cut the throats of all the women and children, and, very properly, crowned the catastrophe by cutting his own. Tragedies such as these are of common occurrence in the history of Indian sieges; but the most approved, and certainly the most complete method of preserving the zenana inviolate was by the summary process of blowing it into the air by means of mines, prepared with providential foresight by the besieged, and exploded by some devoted servant at a preconcerted signal.

Our camp occupied a tolerably level space of ground, dotted with bushes and rocks, within 300 yards of the foot of the Kallinger rock; nor could a more favourable position have been chosen to display to advantage the grand and awful proportions of this formidable stronghold.

The hill on which Kallinger stands is said to be 960 feet above the plain: it stands out in isolated grandeur from the main range, from which it is separated by a deep, rocky, and thickly-wooded valley. The flanks of the mountains are scarped almost perpendicularly on all sides, and are thickly clothed with stunted copse-wood, with the exception of a space of about 50 feet from the summit, which presents a natural wall of bare rock, scarcely needing the solid curtains and bastions of stone surmounting it, and conforming in their curves and angles exactly to the shape of the hill. The circumference of the battlements is computed at 6 miles. The only access to the fort is by a stair-road, as at Gwalior, and, Kallinger being at least as high again as the latter place, the ascent is proportionately more fatiguing. I rode my mountain-mule the greater part of the way, and was just an hour from base to summit. It is a curious fact that the surface of the rock, whose sides are so rugged and steep, presents a nearly level table-land; and the like peculiarity is observable throughout the mountain-fortresses of Bundelcund. There is smooth space, sprinkled with turf, of sufficient extent for the manœuvres of a regiment or a game at cricket; and there are the remains of a capital carriage-road 3½ miles in circuit. The English officers of the garrison, until within these few years, had buggies brought to the summit on the heads of porters, and enjoyed their evening drive 900 feet above the plain. Hill forts usually fail in that most important of munitions, water; but Kallinger, in addition to several spacious tanks, possesses one well which, for aught that is known to the contrary, may reach to the antipodes, for it has never been fathomed.

It appears as though Providence had designed this province for the last refuge of Indian independence, so perfect in their defensive properties are all these natural bulwarks spread throughout the district. It is certain that, though overrun for the space of 14 years by the countless hosts of the Mahrattas, Bundelcund was never fairly subjected; and that the same Kallinger that worsted the repeated and obstinate attacks of the thitherto successful Ali Bahauder, opposed as brilliant a resistance to even British arms, and upheld the standard of liberty long after the whole of the surrounding country had succumbed to the pertinacious ambition of the Company.

The English army invested this fort in 1810, and, getting possession of a small conical hill, a kind of natural outwork, called Kallingeri, erected their batteries thereon. Although the distance of 1200 yards from the nearest point of the battlements was almost too great for the effecting of a good breach, the guns, directed against an angle, brought down considerable masses of masonry; and the storming party, encouraged by these appearances, rushed down from their position, and commenced their arduous progress across the craggy and tangled gorge separating the lesser from the main rock. A murderous fire was poured upon the ascending troops, and huge blocks of granite rolled destruction through their ranks. Nevertheless, they persevered, and, on approaching the work, what was their consternation when they discovered that the brickwork which had been battered down had only served as a facing to the bluff scarped rock! The breach was totally impregnable, and the English were forced back with severe loss. What, however, could not be effected by lead and steel, was speedily accomplished by all-conquering gold—the sinews of diplomacy as well as of war—and the fortress was surrendered by negotiation shortly after our failure.

As I stood on the frowning brow of the positively inaccessible angle which formed the point of attack, my bosom swelled with emotions of pride at the determined hardihood which alone could have brought my countrymen to the hopeless exploit. I gazed from the dizzy height upon the mist-covered jungle below, until I almost fancied I heard the loud huzzas of the impetuous storming party; and I felt that, on the "coigne of vantage" where I stood, I could, with a troop of 20 men and as many old women, and with no other arms than the huge stones which lay in piles around me, have made good my Thermopylæ against tens of thousands and hundreds of thousands!

The antiquity of Kallinger is, like its famous well, unfathomable. Mahomedan historians make mention of Rajahs of Kallinger as far back as A.D. 1008. It was taken by the Emperor Shere Khan about the middle of the 16th century; but its fall was accomplished by the treachery of the garrison, and the conqueror lost his life in the assault by the explosion of a magazine in one of the batteries.

The forests, which spread over the valleys and hills to the south and east of Kallinger, abound in game of every species. The gigantic elk, so rare in India, the leopard and hyæna, are frequently fallen in with and shot by the officers of the three companies forming the garrison of this sequestered fortress. There is little danger in the pursuit of the latter animals, even on foot, for they never attempt resistance, except when too much wounded to escape.

My dâk from Kallinger to Allahabad was duly laid for the evening of this day, *Feb. 1st.* At the latter town it is my intention to embark on the Ganges and sail down its stream as far as Dinapore, to give a meeting to a young relative who has just donned the Honourable Company's uniform. At 9 P.M. my palankeen was reported ready: the bearers were girding up their loins, and jabbering about khanah and peisa,* their never-varying topics; the Mussalgees replenishing and lighting their torches; the broad-shouldered, fierce-looking, bare-legged Burkindass twirled his moustaches, braced his buckler, and shouldered his sheathed sword; my faithful surdar-bearer bustled about, arranging pillows and rezies†—(Oh for an established orthography of current Indian words! for I believe I spell them differently as often as they occur)—the bangy-burdars,‡ after nicely balancing their patarras, had already jogged forward; and syces, khitmutgars, hookahburdars, and other domestic ministers with hard titles and easy offices, were craning about the tent-door, and each in their turn—though previously furnished with orders with a view to save trouble at the last moment—advancing with closed hands and open mouths, to get the Sahib's hookam about horses and baggage and hookahs; or to insinuate a whispered prayer for buckshees; or to put in a "humbly showeth," calligraphized by some erudite camp sircar, setting forth some petty grievance, or petitioning for discharge or increase of pay, backed by well-feigned panic at the prospect of a Calcutta climate!

As I tarried for a moment before the door, to deliver a parting injunction to my major-domo, a crowd of my private bearers suddenly set up a combined yell of complaint,

* Food and payment. † Quilted bed-covering.
‡ Baggage porters.

in which I could just collect that the Khansamah, under the influence of opium, had with his Mussulman fists battered the whole body corporate of the Hindoo officials—the defendant in return alleging that he had been wrought by their gaulee* to commit the assault.

After striving for a few moments to make out the pros and cons of the case, it ended by my sending the whole party to Jehanum, bundling into my palankeen, and drowning their complaints in the chanted *refrain* of my dâk-bearers; whose monotonous chorus, assisted by the cradle-like motion of my equipage, lulled me, in the course of time, into a comfortable sleep. Thus ended my last day in camp; and much did I regret my canvas tabernacle, with its diurnal change of site and prospect; the healthful daily journey, anticipating the sun; the busy bustle of the line of march; the diverging ramble from the direct route with chetahs, greyhounds, or falcons; the amusing visits to royal personages at their glittering courts, and the still more exciting interviews with royal tigers in their jungle realms; the half-sporting, half-reconnoitring stroll in the afternoon, with gun or pencil equally ready for its object; the repast rendered more savoury by exercise, and digested to the "interposing puff" of the cozy, dozy hookah; the evening whist-parties, given in routine by the heads of departments of our migratory microcosm, and graced by the presence of ladies—where camp politics were discussed, or well-digested plans were arranged for the morrow's chasse; the constant and endless variety of climes and countries, customs and characters, scenery, and incident—in a word, the roving, errant, gypsy-like life, in which novelty trips up the heels of ennui, and adventure casts out the blue devils engendered by an enervating climate.

But I left myself asleep in my palankeen, at 9 P.M. on the 1*st of February*. At sunrise, on the 2*nd*, I passed through the pretty town of Turrowah; crossed the Jumna at the village of Mow at 8 P.M.; and reached Allahabad at gunfire n the morning of the 3*rd*; thus accomplishing, in about 32

* Abuse.

hours, the distance that the Head-quarters camp will consume 10 days in performing. I only halted one hour on the road, to make a meal of tea and biscuit; my banqueting-hall was an umbrageous mango-grove; the roof of my palankeen formed a convenient table; and my Hebe was a garrulous old woman, who "for a consideration," purveyed for me, from the neighbouring hamlet, an earthen pot of goat's milk, which had been boiled just too late to prevent its turning sour. At Allahabad I was hospitably received by Captain Mein, the assistant Commissary-General, who introduced me to the budgerow destined for my transport to Calcutta; and in which, in the course of the day, all my goods and chattels were safely deposited. The shore of the Ganges, for many hundred yards under the steep bank on which Captain Mein's house is situated, is lined with the budgerows, horse-boats, office-boats, and cook-boats, forming the fleet of the Head-quarters; and at the mast-head of each officer's galley flaunts a gay-coloured, distinguishing flag.

The important, and, to the Hindoos, holy city of Allahabad is eligibly situated at the confluence of the Ganges and Jumna; and the fort, a place of great extent and strength, commands the navigation of both rivers. The emperor Acbar founded the new city in 1581, and his handiwork came into the clutches of the English in 1765. Here Lord Clive received from Shah Aulum of Delhi—on conditions of protection—the legal possession of the province of Bengal. The Company laid out vast sums of rupees on the fortifications of this important stronghold, and made it the grand depôt of military stores and provincial justice for the upper districts of India. I had not been long at Allahabad ere I received a message from Doorjun Saul, the ex-usurper of Bhurtpore, who is now a state prisoner in the fort. In a dhâllee of fruits, vegetables, and preserves, he insinuated—liked Cleopatra's asp—a letter, in which he besought me, as Mousahib* to the Lord General, to visit him, and to exert my influence at the British court for his

* Aide-de-camp.

liberation—an invitation which I politely declined, preferring a jaunt to the grand fair—now in celebration under the walls of the fort—to being made the auditor of complaints for which I could administer no balm.

The fair—in *fair* company, for such I enjoyed on the occasion—was worth seeing. There was more chaffering and bargaining, and less fighting and love-making, than are seen in England in like assemblies: but after Hurdwar fair, Allahabad had nothing of novelty to show. We passed down the whole street of booths, driving hard bargains with the retailers of trash; and, amongst other valuables, I purchased for one rupee a whole mythology of Hindoo deities.

Budgerow.

Feb. 4th.—At 11 A.M. I stepped into the clumsy, rickety budgerow in which, with the special intervention of Providence, I may hope to navigate 750 miles without becoming food for alligators. My palankeen and half a dozen domestics, with a posse of dogs and goats, were established as outside passengers, on the roof or poop of the vessel: the maungee * gave the word for weighing; the huge bamboos cramped the top-heavy ark from the shore; she swung heavily round; and after carrying away the noses of several figure-heads and jamming in the jilmils † of two or three sister budgerows, my gallant tub rolled gracefully away, like a swan — out of water—followed by a favouring breeze and the hearty execrations of the crews of the injured vessels. My little fleet consisted of this my private yacht, a smaller boat for servants' baggage and kitchen, and a little dinghee, or Ganges wherry. The budgerow, though unwieldy and ungovernable in narrow winding streams and high winds, is really,—considering its primitive construction, for it appears to have been built after Jason's model—very well calculated for Ganges navigation. The accommodation between-decks is even superior to that of a frigate—my sitting-room being 17½ feet by 15 feet and nearly 8 feet high, and the sleeping cabin, more abaft, about 12 feet square. In addition to two large square sails, it is furnished with 14 long sweeps. The voyages are always made by daylight, the numerous shoals of the river rendering night navigation dangerous. Towards sunset the budgerow is, therefore, run ashore in some favourable spot, and the dândies as the boatmen are called, from the word dân, an oar—instantly set about making their little temporary ovens on the bank, to bake their chupâtties, and concoct their curry. The crews are of either sect, Mussulman or Hindoo; the former are, perhaps, the more able-bodied seamen, and stancher at the oar; but they cook their meals on board, and smother the passenger —already stewed by 90° of Fahrenheit—with their savoury steams. The Hindoos, on the contrary, are forbidden by their religion to perform these rites on board, solacing themselves with parched grain and sweetmeats until the anchoring of the vessels gives them the advantage of a legitimate feast. Then, indeed, do these sufferers for religion's

* Boatswain. † Venetian blinds.

sake make up for lost time. An Englishman who pecks at his three or four meals per diem, would stare to see the mountain of rice devoured at a sitting by these hard-working and hungry disciples of Brahmah.

The dândies are generally fine, stout, and sleek figures. In rowing they stand upright, advancing and retiring two or three steps at every stroke; and lightening their labour, as well as preserving the measure, by a song and chorus.

The Ganges, though certainly magnificent as a river, from the great width of its stream and the fineness of its water, must yield the palm of picturesque beauty to the Thames, the Liffy, or the Rhine. Its banks present an unvaried sand-wall on one hand; and on the other are low, flat, and unbroken. This is, however, speaking generally; for there are points and headlands on the great river, which, invested as they are with all the scenic requisites of wood, water, and architecture, afford brilliant subjects for the pencil. Almost every sand-bank—and the Ganges is replete with them—forms the basking-place of some huge alligator. It is not unusual to see a group of 10 or 12 of these monsters lying so motionless, in their enjoyment of the sun, that an unaccustomed eye would mistake them for logs of timber. On the near approach of a boat they tumble clumsily into the water and disappear. There are two species of the alligator, the most common of which, the long-nosed, preys only upon fish. But the short-headed mugger, which grows to the length of 30 feet, extends his tastes to flesh, human or bestial.

About 4 P.M. on the *6th* I sailed past Mirzapore, a large town situated on the right bank of the river. It drives a busy trade in cotton and silk, and is famous for the manufacture of carpeting. The bank of the stream is adorned with several fine ghauts and temples: a little below the town four or five handsome houses mark the Civil Station; and a line of more humble bungalows, the Cantonments.

The ghauts—flights of steps to the river—of which every

town on the Ganges boasts of three or four, always present an animated scene to the aquatic passenger. At all hours of the day, but more particularly in the morning, they are thronged with busy crowds of Hindoos, who are certainly the most cleanly people in the world. The Brahmin may be seen standing up to his knees in the holy stream, with depressed head, and hands in the attitude of prayer; or carefully washing the symbolical thread, the badge of his sacred caste. Women, with their graceful garments, and still more graceful persons, and with their well-poised water-vessels on their heads, glide up and down the steps in execution of their duty, the drudgery of the ménage. It does one's heart good to see these elegant creatures cheerfully performing their domestic offices, and rendering even labour graceful. You may talk of your Frenchwoman's walk — it may be pretty—indeed, it is so; but is it natural? She goes pitter-patting along, as though she feared at each step to burst her shoe. My Indian daughter of nature has no shoe to burst; but she plants a very pretty bare foot with precision, yet lightness; and floats past, unencumbered with the weighty vase, which her slender neck seems almost too fragile to support.

Hindoo woman and child.

A little apart from the town and the public haunts of man, females, singly or in pairs, may be seen stealing down to the river like Musidora, to bathe their "fervent limbs in the refreshing flood;" like her, unconscious of any treacherous Damon, after a hasty glance up the bank and along the shore, they disengage themselves in an instant from their simple garment, and plunge into the stream.

This dress of the women consists of but one piece of cloth, the sarree; it is fastened round the waist, and thrown over the head and across the bosom. Simple though it be, this attire is infinitely more graceful, and even more decent, than the evening costume of the belles of more sophisticated regions.

I have often been amused by, and marvelled at, the total absence of all visible sympathy or gallantry between the Hindoo men and women in public. In Europe, on occasions like these conventions on the Ghaut, there would doubtless be free scope given to badinage, ribaldry, and practical jokes; but the orderly Hindoo plods through his prayers and ablutions perfectly indistrait by the vicinity of his fair neighbour, whom he suffers to raise the ponderous water-vessel to her head, without dreaming of offering assistance.

Feb. 7th.—At 3 P.M. passed the town and fortress of Chunar. The appearance of this place is very striking; and its situation on a bluff rock jutting far into the river, and commanding its navigation, makes it a formidable toll-bar on this great high road of military and commercial communication between Bengal and the upper provinces. This stronghold has been the scene of many sieges and battles. In 1575 it held out against a Mogul army for six months; and in 1764 it surrendered to the English, after having repulsed them in a night attack. The fort of Chunar is the prison of a Mahratta rebel of rank, and the Chelsea of European invalids; and if the one is not speedily emancipated from his chains, and the others from all sublunary—or rather sub-solar—maladies, I shall never more put faith in the dissolving powers of heat; for this bare bright rock must be the hottest spot in the world. The natural productions of Chunar are its fine freestone and famous tobacco. I passed the town without landing, sending the small boat ashore to cater for provisions.

This lonely, lazy, lounging aquatic expedition appears to me somewhat monotonous—though not ungrateful—after the constant action and bustling variety of "life in camp." It is some days since I have heard my own voice, except in the necessary laconic orders to my native attendants: my pretty spaniel, Rustem, with his insinuating wriggle and eloquent whine, seems, indeed, as if he only wanted the gift of utterance to say a great deal; but his visits to his master being regulated more by appetite than duty, he only makes his appearance in the parlour about the time that the cook-boat runs alongside—preferring a romp on deck with the goat to any other less mercurial society. The scuffling attacks of the one, and the repellent butts of the other, come as distinctly home to my senses through the reverberating medium of the thin roof, as though I were an ocular witness of their gambols. The hours float past as smoothly and slowly as the stream of the unruffled and somewhat dilatory Ganges; and my faith in my own fund of resources is sometimes grievously shaken by a longing for the dinner-hour prompted more by ennui than hunger. Yet there is something of luxury and comfort in thus gliding through space with so little trouble to oneself, and in the feeling that you are wending rapidly towards your destination, whilst engaged in your usual pursuits and avocations. I look round my little floating home with a self-hugging complacency; and when I am fairly ensconced in my deep easy chair, with my slippered feet on the sill of the open window, my novel, my book of topographical reference, my hookah, and my sherbet, I would not barter my cozy solitude and the moving panorama constantly before me for any pleasure or scene which would involve the necessity of rising from my seat.

Feb. 8th.—At 10 o'clock this morning the great city of Benares hove in sight. I therefore ordered my chair, my chattah,* and my telescope upon deck, and during the hour which was occupied in sailing past this Indian Babylon I found ample amusement and interest in the busy

* Large umbrella.

scene which the Ganges' bank daily presents at this hour. Great masses of building crowd, one below another, down to the water's edge: splendid modern palaces, gaunt and deserted ruins, Hindoo temples, Mahometan mosques, spacious ghauts alive with moving myriads of bathers; fat Brahmins, lean fakirs, hobbling and squabbling beldames, plump and taper damsels, all seemed to pass in review before me; and I was scarcely tired of laughing and admiring, sketching and spying, ere I found myself at the Raj Ghaut, where I gave orders to shorten sail and drop anchor.

A buggy, sent for me by Mr. Hamilton, the magistrate, was in waiting; I jumped into it and drove to the splendid mansion of Sir Frederic Hamilton (the collector of Benares)—situated near the cantonments, and about 5 miles from the river—where I was most hospitably entreated during two days. Of the town I had only a cursory view. The streets are narrow and dirty, crowded from morn till night with tribes of fakirs, processions, horses, elephants, Brahminee bulls and Brahminee marriages. In this holy Head-quarters of Hindooism the most remarkable and prominent edifice is the great musjed of Aurungzebe, whose lofty minars seem to look down with contempt upon the Lilliputian crowds of Hindoo muts within view of its proud dome. How galling must the Muezzin's call be to the ears of the 500,000 followers of Brahmah who form the chief population of Benares! *

In the English cantonments a house was pointed out to me in which Mr. Cherry, the Resident, and three other English civil-servants were, in 1799, butchered by the emissaries of Vizier Ali, the ex-Nawaub of Oude. The traitors seized the occasion of an amicable visit to attempt the massacre of all the hated British at this station; and they would, doubtless, have fully succeeded in their bloody

* At Benares is the famous Vidalaia, or Hindoo College; where, among other well-established points of science, the students are instructed that the sun revolves round the earth.

designs, had not one gentleman made his escape, and, throwing himself upon a horse, galloped at full speed to the cavalry cantonments of Sultanpore, 8 miles from Benares, turned out a squadron which was fortunately at drill, and returned with it within the hour, and in time to save many of our countrymen's lives. The arrival of this reinforcement was most opportune for Mr. Davis, the judge. When this gentleman's house was beset by the murderers, he sent his family by a spiral turret staircase to the roof of the building, and, when his retreat was discovered, defended himself on the narrow escalier for half an hour, with no better weapon than a hog-spear.

On the evening of the 9*th*, accompanied by a very special round of beef, and an odoriferous dhally of fruits and vegetables, I re-embarked; and at daybreak got under weigh for Dinapore. The wind was strong, and so inveterately in our teeth, that sails, and oars, and current were no match for it. The budgerow, however, has yet another method of locomotion, namely, tracking. A rope is fastened to the mast-head, and the crew, jumping overboard like so many frogs, swim to shore, and drag the vessel along the banks, until a favourable turn in the river or the wind brings them all on board again.

Received this day a packet from Head-quarters, enclosing a letter from Deyra, giving an interesting account of a tiger-hunt. The correspondent was the same gentleman who, with my friend and myself, slew the tigress and cubs, near that town, in last April. As there is a plentiful dearth of log-matter on the river, I shall—with due apologies to the writer for rendering his letter immortal by smuggling it into this important work—take leave to subjoin an extract. "Having obtained pretty certain intelligence that a tiger had taken up his temporary abode in the thick wood jungle about the hill of Kalunga, a party of four of us, assisted by two or three native volunteers, determined to sally out in quest of him. Having no elephants, we proceeded on foot to the spot indicated as his lurking-place; and, after beating about for some time without discovering him, we strolled down the hill, tracking him by his footmarks. Erskine was in front, and I a few yards behind him, when suddenly and without the slightest warning the tiger sprung from a thicket, and seized in his jaws a Goorkah sepoy, who was close to E——. A native policeman, who was at the sepoy's elbow, fired his matchlock, when the tiger instantly dropped his victim, and made at him. Erskine, who all this time had stood firm as a rock, watching his opportunity, now stepped up; and, as the animal was in the act of seizing the second man, within three paces of himself, fired his piece: the ball took effect in the tiger's back, and he dropped dead on the spot. The coolness of Erskine was beyond all praise. The tiger measured nine feet four inches."

On the 12th I brought-to at the town of Gazypore, and sent the crew and servants ashore to buy food. The best rosewater in India is manufactured here; and attar is so rich, that it is sold as high as 100 rupees for the rupee weight. Travellers are usually taken in by sellers of spurious rosewater, and I proved, though duly warned, no wiser than my neighbours. A plausible rascal came on board, and convinced me, in spite of my nose, that the three carbhies, each containing eight or ten quarts, which I bought for nine rupees, were of the very first quality: my hookahburdar, who pretended to be a judge, assisted in making a fool of me: the bargain was struck; the brittle, yet precious carbhies were a constant source of anxiety to me in my passage to Calcutta: there the rosy liquid was carefully run off into quart bottles, to be taken to England; and the first that I stingily opened brought me the satisfactory conviction that I had been humbugged.

The next day an adverse storm raged for several hours, and dispersed my armada. My budgerow, which is surely built expressly to be the laughing-stock of the winds, was driven ashore with a bump that upset my breakfast apparatus; and the crew, after making one or two efforts at tracking, finally ceased their fruitless toil and trouble, and quietly took to their hubble-bubbles,* their never-failing consolation in time of need. As my vessel lay helpless aground, a large fleet of clumsy cotton boats, coming up the stream, took advantage of the gale, and sailed past me in the most triumphant style. I was just envying them their prosperous breeze, and perhaps wishing them a share in my adversity, when a sudden squall swept over the fleet, and left not a sail and scarcely a mast standing. Down drifted these cumbrous specimens of naval architecture with the stream, and one of the hugest of them ran ashore close astern of me with a force that would have crushed my comparatively tiny craft, like a walnut under the heel of a Bath porter.

During this ill-omened day I never lost sight of Buxar. At this town and at Karinta-Dee, just opposite, there is a grand establishment of the Company's stud, the superintendant, Major Hunter, having a pretty house at the latter place. Buxar is chiefly celebrated as the scene of the great victory gained by the British detachment under Major Munro over the countless hosts of Suja ood Doulah and Cossim Khan in 1764. The English army consisted of little more than 7000 Europeans and sepoys, whilst that of the enemy has been computed at 40,000. Our victory was complete, and the capture of 130 pieces of cannon, and an immense booty, rewarded the conquerors.

I passed the greater part of Valentine's day on a shoal in the middle of the river. The weather was dreadfully hot, and the budgerow much out of the perpendicular: the crew standing for two hours in the water with their brawny shoulders applied to the counter of the stubborn vessel, which only responded by a slight heave to their strenuous exertions and vociferated "Allahs!" It was truly a patience-proving predicament. Tired of my passive situation, I at length jumped out of the window, and trusting to a wet towel twisted round my head, as an ægis against the sun's meridional rays, and to the ceaseless ululations of

* Cocoa-nut pipe, so called by the English.

the dândies as a defence against alligators, enjoyed a refreshing bathe. Then dressing myself, and taking a gun and a dog, I got into my dinghee, and, leaving my budgerow to the care of the crew, proceeded to disturb the siestas of several of the above-named monsters of the deep, whose basking forms I had previously reconnoitered with my telescope. I failed in accomplishing the destruction of any of them; though I flattered myself—and so did my native aide-de-camp—that many of them only owed their safety—like Ajax—to their seven-fold shield of a hide. A drop of blood too, on one occasion discovered by my man Friday, on a sand-bank, satisfied me as to the correctness of my aim.

On these sporting trips I was always accompanied by one of the dândies, a plump, smiling little fellow, whose sleek russet skin, Nature's handiwork, was more becoming to him than the most consummate production of Stultz could be to the dandies of my native land. He was a tacit volunteer, and a perfect fanatic in his new pursuit. As a retriever he was invaluable; quite usurping the occupation of my spaniel, who was amusingly jealous. If I shot a wild-duck—and I generally got one for my solitary dinner—the report of my gun was instantly echoed by the plunge of my amphibious attendant, who had generally almost reached his object before his quadruped rival, conquering his natural hydrophobia and urged by despairing emulation, had made up his mind to the dreaded leap. I never saw any natant animal cleave the water with such speed as this fellow, and I remarked that he always swam on his side with his right hand protended, and his left arm vigorously plied as a paddle. This is intelligible: for the keel-like side of a man must oppose much less resistance to the water than the broad "breast of controversy" of the straightforward swimmer.

Feb. 15*th.*—In the morning, a continuation of adverse winds, which, however, lulled towards noon. At 3 p.m. I passed the confluence of the Gogra with the Ganges; it is, next to the Jumna and the Sone, the most powerful of the

Drawn by Captn. G. C. Mundy. Etched by T. Landseer.

Ferry on the Ganges near Kurrah.

London. Pubd. by John Murray. 1858.

tributaries to the queen of rivers. Near the junction was fought—according to Dow—a great battle between the armies of the Emperor Acbar and Daood the rebel governor of Bengal. The latter was beat, and fled to Patna, which he defended. On arriving before this place the emperor, with his customary heroism, offered to stake his empire in a single combat with Daood—a challenge declined by the latter. He had better have accepted it, for he was afterwards taken, and murdered in cold blood.

The next morning, on awaking, I found my gallant bark scudding at the rate of 10 knots an hour before a fresh and favourable gale which brought me safe to my anchorage at Dinapore, after an exhilarating sail of six hours. I immediately landed, and proceeded to the barracks by the back way, hoping to take my relative by surprise. He was out, so I employed myself in guessing at his character and pursuits by the furniture and garniture of his apartment—a test which I have generally found to be, at least, as satisfactory as a first personal interview. I need not detail the conclusions I drew from the following sketch of the young cadet's domicile:—in one corner of the room—"that served him for parlour, and kitchen, and hall"—stood a box full of oats for the horse; in another, a billiard cue, a gig-whip, and some rackets. On the table lay a volume of Shakspeare, its pages unthumbed, and its back impliant; a Persian grammar, which had evidently been half gone through—for only the last half was left; a couple of nearly empty boxes of cigars; and a pair of silk French garters, with the embroidered motto, "Pensez à moi." The pictures which adorned the whitewashed walls were some of "Alken's Symptoms," and two large framed pendants of our first parents in Paradise, and Leda. The awkward schoolboy, whom I had lost sight of for four years, had thrown off the chrysalis of boyhood, and become the gay, comely, and sesquipedalian Ensign. What a change do not these four years, from 12 to 16, bring about! and with what anxious solicitude must the parent—at that interval between the two ages—watch over the dawning qualities of his son, which, good or bad, must now be elicited! During this eventful period boyhood is exchanged for manhood, whims for passions, love of marbles for first love, and, though last not least (in my estimation, as I remember), the jacket for the coat. The sanguine youth, full of dreams of success, vaults at one spring into the arena of life, and commences a series of combats and struggles, in which he probably finds himself the most dangerous of his enemies; sometimes triumphant, at others succumbent, his toils are sooner or later rewarded by the olive-crown of experience.

Dinapore—the name always gives me an appetite!—is situated a few miles below the confluence of the Sone and Ganges. There is little remarkable in the place, except the barracks, erected on a more extensive scale than any other in India, and in which one of his Majesty's regiments and two of the Company's are quartered. The country round about is exceedingly fertile in grain, but not so in rides for the evening airings of the English inhabitants. About half a mile from the barracks is a great victualling establishment, called Deega Farm; the estate is of some extent, and within its limits are contained a beautiful dwelling-house, splendidly furnished, the residence of the farmer; a very extensive Tunbridge-ware shop; immense ranges of stalls, containing about 2000 bullocks and other cattle; wine and store vaults; kitchen ranges; and fruit, vegetable, and flower gardens showily laid out. The owner, an Englishman, having, as I was informed, made some 50,000*l.* by the same species of establishment about eight years ago, set up for a gentleman, went to England—where of course his rupees found him friends—and was persuaded by them to aspire to a seat in the councils of his country. His M. P. plan failed, as did his rupees, and consequently his friends; and Mr. H. returned to India, his poultry, and piggery, where he bids fair soon to realize a second fortune, which—with 50,000*l.* worth of experience—will enable him to enact the independent gentleman to the end of his days.

On the eighth day of my stay at Dinapore the Head-quarters' fleet, with its white sails, flaunting flags, and "pictis puppibus," hove in sight. The pinnace flag-ship, with its 24 first-rate budgerows, store-ships, fire-ships—for so the cook-boats may be styled—and horse-vessels, made really a very imposing appearance as they bore down upon the town before a fresh breeze. The Commander-in-Chief remained at Dinapore the following day to review the brigade, and was entertained in the evening with a fancy-dress ball, where there were many good characters, and some very pretty ones.

Feb. 25th.—The fleet dropped down to Bankipore, the English civil station, near Patna; and the greater portion of our party dined with Sir Charles D'Oyley. Here we met with a hospitable welcome and good cheer, and in the evening we heard some beautiful music, and saw some splendid drawings of the talented baronet. At Bankipore are the extensive opium warehouses of the Company; and near Patna is a huge mountain of a granary, built by the English, and alike remarkable for its size, its expense in building, and its utter inutility. The city of Patna, of which Bankipore may be considered a suburb, extends for many miles along the right bank of the river, which is at this point, in the rainy season, nearly five miles in width. Patna boasts great antiquity, and is one of those numerous cities set up by conflicting English antiquarians as candidates for the site of the great Palibothra of Pliny.

The remains of an old English factory are shown, where about 200 prisoners were butchered by the adventurer Sumroo, whose widow I had the honour of dining with a few weeks ago at Meerut. Late in the evening our party were provided with equipages, and drove down to the fleet, lying at anchor about five miles distant.

At gun-fire on the *26th* the Head-quarters' armada got under weigh, and made a good day's run to the village of Bar, a favourable wind propelling us at the rate of 8 miles an hour. There was a good deal of emulation among the budgerows, and I soon discovered that mine was not among the *crack* sailers. At the windings of the river, the vessels, though there was plenty of sea-room, generally ran aboard of each other; and if one of the leading ships chanced to touch upon a shoal, she was sure to be bumped farther into the mud by the rear attacks of her unwary followers. There was something monstrously provoking, when well placed in the van of the fleet, to be thus suddenly arrested in one's triumphant career: the friends who shot past you laughed at your mishap, and those who backed you up pushed you farther into the scrape—"a plague of such backing!" I say.

With prosperous gales we reached Monghir at 2 p.m. the next day, and remained there during the night. The fortress of Monghir is beautifully situated on a rocky peninsula, formed by a graceful sweep of the river: the walls are of brick, and enclose an area of about three miles. Most of the ancient buildings have fallen to ruin, or been cleared away; and there are now only a few houses and bungalows, and a cantonment for sepoys, within the walls. The remainder of the space is covered with remarkably fine turf, and is employed as a parade-ground. Without the walls, and to the southward of the fort, lies the town, which is of great extent: the country in the neighbourhood is extremely pretty and fertile, and the prospect is backed up by the mountains of Corruckpore. Monghir was much strengthened by Cossim Ali Khan, the Mogul governor of the province, who made strenuous efforts to throw off the yoke of the English: the fort was, however, taken after a siege of only nine days.

The chief *lion* of the place is a hot well, called the Seeta Coond, or Well of Seeta—the Apollo of Indian mythology—about four miles from the fort. It is situated in a pretty wooded dell; and the fact is singular that, within a few feet of the hot well, there are several springs of cold water. The heat of the Seeta Coond is usually about 137° of Fahrenheit: it is painful to keep the hand for more than an instant in the stream; and instances are recorded of persons having been scalded to death by falling into it.

The water, having no mineral admixture in its composition, is extremely pleasant to the taste: and such is its purity and durability that I considered six dozen quarts, sent me by a friend for my voyage to England, an offering at least equivalent to Horace's vaunted "Plenus Albani cadus." The well is considered a spot of great sanctity by the Hindoos, and superstition has invested it with a divine origin. The rock from which the stream gushes once bore the form of a beautiful nymph, who, like Daphne, underwent the metamorphosis to escape from the amorous pursuit of a god.

Monghir is at present an invalid depôt, and is considered a very healthy place. It is famous for its iron-ware and furniture manufactures. Among other articles hawked about the fleet for sale, a very neatly-made fowling-piece was offered me for 20 rupees, or 2*l.*: stock, lock, and barrel appeared to be well finished; but I doubt not that the doctor's bill, consequent upon the firing it off, would have more than counterbalanced the difference of price between the Monghir maker and Wesley Richards of Birmingham—who will doubtless take 20 per cent. off my bill for this recommendation.

Feb. 28th.—The morning being calm, the fleet took its sweeps and fairly rowed itself into a favourable wind, which we picked up about mid-day as we passed through that beautiful estuary of the Ganges spread round the picturesque rocks of Janguira. The main rock is insular, and is crowned with a lofty Hindoo temple and the habitations of a band of Fakirs, whose predecessors have occupied this singular spot time out of mind. Janguira is the scene of a poem by a Mr. Derozio, a young Eurasian of great acquirements, who has been styled the Byron of the East. The situation of the temple is not very unlike that of the Château de Chillon; and the Ganges at this spot is to the full as wide as Lac Leman between Chillon and the Meillerie mountains.

At 3 P.M. the fleet brought-to at Boglipore, and we immediately got out our horses and uniforms, and proceeded with his Excellency to inspect the barracks of his Majesty's 3rd (Buffs), who are quartered here in temporary cantonments. There is also stationed, about four miles from the European barracks, a native local corps, formed entirely of the wild mountaineers of Rajemâl. The country in the vicinity of Boglipore is extremely fertile and luxuriantly wooded, and the vegetation preserves throughout the year that rich verdure caused by the heavy dews peculiar to the provinces of Bahar and Bengal. At a short distance from the cantonments stands a monument—perhaps the only memorial ever dedicated by Indians in gratitude to an European—erected by the natives of the neighbouring hills to the memory of an Englishman, named Cleveland, who was formerly magistrate of the district, and whose short life was devoted to ameliorate the condition of those mountaineers, who at his death showed that they were not ungrateful for the kindness of their benefactor. The cenotaph is of Hindoo architecture, and two Fakirs are employed to keep a lamp eternally burning within the building.

The following morning, after a review and a breakfast with the Buffs, we re-embarked, and, having a good day's run, reached the Colgong Rocks—the Scylla and Charybdis of the Ganges—by 3 P.M. These two strange-looking insular crags stand out in the middle of the steam, opposite a lofty and woody promontory which forces the river from its straight course. They are both more or less clothed with stunted coppice-wood, and are ornamented with carved representations of Hindoo deities, or devils. I landed on one of the sister rocks in pursuit of a curious bird, of a species I never happened to have met with before, and which my companion succeeded in shooting. It was milk white, with two slender feathers, half a foot long, growing out of the back of its head. In size and shape it resembled a small sea-gull.

Looking down from the rock into the pellucid depths of the stream, I could distinguish the dark forms of several huge alligators, who rose at intervals to the surface. As I was stepping into my dinghee, one of these monsters lifted several inches of his snout (which looked like the rough bark of an old oak) above the water, within ten yards of me. I quickly saluted him with a charge of small shot, on which he instantly disappeared. The fleet *luggowed*, about three miles below Colgong, on the bank of a large island, where, in my evening stroll, I found a good deal of game. In addition to a plentiful bag of snipes, I killed a large bird of the partridge kind, which I believe to be the brown chekoar, common in the Rajemâl hills, of whose wooded heights we enjoy from this spot a beautiful view. At the foot of these mountains there is to be had some of the finest shooting in India. In the thickest of the forest the rhinoceros revels in his native swamps. Lord Hastings, with a large party of friends, made a sporting campaign under these hills in 1819, and killed three of the above-named animals. Their skin is so thick as to be almost ball-proof, and they are usually shot with tin or copper bullets or bolts. Elephants have a great dread of the rhinoceros, and few of them will await his charge.

March 2nd.—The thermometer rose to 87° yesterday; but was this morning reduced by a welcome shower to 75°. It is calculated that this seasonable fall of rain will protract the cool season for another fortnight. Shortly after noon we sailed past the point of Sicrigully, one of the great passes between the provinces of Bahar and Bengal. In former days there was a strong fortress defending the pass, and a wall running between the mountains and the river: the former is mentioned as having been stormed by Shah Jehan of Delhi in 1623, when a gallant but unsuccessful defence was made by some Europeans of the garrison, who were finally overpowered and put to the sword. Sicrigully is now nothing more than a small hamlet of huts. The inhabitants of the lowlands of this part of Bahar are dark-coloured, stout-made, and ill-favoured. The Puharrees, like those of the Nepaul mountains, are Tartar-featured, very short in stature, but strong-limbed and active. Being unencumbered with the besetting prejudices of the Hindoos of the plains, these sturdy little highlanders are well formed for soldiers.

We passed the night, which was very tempestuous, under a steep bank about 10 miles above the town of Rajemâl; and the next morning at 9 o'clock we sailed past that city. None of our party landed here, as most of us had inspected its interesting ruins when engaged in a similar voyage two years ago. Rajemâl was, at more than one period, the capital of Bengal. It was entirely consumed by an accidental conflagration, whilst in the possession of Suja,—one of the rebel sons of Shah Jehan, whose misfortunes are so movingly recounted by the historian Dow. Suja then narrowly escaped being burnt: and was, at this same place, 20 years after, defeated by his nephew Mohummet, son and general of the great Aurunzebe. The young Mohummet afterwards deserted his father's cause for love of his beautiful cousin, the daughter of Suja, whom he married; was seized by his remorseless parent, and confined in Gwalior, where he died, probably of poison. His fair and faithful bride broke her heart for sorrow; and the ill-starred Suja, persecuted by the rancour of his imperial brother, took refuge in Arracan, where he was treacherously murdered by the Rajah of that province. Here are materials for a novel! Let the author of the 'Spy' embody them.*

The melancholy ruins of Suja's palace, of which a hall of black marble is the most remarkable feature, still remain as memorials of his unhappy career; but the Ganges, by its silent encroachments, bids fair shortly to obliterate even these vestiges. The great river, nearly two centuries ago, made an important change in its course at this point; deserting Gour, the former capital of Bengal, 12 miles from Rajemâl, and bringing its inconstant waters to wash the more elevated bank of the latter place. Here a pretty solid obstruction to its further migration to the westward is op-

* The writer of the 'Romance of History' might, for the extension of his interesting work, cull rich subjects from Dow's 'History of Hindostan;' yet I almost doubt whether English sympathy could be roused by the exploits or misfortunes of Indian heroes and heroines.

posed by the rocky ground which distinguishes the neighbourhood of Rajemâl, and which ceases abruptly at this point. Immediately below the town the appearance of the country is totally changed: throughout the 250 miles of alluvial plain between Rajemâl and the Bay of Bengal it would be a difficult matter for a mischievous schoolboy to find a pebble big enough to break a window.

The following day, after a fine morning's sail, we reached Bogwangola, a commercial village or town, more remarkable for its importance as a grain-mart than for the durability of its architecture.

As this spot is very subject to the encroachments and derelictions of the capricious Gunga—a goddess as notoriously fickle as Fortune—the habitations and grain-stores are merely temporary erections of bamboos and thatch. In one of the invasions of the river, the tomb of an English officer, who died and was buried near the town, was included in its sweeping attack, and engulfed in the sacred flood.

Bogwangola is situated near the Bhâgiretty river, the most western branch of the Ganges. This stream connects its parent river with the Hooghly, and during the rains, when the navigation is available, it presents the most direct passage to Calcutta. At the present season it is totally impassable by budgerows, and those of our party who are bound straight to Calcutta are consequently obliged to travel dâk.

The main body of the Head-quarters fleet proceeds hence in an easterly direction as far as Dacca, where another detachment will branch off to Calcutta by the Sunderbunds; whilst the Commander-in-Chief, with a few of the heads of departments, extends his voyage by the mouths of the Burrampooter to Chittagong, and thence across the Bay of Bengal to Pooree (a not very fashionable watering-place on the Cuttack coast), where, fanned by the refreshing sea-breezes, we are to pass the three broiling months of April, May and June.

The two following days were so profoundly calm, that

we only made that progress which was attainable by oars. We passed Bauliah, and Surdah where there is a silk manufactory of the Company; and at mid-day on the 7th our fleet quitted the Ganges for a smaller stream, the Pubna, running out of the great river, and preferable to it on account of the dangerous shoals of the latter. We brought-to, this evening, at the village of Comerlee.

The hot weather has fairly set in with the calms; the thermometer ranging for many hours this day at 90°.

March 8th.—Continued our passage along the little Pubna, whose banks are covered as far as the eye can range with all the rich and vivid verdure peculiar to Bengal. This morning, before sunrise, as the fleet was making but slow progress, a party of three, who happened to have horses with us, went ashore with some greyhounds, and had some capital coursing, killing three foxes and a jackal. Some villagers reported a fine wild hog in a clump of bamboos close at hand, and offered to drive him out for us, but we had unluckily not provided ourselves with spears.

Early the next morning we scudded past the village of Viziergunge, and entered the Dullaserry river, which is, in many points, nearly of equal width with the Ganges. After running from 4 A.M. to 7 P.M., the signal—so hungrily hoped for by the crews—was given, and the fleet was in a few minutes snugly laid alongside the bank, near the hamlet of Gwalpara. In another instant the English portion of the party were to be seen stretching their cramped limbs upon the shore, and the momentarily increasing fires betokened the diligence of the dândies and servants in preparing their own or their masters' repasts.

The whole surface of the surrounding country is cut into numberless small islands by the myriads of streams, large and insignificant, intersecting each other at a thousand angles, as they hurry to throw themselves into the sea, or into the sovereign rivers Ganges and Burrampooter.

The chief product of the country is that gold-coining plant, the indigo: and scattered here and there, at intervals of 10 or 20 miles, a snug-looking bungalow and a formal business-like range of brick buildings mark the residence of the hog-hunting, claret-drinking factor, who—to his honour be it spoken—is always most ready to share his sports and his bottle with the chance visitor who may happen to stumble upon his solitude.

March 10th.—During this day's sail we quitted the Dullaserry for the Borigunga river; and at 6 P.M. arrived at a hamlet within three miles of Dacca, where we brought-to for the night, in order that we might reach the great city by daylight the next morning. Accordingly, ere sunrise, we were floating past the 5 miles of half-ruined, half-habitable, half-splendid, half-paltry edifices, which, extending along the edge of the stream, constitute the town of Dacca; and shortly after our fleet was moored opposite the Civil station. Although the city does not boast of very great antiquity, yet its many extensive and interesting ruins—which have been done ample justice to by the pencil of Sir C. D'Oyly—attest its former consequence under the Mogul government. It was at one period the capital of the province of Bengal, and the station of a Mogul fleet of armed cruisers, destined to check the Portuguese pirates at that time ravaging the coasts, and to coerce their troublesome neighbours of Arracan.

Dacca is now a considerable station of Company's servants and Company's elephants, of which latter there is organized here a stud of about 300. Every lady knows that Dacca is famed for the fine texture of its muslins; but owing to the improvement of that branch of manufacture in England, and the consequent decreasing encouragement to the Dacca fabricators, the very important art of composing the finer descriptions of this elegant ingredient of the female wardrobe is in imminent danger of being lost.

The town is closely hemmed in by jungles of hundreds of miles in extent, in some parts totally impenetrable. These fastnesses are the great preserves of tigers, and other of the nobler game, which, without such places of refuge, would probably, long ere this, have been extirpated by the indefatigable ardour of British sportsmen. For miles round the

T 2

town, in the depths of the wildest forests, the explorer will stumble upon the mouldering vestiges of the ancient grandeur of Dacca. Palaces, mosques, and tombs are now become the lurking-places of tigers, leopards, and hyænas: in the more accessible parts of the jungle an immense variety of game is to be found; but the sportsman is not always successful, for the animals, at the first report of a gun, commonly make good their retreat to those tangled regions whither he cannot follow them.

Buffalos, hogs, and deer abound; and the streams are alive with those river-pests, alligators, whose penchant for human flesh renders that chiefest luxury in a tropical climate, bathing, a matter of extreme danger. Yet it is strange to see with what perfect nonchalance the native dândies, in case of necessity, take the water.

A beautiful specimen of an alligator's head was here given by Mr. Alexander to Lord Combermere. He was rather a distinguished monster, having carried off, at different occasions, six or eight brace of men from an indigo factory in the neighbourhood. A native, who had long laid wait for him, at length succeeded in slaying him with poisoned arrows. One of these notoriously ghaut-frequenting alligators is well nigh as rich a prize to the poor native who is fortunate enough to capture him as a Spanish galleon is to a British frigate; for on ripping open his stomach, and overhauling its freight, it is not unfrequently found to contain "a choice assortment"—as the Calcutta advertisers have it—of gold, silver, or brass bangles and anklets, which have not been so expeditiously digested as their fair owners, victims of the monster's voracity. A little fat Brahminee child, "farci au ris," must be a tempting and tender bonne-bouche to these river gourmands. Horrific legends such as the above, together with a great deal of valuable advice on the subject, were quite thrown away upon me; for 90 degrees of Fahrenheit, and the enticing blueness of the water, generally betrayed me into a plunge every evening during my Gangetic voyage.

On the following day his Excellency received the visit

of the Nawaub Shums-ood-Doulah, the only native of rank now resident at Dacca. He was, in times past, in some measure, implicated with Vizier Ali in his treacherous massacre of the English at Benares; and vegetated, in consequence, for many years in the prisons of Calcutta, where he made himself master of the English language, and picked up a respectable smattering of English history and literature. He is now a pensioner of the Company, and still retains some of the insignia of royalty about his court and person.

His Highness—for such is by courtesy his title—is about 60 years of age, of middling stature, with a remarkably fair complexion, and an intelligent and amiable expression of countenance. He was dressed simply yet handsomely, and his silver white hair appeared in short elaborate curls from under his muslin turban. His steps were supported by a thick walking-staff—by which he seemed to set great store—formed of an entire piece of ivory: I have since seen just such another depending from the kid-covered little finger of an Almack's beau.

It is said that Bishop Heber—of whose Journal I have not yet been able to obtain a perusal—has spoken somewhat slightingly of his Highness's royal insignificance; and I was informed that the Nawaub, on hearing that the work was in the possession of a gentleman at Dacca, expressed a wish to read it. The gentleman, willing to spare his feelings, made excuses; but the Nawaub persisted, and was, on turning to that part where himself is spoken of, extremely irate at what he called the ingratitude of Heber, who—as he said in a remonstrative article which he put into the Calcutta newspapers—had requited his attention with ridicule and detraction, or words to that effect.*

March 13th.—A chasse having been previously organized,

* I have, since writing the above, of course found opportunities of reading the lamented Bishop's interesting Journal; and I think that the handsome manner in which the Nawaub's character and acquirements are spoken of ought amply to counterbalance any reflections of the author on his Highness's assumption or retention of royal pomp.

a party of sportsmen started in buggies at 4 A.M. for a point of rendezvous 8 miles from Dacca. After due preparation we entered the jungle, which was in general exceedingly high and thick, with a line of no less than 60 elephants, the most numerous assembly of these animals that I have ever seen convened on a sporting occasion. Those who have witnessed and appreciated the brave show that 30 couple of *hounds* exhibit at the cover side may imagine the enthusiasm with which I reviewed this gallant pack as they, at the word of command, quitted the road and crashed through the yielding jungle. We had 3 hours' very good sport, though the bag was disgracefully disproportionate to the vast expenditure of powder and shot. Two enormous elks, a couple of hogs, several deer, and a few heads of small game were carried home. I shot a curious little animal, in appearance something between a hare and a guinea-pig, of a deep brown colour, and less speedy in its paces than the hare. On picking it up I was surprised, and rather gratified, to find that I had killed it with a bullet, having fired the wrong barrel by mistake. A party of guallahs, or cowherds, had led us, by their reports, to hope for a tiger and some wild buffaloes; but we discovered nothing of them but their footmarks. The weather is at this season not sufficiently sultry to force these animals to the plains in search of water, nevertheless the thermometer rose to 95° this evening in my boat. Later in the year the sporting club of Dacca make very successful expeditions into the neighbouring jungles, residing for two or three days at a time in convenient shooting bungalows established for that purpose.

The afternoon was devoted to returning the visit of the Nawaub, who sent his English carriage (of which he is extremely proud) to convey Lord Combermere to his palace. This vehicle is something in the Lord Mayor's style as to ornaments and painting, and is drawn by 4 dun horses, and followed by as many royally-rigged outriders. It was given to him by the British Government as an acknowledgment for his liberal present of eight fine elephants, which he made to them at the epoch of the Ava war, when these animals were in great request, and were purchased up at ruinous prices. At the conclusion of his Highness's levee the Head-quarters party dined with the military of the station, and the repast was followed by a quadrille party. At 2 in the morning I closed a day which had commenced with me at 3 A.M.

CHAPTER X.

The voyage continued — The Burrampooter — Voyage towards Calcutta — Re-enter the Ganges — Quit the Ganges — A north-wester — Lal-Chittee-ka-Bazaar — Delta of the Ganges — Ballisore river — Enter the Sunderbunds — Culna — The Cherruck Poojah — Scenery of the Sunderbunds — A sporting stroll — Calcutta — Leave Calcutta — Budge-Budge — Kedgeree — Sauger isle — Sea voyage to Pooree — Bay of Bengal — Return to Calcutta — Fresh departure for Pooree — Roop-Narain river — Tumlook — Midnapore — Dâk journey — Dantoon — Balasore — Barrepore — Cuttack — Night journey.

March 14*th*.—AT daylight the reveillie drum raised the yawning dândies from their hard couches on the decks of the budgerows; the maungees' shrill voices summoned them to exertion; their loins were quickly girded, their long elf-locks thrust back behind their ears; the awning, spread over them as a protection against the night dews, was speedily furled, and in 10 minutes the Head-quarters fleet was again under weigh, and proceeding in a body down the river.

The next morning we entered the Burrampooter river, which assumes, at this stage of its course, the name of Megna. At the point where this noble stream received us its width must be equal to that of the lake of Geneva;—would that the temperature of the atmosphere would bear a like comparison! What would I not give at this moment for one hour of the fresh breezes from the Jura, to mitigate the fury of Fahrenheit's 95°! I would even compound for a gust or two of the Bise, tant redoutée, by way of variety.

The vessels sailing along the opposite shore appeared hull-down, and the tops of the trees alone gave evidence of the land. The Burrampooter or Bhramapootra,—whichever name it rejoices in,—although it cannot boast the sanctity of the Ganges, must be acknowledged to be the first river of India. It is supposed to derive its source—like the Rhine and Rhone—from the same group of snowy mountains as the Ganges: after making a sweeping course of upwards of 1600 miles, it again approaches its sacred sister, and the twin rivers pour forth, at the same point, their munificent tribute to the Bay of Bengal.

We had not sailed many miles on the Megna ere the fleet separated into two squadrons. The officers destined to accompany the Commander-in-Chief to Chittagong, having provided themselves at Dacca with pinnaces, as being more seaworthy than the keelless budgerows, continued their descent of the river; whilst the division bound to Calcutta by the Sunderbunds—to which I had the honour to belong—dropped astern, and brought-to at the mouth of a small creek uniting the Megna and Ganges; where we were constrained to wait four hours before the tide had rendered the communication available. A six hours' row brought us to the extremity of the creek, and the boats were luggowed for the night at the point where it joins the Ganges. I took a ramble as usual in search of a "second course," and brought home rather an unusual medley. Let not my reader suspect me of shooting with a long bow, nor of an attempt to classify him with the last-named bird in my list of the slain, when I tell him that, in nine shots, I killed four couple of snipe, three pigeons, one eagle, two nameless birds of the duck tribe, a water-snake, and one gull. The snipes all fell to the first discharge of my two barrels. I fired at two of these birds as they were boring in the mud at the brink of a thin sedge; and a flight of some score immediately sprung from the marsh to receive my second shot. The first had killed six birds, four of which were invisible when I fired.

Early the following morning we were once more floating

on the stream of the Ganges, whom we found much increased in bulk since we took leave of her ten days ago. The goddess river has some cause to complain of our inconstancy, for after having ploughed her broad translucent bosom for three or four hours we again deserted her in favour of a little minx of a rivulet, one of her collateral relations, who seduced us into a hundred scrapes with her shoals, sand-banks, and lee shores.

Too close an acquaintance with the banks of these inlets, some of which are 20 feet high and formed of ill-cemented sand, may be attended with serious consequences. It is common to see huge masses of the superimminent earth, sapped by the agitated water, detach themselves from the bank and plunge into the stream with a force which if brought to bear on the deck of a vessel, would infallibly swamp it.

The next day we fell in with a fine stiff breeze, favourable to us in the greater part of our numerous meanderings; though on some occasions, so tortuous was our course, that it blew right in our teeth.

In some of the serpentinings of the stream the fastest of the budgerows, which were a mile a-head of me in distance by water, showed their gay pennants over the low land on my flank, and were only divided from me by 20 paces of sand; and whilst *my* boat was tracked with difficulty against the fierce wind, the same breeze was propelling my precursors at the rate of 8 knots.

In the afternoon the east wind slunk away before a black phalanx of clouds which suddenly invaded the heavens from an opposite quarter; a sultry and almost stifling interval succeeded; a peculiar odour from the surrounding jungles hung upon the languid air; and every symptom betokened a north-wester. Whilst we deprecated its approach for the sake of our friends, who would have to buffet it in the perilous mouths of the Megna, we could scarce refrain from praying for its cooling influence upon our own land-locked detachment. We had just leisure to make our craft hard and fast by double moorings to the shore, near the village of Burrasal, when the hurricane reached us. It was accompanied by violent rain and thunder and lightning; and in a quarter of an hour it had passed on, leaving us nearly 20° cooler from its visit. The storm brought with it numerous flights of golden plover from the morasses; and the earth teemed with reptiles, tempted from their lurking-places by the inviting shower. In my ramble I killed three couple of these plover, which have the game plumage, and almost the game flavour, of the woodcock. I also shot two snakes, one of which, a cobra di capella, I cut in two in the act of flying at my spaniel, which had disturbed him. The whole reptile and insect world seemed to hold high carnival; the frogs and crickets were perfectly stunning in their exultation; the cockroaches rushed from their retreats, and revelled about my cabin; and swarms of grasshoppers, dragon-flies, and beetles, attracted by the light, almost extinguished the flame that had fascinated them. Whilst dressing for dinner I slew a centipede more than half a foot long, as it was crawling along the wainscot, unfortunately disqualifying it for the spirit-phial, by decapitating it with a paper-cutter, the weapon that I availed myself of in my haste.

March 18th.—The toofaun of yesterday has but half done its work, for the atmosphere has again relapsed into its fever; nor can we for some time expect a repetition of that healing tempest, providentially ordained to pay periodical visits during the hot season, and sweep from the narrow streets of Indian cities, and the tangled marshes of Indian jungles, the infectious diseases and baneful malaria which are therein generated.

At noon we passed a long, straggling, and thoroughly Bengalee wigwam, which the natives called Lal-Chittee-ka-Bazaar. The houses were all formed simply of mats, thatch, palmyra-leaves, and bamboos, but the inhabitants were swarming, like bees, on the shore, and all wore a busy and a thriving air. The hamlet was backed up by a thick curtain of cocoa-trees, palmyras, and plantains, and a long line of timber-stacks indicated the chief staple of its commerce.

Hundreds of boats lay along the shore freighted with wood and grain; many of the larger craft, fine teak-built vessels, were Birmese; and their crews, with their coarse flat features and massive muscular limbs, contrasted strongly with the light, supple, and graceful figures of the Bengalees. We afterwards met one of these huge boats coming up the river. It stood at least 10 feet out of the water, and was propelled by 40 long oars, pulled by men in a standing position. They kept time with the greatest precision, though the measure, two short strokes succeeded by two long ones, appeared rather difficult. The rowers were in full chorus as we passed them.

The nameless creek on which this bazaar is established is, I should judge, at least as wide as the Thames at Windsor; and 100 such streams intersect the Great Delta of the Ganges, rendering roads almost useless.

Although this portion of Bengal is so subject to inundations, and so replete with miasma-fostering jungles, the inhabitants did not strike me as being less healthful than their more northern brethren. Elephantiasis is indeed here more common, but this frightful disease does not disqualify the patient for bodily labour.

To the mind of the traveller journeying from the north there is something remarkably pleasing in the peaceful and almost Utopian constitution of the Bengalee community, as compared with the more warlike character of the tribes he has just left behind. In the upper provinces, in general, the soldier is blended so intimately with the cultivator, that he who guides the plough and casts the seed wears a shield on his shoulder, and at his side a sword which he may have to wield in defence of his harvest. War mixes not with the dreams, nor weapons with the dress, of the purely pastoral Bengalee. He is placid, contented, and unambitious — apathetic and selfish if you please — and must truly and gratefully appreciate that change of government which allows him to eat his bread and worship his gods without fear of invasion from Mussulman or Mahratta, or the rapacity of those predatory hordes whom the British monopoly of power has swept from the face of India.

The next day, after losing some hours by lying-to for the ebb-tide, and redeeming the lost time by stealing "a few hours from the night," thereby enjoying a delightful moonlight sail, we luggowed on the bank of the Ballisore river, a large stream running hence direct to the sea. This we soon deserted; and on the 21st, at 11 a.m., our fleet brought-to at Culna, where it is customary for Calcutta-bound boats to take in anchors and fresh water—all the creeks to the southward being brackish. The anchors, which are strange clumsy machines of bamboos weighted with stones and bound with cocoa ropes, are required at this stage of our voyage by reason of the risk attendant upon the usual system of luggowing, from the tigers which infest the jungles bordering the streams. During the passage of the Sunderbunds (beautiful forests), to which Culna may be said to be the northern entrance, the dândies, having Major Munro's fate before their eyes, can rarely go ashore to cook their evening meal; the budgerows casting anchor in the middle of the stream, where the luxurious traveller may lounge securely, smoke his moonlight chillum, and listen to the roars of the prowling tigers. At this hour, when all nature sleeps, every leaf is at rest, and no harsher sound than the gentle rippling of the water round the prow of the boat disturbs the soft silence of an Indian night, there is something peculiarly awful and startling in the sudden, short, furious, and perhaps near-at-hand voice of the jungle tyrant, whose yellow skin and glaring eyes may sometimes be distinguished through the imperfect light, as he hungrily surveys the floating ark, whose tenants, though barely a dozen paces from his station, are safe from his attacks.

Near this spot, two years ago, on the return of Head-quarters from the siege of Bhurtpore, two boatmen, belonging to an office budgerow, who had rashly determined on the enjoyment of a meal ashore, were themselves made a meal of, ere they had leisure to complete their own.

On this same occasion, during our sojourn of 24 hours at Culna, we had a capital opportunity of witnessing that ingenious religious ceremony of the Hindoos, styled Cherruck Poojah. The spot chosen for the spectacle was a clear space, surrounded by a close screen of lofty and luxuriant foliage, on the outskirts of one of those secluded jungle-hamlets, peculiar to Bengal, whose retired situation, indicated only by a labyrinthian path, the rambling stranger stumbles upon by chance alone, scarcely discovering that he has run his prying nose into a cluster of habitations, until warned of his intrusion by the scuttling flight of a covey of women and children. In the centre of this clearing stood a wooden edifice, some 60 feet high, in appearance something like a quadruple gibbet; the four arms being made to revolve round the centre pole by means of a capstan below. It was as frightful an object as a dentist's chair to the schoolboy with three rows of teeth: four votaries were allowed the advantage of hanging at the same moment. An eminent member of the Medical Board was present with us, and the Brahmins willingly allowed him to witness the mode of placing the hooks. A pair of these terrific-looking weapons were affixed to the end of stout ropes, sheaved through the extremities of the several limbs of the machine; and, after some preparation which I was too late to see, were thrust under the muscles low down on each shoulder-blade of the highly-privileged swingers—linen girths to support some portion of the body's weight being supplied. At a given signal the four performers were nimbly run up to the height of 20 or 30 feet from the ground; when the ropes were belayed, and the capstan was set agoing with right good will, the tortured votaries swinging round with frightful velocity, amid the crash of drums and fiddles, and the cheering acclamations of the assembled crowds. In this fashion did they continue to whirl in mid-air for 10 minutes; their countenances indicating sternly-repressed agony, their hands in the attitude of prayer, and their long hair streaming in the wind. They were then obliged to vacate their merry-go-round to other candidates. Those who have witnessed this cruel penance will allow that the Bengalee has *some* species of courage, an attribute not generally accorded them by English opinion.

During our short and necessary stay at Culna a steamboat, bound to Dacca, ran past the place, defying wind and tide. It is the second that has ever navigated these streams; yet so perfect is the apathy and indifference of the Bengalee to everything that does not immediately concern himself, that the novel sight scarcely excited a symptom of curiosity. Even the better informed natives of Calcutta, where steamers have been common for the last year or two, have never given themselves the trouble to make themselves acquainted with the powers and principle of the vessel; but persevere in styling it the "Dhoorkee-Jehaze," smoke-ship, or "Ag-kee-Jehaze," fire-ship.

22nd.—A fair store of fruit, kids, anchors, and water-vessels, having been stowed on board, we quitted Culna, and resumed our voyage towards Calcutta, distant 7 days' sail. During the greater part of the day we were rowing along a very narrow but exceedingly deep creek, whose banks were so thickly overhung with tangled brushwood, interwoven with the creeping rattan, that it was impossible to go ashore, an enjoyment I felt sorely tempted to indulge in, despite the tigers, in order to escape during the cooler hours from my oven-like budgerow, which in the daytime becomes so thoroughly heated by the sun, that even in the evening it is almost untenable. Thermometer, 5 P.M., 94°.

Nothing can exceed the luxuriant richness of the Sunderbund vegetation. How plentiful must be the dews, which, unassisted by one drop of rain, can for months counteract the parching power of such a sun as now burns above our heads! In the clearer portions of the forest the natural vistas, produced by the numerous clumps of trees dotted over the verdant plain, give so park-like an appearance to the prospect, that one almost expects at the next turn to catch sight of the owner's splendid mansion. Whilst the eye is feasted by the infinite variety of tints in the foliage of the groves and banks, the scent is regaled almost to surfeiting with the spicy breezes which float through the atmosphere, loaded with sweets from the surrounding forests. The woods are chiefly formed of the feathering bamboo, the noble tamarind, with its vivid green and refreshing fruit; the cocoa-nut, palmyra, plantain, areeka or betel-tree, and the cotton-tree, which at this season is devoid of leaves, and brilliantly clothed with crimson tulip-shaped flowers. The thar, or palm-date, from whose stem the exhilarating toddy is extracted, must not be forgotten: the liquor exuding before sunrise is a delightful and innocent beverage, and only gains its intoxicating qualities by being allowed to ferment in the heat of the day. In the latter state, and even rendered still more fiery by the infusion of chillies, it is drunk in great quantities by the English soldiers; and many a liver-complaint, laid to the charge of an Indian climate, in fact owes its origin to this lava-like potation. It is, moreover, so unluckily cheap, that a regular hard-going, dram-drinking campaigner may get dead drunk for the value of a penny.

The following morning—whilst the fleet was performing a wide circuit—three of our party took advantage of a tract of country partially cleared and inhabited to enjoy a good long ramble with our dogs and guns. We mustered a mixed pack of 27 dogs, 17 of them being greyhounds, and made desperate havoc among the jackals and foxes abounding in these regions, and the only wild beasts we met with during our walk. We passed several small portions of cultivated land, which, by the encouragement of government, have been reclaimed from utter waste by small parties of wood-cutters and salt-manufacturers, who are bold enough to dispute possession with the aboriginal inhabitants, the tigers. In the swamps our dogs put up great quantities of remarkably fine snipe; and I soon found myself wading after them, though my enjoyment of the sport was somewhat damped by the recollection of the possibility of myself being made game of by the tigers.

It was near this spot, two years ago, that, whilst following the edge of the river in pursuit of wild-fowl, I was arrested by the loud barking of my terrier—the identical Hector whose fate I have recorded at the commencement of this journal—and on running to the spot, discovered him up to his chin in the mud of the tide-deserted creek, and baying at some object under the hollow bank. I had just time to take post on a little promontory of sward, when a young alligator, of the short-headed or cannibal species, rushed from under the cavity, and made towards the water, literally ventre à terre. At the distance of five paces I delivered my two barrels of shot, one of which, breaking through the soft scales behind the elbow of the animal, killed him on the spot. His length did not exceed six or seven feet.

This and such-like personal anecdotes are, it must be admitted, trifling and egotistical; yet I make no apologies for introducing them: for glimpses of a distant country are often as well afforded to the reader by incidental trifles as by more laboured details; and egotism is necessarily the very essence of a journal.

During the next three days we made good progress; passing Muckterpore — marked on Kingsbury's map — on the 24th; and winding through the serpentines of the Attara Banka on the 26th—thermometer ranging as high as 97° in our cabins. Early on the morning of the *27th March* we found ourselves within eight miles of Calcutta, tightly wedged among the thousands of salt and timber boats which constantly throng the busy channel of Tully's Nullah—a narrow creek running into the Hooghly, half a mile south of Fort William. One tide brought us up to Kidderpore bridge, where an equipage awaited me, and I was soon among the white walls of the City of Palaces, and comfortably installed in apartments in the newly-organized Bengal club.

I sojourned a fortnight in Calcutta, during which time the gay inhabitants, flattering themselves that a remnant of the cool season was still in their possession, were feasting, fiddling, and dancing, in spite of Fahrenheit's warning finger pointing to 90°.

On the 12*th April* two brethren of the Staff and myself put ourselves, servants, and baggage on board the 'Planet' buoy-vessel, of 180 tons, destined—it will be seen how successfully—to convey us to Head-quarters, now convened at Pooree Juggernaut. With the south-west monsoon blowing briskly, our marine prospects were not very cheering, our exit from the river, the treacherous Hooghly, being wholly dependent upon the tides. By mid-day we had commenced that unsatisfactory mode of locomotion styled "dropping down;" and at 3 P.M. our misfortunes—of which we were fated to encounter a series—began by the vessel's running aground at a turn in the stream scarcely out of sight of Calcutta; where, after sundry edifying but futile efforts at extrication, we were constrained to exercise our patience until the next ebb tide, which occurred at 11 o'clock the following morning; the pilot, in the mean time, consoling us with the assurance that, as he knew of no shoal at our "sticking-place," we must have run upon a sunken vessel.

On the evening of the second day we had only reached Budge-Budge—a village whose very name seemed to mock our fruitless attempts at further progress,—where we anchored for the night. On this point there are the remains of an old fortress, which was in 1756 besieged and breached in due form by an English naval and military force. Few instances are recorded of a regularly-appointed fort succumbing to the prowess of a single individual; yet such was the fall of Budge-Budge. During the night preceding the intended assault, a British sailor, prompted by the united influence of Mars and Bacchus, approached the work, staggered up the breach, and fired his pistol among the gallant defenders of this Indian Saragossa, whose terrors, magnifying, or rather multiplying, the solitary tar into a countless storming party, induced them hastily to evacuate the place, leaving Jack to chew the quid of astonishment at the success of his exploit!

The next day—after meeting a steam-vessel which gave us the intelligence of the Commander-in-Chief's arrival at Pooree—we accomplished the passage of the dangerous shoal of the "James and Mary," whereon were grounded two large ships, the 'Exmouth' and the 'Jehangire,' which were obliged the next day to return to Calcutta—although outward bound—to repair damages.

On the 16*th* we anchored opposite Kedgeree, 52 miles from Calcutta, the station of a solitary English officer, whose duty consists in despatching daily shipping news to the capital. The river is, at this point, nearly nine miles across; the country low, marshy, and particularly unhealthy.

In the afternoon of the following day we anchored in Sauger Roads, at the mouth of the Hooghly. The island of Sauger, in spite of the efforts made to reclaim it, is still a most desolate jungle; and vegetation is there so rapid as to defy all chances of effectually clearing it. Sauger is famous for the size and ferocity of its tigers; and it was on its shores that Major Munro, of menagerie memory, was carried off by one of these animals. They owe their impunity from the sportsmen of Calcutta to their island position alone, which precludes the introduction of elephants.

18*th*.—During the whole of this day the wind blew furiously and constantly from the south-west. At 5 P.M. we met a pilot-vessel towing home a buoy which had parted from its moorings; and during the night we sailed past the "Floating Light," and got into blue water.

The next day we made but little way, and during the night the breeze freshened to a gale. Our little craft pitched and rolled violently, and shipped a good deal of water. The state of our native servants, particularly the Hindoos—who had stretched a point in embarking with us—was most pitiable; their excessive sickness being aggravated by their religion exacting that, whilst on board ship, they should feed on dry uncooked food alone. The Mussulmans suffered less, their more sensible creed imposing no such mortifying restrictions on the appetite.

On the *20th*, after remaining a few hours under sail, during which we lost rather than gained anything a-head, the pilot again dropped anchor, and we rode out the gale with 100 fathoms of cable, in 20 fathoms water. The morn broke with evil auspices unabated, the monsoon raging in our teeth, our servants groaning at their hitherto unknown torments, and ourselves, if not sea-sick,—for we were all good sailors,—at least sick of the sea. At noon our observations proved that we were within sixty miles of our destination, but with as little prospect of attaining it as though the distance had been as many thousand leagues. There was a very heavy sea running all day, and we were again doomed to pass the greater part of it at anchor. At length the pilot commanding approached me with a length of visage indicative of a catastrophe. The vessel, he said, was driving, and dragging her best bower. Another anchor was dropped, and the serang, or native boatswain, on going below to "*give her cable*," discovered and reported that the good brig 'Planet'—alas! that my fortunes should be influenced even for a week by so inauspicious a star!—had three feet water in the hold. She had got a strain, as the commander assured me, by carrying so great a press of sail on a wind in a heavy sea; a piece of information which I paid little attention to, as I had already made up my mind, first, that the leak arose from a huge rib of the sunken vessel, before mentioned, having pierced her bottom; secondly, that the aforesaid timber was manifestly and gradually deserting its position; and, thirdly, that we enjoyed a fair prospect of being swamped. The pumps were, however, set a-going, and of the two alternatives, Davy's locker or a run before the wind to Calcutta, we selected the latter. The roaring concert of the sea and winds; the constant jarring of the pumps; and the five hours' Allah-ing! of the lascars, requisite to heave up two anchors with 90 fathoms of cable each, left us but little disposition for sleep.

On the morning of the *2nd* the Planet's head was turned towards Calcutta, and on the same evening we anchored once more at Kedgeree. The next morning, favoured by wind and tide, we ran up the river at the rate of 15 knots an hour; at 3 p.m. we reached Fort William, and—after a fruitless sail of 12 days—

> " . . . . . . where we had got up,
> We did again get down!"

To counterbalance in some degree our many contretems, we found that we had just arrived in time for the grand ball to be given at Government House, in celebration of his Majesty's birthday; where I found the pastime of gliding through a punkah-fanned quadrille with a gentle partner infinitely more to my taste than cutting capers on the stormy waves with the romping, rickety 'Planet,' in whose dangerous society I was very nearly performing a pas de trop.

Having been thus unforeseenly thrust back upon the Presidency, we remained there another fortnight; when, Government having refused our application for a steam-passage to Pooree, we determined to travel dâk to Head-quarters.

Accordingly, on the *6th* of May—our palankeens and patarras having been sent on two days before—a brother A.D.C. and myself once more started for our destination on the sea-coast. We travelled as far as Diamond Harbour in a gig (the vehicle, not the boat, so called); where we embarked on board a beauliah, crossed the harbour, entered the Roop-narain river; and after a prosperous sail of five hours reached the town of Tumlook. I did not survey the turbid waters of the above dangerous river with any very great complacency of retrospect, as they were associated with a disagreeable accident which occurred to me whilst sailing on them two years ago. I was making a little trip for change of air—not for change of elements—when, heedlessly standing on the taffrail whilst the boat was tacking, I was knocked overboard by the boom. The stream was swollen into a fierce torrent by the rains; uprooted trees, drowned cattle, and even an elephant, carried away by the inundation, floated past our vessel. However, a better fate than drowning doubtless awaits me; for being lightly clothed, and a practised swimmer, and the boat being in stays, I reached a rope in a few strokes, and was hauled on board—none the worse for a knock on the head, and an involuntary bath.

During the two days we were detained at Tumlook by the non-arrival of our baggage we were hospitably entertained by Mr. Lindsay, the salt agent, who has formed a little Eden here in the midst of the desert. Time did not hang heavy on our hands in a house were there was a well-stocked library, a billiard-table, mechanic and chemical laboratories, musical instruments of great variety, from the church organ to the Geneva snuff-box (not to forget the musical glasses, upon which our host showed great skill), good cheer, and a hearty welcome. The above pursuits, with a taste for botany, horticulture, and entomology, must be efficient weapons against the ennui which, without these allies, would inevitably overwhelm him, in this unhealthy station, where there are only two Europeans besides himself, and in an office whose details are neither interesting nor laborious. Mr. Lindsay's house is surrounded by a beautiful and scientifically-kept garden; and is situated upon a slight eminence, whose formal declivity, giving evidence of the remains of fortifications, goes far to strengthen the supposition entertained of the great antiquity of Tumlook.

May 7th.—The weather having become distressingly sultry, we came to the determination to travel by night only—passing the heat of the day either at the stage bungalows on the roadside, or with some resident at the stations. I believe I have said before that in India it is the universal and benevolent custom to entertain strangers travelling through a country where shelter and supplies are alike difficult to be obtained.

At 10 p.m.—for not sooner would our kindly host permit

us to leave his roof—we got into our palankeens, and, borne along by the fastest and most musical bearers that I had ever met with in the course of my Indian posting, reached Midnapore by the following morning at 9 o'clock: I was only once dropped on the way—which, considering the vileness of the roads, was excusable. This occurrence, in addition to the probable fracture of the carriage, administers to the dozing traveller a shock nowise inferior to that produced by 20 turns of the electric cylinder. It does not, however, often happen; for when it befalls choleric travellers—a race of beings rife in hot climates—it is apt to produce a reaction upon the backs of the offending bearers, pour encourager les autres—a consequence greatly productive of caution, and preventive of future stumbling. The *prudent* tourist will, however, keep his temper and his cane in subjection, and content himself with a verbal warning, or threats of loss of buckshees; for on the first symptoms of vapulative intentions (we hope they are rarely resorted to!) on the part of the Sahib, the timid bearers are not unlikely to take to their heels, and leave their posed employer to cool his own in the middle of an unfrequented road, under a temperature even more fiery than his temper.

A few miles short of Midnapore we encountered a hurkarah bearing a note of invitation from Mr. D'Oyly, the collector of revenue of the district; in whose mansion we accordingly passed the remainder of the day. The station of Midnapore is one of the most picturesque in India: the civilians' houses are surrounded with spacious parks, or enclosures, ornamented with fine trees; the roads are, from the nature of the soil, remarkably good, and shaded by luxuriant avenues of the teak-tree. A very large portion of the district is covered with thick bush jungle, where the sportsmen not unfrequently find the bear and the leopard. In the town, and, indeed, throughout the district of Midnapore, a great superiority in the conformation of the dwelling-houses of the natives is remarkable; yet in religious edifices—those tasteful acces-

Dâk Travelling

sories to Indian scenery—they fall far short of their northern neighbours.

At 11 at night, after a very merry dinner party, we once more took to our palankeens, declining to admit as fellow-passengers half-a-dozen bottles of champagne, warmly pressed upon us by a certain reverend and mercurial guest of Mr. D'Oyly. The night-journey was accomplished without accident or incident worthy of recital, except, indeed, that I was on one occasion suddenly and startlingly awakened from a doze by the report of a pistol (as I thought) fired close to my ear. I sat up and listened, and my only half-roused senses were perhaps still more alarmed by a sharp hissing sound, like the angry sibillations of the cobra-di-capella, proceeding from behind my pillow! Hastily calling for a torch, I threw aside the cushion, and the first object I beheld was the frothy, foaming mouth of —a bottle of champagne! which, surreptitiously introduced by the above-mentioned kindly clerico, and irritated by the jolting of the palankeen, had thus prematurely ejected its cork. Taking certain obvious measures to preclude a second explosion, I re-corked the intruder, and slept again: a confederate was next morning discovered, in the same suspicious position, in my companion's palankeen.

At 9 A.M. on the 9th we reached the lonely stage bungalow of Dantoon, a rickety and uncomfortable building situated on the brink of a tank. It was with great difficulty that we obtained some milk and eggs for breakfast, and a vile curry for dinner; but our store of champagne, which I was at some pains to cool, made amends for the bad cheer. Soon after sunset our equipages came to the door; our impatient *blacks* pawed the ground, and another night's run of 40 miles brought us to the station of Balasore, where we were immediately invited to share the hospitality of Colonel D'Aguilar, commanding a regiment of local infantry at this place. Balasore, being only 6 miles from the sea, benefits in some degree from its refreshing breezes; and the eye, accustomed to the unvarying flatness of Bengal scenery, is agreeably relieved by the view of a fine range of mountains, only 7 miles to the west of the town, and stretching southwards in the direction of Madras. The station is now inconsiderable; but when first the commerce between Europe and India was opened, this place was considered a seaport of great value. There are, even now, extant the ruins of factories belonging to the English, French, Danish, and Dutch nations; and in the bazaar stands to this day a small Portuguese Roman Catholic chapel.

Balasore was ceded to the Company by the Mahrattas in 1803. I cannot furnish much information regarding the present state of its commerce—although, by-the-bye, I exported from it, myself, a considerable pigeon-pie and a good store of pale ale, the parting presents of our hearty host.

May 11th.—At 9 A.M. we reached the stage-house of Barrepore, after a fatiguing journey of 15 hours. The latter portion of the country through which we passed was very wild-looking, and bears a bad character as to the highway honesty of its inhabitants. Accordingly, at every change of the bearers, I made some display of priming my pistols, —weapons for which the natives entertain a high respect —and nothing beyond the above demonstration proved necessary.

Our hotel—for hotel read hovel—of this day was in such a dilapidated condition, that we were almost afraid of talking loud, lest we should bring down the tottering and semi-transparent roof upon our heads. The old resident Hindoo, who fulfilled the offices of bearer, kitmutgar, and cook, was of a piece with the building: those who have travelled that road will recollect the tall, emaciated figure, with his long arms and legs so bent at the joints as to give him the appearance of an overgrown grasshopper. The pigeon-pie proved a friend in need, for a half-starved fowl "was all the store" that our foraging party could levy for us.

Starting, as usual, about sunset, we journeyed forward, and arrived at the town and station of Cuttack by breakfast-time the next morning. As I shall have another opportunity of describing this place, I shall now be content with saying that we took refuge, during the heat of the day, with Mr. Stockwell, the Commissioner for the Cuttack district, who occupies the handsome Government house; and as soon as the fiery chariot of the "nimium propinqui solis" had turned the corner of the horizon, we minions of the moon resumed our equipages and our march. The road from Cuttack to Pooree-Juggernauth, conducting through a tract greatly liable to inundation, is raised upon a bund, or embankment, nearly the whole distance of 52 miles, and for a considerable extent is shaded by fine old trees. In its construction the British government benefited by the handsome contribution of 16,000*l.* presented for that purpose by a certain pious Hindoo of rank in Calcutta.

During the night we encountered a north-wester, accompanied, as usual, with violent thunder and rain, which latter beat with such violence against the doors of our palankeens, that it was in vain to deny it admittance, and we were well wetted before its attacks ceased. The torches too were extinguished, and the road rendered dangerously slippery; yet the patient bearers, exhorting each other in their chorus, persevered, and, by strenuous exertion, brought us safely to Pooree, which is 311 miles from Calcutta, by 7 o'clock on the morning of the 13th of May.

CHAPTER XI.

Pooree-Juggernauth — Fakirs — Sands of Pooree — Temples of Pooree — Surf-boats — Pastimes — Luxuries — Sports — A tiger-trap — Temple of Juggernauth — Pilgrims — Religious ceremony — The Rath-Jattra — The pilgrim-tax — The Suttee — Hindoo funeral rites — Nocturnal bathing — Trip to the Black Pagoda — Sing Durwasu, or Lion Gate — The antechamber — The Black Pagoda, or Temple of the Sun — Its origin — Return to Pooree — Journey to Calcutta — Cuttack — The Oorias — Fort of Barabati — Gymnastics — Black penitents — The Rath-Jattra — Garden Reach — A day in Calcutta — Arrival of the Pallas.

AT the distance of 5 miles from the town the traveller first catches sight of the far-famed temple of Juggernauth, rising with its ill-proportioned and ungainly tower above the ancient and luxuriant trees; and at the same time, if the wind be favourable, the angry lashing of the surf on the beach comes upon his ear. The town and bazaar are pretty extensive—containing between 5000 and 6000 houses; and the main street, 100 yards in width, and constituted chiefly of the habitations of the ministers of the temple, leads directly up to that stupendous building.

Passing through the town I observed several fine tanks, in which crowds of men, women, and children were bathing —yet one of the bearers assured me that he had often seen large alligators raise their heads above the surface when the weather was sultry. Like other holy places, Juggernauth is infested by those sanctified vagabonds, Fakirs, with the numerous branches of Gossains, Byraghees, Suniassees, &c., into which their important profession ramifies. At every turn, along every dead wall, under each banyan or peepul tree, the naked, squalid, and painted bodies, matted and sunburnt hair, and distorted limbs of this race of Gymnosophists disgust the eye of the traveller; whilst his ear is deafened by their vociferated and often insolent demands for charity. My heart and purse were always alike closed against these chartered mendicants, who reap harvest sufficient from the superstition of their fellow-countrymen.

Immediately below the town the line of vegetation and verdure suddenly ceases, and is succeeded by a huge bank of dazzling sand, extending down to the sea, a distance of about a mile. Along the somewhat elevated crest of this accumulation of arid and barren material is scattered the European colony, consisting of some 15 bungalows and a line of bells of arms for the sepoy detachment. Many of the habitations belong to the English officials at Cuttack, who are in the habit of repairing hither during the very hot weather for change of air. Bad accommodation—difficulty of procuring provisions—(beef of course is, owing to the worshipful nature of the cow, rarely attainable)—a deep and drifting sand, which renders walking impossible and riding an act of cruelty, and which insinuates its tormenting particles into both bed and board—a climate, owing to its situation two degrees nearer the equator, even hotter than Calcutta—all these drawbacks are cheerfully confronted for the counterbalancing advantage of the sea-breeze, which blows fresh and constantly during this monsoon; and is, to lungs accustomed to inhale the jungle-tainted air of Cuttack, refreshing and salubrious in the extreme. Among the sand-hills along the beach are several curious and extensive religious edifices—many of them, from their being surrounded and veiled by strong walls sloping outwards towards the base, bearing the appearance of small fortresses. Within these enclosures there is in some cases an attempt at introducing vegetation, a few stunted shrubs rearing their heads above the parapet. Those temples that are not furnished with walls are for the most part buried up to their domes in drifting sand, which accumulates so rapidly, that the whole station would be swallowed up but for the measures taken to repel its inroads. One of these coast muts, near my bungalow, bears the imposing title of "Duara Swarga," or Gate of Heaven; but the stealthy glimpses, that I sometimes caught through the half-closed entrance, of a horrific group of diabolical idols; the strange, unhallowed noises startling the drowsy ear of night; and the unequal and lurid flashes of light glimmering from within the enclosure when all around was darkness, gave this spot—to Christian senses at least—more the appearance of the Descensus Averni; and "hell," accordingly, was the diametrically contrasting name by which it was familiarly known amongst our party.

The beach of Pooree is most uninteresting; there is not a pebble or shell of any kind to be seen; nor any object worth inspection between the Black Pagoda, 16 miles north of Pooree, and the Chilka lake, as many miles to the southward. In the article of fish, however, the coast abounds, no less than 61 species having been enumerated. Mullets, whiting, oysters, lobsters, and crabs are to be had for the gathering; but they are not to be compared to their namesakes in England.

The surf breaks with such violence on this shore during the monsoon, that no European boat could live for an instant amongst its curling breakers—communication with ships from the shore being carried on, as at Madras, by the native surf-boats. Of these there are two kinds, the mussoola, and the catamaran. The former is deep, spacious, and extremely light, not a particle of iron being used in its construction: the planks are sewed together with thongs, and the sides, though tough, are so elastic, that they yield visibly when struck by a sea. The catamaran, which is not calculated to carry anything but the amphibious being who guides it, is a sort of raft, formed merely of three long timbers rudely bound together with ropes.

Ships bound to Calcutta make a point of sighting the Black Pagoda, or the temple of Juggernauth, which form convenient and lasting landmarks. Thus, as residents in the neighbourhood of a high road extract amusement and interest from the coaches and other equipages daily passing in review, so do the inhabitants of Pooree in like manner make the appearance of a ship in the roads an important epoch in the monotony of their existence. Proud is the fortunate man who first detects the sail in the distant offing; and prouder still, as well as richer, is he who, having backed with a bet his opinion as to the number of the stranger's masts, pockets the gold mohur confirmative of the accuracy of his judgment. Many of the passing ships exchange signals with the harbour-master of Pooree, giving their names, and sometimes heads of news from England.

During the pilgrimage of Head-quarters at Juggernauth,—occupying six weeks,—occasional trips to the Chilka lake, the Black Pagoda, or the temple itself, were the almost only occurrences varying the uniform dulness of our daily routine of employments. A matutinal jog through the fathomless sand on a pony, and an evening *ditto* on an elephant, constituted our only exercise. A billiard-table, which might have been mistaken for a model of the Himalaya mountains, was our only recreation; and a dish of oysters our only luxury in a country luxurious par excellence.

At Pooree glass-windows and punkahs are rare exotics; books still rarer; and the scarcity of game, together with the heaviness of the sand, renders the sport of shooting unequal to the labour. A few wild ducks, and still wilder antelopes, were the extent of the spoils obtained in the chase, even by our crafty poaching old Shikkaree, who made nothing of creeping a league or two on all fours in order to obtain the chance of a shot. In the jungles more inland, however, the tiger and leopard roam unmolested by the English sportsmen; but these proscribed animals often fall victims to the ingenuity of the natives, who, on producing the skin of any destructive wild beast, are entitled to a reward from the Collector of the district. One of these daring hunters, who had been unusually successful, brought to Head-quarters, one morning, two tiger-skins and several leopard-skins, the fruits of five weeks' diligence. He carried with him the weapon employed in his "dreadful trade"—more worthy of the epithet than that of the samphire-gatherer, methinks—and exhibited to us the method in which it was used. It was a large cross-bow formed of double bamboo, fitted into a solid stock, and furnished with a long arrow, or rather a short javelin, armed with a barbed point, at the root of which was tied a spongy substance saturated with a poisonous gum. The united strength of the Shikkaree and his assistant, howbeit artfully applied, barely sufficed to draw the string to the lock: this being at length accomplished, the weapon was laid on the ground, and a cord, attached to the trigger and crossing the supposed path of the tiger, was fastened to a peg firmly fixed in the earth in front of the bow. On striking this thread, the arrow was projected with a force that would have carried it half, if not *quite*, through the body of a man; and so virulent is the poison employed, that the archer related that the wounded animal rarely moves a hundred yards from the spot before he drops and dies. In the skins he showed us, the wounds appear generally about the region of the shoulder, which is the most mortal point.*

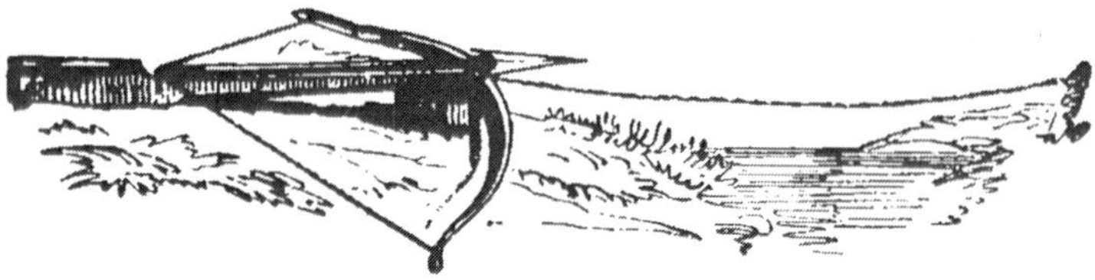

The great temple of Juggernauth—although, at some distance, and particularly from the sea view, it presents an imposing appearance—is, on a closer inspection, neither remarkable for its architecture, nor the materials of which it is composed; the latter being rough stone overlaid with a coating of coarse chunam. The khetr, chief tower, and other minor buildings connected with it, are comprised within a wall surrounding a platform raised high above the ground and no less than 650 feet in length. The height of the tower is 200 feet. According to ancient Brahmanical records preserved in the building, the temple of Sri Jeo, or Juggernauth, existed many centuries before Christ; was destroyed and rebuilt sundry times; and was lastly restored in A.D. 1198, by Rajah Bhim Deo, of Orissa, who is said to have expended nearly 500,000*l.* on the work. Within its holy precincts many inferior deities are provided with lodgings and attendants: but the most revered of the divine occupants are Juggernauth (the Lord of the World), an *alias* of the many-named Vishnu; Buldeo his brother; and their sister, the saffron-coloured Subhadra.

These personages are only twice a year indulged in an airing, which is fortunate, as a team of 1500 men is required

* In the accompanying cut the engraver has erred in giving the appearance of *water* to what was intended by the author to represent the beaten track of the tiger.

to drag each of their carriages. The grand ceremony of the installation of the idol on his triumphal car, styled the Rath Jattra, will take place next month. The usual influx of pilgrims at this epoch is immense: crowds of votaries are already assembled in the town, or are wearily plodding their way towards this Mecca of their hopes; but their numbers decrease yearly, and the sanctity of Juggernauth wanes in proportion to the progress of civilization in India. The mad fanaticism which formerly led hundreds of voluntary victims to immolate themselves beneath the wheels of the idol's car—an offering which is said to extract a ghastly smile of delight from the blood-loving Dagon—is now much sobered down. Sterling mentions that, during the four years in which he witnessed the ceremony, Juggernauth was only propitiated with three sacrifices; and that these wretches, being afflicted with some grievous bodily complaints, merely embraced that method of ridding themselves of a miserable existence, as preferable to the more commonplace suicide of hanging or drowning.

The average number of pilgrims annually resorting to Pooree is said to be about 120,000, many of whom are destined never to return. Thousands of these poor wretches die from famine, over-fatigue during the journey, or from the pernicious climate of the rainy season; and their corpses, thrown on the sands near the English station, are either burnt or left to be devoured by the troops of pariah dogs, jackals, and vultures with which this place, so rich in food for them, swarms. The chaplain of the district assured me that he had himself seen, on the space of half an acre of ground, as many as 150 bodies, with twice as many of the above-named scavengers fighting over their horrid feast,

> "As they lazily mumbled the bones of the dead,
> When they scarcely could rise from the spot where they fed!"

The blood-curdling picture, of which these two lines are only a small part, and which must have been penned by Byron with true zest, I myself saw realized, in all its horrible details, at Bhurtpore; and I think I could have furnished an ingredient that would have given even additional seasoning to the noble poet's already overflowing caldron of horrors. He has, indeed, most vividly portrayed the carnival of the wild dogs, the wolf, and the vulture beneath "the leaguered wall;" but had he, as I have, shudderingly watched the gaunt and famished *swine* rooting and revelling with gory snouts among the "tombless dead," I think he would have devoted a couplet to immortalize *their* deeds!

We had left Pooree before the Rath Jattra took place; but I witnessed some part of the minor and prefatory ceremony of bathing the idols. On hearing that they had been brought out of the temple, and that they were now exhibited to the admiring gaze of the multitude who had travelled so far to pay their respects, I mounted an elephant, and with two or three others of our party repaired to the open marketplace, opposite the platform of the temple. Winning our way carefully through the assembled crowds, we took post in a convenient spot, our exalted situation enabling us to see over the heads of the pedestrian gazers. There is no conveyance through a mob like an elephant; for, although extremely and amiably careful of the lives and limbs of the pigmies surrounding him, his progress is sure and irresistible. What a convenient look-out place one of these animals would make for a general directing the movements of an army; and as a perambulatory hustings, how invaluable would he be to an haranguer of a populace!

Their godships were formed up in line on an elevated terrace within the enclosure, and protected from the night dews by an extensive and gaudy canopy of many-coloured cloths. The evening was dark, and at intervals blue lights were thrown up to enable the spectators to view the ceremony; but the idols being almost constantly hidden by a forest of chowries and hand-punkahs—diligently agitated by the attendant Brahmins to prevent the flies and musquitoes from invading their sacred noses,—we sent a polite message to the Raj-Goru, or chief priest, requesting that he would cause the officials to open out for an instant to the right and left in order to afford us the satisfaction of contemplating the expressive countenances of the worshipful trio. Our embassy succeeded; the crowd fell back from before them; two brilliant lights were illumined, and we saw distinctly three frightful wooden faces, of the respective colours of black, brown, and yellow; the lower portions of the figures being closely swathed in cloth wrappers.

The following day the idols were again consigned to their niches in the temple. Upon this occasion it is the annual custom for Juggernauth to declare himself to be *en petite santé*, from the effects of a severe cold—consequent, probably, upon his bath—which continues to afflict him until the day of the grand ceremony, when, by the wise treatment of his physicians, he is restored to his usual good health!

To such a length as this is carried the blind superstition of this simple people; and carefully is it nourished and fostered by the crafty Brahmins, who doubtless secure to themselves a large share of the offerings paid at the shrine of the idolized but helpless King Log. Many as notorious a *block*-head as friend Juggernauth, however, receives—without the excusing plea of religious superstition—the obsequious homage and adoration of more enlightened idolaters than the unsophisticated Hindoo!

At the festival of the Rath Jattra the idols are conducted in state to visit their country-seat, one mile and a half from Pooree—a journey of *three* days. By all accounts, the method of inducting their worships from the temple to their raths, or cars, is not remarkably ceremonious. Ropes being fastened round their throats, they are dragged "neck-and-heels" down the grand steps, through the mud, and are finally hauled by the same gallows-like process into their respective vehicles, where they are decorated by the priests, and welcomed by shouts of admiration and triumph from the fanatical multitude. The raths on which the monster deities are drawn are of lofty and massive dimensions and clumsy architecture: that of Sri Jeo is nearly 45 feet in height, has a platform of 35 feet square, and moves upon 16 wheels of solid timber.

At first sight it appears even worse than strange and inconsistent, that the same government which encourages the religious endeavours of hundreds of missionaries to convert the Hindoos to the Christian faith, should virtually countenance (as the cavillers against the Company on this much-canvassed point insist that it does) the most revolting idolatry, by making it a source of revenue. It is certain that the E. I. Company, by the pilgrim-tax, secure to themselves an annual average amount of 15,000*l.*; that the collections are made by the Brahmins; and that in return for this extortion—startling fact!—a Christian government agrees to keep in repair, and adorn with silks and broadcloths, a pagan idol; and to support, for the private use of the graven image, a stud of elephants and horses!

The defenders of the system, on the other hand, contend that the interference of the Company is salutary in every respect; that it controls a rapacious and unprincipled priesthood by depriving them of an immense revenue; and that the mode pursued is the one best calculated to bring about the final suppression of the idol. It is, indeed, manifest, that taxation is anything but encouraging to the thing taxed: and it is obvious to every one that open and violent opposition to a rite so firmly rooted in the religious prejudices of the natives might shake the allegiance of our Hindoo sepoys, and thereby involve even the loss of India.

At Pooree, where there is so great a congregation of Brahmins, whose superstition and avarice alike prompt them to uphold the barbarous and inhuman, but to them lucrative custom, it is not surprising that the suttee should flourish. The enactment put forth for its abolition by the English government, supported as it is by the natural love of life and dread of pain so deeply rooted in the bosom of those for whose protection it is ordained, has no doubt materially operated to diminish the number of the sacrifices; yet has it not given so decided a check to the unnatural rite as might have been expected; and heroic widows, perhaps stimulated by the opposition of the higher powers, daily contrive to grill themselves under the very nose of the government which has been so long and so disinterestedly endeavouring to snatch them from the burning.

If, however, disconsolate widows are prevented by one law from going to heaven with their first and, according to Hindoo customs, *sole* husband, it is but just, methinks, that a further edict be framed enabling the willy-nilly surviving lady to take to herself, without consequent loss of caste or character, a second lord, to solace her during her involuntary sojourn in this vale of tears.

During my rambles in India I never chanced to witness

—within distinct eye-range at least—an instance of this savage ritual; though on my passage down the Ganges, a white column of smoke rising above the trees from the burning chitta, accompanied by a distant din of instruments and voices, has more than once been pointed out to me as the apotheosis of some loving pair. One evening, at Pooree, whilst riding with a companion on an elephant along the beach, we descried a large fire at a distance, and, guessing it to be a suttee by its vicinity to the "gate of heaven," we proceeded towards it. On reaching the spot, I was, I trust, not sorry to find that the body which was undergoing cremation had died previous to the ceremony; and that the crowd who were singing and gesticulating round the pyre were merely performing the last offices for a deceased relative, instead of, as I had at first imagined, drowning by their rude music the agonized cries of a living victim.

Pushing our elephant near to the fire, we inquired of an old, emaciated Brahmin, who seemed to take a leading part in the ceremony, "Who it was who had gone to heaven?" He answered readily, and indeed garrulously, that it was his mother, who had died the same morning. On our expressing our wonderment that he, who appeared to be 75 or 80 years old, should have had a mother alive so lately, he said, "My mother was five twenties and four years old: she came thirty years ago, being at the point of death, to Juggernauth, to die on holy ground, but recovered, and lived until this day." The old man then rejoined the group round the pile, and re-commenced clapping his hands, and joining in the shouted chorus of "Hurri bole! hurri bole!" an invocation, I believe, to Vishnu. The whole party seemed to me to be actuated by a strange sort of merriment, very foreign to the occasion; and there was one callous-looking assistant, who, probably with a view to hasten the destruction of the corpse, continually employed himself in striking it with a long bamboo, and turning it over, like a beef-steak upon a gridiron. They were extremely economical of their fuel, throwing the wood on in small quantities, and leaving the pile not more than a foot high.

The scene was altogether wild, horrific, and yet picturesque. The evening was dark and stormy, and thunder-clouds were flying athwart the heavens in all directions: the angry surf dashed and foamed within a few feet of the sand-hill on which was raised the pile, whose bright blaze threw out in strong relief the wild-looking figures of the group, who, with their white garments floating in the winds, were singing and dancing with the most fantastical gestures round the flame. As a background to the picture, the white cupolas and domes of the "gate of heaven," embedded in dusky foliage, were alternately lighted up by the red glare of the funeral pyre and the silvery and fitful gleams of the lightning; and still farther in the distance might be faintly discerned the snowy tower of the great temple of Juggernauth.

On the 8th of June the Hattrass pilot-brig made her appearance off the coast for the purpose of transporting a detachment of the Head-quarters to Calcutta: a second division being destined, towards the latter end of the month, to accompany the Commander-in-Chief by land to the Presidency. The surf ran so high the next day that it was not considered safe for the party to embark; but on the following evening, its fury having somewhat abated, the passengers and baggage were securely stowed in the bottom of the mussoola; the buoyant craft was launched, and bravely surmounting—though sorely buffeted—the impetuous attacks of three successive lines of surf, finally reached the brig in safety. One sea, taking her on the quarter, broke on board, drenching to the skin all the passengers, one of whom was a lady, and sweeping five of the crew overboard. The tenure of these latter on the boat is far from secure, as they sit on the transverse beams *flush* with the gunwale, and have only their paddles, which are fixtures, to hold on by.

In returning, the mussoola was thrown on her beam ends, and nearly the whole of the crew went overboard.

Being, however, all powerful men, expert swimmers, and unembarrassed with excess of clothing, they account this accident an affair of little moment; and in the event of their failing to recover their boat, they are picked up by the attendant catamarans—or by the sharks, which abound on this coast.

On the occasion of a grand nocturnal bathing ceremony, held at the great tank, called the Indra Damân, I went with a party of three or four others to witness the spectacle. The walls surrounding the pool and a cluster of picturesque pavilions in its centre were brilliantly lighted up with hundreds of cheraugs, or small oil-lamps, casting a flickering lustre upon the heads and shoulders of about 500 men, women, and children, who were ducking and praying, *à corps perdu*, in the water. As I glanced over the figures nearest to me, I discovered floating among the indifferent bathers two dead bodies, which had either been drowned in the confusion, or had purposely come to die on the edge of the sacred tank; the cool and apathetic survivors taking not the slightest notice of their soulless neighbours.

June 16*th.*—Having projected a trip to the Black Pagoda—situated 16 miles north of Pooree, near the village of Kanárac,—and having previously sent forward some tents, servants, and provisions, Colonel D. and myself started for that place late in the evening in our palankeens. The night proving rainy and tempestuous, our progress was somewhat retarded: at 2 A.M. however, we forded the river Kusbádra; and at a little before 4 o'clock reached our encampment near the Pagoda. The road lay the whole way over a plain of deep sand slightly sprinkled with some unhappy and intrusive weed; but in the immediate neighbourhood of the temple the scenery is rather improved by the undulating form of the ground, and the fresh verdure of several patches of jungle. Part of this was once the garden attached to the residences of the Fakirs or ministers, whose handiwork has been once more reclaimed by the wilderness.

After breakfast, having summoned for our guidance an

old hirsute Fakir,—who seemed to haunt the ruin like the ghost of its by-gone prosperity—we rambled over this curious and wonderful edifice; the weather fortunately for our antiquarian labours, being cloudy and cool.

The Black Pagoda, or Temple of the Sun, was built by Narsing Deo Langora, Rajah of Orissa, as far back as the year A.D. 1241. The main body, or sanctum sanctorum, has been almost totally destroyed—by lightning as they relate; the only portion remaining upright amid the general wreck being one lofty shapeless pinnacle of stone, which surprisingly retains its erect position, although its height is about 130 feet, its base extremely small, and the inclination of the whole mass decidedly out of the perpendicular. The ante-chamber, however,—a large square building,—is still in excellent preservation, notwithstanding the depredations and wanton ravages of the Mahrattas, who barbarously purloined the stone to erect their own paltry temples, and even extracted most of the iron clamps used, instead of cement, to fasten together the huge materials of the building. These same savages, whose destructive "trail" may be traced throughout all India, and who possessed the province of Orissa for many years antecedent to its cession to the Company, have also mutilated, defaced, and overthrown many of the statues, ornaments, and gateways of the edifice.

The Brahmins, too, of Pooree, assisting in the general pillage, carried away from hence an elegant column—about 35 feet high, formed of a single shaft of black basalt, and of the most graceful proportions and architecture—to adorn their own temple of Juggernauth. In its present situation in front of that heavy clumsy tower, it is quite out of place. Its original position was in front of the eastern gateway of the Black Pagoda. This approach was flanked by two colossal figures, on high pediments, representing a huge lion—whose countenance is the very quintessence of ferocity—trampling upon and subduing an elephant, which cowers under its conqueror.

The group, exclusive of its base, appears to be about

10 feet high by 12 in length. One of these gateposts is alone erect, its fellow having been thrown down. The perpetrators of this mischief must have been at some pains to accomplish their object, as it is formed—as are the supporters of the other entrances—of one solid block of red granite. The following sketch gives an idea of the remaining gatepost; and the well-dressed figure on the right is our conductor, the Fakir.

Lion Gate.

At the western gate lie, overthrown, two gigantic horses in stone, richly caparisoned, and represented in the act of rearing and treading beneath their hoofs the strangely-distorted figure of a man armed with a sword and shield. Although stunted bushes and noisome weeds have almost entirely overgrown these statues, and the monsoons of nearly six centuries have vented their fury upon them, the edge of the sculpture is still sharp and decided,—even the chains of the bridles, and the studs and ornaments of the trappings, remaining uninjured. The same may be remarked throughout the numerous rich carvings of the temple; a peculiarity which may be perhaps attributable to the dryness of the sandy soil.

On another side of the Pagoda I discovered, rolled over among heaps of huge stones and prickly thickets, the two supporters of another gateway. One was much defaced; but the other, in good preservation, portrayed an elephant, ornamented with rich housings, and holding in its curled proboscis the struggling figure of a man—a most spirited composition.

The fourth entrance led from the ante-chamber to the main temple; but it has been nearly closed up by the fall of that building. An immense mound of ruins, overgrown with copse-wood, attests the stupendous proportions of the fallen edifice.

The interior of the still-existing chamber is a square of about 60 feet diameter, the walls about the same in height and nearly 20 feet thick. The dome is conical, and its arch artfully formed by large stones projecting over each other until they approach near enough at the apex to be connected by an enormous keystone of granite.

The floor is, quite unaccountably, covered with a confused pile of large blocks of stone, some of them 12 feet long by 6 feet in diameter; and amongst them are several solid bars of iron, 18 feet in length and nearly a foot square. That they must have *fallen* is apparent; but to what purpose such massive materials could have been applied is extremely problematical. It has been, indeed, conjectured that they might have formed the floor of an intermediate story; but, as there are no windows or other means of admitting light and air to the upper part of the dome, this surmise is not borne out by probability.

Myriads of wild pigeons and bats occupy the dark interior of the lofty cupola; and among the heaped ruins of the main tower a family of bears and a colony of porcupines have found a retreat.

Being armed with guns, we tried to provoke Bruin from his den; but, at home or not, he made no answer to our summons. The Fakir related that on a former occasion two English visitors were more successful in a like attempt: damp straw being ignited at the mouth of the cave, which is not more than 3 feet wide in the bore, the sturdy patriarch of the ursine family, smoked beyond endurance, made a sudden sally from his stronghold; one of the besiegers, stepping back, missed his footing, and fell down some feet among the masses of sculptured stone; and the bear, bent upon following up his advantage, was shot through the head by the second sportsman, who had, with consummate generalship, seized a position just above the gorge of the cavity.

The beauty of this Temple of the Sun is marred by numerous obscene figures and groups, rendering it unfit for any more prominent situation than the lone and savage spot where it stands. Those which fill the niches on the exterior sides of the edifice are as large as life; on the lintels of the doorways they are minute: beyond the remark that some of the statues would scarcely have been unworthy of Canova, these strange features of the Black Pagoda are totally indescribable.

Female Statute.

A sculptor of no mean art and taste must have been employed upon the cornices and other ornamental parts of the temple; the scrolls of leaves and flowers being remarkably easy and beautiful, and the execution displayed in the representation of elephants, boars, bulls, cranes,

&c., extremely spirited. Some of the female figures are especially graceful; although the shape is, perhaps, somewhat caricatured.

I give a pretty exact sketch of one of them which I found half way up the roof snugly sheltered by a projecting eave. It is in alto-relievo, as are all the statues occupying niches.

By clambering up one of the deeply-carved angles of the roof I succeeded in attaining a situation within a few feet of the melon-shaped mass which crowns the summit, from whence I enjoyed an extensive view of sand-plains, ocean, and jungle.

The elephant appears to be the animal most in vogue for ornamenting the cornices; hundreds of these picturesque beasts, in every possible attitude, being disposed throughout the building; and there is, perhaps, more skill and truth to nature displayed in them than in any other subject of the sculpture. Marriage processions, and highly-wrought battles, are likewise portrayed in the same style by way of borders.

It is surprising that so costly an edifice should have been erected in so sequestered a situation, a barren, sandy plain, and far from any town of consequence; but it is thus accounted for—the Rajah, being afflicted with rheumatism, resorted to the sea-shore, where he was cured; and he evinced his gratitude to the gods by building the temple on the spot where his malady left him. It is now about two miles from the sea, which is supposed to have receded considerably from this coast. Like many other ancient Indian buildings, the Black Pagoda has been saddled with sundry and marvellous legends. One of the causes assigned for its desertion by the priesthood is as follows: the summit of the Khetr is said to have been, in times of yore, furnished with a stupendous loadstone, which, attracting the ships passing in the roads, drew them to the shore, where they were wrecked. Some desperate foreigners, having suffered a like catastrophe, stormed the Pagoda, and carried away the magnet. The sanctuary being thus defiled, the shrine was deserted by the Brahmins; and many of its ornaments removed to the temple of Juggernauth.

The jungles in the neighbourhood of Kanárac swarm with antelopes; and buffalos are to be found in the swamps. The old Head-quarters Shikkaree, who generally contrived to enrol himself — among the host of more requisite menials — on all rambling expeditions, succeeded in shooting one of the former animals, whose exceeding wildness and watchfulness defied all attempts of my ardent companion to approach them.

Shikkaree.

The thunder-threatening closeness of the atmosphere having completely spoiled our imported provisions, in the afternoon we took post on each side of the temple with our guns, and, sending in a domestic to drive out the immense flocks of pigeons, soon provided ourselves with an extempore dinner, beside the enjoyment of half an hour's very pretty practice.

In the dusk of the evening we resumed our palankeens, and returned to Pooree; pronouncing the Black Pagoda to be—albeit little known—the finest specimen of Hindoo architecture that we had met with in our peregrinations through the great continent.

June 26*th*.—This day having been fixed for the departure of the first section of the landgoing detachment of Head-quarters for Calcutta; and the adjutant-general, the surgeon, and myself having been "told off" for this section, at 6 P.M. we stepped into our palankeens, and, nothing loth, commenced our retreat from Pooree—that depôt of Brahmins and pilgrims, flies and fakirs, idols and oysters, live sands and dead bodies—leaving nothing behind us worthy of regret, except perhaps the sea-breeze. It would be ungrateful, however, not to admit that almost every individual of the party had derived more or less benefit from the climate during our short residence on the Cuttack coast.

Having now conscientiously accomplished the three great pilgrimages of Benares, Hurdwar, and Juggernauth—the two last of which are 1400 miles apart—it only remains for me to regret that this performance, which would yield the Hindoo such vast claims to respect in this life and beatitude in the life to come, will redound no more to my advantage—perhaps not half so much—as a trip to Cheltenham or Leamington; except indeed that it secures to me the amusing recollections of a long journey, and the power of boring and re-boring my friends hereafter with yet longer descriptions of it.

A pleasant night's run of 12 hours brought us within sight of Cuttack, just as the morning-gun boomed over the waters of the Mahanuddy. The roads were greatly cut up by the rains; but from the same cause the appearance of the country was much improved. The approach to the town is extremely striking; a long avenue of noble trees leading the traveller to the bank of a beautiful stream, which, rushing against the bold angle on which Cuttack is situated, is split into two channels, distinguished by the respective names of Mahanuddy and Cajori. Cuttack being subject to sudden and violent floods, the point of bifurcation is fortified against the abrupt rising of the river by a strong stone revêtement; the town is surrounded with luxuriant groves, and the swelling hills of Koorda afford a pleasing background to the prospect.

The ferry-boats on the river were crowded, almost to sinking, with troops of pilgrims of both sexes travelling towards Juggernauth: among the men there were several dreadfully emaciated objects; but the women were for the most part in good case, and many of them very pretty. Passing through the town, I was kindly welcomed under the roof-tree of a young friend, who, in his lately-achieved capacities of magistrate and Benedict, had newly settled down in this Station.

Cuttack is not considered healthy; the same moisture of the atmosphere which renders the vegetation so verdant and abundant, but ill according with the European constitution. It is perhaps to counteract the bad effects of the damp that the native inhabitants are in the habit of smoking a very substantial cigar, which, when it is not in use, they carry behind the ear, as a clerk does his pen. In the rivers about this neighbourhood, lapidarian research has discovered a great variety of the agate family. I obtained very good specimens of jasper, onyx, and cornelian.

Cuttack is the head-quarters of that useful tribe of men called the Ooria-bearers, who, being looked upon as the best and most trustworthy servants, are much in request among the English of the Presidency. Their masters, without fear, confide large sums of money to their keeping; and almost every little master and little miss of the rising generation of Chowringhee* is attended by one of these bareheaded and almost naked, but very cleanly guardians. I trust that honesty is not necessarily associated with, or the natural offspring of intellectual dulness; but it is certain that Mr. Sterling, in his interesting account of the province of Orissa, applies to its inhabitants the term of "the Bœotians of the East!" I myself attended the Cuttack Kutcherrie, during the examination of some witnesses deposing to an outrage committed amongst the hills; and obtuse and temper-trying as the whole tribe of witnesses notoriously is, the Laputa flapper was never more wanted than in this instance.

June 28th — Cuttack. — His Excellency arrived from

* Quarter of Calcutta exclusively inhabited by the English gentry.

Pooree; and the following morning, a ter a review of a corps of native infantry, I accompanied him on a visit to the fortress of Barabáti, situate near the cantonments. It is of great antiquity, owing its foundation to the ancient Rajahs of Orissa. From the Mahomedans, who seized the country about the middle of the 18th century, it received several additions; and at a later period it fell into the hands of the Mahrattas, from whom it was wrested by the English, after a determined resistance, in 1803—by this conquest the Company obtaining possession of the rich province of Cuttack. In the days of its prosperity Barabáti must have been almost impregnable; and, even in its broken-down old age, its lofty ruins frown formidably upon the surrounding plain. The area of the fort occupies more than a square mile of ground, and it is girt about with double walls of red pudding-stone, in the destruction of which the march of time has been assisted by the ruthless hand of man, and the materials devoted to the repair of the roads. The ditch is scarped with the same stone, and, in the widest part, is no less than 220 feet across: it is always filled with water, and is additionally fortified with a terrific band of alligators, who have, time out of mind, held hereditary sway in its dark cool depths;—a bloody siege would be a gala-time for these ravenous monsters.

The Commander-in-Chief having expressed a wish to witness the athletic and gladiatorial performances of the sepoys of the 39th infantry, 16 of the most skilled in these sciences were drawn from the ranks, and in the cool of the evening repaired to Mr. Stockwell's garden. The place selected for the display was a spot of soft mould about 100 feet in extent; the English spectators were furnished with chairs under the surrounding trees, and the circle was completed by a crowd of the sepoys, who, attired in their own graceful undress, had assembled to view the exploits of their companions.

The games were opened by the sword-players, who, as well as the wrestlers, were entirely naked, with the exception of a cloth bound tightly round the waist, and reaching a few inches down the thighs. Such perfect models of the animal man I never beheld! The first two combatants, who jumped simultaneously into the arena, were armed with a species of single-stick, shorter and heavier than those used in England, and covered with leather to qualify the effect of the blow; bearing in their left hands a small leathern buckler about the circumference of a dinner-plate. After a smiling salaam, they approached each other very cautiously, circling round at the respectful distance of 10 feet, and using the most extraordinary and extravagant gestures—preliminaries which to me appeared absurd and unnecessary, but which an old Jemadar near me described as useful to awe and distract the attention of the antagonist, and to gain the sun of him.

When they at last came to blows they laid about them in real earnest, striking with all their might, and often with both hands. The extreme dexterity which they displayed in warding with the little shield, their crafty feints, and the immense springs they occasionally made to avoid or surprise their adversary, drew loud plaudits from the circle. Towards the end of the combat one of these supple fellows suddenly threw himself upon his knees, in order to cut at the legs of his opponent; and from that apparently helpless position, with the quickness of lightning, sprung back 6 or 8 feet to escape the stroke that was descending on his head. The other, in attempting to retort the same manœuvre, received a blow on the shoulder that echoed through the field; upon which, at a signal from the Subadar directing the sports, the contending couple struck their swords and bucklers together, salaamed in token of amity, and swaggered out of the ring.

The gladiators were succeeded by the wrestlers, whose performances were infinitely more interesting. After rubbing their arms and shoulders with dry mould, the first adverse couple stalked with inflated chests and strutting gait into the arena; and after going through the same preparatory demonstrations as the swordsmen, came at last aux mains. The crouching posture, in which they crept round each other prior to the attack, was occasionally varied by a tremendous leap, as if to prove the vigour of their limbs, and accompanied by a smart clapping noise, produced by striking the hollow of the hand upon the muscular part of the opposite arm. On meeting, they placed their heads firmly together, like butting rams, seized each the other's wrist with one hand, whilst the other was twined round the back of the adversary's neck. In Indian wrestling a fair fall consists in being thrown flat on the back, a consummation which, owing to the extreme agility and suppleness of the wrestlers, is seldom accomplished. A front or side fall is not accounted disgraceful; on the contrary, it is common for the spent combatant to throw himself flat upon his face in order to gain breath; in which position, with outspread arms and legs, he defies the utmost attempts of his adversary to turn him, like a turtle, upon his back.

The most distinguished of the wrestlers was a youth of about 22, who successively bore the palm from six opponents, four of whom were much heavier men than himself. He had a remarkably handsome and classical countenance, with a figure of perfect symmetry; and as he sprung into the circus, looking sternly and confidently round for his first antagonist, I would not have wished for a better representation of a youthful Roman athlete. Loud were the applauses that saluted him from all sides, as, after the overthrow of five competitors, the noble fellow stood panting in the ring, and eagerly awaiting another candidate for the Olympic wreath.

These skilful sepoys seemed to me to understand the mechanical application of their strength better than any British wrestlers that I have seen. The legs were brought much more into play; and at the commencement of the bouts, when the combatants were fresh, the falls were dreadfully heavy. The young Roman, after a series of intricate combinations which I could not trace, twice threw an opponent heavier than himself quite over his head, the faller coming to the ground, on both occasions, upon his crown; and by this same opponent the youth was himself thrown in the same style, and with a violence that extorted a groan from his well-wishers. He nevertheless alighted upon his feet, and soon after threw his man—a perfect Dares in stature—fairly upon his back.

I was much struck by the great similarity of make in the several sepoys who contended—the chief peculiarities in their form being the immense expansion of chest, breadth of shoulder, flatness and hollowness of back, and extreme smallness of waist. In their persons the strength of the lion and the litheness of the serpent are wonderfully united. In the nether limbs, however, their symmetry somewhat fails them. I should like much to see an English wrestler of equal weight pitted against one of these Indian athletes. The stamina of the former would doubtless tell in the end; unless, at the first onset, the comparatively stiff Briton should get some incapacitating wrench or strain from the superior suppleness of the Indian's body and limbs.

At the conclusion of the combats a man stepped forth to show us the practice of the double-edged sword, which in his hands appeared a terrible weapon, though in those unaccustomed to its use it is but an awkward instrument. The blade was full 5 feet long, and encumbered with a clumsy iron hilt reaching half way up the arm, like a gauntlet, thus—

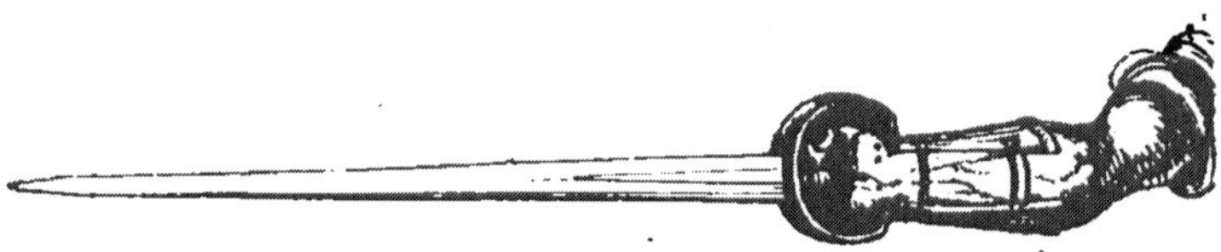

Double-edged Sword.

After a display of sundry sweeping and rotatory cuts that would haye severed a bullock's neck, four small limes were placed on the ground, equidistant round the circle; and the fellow, describing a variety of twirling evolutions, not unlike an exaggerated *waltz*, approached them alternately, and, without pausing in his giddy career, divided each of them in two with a well-aimed horizontal cut.

Shortly after the conclusion of the games, my two companions and myself resumed our dâk journey; and so damaged were the roads by the late rains that we did not reach Bareepore—of comfortless memory—until 12 o'clock the next day. I was oftentimes during the night awakened by the shouted chorus of "Hurribole! hurribole!" with which our bearers were saluted, as they passed, by the groups of pilgrims who were snugly squatting on the roadside with their mat umbrellas spread over their heads to protect them from the heavy night-dew.

Early in the morning I met a more distinguished votary, who had accomplished thus much of his painful journey to Juggernauth, having measured his length all the way from the northern provinces: he had been a fortnight coming from Balasore, a distance of about 55 miles. This human reptile was a young man of very slight form; nevertheless, he did not appear to be much worn or harassed by his quadrupedal journey of nearly a thousand miles. His forehead and breast were soiled with the mud of his unceasing prostrations, at each of which, ere he rose to his feet, he made a mark beyond his head on the ground, in order to be exact in his mensuration.

These cruel penances are sometimes undertaken in propitiation of some heinous sin or sins, and at others in ratification of vows made to the gods to avert grievous afflictions. In the hour of sickness, for instance, the pious husband prays for the preservation of—or perchance his liberation from—his expiring wife; and he backs his prayer with a vow, which is always conscientiously executed.

During the night of the *2nd July* we crossed the Subanreeka river, a fine broad winding stream forming the frontier between the two great provinces of Orissa and Bengal. Its banks are ornamented with some banyan-trees of remarkable growth, but the finest specimen of these wonderful productions of vegetative nature that I have seen in this quarter of India flourishes near the ghaut of the Brahminee river, which we passed two days ago. As my palankeen ran under the arched corridors of this vegetable palace, its hundred stems, faintly lighted up by the passing glare of the torches, might have easily been mistaken for the gray and timeworn columns of some ruined cloister.

In our passage through the hamlet of Dantoon on the evening of the *3rd* our progress was obstructed by a dense crowd employed in celebrating their village edition of the festival of Rath-Jattra. The car was fixed obstinately in the mud of the main street, and the mob were striving with great uproar and little real exertion to remove it. On our approaching the spot the hubbub immediately subsided, the women covered their faces, the populace opened out, and most of them saluted us respectfully as we passed—and thus it is throughout India in general: the Englishman meets with more respect and deference from the natives of the wildest parts of Hindostan than he would from the lower orders of the most civilized portion of his own country. Nor is it merely the lip-homage of the conquered to the conqueror, of the weak to the strong: the Company's government has (by contrast with former possessors of the country) formed to itself a character for moderation, good faith, wisdom, and benevolence, which has secured to it the confidence of its subjects; a feeling extended in greater or lesser degrees—though in some instances, Heaven knows, it is but ill-deserved—to every member of the English community.

More than once, during my sporting rambles, I have been waylaid by old men or women, who have brought sick children to me, and begged me in their simple manner to prescribe for them. Although I never ventured to incur the risk of infanticide, I have often administered to adult patients; whose own faith in the infallibility of a white face is probably more efficacious than the medicine itself. On one occasion, whilst an equally experienced friend and myself were in the act of pouring a dose of brandy down the throat of a youth afflicted with the cholera, he sunk down at our feet and expired.*

July 9th.—The two dâk divisions were convened at Tumlook. On the 10*th* Mr. Lindsay's beautiful beauliah took us to the mouth of the Roopnarain river, where a steamer awaited us, which was to waft us with great expedition to Calcutta by the usual dinner-hour. After three several fractures of the machinery, however, we thought ourselves fortunate in making Garden Reach by 9 P.M. Here we were obliged to cast anchor; and Sir C. Metcalfe brought us off in a boat to his house, where we were all provided with beds.

The next morning, *July* 11*th*, 1829, Head-quarters were once more established at Calcutta, after a rambling and most interesting tour of 20 months.

During the remaining five months of my residence in India I was pretty generally stationary at the Residency; and as the march of my pen seldom outruns that of my person, I find my journal, during this period, blank, except on two occasions; first, where it follows me on an eight days' sporting expedition; and secondly, where it attempts to give a slight sketch of "A day in Calcutta," or more properly Chouringhee—the sonorous name by which the English quarter of the great city is known. The first I shall omit—for it is long. The last I shall subjoin—for it is short.

A DAY IN CALCUTTA.

In the hot weather—and nine months of the twelve *are* hot—the Anglo-Bengalee—unless he has been late at a

* Lest the English reader should be impressed with too exalted an idea of my heroism in thus exposing myself to contact with a cholera-struck patient, I feel obliged to state that in India—where that cruel distemper has been at such pains to make itself known—I never heard even so much as the possibility of its contagion canvassed. In Europe, however, I found a contrary creed established, and the whole collective faculty ready to jump down the throat of the rash sceptic venturing to broach his old-fashioned, exploded, yet comfortable Indian notions.

party the night before, or loves his bed better than his health—is roused by the punctual warning of his bearer, "Sahib! Sahib! it has struck four;" and completing, by the assistance of the same domestic officer, a hasty toilette, he mounts his Arab, and by half-past four is taking his constitutional canter round the dew-freshened race-course. There—unless, as is sometimes the case, he be too languid to be social—he joins company with some of the many acquaintances he is sure to fall *in* with; and discusses the merits of the last batch of claret, "per Petite Louise," from Bordeaux, or the last batch of misses, "per Duchess of Bedford," from England; the last act of Government, or the last dinner at Gunter's. Or, if there be any that he has chanced to fall *out* with, he may on the same spot, under the well-known "Great Tree," discuss his point of honour without danger of interruption. During the months preceding the races, the training of the horses affords the sporting world of Calcutta an additional incitement to the healthful practice of early rising.

At six, or soon after, that arch-enemy of European constitutions, the sun, begins to dart, from above the tall mansions of Chouringhee, its intolerable rays across the hitherto thronged plain; and the "Qui hi" who has any respect for the wellbeing of his liver, shrinks appalled from its increasing disk, sneaks home, delivers his reeking horse to the attendant syce, and, exhausted with the monstrous exertion he has undergone, creeps under his musquito curtain, and dozes, a bearer fanning him, until half-past 8.

A bath—the greatest luxury in India—and perhaps shampooing, wind him up for the breakfast of tea, muffins, and pillau at half-past 9; after which those who are fortunate enough to have offices, repair thither in buggy or palankeen; and, with white jacket on back and punkah over head, earn, *tant bien que mal*, their rupees and their tiffen. This subsidiary meal is a favourite mid-day pastime of both the ladies and men of the Presidency, and is the only repast at which appetite generally presides. A rich hash, or hot curry, followed by a well-cooled bottle of claret, or Hodson's pale ale, with a variety of eastern fruits, are thus despatched at 2 o'clock, forming in fact a dinner, whilst the so-called meal at 8 o'clock would be better named supper.

Idle men employ the above hours in visiting, billiards, or the auction-rooms. In the former ceremonial, should the visitor, going his rounds, find the gates of the "compound" * closed, he is to deduce that the Bebee Sahib † is not visible. Should they be thrown open, on the contrary, he draws a favourable augury—(which, however, may still be negatived by the Cerberus Durwân ‡)—dashes through the portal, draws up sharp under the columned entrance, jumps out, and is received at the door—(there is not a knocker in all India!)—by a respectful but pompous and most deliberate jemadar, who, striding before the Bharkee-Sahib §—the ivory tassels of his dagger rattling as he walks—leads him through a darkened ante-room (where another attendant, within hearing of the delicate "Qui hi!" of the lady, rises wakefully and salaams, or sits sleepily and nods), and finally introduces him by his name (strangely distorted however) into the yet more obscured sanctum. Here, seated in luxurious fauteuil, and fanned by the wavings of the heavy-flounced punkah, the eyes of the visitor (albeit as yet unused to the tender twilight of the hermetically-closed apartment) discover the fair object of his visit. He is seated; obvious topics are despatched, and happy is it for absent acquaintances if the late arrival of a ship, or a new novel, is at hand to furnish external matter for discussion. In default of this diversion, living victims are offered up at the shrine of tittle-tattle—I won't call it scandal; "attentions" and "intentions" are anatomized; flirtations analyzed; couples, as adverse as fire and water, are wedded and bedded; and friends, as attached as twin-brothers, are paraded with "pistols for two" under the "Great Tree." The lady's ivory stiletto, urged by her white fingers rendered still whiter by Indian seclusion, is not more actively employed in torturing her

* Enclosure round the house. † The lady. ‡ Porter.

§ Strange gentleman.

tamboured muslin, than is her tongue in torturing and distorting facts—I won't say characters; the gentleman attacks the men, the lady the women; each defends the opposite sex, and they separate perfectly satisfied with themselves,—not overhearing the exclamation from the neighbouring verandah, "There is Captain A. only just going away from Mrs. B.; what can he have been doing there these three hours, whilst Mr. B. is at office?"—but this smacks of persiflage! To our subject. The tiffen being concluded, many have recourse to a siesta, to recruit their forces and to kill time.

Towards 6, the orb of day, tending towards the western horizon, begins to relax the vigour of his rays; the lengthening shadows give evidence of his decline; and ere he has quite deserted the glowing heavens, the echoes of Calcutta are awakened by the rattling—rattling indeed!—of hundreds of equipages, from the lordly coach-and-four to the less-aspiring but dapper buggy; from the costly Arab charger to the ambling Pegu pony. All hurry to the same point, urged by the desire of seeing and being seen; and indeed those morose few, who are not instigated by these all-potent motives, are obliged to resort to the same mall, as the only well-watered drive. At dusk the Course and Strand are deserted:—except by a few choice spirits, who love to breathe the cool air of moonlight and to listen to the soft whisperings of . . . . . . the evening breeze, rather than the coarse steam of viands and the bubbling of hookahs—the world of Calcutta is dressing for dinner; and by 8 o'clock it is seated at that important, but often untasted meal. In the hospitable mansions of the "upper servants" of the Company the tables groan under the weight of massive plate, and, what is worse, under whole hecatombs of beef and mutton. I have frequently seen—horresco referens!—in a side-dish, which would have been much more appropriately tenanted by an appetizing fricandeau or a tempting ris de veau,—two legs of mutton, or twin-turkeys; yet with all this profusion, scarcely any one has sufficiently recovered from the heavy tiffen despatched at two, to be able even to look without shuddering upon the slaughtered herds—much less to taste two mouthfuls.

Champagne and claret, delightfully cooled with ice or saltpetre, are real luxuries; and ere the last course is well off the table, an isolated bubble announces the first hookah: others drop in, the jingling of Suppooses is heard; a rich, though rather evercoming odour pervades the air; handsome mouth-pieces of amber, gold, silver, or videri, decked with snowy ruffles, insinuate themselves from under the arms of the chairs; and the pauses in the sometimes languid and ill-sustained conversation are deprived of their former awkwardness by the full sonorous *drone* of a dozen of these princely pipes.

The men do not sit so long after the adjournment of the ladies as is the custom in England.

Inveterate smokers have their hookahs transferred to the drawing-room. They are not bad companions in the silence of a whist-table; but prove rather a barbarous accompaniment to the music and singing, in the piano passages of which its monotonous growl chimes rather discordantly. The hookah, however, in a room full of ladies, does not appear to a *griffin* ("young hand," or Johnny Newcome) more out of place, than does the half-naked figure of the punkah-puller. Small parties break up about half-past 10, with a view to the ensuing morning's ride—and lo! a Calcutta day is completed.

Dec. 8th.—This evening, during the accustomed promenade, a flying report of the arrival of the frigate reached the mall. My heart leaped at the glad tidings, and I vented my joy by spurring my astonished Arab at full speed round the lonely race-course. A reaction followed, and as I walked my smoking horse slowly home I sighed at the thought of quitting a country where I had passed four happy and eventful years. Ere nightfall the rumour was confirmed—H.M.S. Pallas, 42, Captain Adolphus Fitz-Clarence, had anchored in the Hooghly, having on board Lord Dalhousie and Staff, and the Right Rev. John Turner, newly appointed Bishop of Calcutta. I received by this conveyance several letters kindly brought from England by Lieutenant Knox, and all of them *beckoning* me home again.

CHAPTER XII.

Voyage from Calcutta to England — Diamond Harbour — The Sand-heads — Pallas at Sea — The frigate — Madras — Government House — The Esplanade — Fort George — The natives — Re-embarkation — Pallas — A funeral at sea — Pallas off the Cape of Good Hope — False Bay — Simon's Bay — Simon's Town — Land in Africa — Drive to Cape Town — Fish-Hook's Bay — Half-way House — Table Bay — Cape Town — Lodging-hunting — The women — The Lion Hill — Cape horses — Cape living — Suburbs of Cape Town — Ride to Simon's Town — Constantia — Wine-stores — Voyage to St. Helena — James's Bay — James Town — Plantation House — Ride round the island — Diana's Peak — Longwood — Napoleon's tomb — Statistic account — Quit St. Helena — Pallas at sea — Isle of Ascension — George Town — Green Mountain — The Azores — English Channel — Spithead — Pallas at anchor — England.

Jan. 6th, 1830.—YESTERDAY Lord Combermere repaired on board the Pallas; and this morning was fixed for the embarkation of the remainder of the home-bound party. A brother *Ex*-A.D.C. and myself breakfasted at Government House; and at 10 o'clock we accompanied the Governor-General and Lady William Bentinck—who intended to honour the frigate with a visit—on board the Hooghly steam-boat, destined to convey us to Diamond Harbour, about 50 miles from Calcutta.

By half-past 10 the City of Palaces was shut out from our view, and we were dashing past the verdant shores of Garden Reach, with its long line of Thames-like villas—under whose roofs I had so often quaffed the cup of hospitality, or "chased the *glowing* hours with flying feet." On rushed the quivering Hooghly, ploughing fiercely through the glossy bosom of her river godmother and namesake; and soon after 4 o'clock she brought us alongside the Pallas, who received the Governor with manned yards, and a thundering salute,—an example followed by all the ships in the harbour.

At 6 o'clock the whole party, about 30 in number, dined on board. The table was spread on the quarter-deck, and canopied over with flags; and the feast afforded us a very satisfactory earnest of the good cheer that we were to expect during our long voyage—expectations that were more than realized by the result. In the evening the Hooghly again received its noble passengers, and the great number of our leave-taking friends; the Ganges steamer remaining to tow us out of the river.

Jan. 7th.—Pallas weighed and made sail from Diamond harbour, towed by the Ganges. Slowly and gradually we floated past the low and marshy shore of Kedgeree, the wild and desert Sauger, and the sandy Edmonstone's Isle; and at sunset we anchored still in sight of land. Among others of our friends who remained on board, with the intention of returning when the steamer left us, was Colonel Skinner, who had brought with him three of his Russuldars (native officers of rank). These men, who had never before quitted dry land, were rapturous in their admiration of the size, cleanliness, and discipline of the ship; nor were they themselves less the objects of wonder to the crew, who eyed them with that sort of knowing smile in which there is more of satire than mere curiosity—and many a wink was exchanged, when, as the sun sunk below the horizon, the tall, showily-attired Mussulmans prostrated themselves on the quarter-deck, and pressed their foreheads against the planks. At dusk Pallas anchored in 5 fathoms of water.

Jan. 8th.—This morning I saw for the last time the sun rise over the low green shores of Bengal; in two hours the tallest palmyras had dipped out of sight; and when our noble frigate had fairly become the nucleus of a wide unbroken circle of sea and sky, the fact was pointed out to the three native officers, who, after deliberately scanning the whole horizon, vented their admiration in a torrent of enthusiastic ejaculations. The Ganges towed us well out of a calm; and at 6 P.M. she cast us off, and, taking the still lingering remnant of our friends on board, turned her head towards the land.

At 8 o'clock we put our pilot on board the "floating light," which is moored at the extreme point of the Sandheads; a fine leading breeze assisted us all night, and in the morning the Pallas was in blue water, and bending her rapid course towards Madras. The England-bound party consisted of Lord Combermere and five of his Staff; each passenger was provided with a comfortable cabin; and during the four months we were on board, our liberal and courteous captain left us nothing to complain of—except, perhaps, occasional indigestions, the fruits of a table but too profuse for the well-being of dyspeptic Indians.

To a *passenger*, a frigate possesses advantages and drawbacks in pretty equal proportions—though, in the eyes of military men, the latter generally preponderate:—but as a *command*, it appears to me the most complete and independent that falls to the lot of men of middling rank.

> "Who would not brave the death fire, and the wreck,
> To move the monarch of her peopled deck?"

The captain of a frigate is the sovereign of a little floating island: he is the tyrant or the father of his subjects, according as his disposition prompts; and with very little management and tact he may make himself the master of the affections, as well as the services, of his officers and crew. To a subordinate, however, the army must necessarily be the most engaging profession.

Jan. 14th.—At 8 o'clock this morning, after a pleasant sail of 5 days, the Pallas anchored in the Madras roads, about 2 miles from the shore, and in 8 fathoms water. The view of this Presidency from the sea is by no means favourable: the shore is flat, the buildings mean in comparison with Calcutta, and the trees scrubby and ill-grown. On more intimate acquaintance with Madras, however, we were agreeably surprised by the picturesque and umbrageous situations of its garden-houses, which are not seen from the sea; yet, on the whole, our parting and collective verdict pronounced it to be a full half-century behind the sister Presidency in the luxuries and conveniences of life.

No sooner had the Pallas swung to her anchor, and the

canvas, quickly furled, disappeared as if by magic from her taper yards, than a mussoula boat was seen to push from the shore; and on coming alongside was found to contain the almost senseless person of a highly embroidered Staff officer, who had come off to arrange about the landing of his Lordship; but so dreadfully sea-sick was the unfortunate man, that ere he reached the Pallas he was lying quite helpless in the bottom of the boat.

About an hour after, the Governor's mussoula boat, decorated with the Honourable Company's flag and furnished with a stern-awning, took us on board. The sea was running very high; and nothing could be finer than the manner in which our buoyant craft bounded over the three surfs, the last of which left us far up, high and dry, on the sand. On landing opposite the Custom-house, our party was immediately accommodated with a variety of equipages, which conveyed us to the Government House, where we were courteously welcomed by the Governor, Mr. Lushington.

The palace, which is about 1½ mile from the Custom-house wharf, is large and commodious, but of anomalous and in elegant architecture: it is well situated near the mouth of a small river, and has some 50 acres of parkish-looking ground around it.

In the afternoon a resident friend drove me in his phaëton to the fashionable Mall. The Esplanade, the road along the beach, and the Mount-road were thronged with well-filled carriages: but *such* carriages! they were even more antediluvian in their construction than the equipages of Calcutta, and contrasted strangely with the smart bonnets of the ladies who tenanted them.

Dined with a very numerous party at Government-house. The servants of Madras are smart and attentive, and have more of the mercurial flippancy of the English waiter than the slow deliberate khitmutgar of Calcutta. They are not so tenacious of caste, and consequently fewer of them are required; for the same domestic who waits at dinner will also condescend to superintend his master's toilet.

I did not see a single hookah at Madras, and I was

informed that this fashionable stimulant, to an old Bengalee almost as necessary as his food, is seldom used here.

Jan. 15th.—Madras.—I was introduced this morning to the famous horse-fancier—Colonel Macdonell, I think—who goes by the familiar sobriquet of *Arab Mac:* he is said at this moment to have a stud of about 60 high-caste Arabs in his stables; two of them, Aurelio and Esterhazy, being considered by the knowing ones to be the best in India.

Went to see "the lions" of Fort George and Black Town. The former, which has been the scene of more than one stubborn fight between the English and French, is laid down agreeably to the rules of modern fortification; its situation is good, but it is much crowded with high buildings in the interior. His Majesty's 26th Regiment is now quartered within the walls. The native town has nothing remarkable in it: it is, however, built more regularly and of more durable materials than is the similar quarter of Calcutta.

The natives of Madras fall short of the Bengalese in delicacy of feature and symmetry of person, although they are perhaps better formed for exertion. The men are smaller, as was manifest on comparing the average standards of the regiments of each Presidency: the women, on the contrary, are, I think, taller, and many of them very handsome. Their costume is becoming, and the poorest have some gold ornament on their persons. The prettiest of their decorations is a small skull-cap of solid filigree gold, which is worn on the crown of the head, and fastened through the hair like a brooch. Another article of fashion, which has since found its way to England, is a belt of solid gold or silver fastened round the waist. Trichinopoli chains are in high vogue both with Europeans and natives: and there is always a profusion of very inferior ones ready to tempt the casual passenger.

The next morning we had a pleasant drive to Palaveram, a military cantonment 12 miles from Madras, where Lord Combermere reviewed four regiments of native infantry. The men are certainly inferior in personal appearance to the Bengal sepoy, but they are well dressed, and are, individually, smarter and more active soldiers than the latter. On our return from the Mount we visited St. George's Church, built by Captain Colvin of the Engineers. It is a beautiful edifice, and the chunam of the columns in the interior is so fine as to have all the polish of white marble. At one entrance there is a very fine monument by Chantrey of Dr. Anderson, a gentleman to whom Madras is indebted for many improvements. It was exhibited in Somerset House before it was sent out to its destination.

At 1 P.M. our party took leave of the Governor and drove down to the busy wharf, where a mussoula boat attended us. An hour's knocking about brought us alongside the Pallas; in another hour we were under all sail, going 9 knots; and by the following midday we had left Madras 183 miles behind us.

After three or four prosperous days, the wind gradually deserted us, and on the 21*st* morning we were nearly becalmed. Croakers—of whom there are always a strong party on board-ship—immediately began to anticipate the usual fortnight's calm weather near the equator, when fortunately a sudden squall came on and completely changed the face of affairs. The gallant ship, which for the last 48 hours had been almost paralyzed, as suddenly resumed her functions, and sprung through the hissing billows at the rate of 9 and 10 knots all night, during which time we crossed the dreaded Line. The next two days this auspicious breeze continued, only abating at intervals. Towards the close of the month the westerly airs grew gradually fainter, and we had very nearly relapsed into a calm, when, on the 4th of February, in latitude 17°, a light breeze from the south-east sprung up, and the barometer of our hopes rose in proportion.

For the last week "all hands" had been impatiently looking out for the south-east Trade-wind, which is usually fallen in with by homeward-bound ships in latitude 11° or 12°, and board-o'-ship superstition had attributed our ill-luck to some Jonah passenger. To corroborate this theory, the bearer of the first intelligence of the Trade having set in, brought likewise, at the same time, to the cabin the report of the death of Sergeant Sawkins (Lord Combermere's orderly for many years), who had embarked in wretched health, the effect of drinking, and had been gradually wasting away. It struck me that these two events were connected in the minds of the seamen!

The next day the little Pallas, under the full influence of the south-east Trade, was gliding along at the rate of 9 knots an hour, and so smoothly that she scarcely appeared to be in motion.

Early in the morning the body of poor Sawkins, shrouded with a flag and weighted with shot, was, in the words of the beautiful funeral service, "committed to the deep." The deceased is the fourth victim dragged by the grim king of terrors from among Lord Combermere's suite since he landed in India. The other three were his aides-de-camp, Colonel Kelly, Captain Stapleton, and Captain Dougan. Had it been pre-revealed to us that so large a portion of our small party were to be stricken, how awful would have been the warning!

Feb. 17*th*, lat. 28° 10′, long. 45° 31′.—This day, at 12 o'clock, we were 156 miles direct south of Cape St. Mary in the Isle of Madagascar, and 1035 miles from Algoa Bay, on the coast of Africa. The trade-wind has hitherto treated us as though its charter were confined to the propulsion of commercial ships, and H.M.S. Pallas consequently not entitled to its assistance. This day, however, it vouchsafed to arrive in real earnest to our aid, and continued with us for a week, advancing us at the rate of 200 miles a day.

23*rd*.—At 5 P.M. the cry of "land ahead," from the look-out aloft, brought us all upon deck, in the hope of seeing *that* which was not made visible to us in our less exalted situation until an hour later, when we were within 30 miles of the shore. The horizon was hazy, but we nevertheless plainly distinguished the line of lofty and bold mountains backing up the Bay of Algoa—the point which is usually made by ships returning from India. At 10 P.M. the ship was only 8 or 9 miles from the land: and large fires, probably the burning of the forests on the hills, were distinctly visible to those on board.

The following day we added 200 miles to our score, and at 8 o'clock P.M. sounded in 55 fathoms, distance from shore 34 miles.

Feb. 25th.—The south-east trade, having fairly carried us into soundings, made its bow, leaving behind it a dead calm, and so heavy a swell that the poor Pallas elbowed the waves at every roll with her studding-sail-booms, and nearly thrashed threadbare a whole suit of canvas. The middies were very busy with their fishing-lines, and were pretty successful. A very good cod of about 15 pounds was caught by dropping the deep-sea lead to the bottom, furnished with hooks baited with meat. It found its way to the Captain's table, the fisherman being too glad to barter his fish for a fine sheep.

26*th.*—At 12 o'clock Cape Lagullas, E.N.E., 5 miles; and Cape Hanglip, N.W. ¼ W., 63 miles—the calm and swell still mocking our endeavours to approach those bold and beautiful mountains, under whose shadow a steam-vessel would place us in a few hours. An occasional "cat's-paw" and the set of the current prevented us, however, from being utterly motionless; and Pallas gradually crept towards her destination. During the day a large whale several times approached the ship, disporting its huge bulk in heavy gambols round us. The weather was delightfully cool, although there was not a single cloud to moderate the rays of the sun.

How diametrically different were the circumstances under which I passed the Cape of Good Hope in August, 1825! My journal, on that occasion, expatiates, with all the eloquence of a first voyage, upon a terrific north-wester; and, as I glance down its sea-washed pages, my eye is arrested by the following catch-words: "violent hailstorm;" "waves half-mast high;" "mainsail split into ribbons;" "quarter boat washed off the davits;" "man overboard;" "fine lunar rainbow," &c.

Feb. 28*th.*—Rounded Cape Hanglip at 5 A.M., and entered False Bay with a fine strong breeze from the south-east. The two points of Hanglip and Good Hope form the horns —if they may be so styled—of the bay; and appear to be distant asunder about 10 miles. They are as bold, bluff, and bleak, as the extreme salient angle of the continent of Africa, exposed and opposed to the unceasing attacks of the great Southern Ocean, has need to be. On entering the bay we skirted swiftly along the western shore, within half a mile of its precipitous and rocky cliffs; and at 8 A.M. Pallas dropped anchor off Simon's Town, in the little bay or inlet of the same name. The anchorage is completely land-locked; and during the south-east trade, which blows with little variation during the whole summer, it is more easily approached than Table Bay—on the western side of the Cape. The only ship that we found in the harbour was the Maidstone frigate, Commodore Schomberg, who commands on this station.

The greatest drawback to Simon's Bay is its distance, 23 miles, from Cape Town. Simon's Town has nothing to recommend it in its appearance; though, from its being generally seen after the tedium of a long voyage, it is, perhaps, regarded by visitors with more complacency than it intrinsically merits. It is situated at the foot of a steep crescent of rock and gravel hills sparely sprinkled with stunted brushwood. The Methodist chapel occupies the most commanding station in the town: next to which will be remarked the Custom-house, the Commodore's residence partially shaded by some dwarfish trees, the hospital, and the clergyman's rus-in-urbe retreat. The warehouses on the wharf contain stores for his Majesty's ships to the amount of 50,000*l.* There is very good fishing in Simon's Bay, particularly in the vicinity of the Roman Rocks—a cluster of surf-washed crags 2 miles from shore—and in an inlet called Fishhook's Bay,* 3 miles beyond Simon's Town.

* "Visch Hoek," *i. e.* Fish Corner.

We had not been five minutes at anchor, ere the ship was surrounded by a swarm of small boats, chiefly filled with Malays, who supplied us largely with grapes, figs, and eggs; the former were unripe; the latter, on the contrary, were "rather too mellow for me." Washermen, too, in abundance, offered their services, and the number of "buck-baskets" lowered into their boats bespoke a thriving business. The exorbitant charges of these ministers to board-o'-ship comfort astonished those of our party who in India had been accustomed to exhaust a whole wardrobe of linen in a day, at the trifling monthly cost of seven or eight rupees.

At noon the Captain, with some of his officers and his passengers, went on shore, where we were hospitably greeted by the worthy Commodore, who entertained us with a capital dinner (which, from its variety of Cape rarities, was as good as a museum to us strangers), and with his merrily-expended fund of high spirits and dry humour. What havoc did we commit upon his vast mounds of delicious fruit! No one who has not been six weeks at sea, can imagine the rapture of a first meeting with a fine, fresh, luscious bunch of grapes. My young friends in the midshipmen's berth can well appreciate the luxury; for it did my heart good to see one of these merry middies—whose bill of fare for so long a period had been "junk," and nothing else but junk—sitting, like a little Bacchus, across a cask, and stripping a bunch of "honey-pods" nearly co-bulky with himself.

The largest house in Simon's Town, and indeed, the greater part of the town itself, belongs to an Englishman of the name of Osmond, who, however, is more generally known by the dignified title of "King John." He was carpenter on board the 60-gun ship Sceptre, which was wrecked off this coast some years ago. Like Juan he escaped the sea, and like Juan he found a Haidee. Being well-favoured and sharp-witted, he won the heart and the hand of a wealthy Dutch widow, whose dollars he afterwards, in some bold but successful speculations, turned to good account. He is said to have laid out 10,000*l.* on these —to every one but himself—inhospita littora. King John is much respected.

March 1*st.*—Captain Fitz-Clarence having signified his intention of remaining a week at the Cape, Lord Combermere, with one of his party, started this morning for the country cottage of the Governor, Sir Lowry Cole; whilst the remaining four projected a trip to Cape Town. In pursuance of our plan, we hired a barouche and six, and a light waggon for our baggage, and by noon we were fairly off. The carriage was of English build, and the six horses were driven in hand by the allied powers of an English coachman and a Hottentot assistant; the former managing the rein department, whilst the province of the latter consisted in wielding a terrific scourge of bamboo and thong, which reached with ease the leading horses. Our coachee's lash, however, sunk into insignificance when we saw the whips used in Cape Town to drive teams of 18 or 20 oxen. We soon found that our carriage, lightly freighted as it was, could not have gone a mile with less than six horses; and even with them we were compelled to alight several times, at points where the road, crossing the heads of little bays, was axle-deep in sand. At one pass the horses struggled so violently that the leaders lost their balance, and both rolled over the side of the road. We kicked open the door, and were out of the vehicle in a moment, and the frightened animals fortunately lay perfectly quiet until we had divested them of their harness. Had they continued their struggles, they must have drawn the whole equipage over the rocky precipice into the boiling surf below. We soon repaired damages, and proceeded, meeting with no further mishaps.

On the sides of the road I remarked the most luxuriant geraniums growing up in company with the rankest weeds. The hills in the neighbourhood abound in a great and curious variety of bulb plants, of which pretty large collections are yearly shipped off to England. At Visch-Hoeks Bay, where there is a tolerably productive whale fishery, the shore is strewed with the gaunt skeletons of several of these giants of the deep: the gardens and enclosures round the cottages of the hamlet are fenced in with the smaller bones; and the beams and uprights—I may not call them timbers—of the habitations themselves are for the most part formed of the vast ribs, which afford a most durable material.

After the first six miles the road deserts the sea-shore, and leads over a sandy plain, which, with very few slight elevations, extends from the head of False Bay to that of Table Bay. The lowness and sandiness of this valley, and the abruptness of the mountains of the Cape and Hottentot Holland on either side of it, give probability to the theory which attempts to prove that the two harbours were once connected by the sea—thus making the Cape an island.

We stopped an hour to bait at the half-way house, a well-situated hotel, kept by Mr. George, the host of the first inn at Cape Town. From the road near this are distinctly discernible the two famous wine farms of Constantia, reclining in the sunny yet sheltered lap of the great Table Mountain, which towers in dark and awful majesty behind them. Its flat summit was entirely shrouded by the "Devil's Table-cloth," which, in spite of the high wind, hung torpid and motionless in its appointed place.

Not far from the halfway-house is situated the pretty village of Wynberg; and, two miles beyond it, embowered in rich groves, is snugly seated Protea, the Governor's country residence. Approaching Cape Town, the country gradually assumes a more smiling aspect; and as the traveller drives between luxuriant hedges of well-grown oaks and firs, and glances down the long umbrageous avenues leading to the villas of the more wealthy Dutch burghers, he almost forgets the arid sands and bleak rocks of Simon's Bay.

Turning sharp round the east shoulder of Table Mountain, in the face of a wind which kept up a continual volley of gravel (for *dust* is no name for its coarse granulation), we came suddenly upon Table Bay and Cape Town. The anchorage was adorned with no less than 16 large vessels: in the centre of the bay we plainly descried the low Robbin Island, which seems to act as a breakwater; and in the right distance was pointed out to us the Blue Berg Hill, near which our troops, under Sir D. Baird, landed at the conquest of the Cape in 1806.

The town is most picturesquely, but most stiflingly, situated under the curving flanks of the Table Mountain and Lion's Hill: the houses are of dazzling whiteness; and the church spires, windmills, and turnpikes carried me in imagination to England. I paid the toll this day with real pleasure, for it was the first that I had paid for five years! After passing the castle (a wretched mud fort), the great barracks, and a well-shaded promenade, in which are situated the public reading-rooms and library, we entered the Heerren Graght (Gentlemen's Walk), a fine wide street, with a deep watercourse and a double row of tall and thick fir-trees in the centre. Turning up this boulevard of Cape Town, our barouche and six rattled up to George's inn, which proved to be quite full: and its thriving host gave us the unwelcome intelligence that the numerous boarding and lodging houses—kept chiefly by Dutch families—were nearly all occupied by the unusual influx of chance visitors. The Lady Holland merchantman had been wrecked a few days before near the bay, and the passengers, who were all saved, were quartered on the town.

We were, however, after some debate, directed to a pension kept by a Dutch gentleman (whose name by six weeks' application I might, perhaps, have learned to pronounce), in one of the three great streets parallel to the Heerren Graght. Two of our quartette remained below to covenant with Mynheer, whilst the third and myself were conducted by an ancient *frau* to inspect the apartments. In our progress she led us calmly through a chamber in which there sat a very comely damsel, attired in a white robe de chambre, her long dark hair unknotted, and abandoned to the tender mercies and the scissors of an Atropos-like barbress. I had half a mind to beg a lock—but the weird coiffeuse looked daggers, and the maiden looked distressed. The apartments were dark as the damsel's tresses: they were also dirty and dismal; and Mynheer conditioning that we should dine at his family hour of 2 o'clock, and keep his bourgeois hours, we failed in coming to terms; although I remarked, and pointed out to our chargé d'affaires, the stupendous chalkstones in our Dutchman's knuckles, which spoke volumes in favour of his cheer; and although his pretty black-eyed daughter paraded her syren charms on the antique balustraded steps in front of the door.

After some further search, which we prolonged rather more than was strictly necessary, we finally engaged apartments, tolerably airy, with well-polished parquets, and as clean as white dimity could make them, in the house of a widowed milliner—the Frau Öst by name—and we boarded at the inn. Our landlady and her assistant sempstresses spoke English pretty fluently:—one of them, a slender, melancholy, Spanish-looking girl, who seldom made her appearance in the shop, was exceedingly beautiful—a sort of creature that one makes out a story for at first sight.

Being fresh landed from a six weeks' voyage, during which I had seen nothing less delicate than the bronzed cheek—*Bacchi* plenus!—of the tar at the wheel, I somewhat distrusted the acumen of my taste for beauty, and I made due allowance for the same; be it as it may, we were all much struck by the uncommon comeliness of the Dutch women in general. There was scarcely a window that had not its pretty face—but it is said that their beauty is not lasting; premature old age and wrinkles soon destroying the charms of a face whose perfections are more those of complexion than of feature.

In the afternoon we repaired to the promenades. The weather was heavenly; and the Heerren Gracht was thronged with gay crowds. Passing up its shady street, we entered the Company's garden, through the centre of which, in continuation of the "gentlemen's walk," runs a gravelled promenade a mile in length, and delightfully shaded with oaks meeting overhead. Within the extent of the walls are the Government House, and a fine menagerie of lions and tigers: but the largest lion perhaps ever seen belongs to Monsieur Villet, a vender of natural curiosities. I went to see it at his country-house at Green Point, a short distance out of town, where he has several curious animals.

The variety of nations, and the numerous shades of complexion, among the people in the streets of Cape Town, are very striking to a stranger. First may be remarked the substantial Dutchman, with his pretty, smiling, round-faced, and particularly well-dressed daughter: then the knot of "Qui hi's," sent to the Cape, per doctor's certificate, to husband their threadbare constitutions, and lavish their rupees: next the obsequious, smirking, money-making Chinaman, with his poking shoulders and whip-like pig-tail: then the stout squat Hottentots—who resemble the Dutch in but one characteristic!—and half-castes of every intermediate tint between black and white. These are well relieved and contrasted by the tall warlike figures and splendid costume of His Majesty's 72nd Highlanders, who, with the 98th regiment, form the garrison of Cape Town.

March 2nd.—Having engaged from Mr. Stone's livery-stables a very smart and serviceable hack, I rode this morning round the Lion's Hill, so called from its rude resemblance to the couchant form of the brute king. It is a spur, running out at right angles from the Table and abutting upon the sea. A semaphoric post, on that part of the hill styled the Lion's Rump, commands a very extensive prospect. The road is not accessible to carriages, but it affords a delightful ride for the inhabitants of the town. That portion of it which skirts round the bluff promontory of rock overhanging the sea reminded me a good deal of some points in the mail-road between Conway and Bangor, in Carnarvonshire. The view from the lofty Kloof or Pass, separating the Lion's Head and Table Mountain, is beautiful in the extreme, and the more so from the suddenness with which the traveller comes upon it. Below us, about 2 miles distant, lay the town, with its white buildings, parallel streets, and verdant promenades spread out like a map; beyond, the thronged harbour, and the sunny bay spangled with distant sails—one of which, by-the-by, proved to be the 'Minerva' Company's ship, which sailed two days after the 'Pallas' from Calcutta, and had thus kept pace with her frigate namesake. The graceful crescent of the bay is closed by the low outline of the Blue Berg Hill, and the extreme distance of the picture is filled up by the lofty mountains of Hottentot Holland.

The horses of the Cape of Good Hope are in general very good, all the better bred ones having English blood in them. I have seen a Cape horse, with 16 stone on his back, leading the field with the Calcutta hounds; and, returning from my ride to-day, I overtook a brick-waggon, drawn by a team of four bays, which would not have shamed the carriage of Lord Sefton himself. The driver told me that the wheelers, which were skittish, and much above their work, cost 1000 rix-dollars* or 75*l.* each. The price of hacks per day is 5 rix-dollars, or 7*s.* 6*d.* Board and lodging in a Dutch family, including Cape wines, only 6 dollars a day. Provisions and fruit are very cheap, but the inns—there are only two—are exorbitant. My landlady brought every morning, for 2*d.*, more than enough grapes for her four lodgers: the honey-pod and crystal are the best for the table. Grapes, horses, women, and whips are the objects best meriting admiration at the Cape; but for the wine I cannot say so much. The common Cape wine is bad Madeira; the Pontac bad port; but the Frontignac and Constantia are rich and luscious sweet wines.

In the field-sports of the Cape I had no opportunity of mixing, but I am informed that it yields to no part of the world in quantity and variety of game. At the distance of 20 or 30 miles from Cape Town may be had excellent shooting; quails, snipes, partridges, hares, wild ducks, and

* The rix-dollar is a nominal coin, worth here one shilling and sixpence; the Spanish dollar is worth three of the above.

guinea-fowls greatly abounding: but for *gros gibier*, such as leopards, lions, the rhinoceros, hippopotamus, zebra, and the larger species of antelope, the sportsman must make a trip to the frontier of the colony, on the borders of Caffraria, where in the earlier days of the Dutch settlement a Caffre or a brace of Bushmen were not uncommonly added to the game-bag.

Near Cape Town are kept two packs of foxhounds, which hunt the flats and sandhills between that town and Tiger Bay, and the mountains of Hottentot Holland. (The fixtures would sound strange in Meltonian ears!) The heat compels them to meet, even in winter, at daybreak. Foxes are plentiful, and generally run stout and straight. Sportsmen are, and have need to be, well mounted, for there is nothing to stop the speed of the hounds; and nature, in default of fences, has kindly furnished the horseman with the necessary degree of risk in the furrows of the great Cape mole, in which tumbles may be obtained suited to the capacity of almost any neck or skull, as I myself had afterwards an opportunity of personally judging.

March 3rd.—In the morning I rode out in the direction of the Table Mountain, and was surprised to find how much more there is of sloping space between its scarped and frowning flanks and the town than appeared at first sight. I soon found myself in an extensive suburb, chiefly formed of pretty villas, well sheltered and screened from the road, but commanding extensive prospects to the seaward. Some of these secluded dwellings nearest to the mountain reminded me of those full-dress cottages under Abraham's Height at Matlock—but Abraham's Height is but a mole-hill compared with the Table. The road was thronged with busy washerwomen, black and white, who had been far up the hill to pound the linen of their employers in the little runnels which ooze but scantily from the sides of the mountain; and the Hottentot individuals of the party presented, I think, the most awful specimens of womankind that I ever in my rambles had the misfortune to encounter.

In the afternoon we examined the collections of stuffed animals by Messrs. Villet and Verreau—the latter of whom is peculiarly happy in giving the natural character and expression to his birds and beasts. I dined with the 72nd Highlanders, who live in very good style; and the officers did not speak so well of Cape Town as a quarter as I had expected. It appears that the Dutch and English do not mix much in society—the former certainly enjoy their own, if I might judge by the "sounds of revelry by night" which I heard in some of the larger houses as I passed through the streets.

March 4th.—Advertisement in the Cape paper.—"To be let—A slave boy of able body and good disposition, equal to any common household work." A few days ago, as I was informed, a beautiful girl was put up and sold by auction for 1000 rix-dollars; an emigrant to the Swan River being her purchaser.* With this vile slave system in full force, it is not surprising that Cape Town is by no means famous for rigidity of morals.

The next morning one of our party received a polite note from Mynheer Colyn of Little Constantia, expressing his happiness to see us at his wine-farm on our road to Simon's Town to-morrow. This being my last day at Cape Town, I determined to leave it with the fairest impressions: I therefore went in the afternoon to pay a visit to the much-lauded beauty of the Cape, Helen Bestandig. She is the daughter of the hostess of a fashionable boarding-house, and is, in truth, surprisingly handsome. Though only fifteen, she has already, says report, doomed many English and Dutch swains to wear the willow.

March 6th.—Having paid our bills through all the perplexing intricacies of rix and Spanish dollars, schellings and shillings, and taken a warm farewell of the good widow and her pretty aides-de-camp—or rather "de boutique"—we mounted our hacks to ride to Simon's Town. An

* I am assured, however, of the existence of a law, difficult of evasion, prohibiting the sale of slaves for exportation.

8-horse waggon, driven in hand, trotted away with our baggage, and beat us in.

The dexterity of the Hottentot drivers is admirable. It is wonderful to see how well they keep eight in hand together, as they rattle through the narrow and crowded streets at a long trot.

Cantering merrily along, we reached the halfway-house —9½ miles—in an hour, and breakfasted there with two gentlemen of the Honourable Company's Civil Service, or *Hindoos*, as they are here styled. Having refreshed ourselves and horses, we made for Constantia, which took us about six miles out of our road; but the fame of its wines and its vines, and the civility of its master, are sufficient inducements to visitors. After riding by ill-defined paths across a common thickly covered with low heather and jungle, we passed the gate of "Groot Constantia," the property of Mynheer Cloety, and, descending a rustic lane, like those of Surrey, and diving under a dark and beautiful arcade of oaks, we came suddenly upon the goodly mansion of Mr. Colyn. He received us most urbanely, and introduced us to his mother, sister, and wife; the last of whom bears in her comely countenance as much of the purpurea juventas as her own bloom-grapes. Mr. Colyn then conducted us to his vineyards, which are situated on gently undulating ground, exposed to the south, and protected by the mountain from the north and west winds. They are also surrounded by a leafy screen of fine tall oaks, bearing the largest acorns I ever saw. We tasted his several kinds of grape, the Muscadell, Frontignac, red and white Constantia, &c.,—the latter I thought the best flavoured. I was surprised at the extreme lowness of the plants, few of them being higher than two feet, though some of them had been in the ground 100 years. This mode of pruning down the Constantia vine is, however, very advantageous, for the fruit hangs so near the ground, that the reflection of the sun from the white earth is nearly as powerful as its rays from above. For sweet wines the grapes are allowed to remain on the tree until they become half raisins. It is quite true that the Constantia grape will not attain perfection when planted even 20 paces on either side of its own exclusive vineyard;—the common Cape grape is therefore introduced in preference. A pointer dog that accompanied us devoured several large bunches with great apparent zest.

After roaming for half an hour through the sunny vines, we went to see the vats in store—a most formidable array! —and tasted the Frontignac and the two Constantias; they are all expensive, the former especially. Our visit concluded with a capital luncheon—I must forget the Indian "tiffin"—and in return for all his civility, Mr. Colyn only requested us to record our names in a book which he keeps for that purpose, and which contains a rare variety of autographs. He afterwards sent a vast quantity of beautiful grapes to one of our party on board the Pallas, who, in return, despatched to the fair vigneronne a present of fine Dacca muslins.

At 2 o'clock we again mounted our horses, and having received precise injunctions from Mr. C. not to leave the high road, on account of the dangerous quicksands, we bade adieu to the blooming Constantia, and resumed our journey towards the bleak and dreary Simon's Bay. I know not whether the sipping of so many wines under a hot sun had obfuscated our vision, and confused our notions of right and left, or right and wrong—but certain it is that we started off at a most "larking" pace; soon lost our way, and suddenly found ourselves floundering in a bog. My horse, which was leading, refused to advance; but they were all soon forced through the quag by some Hottentot slaves whom we called to our aid. These fellows jumped into the saddles, and, laughing and flogging, crammed them fearlessly at the black and deep morass; whilst we walked across on a narrow artificial ridge—a performance which fully satisfied us as to the stability of our brains!

After riding about three miles farther, across a country dangerously undermined by a large and beautiful species of mole, we gained the turnpike-road, and reached Simon's Town at 5 P.M. Lord Combermere, accompanied by Sir L. Cole, arrived soon after; the whole party dined with the gallant Commodore; and late in the evening we were again assembled in the cabin of the Pallas, having passed six very pleasant days at the Cape. For myself, I never was more agreeably surprised in any place: the climate is heavenly; and although this is the summer season, none of our party felt the worse for having rode 30 miles in the heat of the day.

March 7th.—11 A.M. weighed and made sail, beating out of False Bay against a light south-west breeze. At sunset Pallas rounded the rugged point of Good Hope, and turned her head towards St. Helena, 1700 miles from the Cape, a distance usually performed in from 10 to 14 days.

As we looked back through the obscurity of the night, towards the land that we had just quitted, our eyes were arrested by a most brilliant and curious spectacle—a long and tortuous train of flame, caused by an accidental conflagration of the jungle, wound up the back of the Table Mountain, which being invisible through the gloom, the blazing line bore all the appearance of a vast fiery serpent, rearing itself out of the dark ocean.

On the third day we overtook, and administered the *go-by* to, the Minerva, which had weighed and made sail from Table Bay about the same time that Pallas quitted Simon's Bay.

March 20th.—At mid-day St. Helena was visible from the deck, distant 42 miles, and we were drawing near to it with a fine south-east breeze, at the rate of 8 knots an hour. When I first caught sight of it, it appeared like a single filmy cloud lingering on the edge of the horizon, whose wide expanse was clear of vapours, yet hazy from excessive heat. In a few hours, however, it assumed a darker and more solid form, and ere sunset we were near enough to scan its rugged features.

Nothing can be more repulsive than the appearance of St. Helena from the sea: many hundred miles from any continent, it looks as though it had been divorced from the mass of the habitable world. It starts abruptly out of the deep, in a confused heap of bare and craggy rocks, of which the southern side is, perhaps, the most savage and desolate part.

It is impossible for the most apathetic to approach the prison and tomb of the most wonderful man Europe ever produced, and the most powerful enemy England ever had, without feelings of the highest interest. As I gazed on the black and sea-worn flanks of this bastile of Nature, I imagined to myself the chilly horror with which the Imperial captive must have contemplated, from the deck of the Northumberland, his destined abode. Precipitously scarped all round, it looks as though it had been formed expressly to be the iron cage of some gigantic Bajazet.

As we sailed round the bluff, round-headed point, called from its structure "the *Barn*," we gradually neared the shore; and just as the shades of evening were closing around us we ran close under a battery, situated on a lofty salient angle of rock, and styled with true English vulgarity and ineptitude of nomenclature, "Buttermilk Point."

A hoarse voice from the battery hailed us as we passed, demanded the ship's name, and gave the necessary permission to anchor in James's Bay after sunset. From this point we could distinctly see the forest of masts in the harbour, and the lights in James's Town and in the surrounding batteries; and, strongly relieved against the yet ruddy evening sky, we descried two large ships quitting the roads.

At half-past 7 Pallas shortened sail, and dropped anchor about half a mile from shore, in 20 fathoms. Within a few hundred yards of us lay the Sybèle frigate, carrying the broad pennant of Commodore Collyer. This ship was in quarantine, having just returned from that very efficient drain on England's excessive population, Fernando Po; where the work of saving black men, at the price of killing whites, is going on as merrily as ever.

March 21st.—Rose early to have a view of James's Town

and Bay. The former is snugly niched in a narrow ravine between two towering cliffs, and consists of one long street running up towards the centre of the island. Strong batteries, with a ditch and drawbridge, are drawn across the defile from cliff to cliff; and the summits and flanks of the rocks on either hand are strengthened with numerous posts bristling with heavy guns. Ladder Hill, 800 feet high, on the right of the town, is the most considerable battery; and the Governor has lately improved its communication with the arsenal by means of a direct flight of steps from the summit to the base, flanked by two railroads, up which any quantity of stores or ammunition may be raised in a few minutes by a windlass.

At 9 A.M. Lord Combermere and his party landed. The Governor, Brigadier-General Dallas, received him on the pier, and we were all quickly furnished with horses to carry us to Plantation House, distant 3½ miles from James Town. A salute rattled from the batteries; the little garrison drawn up in line presented arms; an excellent band pealed forth the national anthem, and I could hardly believe that we were on a little barren rock in the midst of the Atlantic, and so far removed from the civilized parts of the world.

On clearing the town we climbed by a steep zigzag, but wide and safe road, up to the post of Ladder Hill, the Governor's carriage and four following us. From the battery at this point, a heavy shot, taking effect on a ship in the bay, would make its entry through the upper deck and its exit through the bottom of the vessel. Leaving Ladder Hill, we passed the artillery barracks, and soon after came upon a most sterile slope, cut up into ravines, and thinly inoculated with the cactus-plant. This desert, I was surprised to hear, is the preserve—the partridges breeding there in preference to the most woody parts of the island. Pheasants and rabbits are also found there.

Passing upwards over the crest of the hill, we had a pleasant canter through about a quarter of a mile of fir plantation, and came suddenly upon Plantation House, the

Governor's residence. Here Nature is decked out in her holiday attire: the mansion, a good square English-looking building, is delightfully situated in the gorge of a wide ravine, surrounded on three sides by woods, and with a verdant lawn in front. Beyond this the eye ranges uninterruptedly down to the ocean. From the drawing-room windows a ship a mile out at sea is seen through the wire fence at the end of the lawn. Pleasant shady walks are cut through the woody arms of the ravine which enclose the view on either side. Here the oak and bamboo, fir and plantain, natives of such widely-distant climes, mingle branches; and the myrtle aspires to the dignity of a timber tree. Geranium is a weed. Peaches and grapes, the fig and the loquot, the pear, potato, and brinjâl, all flourish together in the gardens. The house is roomy and cheerful, and a neat chapel is situated 300 yards farther up the hill, in the rear. From the unpromising appearance of the exterior of the isle, no visitor would be led to expect so pretty a domain and so comfortable a residence as Plantation presents. The Governor's family consists of his lady and three fair daughters—the Mirandas of this sainted isle: with a military secretary and an aide-de-camp, both island-born, or "Yam-stocks," as the natives are technically styled.

We were received most kindly by the family, and hospitably and pleasantly entertained during three days. The number of visitors of every nation, whether in the pursuit of business or of pleasure, who cross the threshold of the Governor's ever-open door, is immense. Nine vessels were telegraphed this morning early, and four more soon afterwards.

Hallowed as this isle is in their eyes, as being the resting-place of the remains of their demigod, the French are naturally the most numerous visitors. One of this nation, a very clever fellow, sat next to me at dinner today, and I had much interesting converse with him regarding Napoleon. He said he had come from the Mauritius expressly to make a "pélerinage au tombeau du plus grand des hommes," and moralized on the déchéance of human greatness with tears in his eyes.

March 22nd.—After breakfast, a fine shower of rain having cleared the atmosphere, a party of ten started on an equestrian ramble round the island. Passing through the gateway at the back of Government House, we came directly upon a series of verdant and beautiful valleys, which, crossing each other in every direction, occupy the concave centre of the isle, and seem to emanate from the great mountain of Diana's Peak.

The roads are very good, though the rider is too constantly interrupted by the multitudes of gates (not turnpikes, for the roads are kept up by taxes on horses, dogs, guns, &c.), which, when they occur in a narrow path, with a fathomless precipice on one or both hands, are troublesome obstructions. In our case they were rendered still worse by the number and insubordinate conduct of our horses.

We soon reached the top of a steep ridge, from whence we enjoyed a most beautiful prospect of what may be called the southern division of the island. For a mile in our front lay a foreground of the richest green—forests of firs, knolls covered with gorse in full blossom, with here and there cottages or more considerable houses peeping from the midst of groves or perched on the very brow of the abrupt but verdant hills. Among these, the mansion of Sir William Doveton is the most prominent, and most picturesque in situation. The owner is an old resident of the island, and was knighted by the king as the bearer of some loyal address from the islanders. He is a very fine old man, in the full possession of all his faculties at the age of 78, and is in himself an eloquent proof of the goodness of that climate which was so much vituperated by Napoleon and his followers. On this point the dissatisfaction of the great prisoner seems decidedly unfounded — the thermometer ranges at a mean between 58° and 78°, seldom higher or lower—the "Yam-stocks" are usually stout and florid in appearance; and certainly, during this day (and we were out from 10 till 5 o'clock), it was impossible to say that it was either disagreeably hot or cold. The very few deaths in the Emperor's family, during the five years of his residence, afford fair presumption of the healthiness of the climate; for, of 50 persons, I believe only one died, and he was a consumptive subject. But to resume our sketch.

Immediately beyond the above-described vivid and luxuriant foreground, the eye of the spectator loses itself amongst a chaos of parched, cragged, and precipitous ravines, which, unadorned by a single blade of vegetation, run down towards Sandy Bay, one of the very few accessible points of the isle. The bare and forked peaks of the southern extremity of the island close the landscape; but beyond them, on a clear day, 20 leagues of the blue ocean are visible.

Continuing our ride, we soon reached Diana's Peak, the loftiest pinnacle of St. Helena, about 2700 feet above the sea, or co-equal with the Cheviot mountains in Scotland. It is thickly clothed with shrubs up to the extremest summit, and the road is hedged in with the cabbage-tree, the gum-tree, and the most luxuriant blackberries. This path, which is certainly very narrow, was cut expressly for, and dedicated exclusively to, Buonaparte; and he, always ready with objections, complained that it was formed for the express purpose of breaking his neck. Each lofty point has its signal-post, so that the prisoner's every movement was overlooked, a measure which must have been galling enough, but no less necessary. Even now, so vigilant are the watchmen, that they seldom fail to discover vessels at 20 leagues' distance. They have orders to fire a warning-gun if three ships are seen approaching, as if in company. Captain D. told me that one of these look-out posts telescoped and telegraphed him to Government House as *poaching* in the preserve, when he thought himself quite secure from observation.

We soon came in sight of the level plateau of the Longwood estate, the residence of the late emperor, and six miles from Plantation House. Here the country gradually assumes a more desolate and a wilder look; and the English visitor arrives at the unfortunate and unwelcome conclusion that the best part of the island was not given to the illustrious captive. One cannot avoid agreeing with Sir W. Scott, that Plantation House should have been accorded to him, in spite of the deterring reasons of its vicinity to the sea, and its sequestered situation. Longwood, however, has better roads, more space for riding or driving, and in summer must have been much cooler than the less open parts of the isle.

As we turned through the lodges the old house appeared at the end of an avenue of scrubby and weather-worn trees.

It bears the exterior of a respectable farm-house, but is now fast running to decay. On entering a dirty court-yard, and quitting our horses, we were shown by some idlers into a square building, which once contained the bed-room, sitting-room, and bath of the Empereur des Français. The partitions and floorings are now thrown down and torn up, and the apartments occupied for six years by the hero before whom kings, emperors, and popes had quailed, are now tenanted by cart-horses!

Passing on with a groan, I entered a small chamber with two windows looking towards the north. Between these windows are the marks of a fixed sofa: on that couch Napoleon died. The apartment is now occupied by a threshing-machine; "No bad emblem of its former tenant!" said a sacrilegious wag. Hence we were conducted onwards to a large room, which formerly contained a billiard-table, and whose front looks out upon a little latticed veranda, where the imperial peripatetic—I cannot style him philosopher—enjoyed the luxury of six paces to and fro,—his favourite promenade. The whitewashed walls are scored with names of every nation; and the paper of the ceiling has been torn off in strips, as holy relics. Many couplets, chiefly French, extolling and lamenting the departed hero, adorn or disfigure (according to their qualities) the plaster walls. The only lines that I can recall to mind—few are worth it—are the following, written over the door, and signed "* * * * * * *, Officier de la Garde Impériale."

> "Du grand Napoléon le nom toujours cité
> Ira de bouche en bouche à la postérité !"

The writer doubtless possessed more spirit as a sabreur than as a poet.

The emperor's once well-kept garden,

> "And still where many a garden-flower grows wild,"

is now overgrown and choked with weeds. At the end of a walk still exists a small mound, on which it is said the hero of Lodi, Marengo, and Austerlitz amused himself by erecting a mock battery. The little chunamed tank, wherein he fed some freshwater fish, is quite dried up; and the mud wall, through a hole in which he reconnoitred passers-by, is, like the great owner, returned to earth!

It is difficult now to judge of what Longwood was when in repair; but I cannot think that it could, in its *best* days, have been worthy of the illustrious occupant, even in his *worst.* A little lower down the hill, and much better situated than the old house, stands the new one, which was not finished when Napoleon died.

The erection of this commodious and handsome building shows a willingness to accommodate Bonaparte, which is highly creditable to our government, and affords a good proof of the same to his compatriots. It is built according to his expressed wish, "without dark passages," and with a fine suite of rooms leading into each other. He, however, preferred the old incommodious house, with its concomitant grievance, to the new one, which would have left him little to complain of. No one can remember without regret the unhappy subjects of dispute which embittered the communion between the distinguished exile and his governors, and the undignified and unmanly schemes which he concocted for the annoyance of his unlucky keeper. There was doubtless blame on both sides.

As we English never do anything without eating, our party lunched in the spacious veranda of new Longwood House, and then repaired to the St. Helena museum, distant a quarter of a mile: it is a small collection, but valuable to science.

Having passed two hours on the spot where Napoleon lived and died, we rode onwards to the vale which contains his bones: it is about half a mile from Longwood, and within a few hundred yards of the cottage of Madame Bertrand, to whom he indicated the spot in which he desired to rest, should the English not allow his remains to lie on the banks of the Seine. Soon after leaving Bertrand's house, we caught sight of the tomb, at the bottom of the ravine called Slane's valley, and, descending a zigzag path, we quickly reached the spot. About half an acre round the grave is railed in. At the gate we were received by an old corporal of the St. Helena corps, who has the care of the place. The tomb itself consists of a square stone, about 10 feet by 7, surrounded with a plain iron railing. Four or five weeping-willows, their stems leaning towards the grave, hang their pensile branches over it.

Who could contemplate without interest the little spot of earth which covers all that remains of mortal of the man who made Europe tremble! who carried his victorious arms from the Nile to the Elbe, from Moscow to the Pillars of Hercules; who bore his eagles triumphantly through Vienna, Rome, Berlin, Madrid! Beneath our feet lay he who " du monde entre ses mains a vu les destinées"—

> " The desolator desolate, the victor overthrown ! "

" They that see thee," saith the inspired prophet, " they that see thee shall narrowly look upon thee, and consider thee, saying, Is this the man that made the earth to tremble, and did shake kingdoms; that made the world as a wilderness, and destroyed the cities thereof; that opened not the house of his prisoners? All the kings of the nations, even all of them, lie in glory, every one in his own house. Thou shalt not be joined with them in burial, because thou hast destroyed thy land, and slain thy people; the seed of evil-doers shall never be renowned."*

The willows are decaying fast, and one of them rests upon the sharp spears of the railing, which are buried in its trunk—as though it were committing suicide for very grief! The foliage of the rest is thinned and disfigured by the frequent and almost excusable depredations of visitors. Fresh cuttings have, however, been planted by the Governor, who intends, moreover, to set cypresses round the outer fence. Madame Bertrand's immortelles have proved, alas! mortal.

The fine, tall, old corporal, who came out from England with the ex-emperor, was full of his praises: "I saw the General often," said the old fellow; "he had an eye in his head like an eagle!" He described the visit of the French pilgrims to this spot—their Kibla—as most affecting. Some are extravagant beyond measure in their grief, falling on their faces round the railing (which they never enter, as foreigners do), praying, weeping, and even tearing their hair. Whilst we were there my friend of yesterday came towards the spot; but when he saw our large, and, I fear me, rather unimpressed party, he turned upwards and disappeared. After inscribing our names in a book—into which also appropriate poetry, as well as ribald nonsense, finds its way—we drank to Napoleon's immortal memory in his own favourite spring, and, mounting our steeds, spurred towards Plantation House.

On the road, we passed within view of "the Briars," where the chief resided during the building of Longwood; and where he—

> "Whose game was kingdoms, and whose stakes were thrones,
> His table earth, his dice were human bones!—

played at whist with the owner, Mr. Balcombe, for *sugar-plums!*

March 23*rd*.—St. Helena was discovered by the Portuguese in 1502, and by them soon deserted. It was taken

* Isaiah xiv. 16, 17, 18, 20.

possession of by the East India Company in 1651, and granted to them by charter of Charles II. in 1661. In 1672 it was taken by the Dutch, and was recovered by the English the following year.

St. Helena is highly important to the Company as an entrepôt for their stores, &c., and in the hands of an enemy would be a thorn in the side of their commerce. In other respects it is far from profitable; the expenses amounting to nearly 80,000*l.* a year, whilst the revenue is scarcely 5000*l.*

A governor and two members of council, invested with both judicial and executive power, form the government of the isle. The inhabitants, including the garrison, are 5000; the infantry and artillery amount to 800 men; and 700 volunteers can be raised at a moment's warning. The island batteries mount about 200 heavy guns; and there are besides some 16 moveable pieces.

St. Helena is 23 miles in circumference. This miniature microcosm boasts of numerous public institutions; amongst others, Horticultural and Agricultural Societies, a Widows' Fund, and a Free-school, educating 500 children.

After an early dinner at Plantation House our party took leave of the Governor and his fair daughters—who seem to rejoice in their truly halcyon home—and rode down to the town. The St. Helena regiment, dressed like the Guards, was drawn up, and presented arms; and as we stepped into the Governor's barge the people on the wharf and on the batteries gave us three cheers. By the time we reached the Pallas it was quite dark. At that moment the batteries opened a salute, a rocket going up with every gun, and blue lights burning along the rocks; Pallas returned the salute, and blue lights were burnt at all her yard-arms.

Nine o'clock, up anchor, made all sail.

Our pertinacious synonyme, the Minerva, who left the Cape the same day as the Pallas, arrived at St. Helena only six hours after her, and quitted James's Bay a few hours before her.

Two days' sailing again brought us up with her, and we

passed at speaking distance. As we glided briskly past her, we exchanged greetings with the passengers on her poop, and her crew manned the rigging and gave us three cheers, the band striking up 'Rule Britannia'—a compliment returned with interest by Captain Fitz-Clarence. I felt proud of the Pallas, as her gallant ship's company, dressed in their neat summer uniform of white shirts and trowsers and straw hats, sprung simultaneously from the deck, spread themselves nimbly over the shrouds of the three masts, suddenly faced outwards, doffed hats, and poured forth a shout that made the heavens echo again.

March 27th.—At mid-day descried the Isle of Ascension, 35 miles north; and at 7 P.M. anchored in seven fathoms, in a small bay, off the settlement. Our passage was very good, being rather under four days. The island is even more forbidding in its external appearance than the one we have just quitted. For a concise and apt definition of the two isles, St. Helena is a *Rock*—Ascension a *Cinder*. Approaching the south end, it bears the appearance of a succession of brick-kilns and lime-kilns, according to their hues, but of Brobdignagian proportions—these elevations being in fact extinct volcanoes. In the centre of the isle is the lofty "Green Mountain," which—lucus a non lucendo—but little deserves its epithet. Near its cloud-capped summit we readily distinguished a line of white buildings, from which the flash and smoke of a signal gun were visible as we neared the shore. The side of Ascension on which the settlement is situated, is considerably lower than the southern extremity of the isle; and as we ran along it we saw several turtle bays, which are merely small inlets of sandy beach between the rocks. In these spots the turtles lay their eggs, which are hatched by the sun, three times a year, each animal having a progeny of some 200. The number of their enemies, however, prevents the undue increase of their population: as the new-hatched turtles crawl to the sea, their migration is intercepted by the clouds of sea-birds which infest the island; and of those that are fortunate enough to reach the water, many are cut off in their prime by the conger-eel and other marine foes. At a more advanced period of their eventful existence, when their bulk protects them against other carnivorous animals, the Corporation of London are said to be no insignificant exterminators of the breed.

March 28th.—Landed early. On the little rocky pier we were received by the second in command; the Governor, Captain Bate, R.M., having received some distressing news by the Pallas. The settlement—though it only consists of a few houses and huts for the accommodation of the garrison, 140 marines—is dignified with the loyal title of George Town. Two captains and two subalterns of Marines, with two surgeons and a victualler, form the aristocracy of Ascension. The Governor draws from the Treasury of England—Mr. Hume! does your lynx-eyed economy doze? —a revenue amounting to 4*s.* per diem! The second in command receives 2*s.* 6*d.*, and the subalterns 1*s.* each, extra!

The only "lion" of the town is the turtle crawl, or kraal, a walled-in creek, in which the tide ebbs and flows, and where hundreds of these "delicate monsters" are imprisoned. I saw one there which was said to weigh 830 pounds. One of 900 pounds was sent to the King last year.—(N.B. A fine bullock was killed at the Cape, for the use of the ship's company, which only weighed 600 pounds.) —The West Indian turtle, I am told, rarely exceed 2 hundred-weight. The turtle of Ascension, the only produce of the island, constitute its sole revenue; but the inhabitants are permitted to use as much as they can consume. It is considered very wholesome food. One hundred and fifty turtles have been *turned* in a night here.

All the horses (seven in number) of the isle being pressed into our service, we rode up to the station on Green Mountain, six miles from George Town, where the little cultivation that this barren spot is susceptible of is carried on. The road, which is safe and formed with some art, leads over a series of hills and valleys of volcanic ashes, whose loose, crisp surface is guiltless of a single blade of vegetation. As we approached the station in our toilsome ascent, we however met with scanty sprinklings of the Indian gooseberry, wild tomata, and coarse grass.

The little mountain hamlet, consisting of some half-dozen houses and cabins, small but comfortable, is seated, like the eyrie of an eagle, on a sunny shelf, 300 or 400 ft. below the summit of the hill, and forms the residence of two officers and a few soldiers, whose florid countenances testify the salubrity of this exalted climate. The gentlemen gave us a capital breakfast of beef-steaks and veal-cutlets—really not misnamed—both made of turtle: and afterwards acted as our guides in a ramble of six miles round the Green Mountain. The road, which is as yet but half formed, and in some points practised in the obstructing rock, is dangerous, but not *otherwise* interesting; unless it be so to see the struggles these good people are making against nature to cultivate a few fruits and vegetables.

About 800 or 1000 acres of land—if the meagre deposit of half mould half cinder may be so called—are capable of arability; at least so say the sanguine settlers, who are naturally anxious to make the best of their colony.

English and sweet potatoes, Indian corn, and a few pumpkins and plantains, are all that their incipient farm has hitherto produced. The Palma Christi, or castor-oil plant, whose fine vine-like leaf and grateful shade are more pleasing than its associations, is the only vegetable production that affects the tree. Nasturtium grows, as wild and as thick as heather, in the ravines.

There are wild goats and guinea-fowls in abundance on the mountain. Three brace of the latter were turned out three or four years ago: last year the settlers killed nearly 2000 head of them; and this day, in our walk, I did not see fewer than 200 brace. They got up in coveys, and flew as strong as pheasants. We had no guns with us, or might have had fine sport. Wild cattle also formerly inhabited the mountain, but they were exterminated on account of their fierceness.

From the Station on Green Mountain the lower region of

the island has, literally speaking, a most infernal appearance —not fewer than 50 craters of exhausted volcanoes having been counted. The lava is from the brightest red to the deepest black in colour; and the latter, of which I procured a good specimen, is susceptible of a high polish. Water is the scarcest commodity, niggard Nature having only vouchsafed two dribbling springs to Ascension: magnificent tanks, as reservoirs for the rain-water, are, however, in progress, one of which is calculated to contain about 550 tuns.

At 3 P.M. we reached the ship, well fatigued, and eager to bid adieu to this desolate shore. It would, I think, have gone far towards reconciling Napoleon to his island prison had they given him a glimpse of Ascension before they carried him to St. Helena. Royal indeed must be the revenue that would tempt me to become "monarch of all I survey," in this "horrible place!" Should, however, in the march of these king-making and king-marring times, the crown of Ascension chance to be forced on my acceptance, I shall rob Shah Jehan of his inflated motto, and, varying only one word of his inscription, adapt it to *my* hall of audience—"If there be a h—ll upon earth, it is this! it is this!"*

At 7 P.M., having stowed ourselves and 19 large turtle on board, we weighed anchor, and made all sail from Ascension, leaving in the bay the 10-gun brig Chanticleer, whose commander, Captain Forster,† is at present employed upon the island in a course of experiments to ascertain, by the pendulum, the sphericity of the globe at different points upon its surface.

April 1st.—Pallas re-crossed the Line. On the 4th the north-east Trade-wind declared for us, and continued to lend

* This well-known inscription—adverted to by Moore in his 'Lalla Rookh' —still remains in the Dewânee Khâs at Delhi:—

"If there be a Paradise upon earth,
It is this! it is this!"

† The newspapers of September, 1831, announced the untimely death of this talented and enterprising officer.

us efficient aid until the 15th. With a pretty equal alternation of calms and stiff breezes, we reached the Azores, or Western Isles, on the 21st, and ran swiftly through the group. At 8 A.M. we passed Pico, a fine island, highly cultivated, 30 miles in length. Its main feature is the Peak mountain, whence its name. It is 7000 feet high, its summit capped with snow. Pico produces yearly 20,000 pipes of wine, a fair portion of which doubtless finds its way to England as Madeira.

We soon after passed in our rapid course the Isles of St. George and Graciosa, the former in high culture, the latter small and rugged. At mid-day we came in sight of the much-talked-of island of Terceira; it is exceedingly high, and as pretty as luxuriant woods, many-tinted cultivation, and bold cliffs can make it. The capital town, Angra—situated behind a bluff promontory of rock greatly capable of fortification—appears tolerably extensive; and numbers of snow-white villages and lone houses are dotted over the face of the slope. The anchorage of this isle, as well as of the rest of the Azores, is very unsafe.

April 26th.—For the last week we have been favoured by fresh and prosperous gales. The little Pallas, sympathizing with our eagerness to reach home, "keeps pace with our expectancy, and flies." In eight days she has run over a distance of 1732 miles!

By mid-day on the *27th* we had struck off 185 miles from the yet remaining small score; and had the breeze proved constant, five hours more would have sufficed to place us out of danger from its further fickleness. At 12 o'clock Eddystone lighthouse and Mount Edgecombe were only distant from us 10 miles, when the wind, deserting our cause, *ratted*, and blew directly in our teeth. Plymouth lay most invitingly to leeward; we could have been there in an hour; but Portsmouth is our destination, and to Portsmouth must we go. At sunset Pallas exchanged numbers with a line-of-battle ship in Plymouth Sound.

28th.—Beating-up the Channel. In the night weathered Portland Bill.

29th.—Beating up Channel. Oh, hope deferred, how dost thou clog the hours! At 10 A.M. we had a fine view of Lulworth Castle (Mr. Weld's), since better known as the retreat of the ex-King of France; and at 12 o'clock we caught the first glimpse of the Isle of Wight.

30th April, 1830.—About two bells in the morning watch (5 o'clock) I was awakened from a deep dream, in which "England, Home, and Beauty" formed the leading features, by the ear-piercing pipe of the boatswain, closely followed up by his hoarse roar of "All hands, bring ship to an anchor;" a call which was speedily re-echoed by the ready mates as they tripped down the hatchways from the main-deck, to hurry up the (on this occasion) doubly willing crew, whose hearts, doubtless, yearned towards that "point" with which so many of their tenderest recollections were associated.

In the prosecution of this nautical réveillé, the following delicate yet highly characteristic expressions came quaintly enough upon a landsman's ear: "heave out there;" "rouse and bit;" "show a leg, and save the tide," &c.

In a few minutes the deck was alive with the assembled people; and, the hammocks being stowed, they flew to their appointed stations. As we approached the well-known anchorage a dead silence reigned around, and all eyes seemed riveted on the Captain, who, mounted on a gun, now gave, in a clear voice, the word of command to "shorten sail." The pipes of the boatswain and his mates pealed out a shrill response, which was distinctly heard above the creaking of blocks and tackles, and the stamp of the seamen as they "run up" the various gear. In an instant the sails, so lately asleep and swelling before the gentle breeze, were clewed up and gathered to the yards by the topmen ready stationed aloft: another moment, and the order to "stand clear the cable" was given; and ere the warning could well be obeyed, the plunge of the "best bower," and the harsh grating of the chain, announced the completion of our voyage.

England welcomed her long-absent sons with her brightest smiles. The sea was as smooth and unruffled as a lake; the beautiful Isle of Wight was decked out in all the tender verdure of young Spring; and the sky appeared almost Indian in its freedom from clouds and its intensity of blue. At 12 o'clock I sprung on to the shore of my father-land, after an absence of nearly five years.

In the words of some bard, whose name I remember not, I might say—

"I've wander'd where the scorching sun
Blights the fair flower it smiles upon;—
I've seen the hunted elephant
Deep in the trampled jungle pant:—
I've seen the lonely vulture fly
With blood-stain'd beak, but hungry eye;
Have mark'd the desert serpent's coil,
The lion's track imprint the soil;—
I've seen the ling'ring daylight set
O'er mosque and arrowy minaret;
Have mark'd its brighter dawning deck
Some column'd temple's marble wreck;
Have felt its noontide radiance shine
Through the pagoda's sandal shrine," &c.

All this, and much more, have I seen since my departure from England; but I doubt if any transmarine spectacle gave me half so much pleasure as did the sight of the jolly, red, weather-beaten face of the first *bumboatwoman* who came alongside our gallant frigate at Spithead!

THE END.

LONDON: PRINTED BY W. CLOWES AND SONS, STAMFORD STREET, AND CHARING CROSS.

ALBEMARLE STREET, LONDON.
February, 1857.

MR. MURRAY'S

GENERAL LIST OF WORKS.

ABBOTT'S (REV. J.) Philip Musgrave; or, Memoirs of a Church of England Missionary in the North American Colonies. Post 8vo. 2*s*. 6*d*.

ABERCROMBIE'S (JOHN, M.D.) Enquiries concerning the Intellectual Powers and the Investigation of Truth. *Fifteenth Edition*. Fcap. 8vo. 6*s*. 6*d*.

——— Philosophy of the Moral Feelings. *Tenth Edition*. Fcap. 8vo. 4*s*.

——— Pathological and Practical Researches on the Diseases of the Stomach, the Intestinal Canal, the Liver, and other Viscera of the Abdomen. *Third Edition*. Fcap. 8vo. 6*s*.

ACLAND'S (REV. CHARLES) Popular Account of the Manners and Customs of India, Illustrated with Numerous Anecdotes. Post 8vo. 2*s*. 6*d*.

ADDISON'S WORKS. A New Edition, with a New Life and Notes. By REV. WHITWELL ELWIN. 4 Vols. 8vo. *In Preparation*.

ÆSCHYLUS. (The Agamemnon and Choephoræ.) *A New Edition* of the Text, with Notes, Critical, Explanatory, and Philological, for the Use of Students. By Rev. W. PEILE, D.D. *Second Edition*. 2 Vols. 8vo. 9*s*. each.

ÆSOP'S FABLES. A New Version, chiefly from the Original Greek. By Rev. THOMAS JAMES, M.A. Illustrated with 100 Woodcuts, by JOHN TENNIEL. 21*st Edition*. Post 8vo. 2*s*. 6*d*.

AGRICULTURAL (THE) JOURNAL. Published (half-yearly) by the Royal Agricultural Society of England. 8vo. 10*s*.

AMBER-WITCH (THE). The most interesting Trial for Witchcraft ever known. Edited by Dr. MEINHOLD. Translated from the German by LADY DUFF GORDON. Post 8vo. 2*s*. 6*d*.

ARABIAN NIGHTS. A New Translation, with Explanatory Notes. By E. W. LANE. *Third Edition*. Woodcuts. Medium 8vo. 21*s*.

ARISTOPHANES. The Birds and the Clouds. Translated from SUVERN by W. R. HAMILTON, F.R.S. 2 Vols. Post 8vo. 9*s*.

ARTHUR'S (LITTLE) History of England. By LADY CALLCOTT. *Eighteenth Edition*. With 20 Woodcuts. Fcap. 8vo. 2*s*. 6*d*.

AUNT IDA'S Walks and Talks; a Story Book for Children. By a LADY. Woodcuts. 16mo. 5*s*.

B

ADMIRALTY PUBLICATIONS; Issued by direction of the Lords Commissioners of the Admiralty:—

1. A MANUAL OF SCIENTIFIC ENQUIRY, for the Use of Officers in H.M. Navy and Travellers in General. By Various Hands. Edited by SIR J. F. HERSCHEL, Bart. *Second Edition.* Post 8vo. 10*s.* 6*d.*
2. AIRY'S ASTRONOMICAL OBSERVATIONS MADE AT GREENWICH. 1836 to 1847. Royal 4to. 50*s.* each.
3. ——— APPENDIX TO THE ASTRONOMICAL OBSERVATIONS. 1836, 1837, 1842, 8*s.* each; and 1847, 14*s.* Royal 4to.

CONTENTS.

1836.—Bessel's Refraction Tables.
Tables for converting Errors of R.A. and N.P.D. into Errors of Longitude and Ecliptic P.D.
1837.—Logarithms of Sines and Cosines to every Ten Seconds of Time.
Table for converting Sidereal into Mean Solar Time.
1842.—Catalogue of 1439 Stars.
1847.—Twelve Years' Catalogue of Stars.

4. ——— MAGNETICAL AND METEOROLOGICAL OBSERVATIONS. 1840 to 1847. Royal 4to. 50*s.* each.
5. ——— ASTRONOMICAL, MAGNETICAL, AND METEOROLOGICAL OBSERVATIONS, 1848 to 1854. Royal 4to. 50*s.* each.
6. ——— REDUCTION OF THE OBSERVATIONS OF PLANETS. 1750 to 1830. Royal 4to. 50*s.*
7. ——— LUNAR OBSERVATIONS. 1750 to 1830. 2 Vols. Royal 4to. 50*s.* each.
8. BERNOULLI'S SEXCENTENARY TABLE. *London*, 1779. 4to. 5*s.*
9. BESSEL'S AUXILIARY TABLES FOR HIS METHOD OF CLEARING LUNAR DISTANCES. 8vo.
10. ——— FUNDAMENTA ASTRONOMIÆ: *Regiomontii*, 1818. Folio. 60*s.*
11. BIRD'S METHOD OF CONSTRUCTING MURAL QUADRANTS. *London*, 1768. 4to. 2*s.* 6*d.*
12. ——— METHOD OF DIVIDING ASTRONOMICAL INSTRUMENTS. *London*, 1767. 4to. 2*s.* 6*d.*
13. COOK, KING, AND BAYLY'S ASTRONOMICAL OBSERVATIONS. *London*, 1782. 4to. 21*s.*
14. EIFFE'S ACCOUNT OF IMPROVEMENTS IN CHRONOMETERS. 4to. 2*s.*
15. ENCKE'S BERLINER JAHRBUCH, for 1830. *Berlin*, 1828. 8vo. 9*s.*
16. GROOMBRIDGE'S CATALOGUE OF CIRCUMPOLAR STARS. 4to. 10*s.*
17. HARRISON'S PRINCIPLES OF HIS TIME-KEEPER. PLATES. 1767. 4to. 5*s.*
18. HUTTON'S TABLES OF THE PRODUCTS AND POWERS OF NUMBERS. 1781. Folio. 7*s.* 6*d.*
19. LAX'S TABLES FOR FINDING THE LATITUDE AND LONGITUDE. 1821. 8vo. 10*s.*
20. LUNAR OBSERVATIONS at GREENWICH. 1783 to 1819. Compared with the Tables, 1821. 4to. 7*s.* 6*d.*
21. ——— DISTANCES of the MOON'S CENTRE from the PLANETS. 1822, 3*s.*; 1823, 4*s.* 6*d.* 1824 to 1835, 8vo. 4*s.* each.
22. MASKELYNE'S ACCOUNT OF THE GOING OF HARRISON'S WATCH. 1767. 4to. 2*s.* 6*d.*
23. MAYER'S THEORIA LUNÆ JUXTA SYSTEMA NEWTONIANUM. 4to. 2*s.* 6*d.*
24. ——— TABULÆ MOTUUM SOLIS ET LUNÆ. 1770. 4to. 5*s.*
25. ——— ASTRONOMICAL OBSERVATIONS MADE AT GOTTINGEN, from 1756 to 1761. 1826. Folio. 7*s.* 6*d.*

ADMIRALTY PUBLICATIONS—*continued.*

26. NAUTICAL ALMANACS, from 1767 to 1860. 8vo. 2*s.* 6*d.* each.

27. ———————— SELECTIONS FROM THE ADDITIONS up to 1812. 8vo. 5*s.* 1834-54. 8vo. 5*s.*

28. ———————— SUPPLEMENTS, 1828 to 1833, 1837 and 1838. 8vo. 2*s.* each.

29. ———————— TABLE requisite to be used with the N.A. 1781. 8vo. 5*s.*

30. POND'S ASTRONOMICAL OBSERVATIONS. 1811 to 1835. 4to. 21*s.* each.

31. RAMSDEN'S ENGINE for DIVIDING MATHEMATICAL INSTRUMENTS. 4to. 5*s.*

32. ———— ENGINE for DIVIDING STRAIGHT LINES. 4to. 5*s.*

33. SABINE'S PENDULUM EXPERIMENTS to DETERMINE THE FIGURE OF THE EARTH. 1825. 4to. 40*s.*

34. SHEPHERD'S TABLES for CORRECTING LUNAR DISTANCES. 1772. Royal 4to. 21*s.*

35. ———— TABLES, GENERAL, of the MOON'S DISTANCE from the SUN, and 10 STARS. 1787. Folio. 5*s.* 6*d.*

36. TAYLOR'S SEXAGESIMAL TABLE. 1780. 4to. 15*s.*

37. ———— TABLES OF LOGARITHMS. 4to. 3*l.*

38. TIARK'S ASTRONOMICAL OBSERVATIONS for the LONGITUDE of MADEIRA. 1822. 4to. 5*s.*

39. ———— CHRONOMETRICAL OBSERVATIONS for DIFFERENCES of LONGITUDE between DOVER, PORTSMOUTH, and FALMOUTH. 1823 4to. 5*s.*

40. VENUS and JUPITER: OBSERVATIONS of, compared with the TABLES. *London*, 1822. 4to. 2*s.*

41. WALES' AND BAYLY'S ASTRONOMICAL OBSERVATIONS. 1777. 4to. 21*s.*

42. WALES' REDUCTION OF ASTRONOMICAL OBSERVATIONS MADE IN THE SOUTHERN HEMISPHERE. 1764—1771. 1788. 4to. 10*s.* 6*d.*

AUSTIN'S (SARAH) Fragments from German Prose Writers. Translated, with Biographical Notes. Post 8vo. 10*s.*

———— Translation of Ranke's Political and Ecclesiastical History of the Popes of Rome. *Third Edition.* 2 Vols. 8vo. 24*s.*

BABBAGE'S (CHARLES) Economy of Machinery and Manufactures. *Fourth Edition.* Fcap. 8vo. 6*s.*

———— Table of the Logarithms of the Natural Numbers from 1 to 108000. *Fourth Edition.* Royal 8vo. 6*s.*

———— Ninth Bridgewater Treatise. *Second Edition.* 8vo. 9*s.* 6*d.*

———— Reflections on the Decline of Science in England, and on some of its Causes. 4to. 7*s.* 6*d.*

———— Views of the Industry, the Science, and the Government of England, 1851. *Second Edition.* 8vo. 7*s.* 6*d.*

BAIKIE'S (W. B.) Narrative of an Exploring Voyage up the Rivers Quorra and Tshadda in 1854. Map. 8vo. 16*s.*

BANKES' (GEORGE) STORY OF CORFE CASTLE, with documents relating to the Time of the Civil Wars, &c. Woodcuts. Post 8vo. 10*s.* 6*d.*

BASSOMPIERRE'S Memoirs of his Embassy to the Court of England in 1626. Translated with Notes. 8vo. 9*s.* 6*d.*

BARROW'S (SIR JOHN) Autobiographical Memoir, including Reflections, Observations, and Reminiscences at Home and Abroad. From Early Life to Advanced Age. Portrait. 8vo. 16*s.*

——— Voyages of Discovery and Research within the Arctic Regions, from 1818 to the present time, in search of a North-West Passage: with Two Attempts to reach the North Pole. Abridged and arranged from the Official Narratives. 8vo. 15*s.*

——— (SIR GEORGE) Ceylon; Past and Present. Map. Post 8vo. 6*s.*

——— (JOHN) Naval Worthies of Queen Elizabeth's Reign, their Gallant Deeds, Daring Adventures, and Services in the infant state of the British Navy. 8vo. 14*s.*

——— Life and Voyages of Sir Francis Drake. With numerous Original Letters. Post 8vo. 2*s.* 6*d.*

BEES AND FLOWERS. Two Essays, reprinted from the "Quarterly Review." Fcap. 8vo. 1*s.* each.

BELL'S (SIR CHARLES) Anatomy and Philosophy of Expression as connected with the Fine Arts. *Fourth Edition.* Plates. Impl. 8vo. 21*s.*

——— Mechanism and Vital Endowments of the Hand as evincing Design. The Bridgewater Treatise. *Sixth Edition.* Woodcuts. Post 8vo. 7*s.* 6*d.*

BENEDICT'S (JULES) Sketch of the Life and Works of Felix Mendelssohn Bartholdy. *Second Edition.* 8vo. 2*s.* 6*d.*

BERTHA'S Journal during a Visit to her Uncle in England. Containing a Variety of Interesting and Instructive Information. *Seventh Edition.* Woodcuts. 12mo. 7*s.* 6*d.*

——— The Heiress in her Minority; or, the Progress of Character. By Author of "BERTHA'S JOURNAL." 2 Vols. 12mo. 18*s.*

BIRCH'S (SAMUEL) History of Ancient Pottery: Egyptian, Asiatic, Greek, Roman, Etruscan, and Celtic. With 200 Illustrations. 2 Vols. Medium 8vo.

BIRT'S (W. R.) Hurricane Guide. Being an Attempt to connect the Rotatory Gale, or Revolving Storm, with Atmospheric Waves. With Circles on Cards. Post 8vo. 3*s.*

BIOSCOPE (THE); or, the Dial of Life explained. By GRANVILLE PENN. *Second Edition.* With Plate. 12mo. 12*s.*

BLUNT'S (REV. J. J.) Undesigned Coincidences in the Writings of the Old and New Testament, an Argument of their Veracity: with an Appendix containing Undesigned Coincidences between the Gospels, Acts, and Josephus. *Fifth Edition.* 8vo. 9*s.*

——— History of the Church in the First Three Centuries. *Second Edition.* 8vo. 9*s.* 6*d.*

——— Duties, Acquirements and Obligations of the Parish Priest. *Second Edition.* Post 8vo. 7*s.* 6*d.*

——— Thirty-Six Plain Sermons Preached to a Country Congregation. Post 8vo. 7*s.* 6*d.*

——— Principles for the proper understanding of the Mosaic Writings, stated and applied, together with an Incidental Argument for the truth of the Resurrection of our Lord. Being the HULSEAN LECTURES for 1832. Post 8vo. 6*s.* 6*d.*

BLACKSTONE'S (SIR WILLIAM) Commentaries on the Laws of England. A New Edition, adapted to the present state of the law. By R. MALCOLM KERR. 4 Vols. 8vo. 42*s*.

BLAINE (ROBERTON) on the Laws of Artistic Copyright and their Defects, for Artists, Engravers, Printsellers, &c. 8vo. 3*s*. 6*d*.

BOOK OF COMMON PRAYER. With 1000 Illustrations of Borders, Initials, and Woodcut Vignettes. *A New Edition.* Medium 8vo. 21*s*. cloth, 31*s*. 6*d*. calf, or 42*s*. morocco.

BOSWELL'S (JAMES) Life of Dr. Samuel Johnson. Including the Tour to the Hebrides, with Notes by SIR W. SCOTT. Edited by the Right Hon. JOHN WILSON CROKER. *Third Edition.* Portraits. One Volume. Royal 8vo. 15*s*.

BORROW'S (GEORGE) Lavengro; The Scholar—The Gipsy—and the Priest. Portrait. 3 Vols. Post 8vo. 30*s*.

———— Bible in Spain; or the Journeys, Adventures, and Imprisonments of an Englishman in an Attempt to circulate the Scriptures in the Peninsula. 3 Vols. Post 8vo. 27*s*., or *Cheap Edition*, 16mo, 6*s*.

———— Zincali, or the Gipsies of Spain; their Manners, Customs, Religion, and Language. 2 Vols. Post 8vo. 18*s*., or *Cheap Edition*, 16mo, 6*s*.

BRAY'S (MRS.) Life of Thomas Stothard, R.A. With Personal Reminiscences. Illustrated with Portrait and 60 Woodcuts of his chief works. 4to. 21*s*.

BREWSTER'S (SIR DAVID) Martyrs of Science, or the Lives of Galileo, Tycho Brahe, and Kepler. *Second Edition.* Fcap. 8vo. 4*s*. 6*d*.

———— More Worlds than One. The Creed of the Philosopher and the Hope of the Christian. *Seventh Thousand.* Post 8vo. 6*s*.

———— Stereoscope: Its History, Theory, Construction, and Application to the Arts, and to Education. *Second Edition.* Woodcuts. 12mo. 5*s*. 6*d*.

BRITISH CLASSICS (MURRAY'S). A New Series of Standard English Authors, printed from the most correct text, and edited with elucidatory notes. Published in demy 8vo. Volumes, 7*s*. 6*d*. each.

Already Published.

GOLDSMITH'S WORKS. Edited by PETER CUNNINGHAM, F.S.A. Vignettes. 4 Vols.

GIBBON'S DECLINE AND FALL OF THE ROMAN EMPIRE. Edited by WILLIAM SMITH, LL.D. Portrait and Maps. 8 Vols.

JOHNSON'S LIVES OF THE ENGLISH POETS. Edited with Notes, By PETER CUNNINGHAM, F.S.A. 3 Vols.

BYRON'S POETICAL WORKS. Edited, with Notes. 6 vols.

In Preparation.

WORKS OF ALEXANDER POPE. Edited by the RIGHT HON. JOHN WILSON CROKER. Assisted by PETER CUNNINGHAM, F.S.A.

WORKS OF DRYDEN. Edited, with Notes.

HUME'S HISTORY OF ENGLAND. Edited, with Notes.

WORKS OF SWIFT. Edited, with Notes.

WORKS OF JOSEPH ADDISON. Edited, with Notes.

BRITISH ASSOCIATION REPORTS. 8vo. York and Oxford, 1831-32, 13*s.* 6*d.* Cambridge, 1833, 12*s.* Edinburgh, 1834, 15*s.* Dublin, 1835, 13*s.* 6*d.* Bristol, 1836, 12*s.* Liverpool, 1837, 16*s.* 6*d.* Newcastle, 1838, 15*s.* Birmingham, 1839, 13*s.* 6*d.* Glasgow, 1840, 15*s.* Plymouth, 1841, 13*s.* 6*d.* Manchester, 1842, 10*s.* 6*d.* Cork, 1843, 12*s.* York, 1844, 20*s.* Cambridge, 1845, 12*s.* Southampton, 1846, 15*s.* Oxford, 1847, 18*s.* Swansea, 1848, 9*s.* Birmingham, 1849, 10*s.* Edinburgh, 1850, 15*s.* Ipswich, 1851, 16*s.* 6*d.* Belfast, 1852, 15*s.* Hull, 1853, 10*s.* 6*d.* Liverpool, 1854, 18*s.* Glasgow, 1855, 15*s.*

BROGDEN'S (Rev. Jas.) Illustrations of the Liturgy and Ritual of the United Church of England and Ireland. Being Sermons and Discourses selected from the Works of eminent Divines of the 17th Century. 3 Vols. Post 8vo. 27*s.*

——— Catholic Safeguards against the Errors, Corruptions, and Novelties of the Church of Rome. Being Sermons and Tracts selected from the Works of eminent Divines of the 17th Century. *Second Edition.* With Preface and Index. 3 Vols. 8vo. 36*s.*

BROOKE'S (Sir James) Journals of Events in Borneo, including the Occupation of Labuan, and a Visit to the Celebes. Together with the Expedition of H.M.S. Iris. By Capt. Rodney Mundy, R.N. Plates. 2 Vols. 8vo. 32*s.*

BROUGHTON'S (Lord) Journey through Albania and other Provinces of Turkey in Europe and Asia, to Constantinople, 1809—10. *Second Edition.* Maps and Woodcuts. 2 Vols. 8vo. 30*s.*

BUBBLES FROM THE BRUNNEN OF NASSAU. By an Old Man. *Sixth Edition.* 16mo. 5*s.*

BUNBURY'S (C. J. F.) Journal of a Residence at the Cape of Good Hope; with Excursions into the Interior, and Notes on the Natural History and Native Tribes of the Country. Woodcuts. Post 8vo. 9*s.*

BUNYAN (John) and Oliver Cromwell. Select Biographies. By Robert Southey. Post 8vo. 2*s.* 6*d.*

BUONAPARTE'S (Napoleon) Confidential Correspondence with his Brother Joseph, sometime King of Spain. 2 vols. 8vo. 26*s.*

BURGHERSH'S (Lord) Memoir of the Operations of the Allied Armies under Prince Schwarzenberg and Marshal Blucher during the latter end of 1813—14. 8vo. 21*s.*

——— Early Campaigns of the Duke of Wellington in Portugal and Spain. 8vo. 8*s.* 6*d.*

BURN'S (Lieut.-Col.) French and English Dictionary of Naval and Military Technical Terms. *Third Edition.* Crown 8vo. 15*s.*

BURNES' (Sir Alexander) Journey to the City of Cabool. *Second Edition.* Plates. 8vo. 18*s.*

BURNS' (Robert) Life. By John Gibson Lockhart. Fifth *Edition.* Fcap. 8vo. 3*s.*

BURR'S (G. D.) Instructions in Practical Surveying, Topographical Plan Drawing, and on sketching ground without Instruments. *Second Edition.* Woodcuts. Post 8vo. 7*s.* 6*d.*

BUXTON'S (Sir Fowell) Memoirs. With Selections from his Correspondence. By his Son. *Fifth Edition.* 8vo. 16*s.*; or, *Popular Edition,* Post 8vo. 8*s.* 6*d.*

BYRON'S (LORD) Life, Letters, and Journals. By THOMAS MOORE. Plates. 6 Vols. Fcap. 8vo. 18s.

——— Life, Letters, and Journals. By THOMAS MOORE. Portrait and Vignette. One Volume, royal 8vo. 12s.

——— Poetical Works. Library Edition. Portrait. 6 Vols. Demy 8vo. 45s.

——— Poetical Works. Plates. 10 Vols. Fcap. 8vo. 30s.

——— Poetical Works. Portrait and Vignette. One Volume, royal 8vo. 12s.

——— Poetical Works. One Compact Volume. For the use of Travellers. Portrait. Crown 8vo, 9s.

——— Poetical Works. Pocket Edition. 8 Vols. 24mo. 20s. *Or separately as follows:*—Childe Harold, 1 Vol.; Dramas, 2 Vols.; Tales and Poems, 1 Vol.; Miscellanies, 2 Vols.; Beppo and Don Juan, 2 Vols. 2s. 6d. Each Volume.

——— Childe Harold's Pilgrimage. Illustrated Edition. With 30 Vignettes. Crown 8vo. 10s. 6d.

——— Beauties. Poetry and Prose. Fcap. 8vo. 3s.

CALVIN'S (JOHN) Life. With Extracts from his Correspondence. By THOMAS H. DYER. Portrait. 8vo. 15s.

CALLCOTT'S (LADY) Little Arthur's History of England. *18th Edition.* With 20 Woodcuts. Fcap. 8vo. 2s. 6d.

CARMICHAEL'S (A. N.) Greek Verbs. Their Formations, Irregularities, and Defects. *Second Edition.* Post 8vo. 8s. 6d.

CARNARVON'S (LORD) Portugal, Gallicia, and the Basque Provinces. From Notes made during a Journey to those Countries. *Third Edition.* Post 8vo. 6s.

CAMPBELL'S (LORD) Lives of the Lord Chancellors and Keepers of the Great Seal of England. From the Earliest Times to the Death of Lord Eldon in 1838. *4th Edition.* 10 Vols. Crown 8vo. 6s. each.

——— Life of Lord Bacon. Reprinted from the Lives of the Chancellors. Fcap. 8vo. 2s.

——— Lives of the Chief Justices of England. From the Norman Conquest to the Death of Lord Mansfield. 2 Vols. 8vo. 30s.

——— Lives of Lords Kenyon, Ellenborough, and Tenterden, Forming the Third Volume of the "Lives of the Chief Justices of England." 8vo.

——— (GEORGE) Modern India. A Sketch of the System of Civil Government. With some Account of the Natives and Native Institutions. *Second Edition.* 8vo. 16s.

——— India as it may be. An Outline of a proposed Government and Policy. 8vo. 12s.

——— (THOS.) Short Lives of the British Poets. With an Essay on English Poetry. Post 8vo. 6s.

CASTLEREAGH (THE) DESPATCHES, from the commencement of the official career of the late Viscount Castlereagh to the close of his life. Edited by the MARQUIS OF LONDONDERRY. 12 Vols. 8vo. 14s. each.

CATHCART'S (Sir George) Commentaries on the War in Russia and Germany, 1812-13. Plans. 8vo. 14s.

———— Military Operations in Kaffraria, which led to the Termination of the Kaffir War. 8vo. 12s.

CAVALCASELLE (G. B.) Notices of the Early Flemish Painters; Their Lives and Works. Woodcuts. Post 8vo. 12s.

CHARMED ROE (The); or, The Story of the Little Brother and Sister. By Otto Speckter. Plates. 16mo. 5s.

CLARENDON (Lord Chancellor); Lives of his Friends and Contemporaries, illustrative of Portraits in his Gallery. By Lady Theresa Lewis. Portraits. 3 Vols. 8vo. 42s.

CLAUSEWITZ'S (Carl Von) Campaign of 1812, in Russia. Translated from the German by Lord Ellesmere. Map. 8vo. 10s. 6d.

CLIVE'S (Lord) Life. By Rev. G. R. Gleig, M.A. Post 8vo. 6s.

COLERIDGE (Samuel Taylor). Specimens of his Table-Talk. *Fourth Edition.* Portrait. Fcap. 8vo. 6s.

———— (Henry Nelson) Introductions to the Study of the Greek Classic Poets. *Third Edition.* Fcap. 8vo. 5s. 6d.

COLONIAL LIBRARY. [See Home and Colonial Library.]

COMBER'S (Dean) Friendly Advice to the Roman Catholics of England. By Rev. Dr. Hook. Fcap. 8vo. 3s.

COOKERY (Domestic). Founded on Principles of Economy and Practical Knowledge, and adapted for Private Families. *New Edition.* Woodcuts. Fcap. 8vo. 5s.

CORNWALLIS (The) PAPERS. Being the Public and Private Correspondence of Charles, Marquis Cornwallis, during the American War,—his two Administrations in India,—the Union with Ireland, and the Peace of America. From Papers in possession of the Family, &c. Edited by Charles Ross. 2 Vols. 8vo. *In Preparation.*

CRABBE'S (Rev. George) Life, Letters, and Journals. By his Son. Portrait. Fcap. 8vo. 3s.

———— Life, Letters, Journals, and Poetical Works. Plates. 8 Vols. Fcap. 8vo. 24s.

———— Life, Letters, Journals, and Poetical Works. Plates. One Volume. Royal 8vo. 10s. 6d.

CRAIK'S (G. L.) Pursuit of Knowledge under Difficulties. *New Edition.* 2 Vols. Post 8vo.

CUMMING'S (R. Gordon) Five Years of a Hunter's Life in the Far Interior of South Africa. *Fifth Edition.* Woodcuts. Post 8vo. 5s.

CURZON'S (Hon. Robert) Visits to the Monasteries of the Levant. *Fourth Edition.* Woodcuts. Post 8vo. 15s.

———— Armenia and Erzeroum. A Year on the Frontiers of Russia, Turkey, and Persia. *Third Edition.* Woodcuts. Post 8vo. 7s. 6d.

CUNNINGHAM'S (ALLAN) Life of Sir David Wilkie. With his Journals and Critical Remarks on Works of Art. Portrait. 3 Vols. 8vo. 42*s.*

——— Poems and Songs. Now first collected and arranged, with Biographical Notice. 24mo. 2*s.* 6*d.*

——— (CAPT. J. D.) History of the Sikhs. From the Origin of the Nation to the Battle of the Sutlej. *Second Edition.* Maps. 8vo. 15*s.*

——— (PETER) London—Past and Present. A Handbook to the Antiquities, Curiosities, Churches, Works of Art, Public Buildings, and Places connected with interesting and historical associations. *Second Edition.* Post 8vo. 16*s.*

——— Modern London. A complete Guide for Visitors to the Metropolis. Map. 16mo. 5*s.*

——— Westminster Abbey. Its Art, Architecture, and Associations. Woodcuts. Fcap. 8vo. 1*s.*

——— Works of Oliver Goldsmith. Edited with Notes. Vignettes. 4 vols. 8vo. 30*s.* (Murray's British Classics.)

——— Lives of Eminent English Poets. By SAMUEL JOHNSON, LL.D. Edited with Notes. 3 vols. 8vo. 22*s.* 6*d.* (Murray's British Classics.)

CROKER'S (RIGHT HON. J. W.) Progressive Geography for Children. *Fifth Edition.* 18mo. 1*s.* 6*d.*

——— Stories for Children, Selected from the History of England. *Fifteenth Edition.* Woodcuts. 16mo. 2*s.* 6*d.*

——— Boswell's Life of Johnson. Including the Tour to the Hebrides. *Third Edition.* Portraits. Royal 8vo. 15*s.*

——— LORD HERVEY'S Memoirs of the Reign of George the Second, from his Accession to the death of Queen Caroline. Edited with Notes. *Second Edition.* Portrait. 2 Vols. 8vo. 21*s.*

——— Historical Essay on the Guillotine. Fcap. 8vo. 1*s.*

CROMWELL (OLIVER) and John Bunyan. Select Biographies. By ROBERT SOUTHEY. Post 8vo. 2*s.* 6*d.*

CROWE'S (J. A.). Notices of the Early Flemish Painters; Their Lives and Works. Woodcuts. Post 8vo. 12*s.*

DARWIN'S (CHARLES) Journal of Researches into the Natural History and Geology of the Countries visited during a Voyage round the World. Post 8vo. 8*s.* 6*d.*

DAVY'S (SIR HUMPHRY) Consolations in Travel; or, Last Days of a Philosopher. *Fifth Edition.* Woodcuts. Fcap. 8vo. 6*s.*

——— Salmonia; or, Days of Fly Fishing. With some Account of the Habits of Fishes belonging to the genus Salmo. *Fourth Edition.* Woodcuts. Fcap. 8vo. 6*s.*

DENNIS' (GEORGE) Cities and Cemeteries of Etruria; or, the extant Local Remains of Etruscan Art. Plates. 2 Vols. 8vo. 42*s.*

DEVEREUX'S (HON. CAPT., R.N.) Lives and Letters of the Devereux Earls of Essex, in the Reigns of Elizabeth, James I., and Charles I., 1540—1646. Chiefly from unpublished documents. Portraits. 2 Vols. 8vo. 30*s.*

DODGSON'S (Rev. C.) **Controversy of Faith; or, Advice to Candidates for Holy Orders.** Containing an Analysis and Exposition of the Argument by which the Catholic Interpretation of the Baptismal Services is to be vindicated. 12mo. 3*s*.

DOG-BREAKING; the Most Expeditious, Certain, and Easy Method, whether great excellence or only mediocrity be required. By Lieut.-Col. Hutchinson. *Third Edition.* Revised and enlarged. Woodcuts. Post 8vo. 9*s*.

DOMESTIC MODERN COOKERY. Founded on Principles of Economy and Practical Knowledge, and adapted for Private Families. *New Edition.* Woodcuts. Fcap. 8vo. 5*s*.

DOUGLAS'S (General Sir Howard) **Treatise on the Theory and Practice of Gunnery.** *Fourth Edition.* Plates. 8vo. 21*s*.

——— **Treatise on the Principle and Construction of Military Bridges,** and the Passage of Rivers in Military Operations. *Third Edition.* Plates. 8vo. 21*s*.

DRAKE'S (Sir Francis) **Life, Voyages, and Exploits, by Sea and Land.** By John Barrow. *Third Edition.* Post 8vo. 2*s*. 6*d*.

DRINKWATER'S (John) **History of the Siege of Gibraltar,** 1779-1783. With a Description and Account of that Garrison from the Earliest Periods. Post 8vo. 2*s*. 6*d*.

DRYDEN'S (John) **Works.** A New Edition, based upon Sir Walter Scott's Edition, entirely revised. 8vo. *In Preparation.*

DUDLEY'S (Earl of) **Letters to the late Bishop of Llandaff.** *Second Edition.* Portrait. 8vo. 10*s*. 6*d*.

DURHAM'S (Admiral Sir Philip) **Naval Life and Services.** By Capt. Alexander Murray. 8vo. 5*s*. 6*d*.

DYER'S (Thomas H.) **Life and Letters of John Calvin.** Compiled from authentic Sources. Portrait. 8vo. 15*s*.

EASTLAKE (Sir Charles) **The Schools of Painting in Italy.** From the Earliest times. From the German of Kugler. Edited, with Notes. *Third Edition.* Illustrated with 100 Engravings from the Old Masters. 2 Vols. Post 8vo. 30*s*.

EDWARDS' (W. H.) **Voyage up the River Amazon, including a Visit to Para.** Post 8vo. 2*s*. 6*d*.

EGERTON'S (Hon. Capt. Francis) **Journal of a Winter's Tour in India;** with a Visit to Nepaul. Woodcuts. 2 Vols. Post 8vo. 18*s*.

ELDON'S (Lord Chancellor) **Public and Private Life,** with Selections from his Correspondence and Diaries. By Horace Twiss. *Third Edition.* Portrait. 2 Vols. Post 8vo. 21*s*.

ELLESMERE'S (Lord) **Two Sieges of Vienna by the Turks.** Translated from the German. Post 8vo. 2*s*. 6*d*.

——— **Second Campaign of Radetzky in Piedmont.** The Defence of Temeswar and the Camp of the Ban. From the German. Post 8vo. 6*s*. 6*d*.

——— **Life and Character of the Duke of Wellington;** a Discourse. Fcap. 8vo. 6*d*.

——— **Campaign of 1812 in Russia,** from the German of General Carl Von Clausewitz. Map. 8vo. 10*s*. 6*d*.

——— **Pilgrimage, and other Poems.** Illustrated. Crown 4to. 24*s*.

ELIOT'S (Hon. W. G. C.) Khans of the Crimea. Being a Narrative of an Embassy from Frederick the Great to the Court of Krim Gerai. Translated from the German. Post 8vo. 6*s*.

ELLIS (Mrs.) On the Education of Character, with Hints on Moral Training. Post. 8vo. 7*s*. 6*d*.

ELPHINSTONE'S (Hon. Mountstuart) History of India—the Hindoo and Mahomedan Periods. *Third Edition*. Map. 8vo. 18*s*.

ELWIN'S (Rev. W.) Lives of Eminent British Poets. From Chaucer to Wordsworth. 4 Vols. 8vo. *In Preparation*.

ENGLAND (History of) from the Peace of Utrecht to the Peace of Versailles, 1713—83. By Lord Mahon. *Library Edition*, 7 Vols. 8vo, 93*s*.; or, *Popular Edition*, 7 Vols. Post 8vo, 42*s*.

———— From the First Invasion by the Romans, down to the 14th year of Queen Victoria's Reign. By Mrs. Markham. *98th Edition*. Woodcuts. 12mo. 6*s*.

———— As it is: Social, Political, and Industrial, in the Middle of the 19th Century. By W. Johnston. 2 Vols. Post 8vo. 18*s*.

———— and France under the House of Lancaster. With an Introductory View of the Early Reformation. *Second Edition*. 8vo. 15*s*.

ENGLISHWOMAN IN AMERICA. Post 8vo. 10*s*. 6*d*.

———— RUSSIA: or, Impressions of Manners and Society during a Ten Years' Residence in that Country. *Fifth Thousand*. Woodcuts. Post 8vo. 10*s*. 6*d*.

ERSKINE'S (Capt., R.N.) Journal of a Cruise among the Islands of the Western Pacific, including the Fejees, and others inhabited by the Polynesian Negro Races. Plates. 8vo. 16*s*.

ESKIMAUX (The) and English Vocabulary, for the use of Travellers in the Arctic Regions. 16mo. 3*s*. 6*d*.

ESSAYS FROM "THE TIMES." Being a Selection from the Literary Papers which have appeared in that Journal. *7th Thousand*. 2 vols. Fcap. 8vo. 8*s*.

EXETER'S (Bishop of) Letters to the late Charles Butler, on the Theological parts of his Book of the Roman Catholic Church; with Remarks on certain Works of Dr. Milner and Dr. Lingard, and on some parts of the Evidence of Dr. Doyle. *Second Edition*. 8vo. 16*s*.

FAIRY RING (The), A Collection of Tales and Stories for Young Persons. From the German. By J. E. Taylor. Illustrated by Richard Doyle. *Second Edition*. Fcap. 8vo.

FALKNER'S (Fred.) Muck Manual for the Use of Farmers. A Treatise on the Nature and Value of Manures. *Second Edition*, with a Glossary of Terms and an Index. Fcap. 8vo. 5*s*.

FAMILY RECEIPT-BOOK. A Collection of a Thousand Valuable and Useful Receipts. Fcap. 8vo. 5*s*. 6*d*.

FANCOURT'S (Col.) History of Yucatan, from its Discovery to the Close of the 17th Century. With Map. 8vo. 10*s*. 6*d*.

FARINI'S (Luigi Carlo) History of the Roman State, 1815-50. Translated from the Italian. By Right Hon. W. E. Gladstone. 4 Vols. 8vo. 12*s*. each.

FEATHERSTONHAUGH'S (G. W.) Tour through the Slave States of North America, from the River Potomac, to Texas and the Frontiers of Mexico. Plates. 2 Vols. 8vo. 26*s.*

FELLOWS' (SIR CHARLES) Travels and Researches in Asia Minor, more particularly in the Province of Lycia. *New Edition.* Plates. Post 8vo. 9*s.*

FERGUSSON'S (JAMES) Palaces of Nineveh and Persepolis Restored: an Essay on Ancient Assyrian and Persian Architecture. With 45 Woodcuts. 8vo. 16*s.*

——— Handbook of Architecture. Being a Concise and Popular Account of the Different Styles prevailing in all Ages and Countries in the World. With a Description of the most remarkable Buildings. With 850 Illustrations. 2 Vols. 8vo. 36*s.*

FERRIER'S (T. P.) Caravan Journeys in Persia, Affghanistan, Herat, Turkistan, and Beloochistan, with Descriptions of Meshed, Balk, and Candahar, and Sketches of the Nomade Tribes of Central Asia. *Second Edition.* Map. 8vo. 21*s.*

FEUERBACH'S Remarkable German Crimes and Trials. Translated from the German by Lady DUFF GORDON. 8vo. 12*s.*

FISHER'S (REV. GEORGE) Elements of Geometry, for the Use of Schools. *Third Edition.* 18mo.

——— First Principles of Algebra, for the Use of Schools. *Third Edition.* 18mo.

FLOWER GARDEN (THE). An Essay reprinted from the "Quarterly Review." Fcap. 8vo. 1*s.*

FORD'S (RICHARD) Handbook for Spain, Andalusia, Ronda, Valencia. Catalonia, Granada, Gallicia, Arragon, Navarre, &c. *Third Edition.* 2 Vols. Post 8vo. 30*s.*

——— Gatherings from Spain. Post 8vo. 6*s.*

FORSYTH'S (WILLIAM) Hortensius, or the Advocate: an Historical Essay on the Office and Duties of an Advocate. Post 8vo. 12*s.*

——— History of Napoleon at St. Helena. From the Letters and Journals of SIR HUDSON LOWE. Portrait and Maps. 3 Vols. 8vo. 45*s.*

FORTUNE'S (ROBERT) Narrative of Two Visits to China, between the years 1843-52, with full Descriptions of the Culture of the Tea Plant. *Third Edition.* Woodcuts. 2 Vols. Post 8vo. 18*s.*

FRANCE (HISTORY OF). From the Conquest by the Gauls to the Death of Louis Philippe. By MRS. MARKHAM. *40th Thousand.* Woodcuts. 12mo. 6*s.*

FRENCH (THE) in Algiers; The Soldier of the Foreign Legion—and the Prisoners of Abd-el-Kadir. Translated by Lady DUFF GORDON. Post 8vo. 2*s.* 6*d.*

GALTON'S (FRANCIS) Art of Travel; or, Hints on the Shifts and Contrivances available in Wild Countries. *Second Edition.* Woodcuts. Post 8vo. 6*s.*

GEOGRAPHICAL (THE) Journal. Published by the Royal Geographical Society of London. 8vo.

GERMANY (HISTORY OF). From the Invasion by Marius, to the present time. On the plan of Mrs. MARKHAM. *6th Thousand.* Woodcuts. 12mo. 6*s*.

GIBBON'S (EDWARD) Decline and Fall of the Roman Empire. *A New Edition.* Preceded by his Autobiography. Edited with Notes by Dr. WM. SMITH. Maps. 8 Vols. 8vo. 60*s*.

——— The Student's Gibbon; Being the History of the Decline and Fall, Abridged, incorporating the Researches of Recent Commentators. By Dr. WM. SMITH. Woodcuts. Post 8vo. 7*s*. 6*d*.

GIFFARD'S (EDWARD) Deeds of Naval Daring; or, Anecdotes of the British Navy. 2 Vols. Fcap. 8vo.

GISBORNE'S (THOMAS) Essays on Agriculture. *Third Edition.* Post 8vo.

GLADSTONE'S (W. E.) Prayers arranged from the Liturgy for Family Use. *Second Edition.* 12mo. 2*s*. 6*d*.

——— History of the Roman State. Translated from the Italian of LUIGI CARLO FARINI. 4 Vols. 8vo. 12*s*. each.

GOLDSMITH'S (OLIVER) Works. A New Edition. Printed from the last editions revised by the Author. Edited by PETER CUNNINGHAM. Vignettes. 4 Vols. 8vo. 30*s*. (Murray's British Classics.)

GLEIG'S (REV. G. R.) Campaigns of the British Army at Washington and New Orleans. Post 8vo. 2*s*. 6*d*.

——— Story of the Battle of Waterloo. Compiled from Public and Authentic Sources. Post 8vo. 5*s*.

——— Narrative of Sir Robert Sale's Brigade in Afghanistan, with an Account of the Seizure and Defence of Jellalabad. Post 8vo. 2*s*. 6*d*.

——— Life of Robert Lord Clive. Post 8vo. 5*s*.

——— Life and Letters of General Sir Thomas Munro. Post 8vo. 5*s*.

GORDON'S (SIR ALEX. DUFF) Sketches of German Life, and Scenes from the War of Liberation. From the German. Post 8vo. 6*s*.

——— (LADY DUFF) Amber-Witch: the most interesting Trial for Witchcraft ever known. From the German. Post 8vo. 2*s*. 6*d*.

——— French in Algiers. 1. The Soldier of the Foreign Legion. 2. The Prisoners of Abd-el-Kadir. From the French. Post 8vo. 2*s*. 6*d*.

———Remarkable German Crimes and Trials. From the German of Fuerbach. 8vo. 12*s*.

GOSPEL STORIES FOR CHILDREN. An Attempt to render the Chief Events of the Life of Our Saviour intelligible and profitable. *Second Edition.* 18mo. 3*s*. 6*d*.

GRANT'S (ASAHEL) Nestorians, or the Lost Tribes; containing Evidence of their Identity, their Manners, Customs, and Ceremonies; with Sketches of Travel in Ancient Assyria, Armenia, and Mesopotamia; and Illustrations of Scripture Prophecy. *Third Edition.* Fcap. 8vo. 6*s*.

GRENVILLE (THE) PAPERS. Being the Public and Private Correspondence of George Grenville, his Friends and Contemporaries, during a period of 30 years.—Including his DIARY OF POLITICAL EVENTS while First Lord of the Treasury. Edited, with Notes, by W. J. SMITH. 4 Vols. 8vo. 16*s*. each.

GREEK GRAMMAR FOR SCHOOLS. Abridged from Matthiæ. By the BISHOP OF LONDON. *Eighth Edition*, revised by Rev. J. EDWARDS. 12mo. 3*s*.

GREY'S (SIR GEORGE) Polynesian Mythology, and Ancient Traditional History of the New Zealand Race. Woodcuts. Post 8vo. 10*s*. 6*d*.

GROTE'S (GEORGE) History of Greece. From the Earliest Times to the close of the generation contemporary with the death of Alexander the Great. Maps and Index. 12 vols. 8vo. 16*s*. each.

GROSVENOR'S (LORD ROBERT) Leaves from my Journal during the Summer of 1851. *Second Edition*. Plates. Post 8vo. 3*s*. 6*d*.

GURWOOD'S (COL.) Despatches of the Duke of Wellington during his various Campaigns. Compiled from Official and Authentic Documents. *New Edition*. 8 vols. 8vo. 21*s*. each.

——— Selections from the Wellington Despatches, and General Orders. *New Edition*. 8vo. 18*s*.

——— Speeches in Parliament of the Duke of Wellington. 2 Vols. 8vo. 42*s*.

GUSTAVUS VASA (History of), King of Sweden. With Extracts from his Correspondence. Portrait. 8vo. 10*s*. 6*d*.

HALLAM'S (HENRY) Constitutional History of England, from the Accession of Henry the Seventh to the Death of George the Second. *Seventh Edition*. 3 Vols. 8vo. 30*s*.

——— History of Europe during the Middle Ages. *Tenth Edition*. 3 Vols. 8vo. 30*s*.

——— Introduction to the Literary History of Europe, during the 16th, 17th, and 18th Centuries. *Fourth Edition*. 3 Vols. 8vo. 36*s*.

——— Literary Essays and Characters. Selected from the last work. Fcap. 8vo. 2*s*.

——— Historical Works; Complete and Uniform Edition. 10 Vols. Post 8vo. 6*s*. each.

HAMILTON'S (JAMES) Wanderings in Northern Africa, Benghazi, Cyrene, the Oasis of Siwah, &c. Woodcuts. Post 8vo. 12*s*.

——— (WALTER) Hindostan, Geographically, Statistically, and Historically. Map. 2 Vols. 4to. 94*s*. 6*d*.

——— (W. J.) Researches in Asia Minor, Pontus, and Armenia; with some Account of the Antiquities and Geology of those Countries. Plates. 2 Vols. 8vo. 38*s*.

HAMPDEN'S (BISHOP) Essay on the Philosophical Evidence of Christianity, or the Credibility obtained to a Scripture Revelation from its Coincidence with the Facts of Nature. 8vo. 9*s*. 6*d*.

HARCOURT'S (EDWARD VERNON) Sketch of Madeira; with Map and Plates. Post 8vo. 8*s*. 6*d*.

HART'S ARMY LIST. (*Quarterly and Annually.*) 8vo. 7*s*. 6*d*. and 20*s*. each.

HAY'S (J. H. DRUMMOND) Western Barbary, its wild Tribes and savage Animals. Post 8vo. 2*s*. 6*d*.

HAND-BOOKS (MURRAY'S); TRAVEL-TALK; or, Conversations in English, German, French, and Italian. 18mo. 3s. 6d.

——— NORTH GERMANY—HOLLAND, BELGIUM, and the Rhine to Switzerland. Map. Post 8vo. 9s.

——— SOUTH GERMANY—Bavaria, Austria, Salzberg, the Austrian and Bavarian Alps, the Tyrol, and the Danube, from Ulm to the Black Sea. Map. Post 8vo. 9s.

——— SWITZERLAND—the Alps of Savoy, and Piedmont. Maps. Post 8vo. 7s. 6d.

——— FRANCE—Normandy, Brittany, the French Alps, the Rivers Loire, Seine, Rhone, and Garonne, Dauphiné, Provence, and the Pyrenees. Maps. Post 8vo. 9s.

——— SPAIN—Andalusia, Ronda, Granada, Valencia, Catalonia, Gallicia, Arragon, and Navarre. Maps. 2 Vols. Post 8vo. 30s.

——— PORTUGAL, LISBON, &c. Map. Post 8vo. 9s.

——— PAINTING—the German, Dutch, Spanish, and French Schools. From the German of KUGLER. Edited by SIR EDMUND HEAD. Woodcuts. 2 Vols. Post 8vo. 24s.

——— NORTH ITALY—Florence, Sardinia, Genoa, the Riviera, Venice, Lombardy, and Tuscany. Map. Post 8vo. 2 Vols. 12s.

——— CENTRAL ITALY—SOUTH TUSCANY and the PAPAL STATES. Map. Post 8vo. 7s.

——— ROME—AND ITS ENVIRONS. Map. Post 8vo. 7s.

——— SOUTH ITALY—Naples, Pompeii, Herculaneum, Vesuvius, &c. Map. Post 8vo. 10s.

PAINTING—the Italian Schools. From the German of KUGLER. Edited by Sir CHARLES EASTLAKE. Woodcuts. 2 Vols. Post 8vo. 30s.

——— PICTURE GALLERIES OF ITALY. Being a short Biographical Dictionary of Italian Painters. With a Chart. Post 8vo. 6s. 6d.

— GREECE—the Ionian Islands, Albania, Thessaly, and Macedonia. Maps. Post 8vo. 15s.

——— TURKEY—MALTA, ASIA MINOR, CONSTANTINOPLE, Armenia, Mesopotamia, &c. Maps. Post 8vo. 10s.

——— EGYPT—Thebes, the Nile, Alexandria, Cairo, the Pyramids, Mount Sinai, &c. Map. Post 8vo. 15s.

——— DENMARK—NORWAY and SWEDEN. Maps. Post 8vo. 12s.

——— RUSSIA—THE BALTIC AND FINLAND. Maps. Post 8vo. 12s.

——— LONDON, PAST AND PRESENT. Being an Alphabetical Account of all the Antiquities, Curiosities, Churches, Works of Art, Places, and Streets connected with Interesting and Historical Associations. Post 8vo. 16s.

——— MODERN LONDON. A Guide to all objects of interest in the Metropolis. Map. 16mo. 5s.

——— ENVIRONS OF LONDON. Including a Circle of 30 Miles round St. Paul's. Maps. Post 8vo. (*In preparation.*)

HANDBOOKS (MURRAY'S); DEVON AND CORNWALL. Maps. Post 8vo. 6*s.*

——— WILTS, DORSET, AND SOMERSET. Map. Post 8vo. 6*s.*

——— BRITISH MUSEUM; ITS ANTIQUITIES AND SCULPTURE. *New Edition.* Woodcuts. Post 8vo.

——— WESTMINSTER ABBEY—its Art, Architecture, and Associations. Woodcuts. 16mo. 1*s.*

——— PARIS. Post 8vo.

——— INDIA. Post 8vo.

——— CATHEDRALS OF ENGLAND. Post 8vo. *In Preparation.*

——— CHURCH AND STATE. Giving an Historical Account of the Duties attached to the various Civil and Ecclesiastical Departments of the Government. Post 8vo. 6*s.*

——— FAMILIAR QUOTATIONS. Chiefly from English Authors. A New Edition, with an Index. Fcap. 8vo. 5*s.*

——— ARCHITECTURE. Being a Concise and Popular Account of the Different Styles prevailing in all Ages and Countries By JAMES FERGUSSON. With 850 Illustrations. 2 Vols. 8vo. 36*s.*

——— ARTS OF THE MIDDLE AGES AND RENaissance. By M. Jules Labarte. With 200 Illustrations. 8vo. 18*s.*

HEAD'S (SIR FRANCIS) Rough Notes of some Rapid Journeys across the Pampas and over the Andes. Post 8vo. 2*s.* 6*d.*

——— Descriptive Essays: contributed to the "Quarterly Review." 2 Vols. Post 8vo. 18*s.*

——— Bubbles from the Brunnen of Nassau. By an OLD MAN. *Sixth Edition.* 16mo. 5*s.*

——— Emigrant. *Sixth Edition.* Fcap. 8vo. 2*s.* 6*d.*

——— London and North-Western Railway. Post 8vo. 2*s.* 6*d.*

——— Defenceless State of Great Britain. Contents—1. Military Warfare. 2. Naval Warfare. 3. The Invasion of England. 4. The Capture of London by a French Army 5. The Treatment of Women in War. 6. How to Defend Great Britain. Post 8vo. 12*s.*

——— Sketches of Paris, or Faggot of French Sticks. *New Edition.* 2 Vols. Post 8vo. 12*s.*

——— Fortnight in Ireland. *Second Edition.* Map. 8vo. 12*s.*

——— (SIR GEORGE) Forest Scenes and Incidents in Canada. *Second Edition.* Post 8vo. 10*s.*

——— Home Tour through the Manufacturing Districts of England, Scotland, and Ireland, including the Channel Islands, and the Isle of Man. *Third Edition.* 2 Vols. Post 8vo. 12*s.*

——— (SIR EDMUND) Handbook of Painting—the German, Dutch, Spanish, and French Schools. Partly from the German of KUGLER. With Illustrations. 2 Vols. Post 8vo. 24*s.*

——— Shall and Will; or, Two Chapters on Future Auxiliary Verbs. Fcap. 8vo. 3*s.*

HEBER (BISHOP) Parish Sermons; on the Lessons, the Gospel, or the Epistle, for every Sunday in the Year, and for Week-day Festivals. *Sixth Edition.* 2 Vols. Post 8vo. 16*s.*

———— Sermons Preached in England. *Second Edition.* 8vo. 9*s.* 6*d.*

———— Hymns written and adapted for the weekly Church Service of the Year. *Twelfth Edition.* 16mo. 2*s.*

———— Poetical Works. *Fifth Edition.* Portrait. Fcap. 8vo. 7*s.* 6*d.*

———— Journey through the Upper Provinces of India, From Calcutta to Bombay, with a Journey to Madras and the Southern Provinces. 2 Vols. Post 8vo. 10*s.*

HEIRESS (THE) in Her Minority; or, The Progress of Character. By the Author of "BERTHA'S JOURNAL." 2 Vols. 12mo. 18*s.*

HERODOTUS. A New English Version. Translated from the Text of GAISFORD, and Edited with Notes, illustrating the History and Geography of Herodotus, from the most recent sources of information. By Rev. G. RAWLINSON, COLONEL RAWLINSON, and SIR J. G. WILKINSON. 4 Vols. 8vo. *In Preparation.*

HERSCHEL'S (SIR J. W. F.) Manual of Scientific Enquiry, for the Use of Travellers. By various Writers. *Second Edition.* Post 8vo. 10*s.* 6*d.*

HERVEY'S (LORD) Memoirs of the Reign of George the Second, from his Accession to the Death of Queen Caroline. Edited, with Notes, by Right Hon. J. W. CROKER. *Second and Cheaper Edition.* Portrait. 2 Vols. 8vo. 21*s.*

HICKMAN'S (WM.) Treatise on the Law and Practice of Naval Courts Martial. 8vo. 10*s.* 6*d.*

HILL (FREDERIC) On Crime: its Amount, Causes, and Remedies. 8vo. 12*s.*

HILLARD'S (G. S.) Six Months in Italy. 2 Vols. Post 8vo. 16*s.*

HISTORY OF ENGLAND AND FRANCE UNDER THE HOUSE OF LANCASTER. With an Introductory View of the Early Reformation. *Second Edition.* 8vo. 15*s.*

HOLLAND'S (REV. W. B.) Psalms and Hymns, selected and adapted to the various Solemnities of the Church. *Third Edition.* 24mo. 1*s.* 3*d.*

HOLLWAY'S (J. G.) Month in Norway. Fcap. 8vo. 2*s.*

HONEY BEE (THE). An Essay. Reprinted from the "Quarterly Review." Fcap. 8vo. 1*s.*

HOOK'S (REV. DR.) Church Dictionary. *Seventh Edition.* 8vo. 16*s.*

———— Discourses on the Religious Controversies of the Day. 8vo. 9*s.*

———— (THEODORE) Life. An Essay. Reprinted from the "Quarterly Review." Fcap. 8vo. 1*s.*

HOME AND COLONIAL LIBRARY. Complete in 76 Parts.

Post 8vo, 2s. 6d. each, or bound in 37 Volumes, cloth.

CONTENTS OF THE SERIES.

THE BIBLE IN SPAIN. By George Borrow.
JOURNALS IN INDIA. By Bishop Heber.
TRAVELS IN THE HOLY LAND. By Captains Irby and Mangles.
THE SIEGE OF GIBRALTAR. By John Drinkwater.
MOROCCO AND THE MOORS. By J. Drummond Hay.
LETTERS FROM THE BALTIC. By a Lady.
THE AMBER-WITCH. By Lady Duff Gordon.
OLIVER CROMWELL & JOHN BUNYAN. By Robert Southey.
NEW SOUTH WALES. By Mrs. Meredith.
LIFE OF SIR FRANCIS DRAKE. By John Barrow.
FATHER RIPA'S MEMOIRS OF THE COURT OF CHINA.
A RESIDENCE IN THE WEST INDIES. By M. G. Lewis.
SKETCHES OF PERSIA. By Sir John Malcolm.
THE FRENCH IN ALGIERS. By Lady Duff Gordon.
BRACEBRIDGE HALL. By Washington Irving.
VOYAGE OF A NATURALIST. By Charles Darwin.
HISTORY OF THE FALL OF THE JESUITS.
LIFE OF LOUIS PRINCE OF CONDE. By Lord Mahon.
GIPSIES OF SPAIN. By George Borrow.
THE MARQUESAS. By Hermann Melville.
LIVONIAN TALES. By a Lady.
MISSIONARY LIFE IN CANADA. By Rev. J. Abbott.
SALE'S BRIGADE IN AFFGHANISTAN. By Rev. G. R. Gleig.
LETTERS FROM MADRAS. By a Lady.
HIGHLAND SPORTS. By Charles St. John.
JOURNEYS ACROSS THE PAMPAS. By Sir F. B. Head.
GATHERINGS FROM SPAIN. By Richard Ford.
SIEGES OF VIENNA BY THE TURKS. By Lord Ellesmere.
SKETCHES OF GERMAN LIFE. By Sir A. Gordon.
ADVENTURES IN THE SOUTH SEAS. By Hermann Melville.
STORY OF BATTLE OF WATERLOO. By Rev. G. R. Gleig.
A VOYAGE UP THE RIVER AMAZON. By W. H. Edwards.
THE WAYSIDE CROSS. By Capt. Milman.
MANNERS & CUSTOMS OF INDIA. By Rev. C. Acland.
CAMPAIGNS AT WASHINGTON. By Rev. G. R. Gleig.
ADVENTURES IN MEXICO. By G. F. Ruxton.
PORTUGAL AND GALLICIA. By Lord Carnarvon.
LIFE OF LORD CLIVE. By Rev. G. R. Gleig.
BUSH LIFE IN AUSTRALIA. By H. W. Haygarth.
THE AUTOBIOGRAPHY OF HENRY STEFFENS.
TALES OF A TRAVELLER. By Washington Irving.
SHORT LIVES OF THE POETS. By Thomas Campbell.
HISTORICAL ESSAYS. By Lord Mahon.
LONDON & NORTH-WESTERN RAILWAY. By Sir F. B. Head.
ADVENTURES IN THE LIBYAN DESERT. By Bayle St. John.
A RESIDENCE AT SIERRA LEONE. By a Lady.
LIFE OF GENERAL MUNRO. By Rev. G. R. Gleig.
MEMOIRS OF SIR FOWELL BUXTON. By his Son.
LIFE OF OLIVER GOLDSMITH. By Washington Irving.

HOOKER'S (Dr. J. D.) Himalayan Journals; or, Notes of an Oriental Naturalist in Bengal, the Sikkim and Nepal Himalayas, the Khasia Mountains, &c. *Second Edition.* Woodcuts. 2 vols. Post 8vo. 18*s.*

HOOPER'S (Lieut.) Ten Months among the Tents of the Tuski; with Incidents of an Arctic Boat Expedition in Search of Sir John Franklin. Plates 8vo. 14*s.*

HORACE (Works of). Edited by Dean Milman. With 300 Woodcuts. Crown 8vo. 21*s.*

——— (Life of). By Dean Milman. Woodcuts, and coloured Borders. 8vo. 9*s.*

HORNER'S (Francis) Memoirs and Letters. By his Brother. *Second Edition.* Portrait. 2 Vols. 8vo.

HOSPITALS AND SISTERHOODS. Fcap. 8vo. 5*s.*

HOUSTOUN'S (Mrs.) Yacht Voyage to Texas and the Gulf of Mexico. Plates. 2 Vols. Post 8vo. 21*s.*

HUTCHINSON (Colonel) on Dog-Breaking; the most expeditious, certain, and easy Method, whether great Excellence or only Mediocrity be required. *Third Edition.* Revised and enlarged. Woodcuts. Post 8vo. 9*s.*

INKERSLEY'S (Thos.) Gothic Architecture in France; Being an Inquiry into the Chronological Succession of the Romanesque and Pointed Styles; with Notices of some of the principal Buildings, and an Index. 8vo. 12*s.*

IRBY AND MANGLES' Travels in Egypt, Nubia, Syria, and the Holy Land, including a Journey round the Dead Sea, and through the Country east of the Jordan. Post 8vo. 2*s.* 6*d.*

JAMES' (Rev. Thomas) Fables of Æsop. A New Version, chiefly from the Original Greek. With 100 Original Designs, by John Tenniel. *Twenty-first Edition.* Post 8vo. 2*s.* 6*d.*

JAPAN AND THE JAPANESE. Described from the Accounts of Recent Dutch Travellers. *New Edition.* Post 8vo. 6*s.*

JARDINE'S (David) Narrative of the Gunpowder Plot. Post 8vo. 7*s.* 6*d.*

JERVIS'S (Capt.) Manual of Operations in the Field, for the Use of Officers. Post 8vo. 9*s.* 6*d.*

JESSE'S (Edward) Visits to Spots of Interest in the Vicinity of Windsor and Eton. Woodcuts. Post 8vo. 12*s.*

——— Scenes and Occupations of Country Life. With Recollections of Natural History. *Third Edition.* Woodcuts. Fcap. 8vo. 6*s.*

——— Gleanings in Natural History. With Anecdotes of the Sagacity and Instinct of Animals. *Eighth Edition.* Fcap. 8vo. 6*s.*

JOHNSON'S (Dr. Samuel) Life: By James Boswell. Including the Tour to the Hebrides, with Notes by Sir W. Scott. Edited by the Right Hon. John Wilson Croker. *Third Edition.* 1 Vol. Portraits. Royal 8vo. 15*s.*

——— Lives of the most eminent English Poets. A New Edition. Edited by Peter Cunningham. 3 vols. 8vo. 22*s.* 6*d.* (Murray's British Classics.)

JOHNSTON'S (WM.) England as it is: Social, Political, and Industrial, in the Middle of the 19th Century. 2 Vols. Post 8vo. 18s.

——— (KEITH) Atlas of the United States, British and Central America, showing the Area and Population of the Free and Slaveholding States; with Plans of Cities, Seaports, &c. By PROF. ROGERS, of Boston, U.S., and A. KEITH JOHNSTON, F.R.S.E. 27 Plates. Folio.

JOURNAL OF A NATURALIST. *Fourth Edition.* Woodcuts. Post 8vo. 9s. 6d.

JOWETT'S (Rev. B.) Commentary on St. Paul's Epistles to the Thessalonians, Galatians, and Romans. With Notes and Dissertations. *Second Edition.* 8vo.

KEN'S (BISHOP) Life. By A LAYMAN. *Second Edition.* Portrait. 2 Vols. 8vo. 18s.

——— Exposition of the Apostles' Creed. Extracted from his "Practice of Divine Love." *New Edition.* Fcap. 1s. 6d.

——— Approach to the Holy Altar. Extracted from his "Manual of Prayer" and "Practice of Divine Love." *New Edition.* Fcap. 8vo. 1s. 6d.

KING EDWARD VIth's Latin Grammar; or, an Introduction to the Latin Tongue, for the Use of Schools. *Tenth Edition.* 12mo. 3s. 6d.

——— First Latin Book; or, the Accidence, Syntax and Prosody, with an English Translation for the Use of Junior Classes. *Second Edition.* 12mo. 2s.

KNIGHT'S (CHARLES) Knowledge is Power: a View of the Productive forces of Modern Society, and the results of Labour, Capital, and Skill. Woodcuts. Fcap. 8vo. 7s. 6d.

——— Once upon a Time. 2 Vols. Fcap. 8vo. 10s.

——— Old Printer and Modern Press. Woodcuts. Fcap. 8vo. 5s.

KOCH'S (PROFESSOR) Crimea and Odessa; their Climate and Resources, described from personal knowledge. Map. Post 8vo. 10s. 6d.

KUGLER'S (Dr. FRANZ) Handbook to the History of Painting (the Italian Schools). Translated from the German. Edited, with Notes, by SIR CHARLES EASTLAKE. *Third Edition.* With Woodcuts from the Old Masters. 2 Vols. Post 8vo. 30s.

——— (the German, Dutch, Spanish, and French Schools). Partly Translated from the German. Edited, with Notes, by SIR EDMUND HEAD, Bart. With Woodcuts from the Old Masters. 2 Vols. Post 8vo. 24s.

LABARTE'S (M. JULES) Handbook of the Arts of the Middle Ages and Renaissance. With 200 Woodcuts. 8vo. 18s.

LABORDE'S (LEON DE) Journey through Arabia Petræa, to Mount Sinai, and the Excavated City of Petræa,—the Edom of the Prophecies. *Second Edition.* With Plates. 8vo. 18s.

LAMBERT'S (Miss) Church Needlework. With Practical Remarks on its Preparation and Arrangement. Plates. Post 8vo. 9s. 6d.

——— Knitting Book. Woodcuts. *Two Parts.* 16mo. 1s. 6d. each.

——— Crochet Sampler. Woodcuts. *Two Parts.* 16mo. 4s.

——— Hints on Decorative Needlework. 16mo. 1s. 6d.

LANE'S (E. W.) Arabian Nights. Translated, with Explanatory Notes. With Woodcuts. Royal 8vo. 21*s.*

LATIN GRAMMAR (KING EDWARD THE VITH'S.) For the Use of Schools. *Tenth Edition.* 12mo. 3*s.* 6*d.*

——— First Book (KING EDWARD VI.); or, the Accidence, Syntax, and Prosody, with English Translation for Junior Classes. *Second Edition.* 12mo. 2*s.*

LAYARD'S (A. H.) Nineveh and its Remains. Being a Narrative of Researches and Discoveries amidst the Ruins of Assyria. With an Account of the Chaldean Christians of Kurdistan; the Yezedis, or Devil-worshippers; and an Enquiry into the Manners and Arts of the Ancient Assyrians. *Sixth Edition.* Plates and Woodcuts. 2 Vols. 8vo. 36*s.*

——— Nineveh and Babylon; being the Result of a Second Expedition to Assyria. *Fourteenth Thousand.* Plates. 8vo. 21*s.* Or Fine Paper, 2 Vols. 8vo. 30*s.*

——— Popular Account of Nineveh. 15*th Edition.* With Woodcuts. Post 8vo. 5*s.*

——— Monuments of Nineveh. *First and Second Series.* Illustrated by One Hundred and Seventy Engravings. 2 Vols. Imperial Folio, 10*l.* 10*s.* each.

LEAKE'S (COL. W. MARTIN) Topography of Athens, with Remarks on its Antiquities; to which is added, the Demi of Attica. *Second Edition.* Plates. 2 Vols. 8vo. 30*s.*

——— Travels in Northern Greece. Maps. 4 Vols. 8vo. 60*s.*

——— Disputed Questions of Ancient Geography. Map. 8vo. 6*s.* 6*d.*

——— Numismata Hellenica. A Catalogue of Greek Coins. With Map and Appendix. 4to. 63*s.*

——— Peloponnesiaca: A Supplement to Travels in the Morea. 8vo. 15*s.*

——— Thoughts on the Degradation of Science in England. 8vo. 3*s.* 6*d.*

LESLIE'S (C. R.) Handbook for Young Painters. With Illustrations. Post 8vo. 10*s.* 6*d.*

LETTERS FROM THE SHORES OF THE BALTIC. By a LADY. Post 8vo. 2*s.* 6*d.*

——— Madras; or, First Impressions of Life and Manners in India. By a LADY. Post 8vo. 2*s.* 6*d.*

——— Sierra Leone, written to Friends at Home. By a LADY. Edited by MRS. NORTON. Post 8vo. 6*s.*

——— Head Quarters; or, The Realities of the War in the Crimea. By an OFFICER OF THE STAFF. *Second Edition.* Portrait of Lord Raglan and Plans. 2 vols. Post 8vo. 24*s.*

LEXINGTON (THE) PAPERS; or, Some Account of the Courts of London and Vienna at the end of the 17th Century. Edited by HON. H. MANNERS SUTTON. 8vo. 14*s.*

LEWIS' (SIR G. C.) Essay on the Government of Dependencies. 8vo. 12*s.*

—— Glossary of Provincial Words used in Herefordshire and some of the adjoining Counties. 12mo. 4*s.* 6*d.*

—— (LADY THERESA) Friends and Contemporaries of the Lord Chancellor Clarendon, illustrative of Portraits in his Gallery. With a Descriptive Account of the Pictures, and Origin of the Collection. Portraits. 3 Vols. 8vo. 42*s.*

—— (M. G.) Journal of a Residence among the Negroes in the West Indies. Post 8vo. 2*s.* 6*d.*

LIDDELL'S (DEAN) History of Rome. From the Earliest Times to the Establishment of the Empire. With the History of Literature and Art. *Library Edition.* 2 Vols. 8vo. 28*s.*

—— SCHOOL HISTORY OF ROME. Abridged from the Larger Work. With 100 Woodcuts. Post 8vo. 7*s.* 6*d.* [*Uniform with* DR. WM. SMITH'S HISTORY OF GREECE].

LINDSAY'S (LORD) Lives of the Lindsays; or, a Memoir of the Houses of Crawford and Balcarres. With Extracts from Official Papers and Personal Narratives. 3 Vols. 8vo. 42*s.*

—— Report of the Claim of James, Earl of Crawfurd and Balcarres, to the Original Dukedom of Montrose, created in 1488. Folio. 15*s.*

—— (REV. HENRY) Practical Lectures on the Historical Books of the Old Testament. 2 Vols. 16mo. 10*s.*

LITTLE ARTHUR'S HISTORY OF ENGLAND. By LADY CALLCOTT. *Eighteenth Edition.* With many Woodcuts. Fcap. 8vo. 2*s.* 6*d.*

LIVINGSTON'S (REV. DR.) Exploratory Journeys of a Missionary in South Africa, and across that Continent from West to East. Map and Plates. 8vo.

LIVONIAN TALES.—The Disponent.—The Wolves.—The Jewess. By the Author of "Letters from the Baltic." Post 8vo. 2*s.* 6*d.*

LOCKHART'S (J. G.) Ancient Spanish Ballads. Historical and Romantic. Translated, with Notes. *Illustrated Edition.* 4to. 42*s.* Or, Popular Edition, Post 8vo. 2*s.* 6*d.*

—— Life of Robert Burns. *Fifth Edition.* Fcap. 8vo. 3*s.*

LOUDON'S (MRS.) Instructions in Gardening for Ladies. With Directions and Calendar of Operations for Every Month. *Eighth Edition.* Woodcuts. Fcap. 8vo. 5*s.*

—— Modern Botany; a Popular Introduction to the Natural System of Plants. *Second Edition.* Woodcuts. Fcap. 8vo. 6*s.*

LOWE'S (SIR HUDSON) Letters and Journals, during the Captivity of Napoleon at St. Helena. By WILLIAM FORSYTH. Portrait. 3 Vols. 8vo. 45*s.*

LYELL'S (SIR CHARLES) Principles of Geology; or, the Modern Changes of the Earth and its Inhabitants considered as illustrative of Geology. *Ninth Edition.* Woodcuts. 8vo. 18*s.*

—— Manual of Elementary Geology; or, the Ancient Changes of the Earth and its Inhabitants illustrated by its Geological Monuments. *Fifth Edition.* With a Postscript. Woodcuts. 8vo.

—— Visits to the United States, 1841-46. *Second Edition.* Plates. 4 Vols. Post 8vo. 24*s.*

MAHON'S (LORD) History of England, from the Peace of Utrecht to the Peace of Versailles, 1713—83. *Fourth Edition.* 7 Vols. 8vo. 93s.

——— History of England 1713—83. *Popular Edition.* 7 Vols. Post 8vo. 42s.

——— "Forty-Five;" a Narrative of the Rebellion in Scotland. Post 8vo. 3s.

——— History of the War of the Succession in Spain. *Second Edition.* Map. 8vo. 15s.

——— Spain under Charles the Second; or, Extracts from the Correspondence of the Hon. ALEXANDER STANHOPE, British Minister at Madrid from 1690 to 1700. *Second Edition.* Post 8vo. 6s. 6d.

——— Life of Louis Prince of Condé, surnamed the Great. Post 8vo. 6s.

——— Life of Belisarius. *Second Edition.* Post 8vo. 10s. 6d.

——— Historical and Critical Essays. Post 8vo. 6s.

——— Story of Joan of Arc. Fcap. 8vo. 1s.

——— Address Delivered at Manchester, Leeds, and Birmingham. Fcap. 8vo. 1s.

McCULLOCH'S (J. R.) Collected Edition of RICARDO'S Political Works. With Notes and Memoir. *Second Edition.* 8vo. 16s.

MALCOLM'S (SIR JOHN) Sketches of Persia. *Third Edition.* Post 8vo. 6s.

MANTELL'S (GIDEON A.) Thoughts on Animalcules; or, the Invisible World, as revealed by the Microscope. *Second Edition.* Plates. 16mo. 6s.

MANUAL OF SCIENTIFIC ENQUIRY, Prepared for the Use of Officers and Travellers. By various Writers. Edited by SIR J. HERSCHEL, Bart. *Second Edition.* Maps. Post 8vo. 10s. 6d. (*Published by order of the Lords of the Admiralty.*)

MARKHAM'S (MRS.) History of England. From the First Invasion by the Romans, down to the fourteenth year of Queen Victoria's Reign. *98th Edition.* Woodcuts. 12mo. 6s.

——— History of France. From the Conquest by the Gauls, to the Death of Louis Philippe. *58th Edition.* Woodcuts. 12mo. 6s.

——— History of Germany. From the Invasion by Marius, to the present time. *6th Edition.* Woodcuts. 12mo. 6s.

——— History of Greece. From the Earliest Times to the Roman Conquest. With the History of Literature and Art. By Dr. WM. SMITH. *Seventh Edition.* Woodcuts. 12mo. 7s. 6d. (Questions. 12mo. 2s.)

——— History of Rome, from the Earliest Times to the Establishment of the Empire. With the History of Literature and Art. By DEAN LIDDELL. Woodcuts. 12mo. 7s. 6d.

——— Sermons for Children. *Second Edition.* Fcap. 8vo. 3s.

MARKLAND'S (J. H.) Remarks on English Churches, and Sepulchral Memorials. *Fourth Edition.* Woodcuts. Fcap. 8vo. 6s. 6d.

——— Reverence due to Holy Places. *Third Edition.* Fcap. 8vo. 2s.

MARRYAT'S (Joseph) History of Modern and Mediæval Pottery and Porcelain. With a Description of the Manufacture, a Glossary, and a List of Monograms. *Second Edition.* Revised. With additional Chapters and Coloured Plates and Woodcuts. 8vo.

MATTHIÆ'S (Augustus) Greek Grammar for Schools. Abridged from the Larger Grammar. By Blomfield. *8th Edition.* Revised by Edwards. 12mo. 3*s.*

MAUREL'S (Jules) Essay on the Character, Actions, and Writings of the Duke of Wellington. *Second Edition.* Fcap. 8vo. 1*s.* 6*d.*

MAWE'S (H. L.) Journal of a Passage from the Pacific to the Atlantic, crossing the Andes in the Northern Provinces of Peru, and descending the great River Maranon. 8vo. 12*s.*

MAXIMS AND HINTS for an Angler, and the Miseries of Fishing. By Richard Penn. *New Edition.* Woodcuts. 12mo. 1*s.*

MAYO'S (Dr.) Pathology of the Human Mind. Fcap. 8vo. 5*s.* 6*d.*

MELVILLE'S (Hermann) Typee and Omoo; or, Adventures amongst the Marquesas and South Seas. 2 Vols. Post 8vo.

MENDELSSOHN'S (Felix Bartholdy) Life. By Jules Benedict. 8vo. 2*s.* 6*d.*

MERRIFIELD (Mrs.) on the Arts of Painting in Oil, Miniature, Mosaic, and Glass; Gilding, Dyeing, and the Preparation of Colours and Artificial Gems, described in several old Manuscripts. 2 Vols. 8vo. 30*s.*

MEREDITH'S (Mrs. Charles) Notes and Sketches of New South Wales, during a Residence from 1839 to 1844. Post 8vo. 2*s.* 6*d.*

——— Tasmania, during a Residence of Nine Years. With Illustrations. 2 Vols. Post 8vo. 18*s.*

MILLS (Arthur) On Colonial Constitutions. An Outline of the History of British Dependencies. Map. 8vo. 14*s.*

MITCHELL'S (Thomas) Plays of Aristophanes. With English Notes. 8vo.—1. CLOUDS, 10*s.*—2. WASPS, 10*s.*—3. FROGS, 15*s.*

MODERN DOMESTIC COOKERY. Founded on Principles of Economy and Practical Knowledge, and adapted for Private Families. *New Edition.* Woodcuts. Fcap. 8vo. 5*s.*

MILMAN'S (Dean) History of Christianity, from the Birth of Christ to the Extinction of Paganism in the Roman Empire. 3 Vols. 8vo. 36*s.*

——— History of Latin Christianity; including that of the Popes to the Pontificate of Nicholas V. 6 Vols. 8vo. 78*s.*

——— Character and Conduct of the Apostles considered as an Evidence of Christianity. 8vo. 10*s.* 6*d.*

——— Life and Works of Horace. With 300 Woodcuts. *New Edition.* 2 Vols. Crown 8vo. 30*s.*

——— Poetical Works. Plates. 3 Vols. Fcap. 8vo. 18*s.*

——— Fall of Jerusalem. Fcap. 8vo. 1*s.*

——— (Capt. E. A.) Wayside Cross; or, the Raid of Gomez. A Tale of the Carlist War. Post 8vo. 2*s.* 6*d.*

MONASTERY AND THE MOUNTAIN CHURCH. By Author of "Sunlight through the Mist." Woodcuts. 16mo. 4*s.*

MOLTKE'S (BARON) Russian Campaigns on the Danube and the Passage of the Balkan, 1828—9. Plans. 8vo. 14*s.*

MOORE'S (THOMAS) Life and Letters of Lord Byron. Plates. 6 Vols. Fcap. 8vo. 18*s.*

——— Life and Letters of Lord Byron. With Portrait and Vignette. One Volume. Royal 8vo. 12*s.*

MOZLEY'S (REV. J. B.) Treatise on the Augustinian Doctrine of Predestination. 8vo. 14*s.*

——— Primitive Doctrine of Baptismal Regeneration. 8vo. 8*s.* 6*d.*

MUCK MANUAL (The) for the Use of Farmers. A Practical Treatise on the Chemical Properties, Management, and Application of Manures. By FREDERICK FALKNER. *Second Edition.* Fcap. 8vo. 5*s.*

MUNDY'S (CAPT. RODNEY) Events in Borneo, including the Occupation of Labuan and Visit to the Celebes. Plates. 2 Vols. 8vo. 32*s.*

MUNRO'S (GENERAL SIR THOMAS) Life and Letters. By the REV. G. R. GLEIG. Post 8vo. 6*s.*

MURCHISON'S (SIR RODERICK) Russia in Europe and the Ural Mountains; Geologically Illustrated. With Coloured Maps, Plates, Sections, &c. 2 Vols. Royal 4to. 8*l.* 8*s.*

——— Siluria; or, a History of the Oldest Rocks containing Organic Remains. With Map and Plates. 8vo. 30*s.*

MURRAY'S (CAPT. A.) Naval Life and Services of Admiral Sir Philip Durham. 8vo. 5*s.* 6*d.*

MURRAY'S RAILWAY READING. Published occasionally; varying in size and price, and suited for all classes of Readers.

[*The following are published:*]

WELLINGTON. By LORD ELLESMERE. 6*d.*
NIMROD ON THE CHASE, 1*s.*
ESSAYS FROM "THE TIMES." 2 Vols. 8*s.*
MUSIC AND DRESS. 1*s.*
LAYARD'S ACCOUNT OF NINEVEH. 5*s.*
MILMAN'S FALL OF JERUSALEM. 1*s.*
MAHON'S "FORTY-FIVE." 3*s.*
LIFE OF THEODORE HOOK. 1*s.*
DEEDS OF NAVAL DARING. 2 Vols. 5*s.*
THE HONEY BEE. 1*s.*
JAMES' ÆSOP'S FABLES. 2*s.* 6*d.*
NIMROD ON THE TURF. 1*s.* 6*d.*
OLIPHANT'S NEPAUL. 2*s.* 6*d.*
ART OF DINING. 1*s.* 6*d.*
HALLAM'S LITERARY ESSAYS. 2*s.*
MAHON'S JOAN OF ARC. 1*s.*
HEAD'S EMIGRANT. 2*s.* 6*d.*
NIMROD ON THE ROAD. 1*s.*
WILKINSON'S ANCIENT EGYPTIANS. 12*s.*
CROKER ON THE GUILLOTINE. 1*s.*
HOLLWAY'S NORWAY. 2*s.*
MAUREL'S WELLINGTON. 1*s.* 6*d.*
CAMPBELL'S LIFE OF BACON. 2*s.*
THE FLOWER GARDEN. 1*s.*
LOCKHART'S SPANISH BALLADS. 2*s.* 6*d.*
LUCAS ON HISTORY. 6*d.*
BEAUTIES OF BYRON. 3*s.*
TAYLOR'S NOTES FROM LIFE. 2*s.*
REJECTED ADDRESSES. 1*s.*
PENN'S HINTS ON ANGLING. 1*s.*

MUSIC AND DRESS. Two Essays, by a Lady. Reprinted from the "Quarterly Review." Fcap. 8vo. 1*s.*

NAPIER'S (SIR WM.) English Battles and Sieges of the Peninsular War. With Portrait. Post 8vo. 10*s.* 6*d.*

——— Life and Opinions of General Sir Charles Napier; chiefly derived from his Journals, Letters, and Familiar Correspondence. Portraits. Vols. 1 and 2. Post 8vo. 24*s.*

——— Administration of Scinde, under General Sir Charles Napier. *Second Edition.* Plates. 8vo. 15*s.*

NAUTICAL ALMANACK (The). (*Published Annually by* Order of the *Lords Commissioners of the Admiralty.*) Royal 8vo. 2*s.* 6*d.*

NAVY LIST (The Royal). (*Published Quarterly, by Authority.*) 12mo. 2*s*. 6*d*.

NEWBOLD'S (Lieut.) Straits of Malacca, Penang, and Singapore. 2 Vols. 8vo. 26*s*.

NEWDEGATE'S (C. N.) Customs' Tariffs of all Nations; collected and arranged up to the year 1855. 4to. 30*s*.

NICHOLLS' (Sir George) History of the British Poor: Being an Historical Account of the English, Scotch, and Irish Poor Law: in connection with the Condition of the People. 4 Vols. 8vo.

The work may also be had separately:—

History of the English Poor. 2 Vols. 8vo. 28*s*.

History of the Scotch Poor. 8vo. 12*s*.

History of the Irish Poor. 8vo. 14*s*.

NICOLAS' (Sir Harris) Historic Peerage of England. Exhibiting, under Alphabetical Arrangement, the Origin, Descent, and Present State of every Title of Peerage which has existed in this Country since the Conquest. Being a New Edition of the "Synopsis of the Peerage." Revised, Corrected, and Continued to the Present Time. By William Courthope, Somerset Herald. 8vo. 30*s*.

NIMROD On the Chace—The Turf—and The Road. Reprinted from the "Quarterly Review." Woodcuts. Fcap. 8vo. 3*s*. 6*d*.

NORTON'S (Hon. Caroline) Letters from Sierra Leone, to Friends at Home. By a Lady. Edited by Mrs. Norton. Post 8vo. 6*s*.

O'CONNOR'S (R.) Field Sports of France; or, Hunting, Shooting and Fishing on the Continent. Woodcuts. 12mo. 7*s*. 6*d*.

OLIPHANT'S (Laurence) Journey to Katmandu, with Visit to the Camp of the Nepaulese Ambassador. Fcap. 8vo. 2*s*. 6*d*.

OXENHAM'S (Rev. W.) English Notes for Latin Elegiacs; designed for early Proficients in the Art of Latin Versification, with Prefatory Rules of Composition in Elegiac Metre. *Second Edition.* 12mo. 4*s*.

PAGET'S (John) Hungary and Transylvania. With Remarks on their Condition, Social, Political, and Economical. *Third and Cheaper Edition.* Woodcuts. 2 Vols. 8vo. 18*s*.

PARISH'S (Sir Woodbine) Buenos Ayres and the Provinces of the Rio de la Plata. Their First Discovery and Conquest, Present State, Trade, Debt, &c. *Second Edition.* Map and Woodcuts. 8vo. 15*s*.

PARKYNS' (Mansfield) Personal Narrative of Three Years' Residence and Adventures in Abyssinia. Woodcuts. 2 Vols. 8vo. 30*s*.

PEEL'S (Sir Robt.) MEMOIRS. Left in MSS. Edited by Earl Stanhope and the Right Hon. Edward Cardwell. 2 Vols. Post 8vo. 7*s*. 6*d*. each.

PEILE'S (Rev. Dr.) Agamemnon and Choephorœ of Æschylus. A New Edition of the Text, with Notes, Critical, Explanatory, and Philological, for the Use of Students. *Second Edition.* 2 Vols. 8vo. 9*s*. each.

PENN'S (Richard) Maxims and Hints for an Angler, and the Miseries of Fishing. To which is added, Maxims and Hints for a Chess-player. *New Edition.* Woodcuts. Fcap. 8vo. 1*s*.

——— (Granville) Bioscope; or, Dial of Life Explained. To which is added, a Translation of St. Paulinus' Epistle to Celantia, on the Rule of Christian Life; and an Elementary View of General Chronology. *Second Edition.* With Dial Plate. 12mo. 12*s*.

PENROSE'S (Rev. John) Faith and Practice; an Exposition of the Principles and Duties of Natural and Revealed Religion. Post 8vo. 8*s*. 6*d*.

—— (F. C.) Principles of Athenian Architecture, and the Optical Refinements exhibited in the Construction of the Ancient Buildings at Athens, from a Survey. With 40 Plates. Folio. 5*l*. 5*s*. (*Published under the direction of the Dilettanti Society.*)

PERRY'S (Sir Erskine) Bird's-Eye View of India. With Extracts from a Journal kept in the Provinces, Nepaul, &c. Fcap. 8vo. 5*s*.

PHILLIPS' (John) Memoirs of William Smith, LL.D. (the Geologist). Portrait. 8vo. 7*s*. 6*d*.

—— —— Geology of Yorkshire, The Yorkshire Coast, and the Mountain-Limestone District. Plates 4to. Part I., 20*s*.—Part II., 30*s*.

—— —— Rivers, Mountains, and Sea Coast of Yorkshire. With Essays on the Climate, Scenery, and Ancient Inhabitants of the Country. *Second Edition*, with 36 Plates. 8vo. 15*s*.

PHILOSOPHY IN SPORT MADE SCIENCE IN EARNEST; or, the First Principles of Natural Philosophy inculcated by aid of the Toys and Sports of Youth. *Eighth Edition.* Revised and enlarged. Woodcuts. Post 8vo. 9*s*.

PHILPOTT'S (Bishop) Letters to the late Charles Butler, on the Theological parts of his "Book of the Roman Catholic Church;" with Remarks on certain Works of Dr. Milner and Dr. Lingard, and on some parts of the Evidence of Dr. Doyle. *Second Edition.* 8vo. 16*s*.

PHIPPS' (Hon. Edmund) Memoir, Correspondence, Literary and Unpublished Diaries of Robert Plumer Ward. Portrait. 2 Vols. 8vo. 28*s*.

POOLE'S (R. S.) Horæ Egyptiacæ: or, the Chronology of Ancient Egypt, discovered from Astronomical and Hieroglyphic Records upon its Monuments. Plates. 8vo. 10*s*. 6*d*.

POPE'S (Alexander) WORKS. An entirely New Edition. Edited by the Right Hon. John Wilson Croker, assisted by Peter Cunningham, F.S.A. 8vo. *In the Press.*

PORTER'S (Rev. J. L.) Five Years in Damascus. With Travels to Palmyra. Lebanon, and other Scripture Sites. Map and Woodcuts. 2 vols. Post 8vo. 21*s*.

—— (Mrs. G. R.) Rational Arithmetic for Schools and for Private Instruction. 12mo. 3*s*. 6*d*.

PRAYER-BOOK (The Illustrated), with 1000 Illustrations of Borders, Initials, Vignettes, &c. Medium 8vo. Cloth, 21*s*.; Calf, 31*s*. 6*d*. Morocco, 42*s*.

PROGRESS OF RUSSIA IN THE EAST. An Historical Summary, continued to the Present Time. With Map by Arrowsmith. *Third Edition.* 8vo. 6*s*. 6*d*.

PUSS IN BOOTS. With 12 Illustrations; for Old and Young. By Otto Speckter. *A New Edition.* 16mo. 1*s*. 6*d*.

QUARTERLY REVIEW (The). 8vo. 6*s*.

RANKE'S (Leopold) Political and Ecclesiastical History of the Popes of Rome, during the Sixteenth and Seventeenth Centuries. Translated from the German by Mrs. Austin. *Third Edition.* 2 Vols. 8vo. 24*s*.

RAWLINSON'S (Rev. George) Herodotus. A New English Version. Translated from the Text of Gaisford, and Edited with Notes, illustrating the History and Geography of Herodotus, from the most recent sources of information, embodying the chief Results, Historical and Ethnographical, which have been arrived at in the progress of Cuneiform and Hieroglyphical Discovery. Assisted by Colonel Rawlinson and Sir J. G. Wilkinson. 4 Vols. 8vo. [*In Preparation.*

REJECTED ADDRESSES (The). By James and Horace Smith. With Biographies of the Authors, and additional Notes. *New Edition, with the Author's latest Corrections.* Fcap. 8vo. 1*s.*, or *Fine Paper*, with Portrait. Fcap. 8vo. 5*s.*

RENNIE'S (James) Insect Architecture. To which are added Chapters on the Ravages, the Preservation, for Purposes of Study, and the Classification of Insects. *New Edition.* Woodcuts. Post 8vo.

RICARDO'S (David) Political Works. With a Notice of his Life and Writings. By J. R. M'Culloch. *New Edition.* 8vo. 16*s.*

RIPA'S (Father) Memoirs during Thirteen Years' Residence at the Court of Peking, in the Service of the Emperor of China. Translated from the Italian. By Fortunato Prandi. Post 8vo. 2*s.* 6*d.*

ROBERTSON'S (Rev. J. C.) History of the Christian Church, From the Apostolic Age to the Pontificate of Gregory the Great, A.D. 590. 8vo. 12*s.*

——— Second Period, from A.D. 590 to the Concordat of Worms. A.D. 1123. 8vo. 18*s.*

ROBINSON'S (Rev. Dr.) Biblical Researches in the Holy Land. Being a Journal of Travels in 1838, and of Later Researches in 1852. With New Maps. 3 Vols. 8vo. 36*s.*

*** *The "Later Researches" may be had separately.* 8vo. 15*s.*

ROMILLY'S (Sir Samuel) Memoirs and Political Diary. By his Sons. *Third Edition.* Portrait. 2 Vols. Fcap. 8vo. 12*s.*

ROSS'S (Sir James) Voyage of Discovery and Research in the Southern and Antarctic Regions during the years 1839-43. Plates. 2 Vols. 8vo. 36*s.*

RUNDELL'S (Mrs.) Domestic Cookery, founded on Principles of Economy and Practice, and adapted for Private Families. *New and Revised Edition.* Woodcuts. Fcap. 8vo. 5*s.*

RUXTON'S (George F.) Travels in Mexico; with Adventures among the Wild Tribes and Animals of the Prairies and Rocky Mountains. Post 8vo. 6*s.*

SALE'S (Lady) Journal of the Disasters in Affghanistan. *Eighth Edition.* Post 8vo. 12*s.*

——— (Sir Robert) Brigade in Affghanistan. With an Account of the Seizure and Defence of Jellalabad. By Rev. G. R. Gleig. Post 8vo. 2*s.* 6*d.*

SANDWITH'S (Humphry, M.D.) Narrative of the Siege of Kars and of the Six Months' Resistance by the Turkish Garrison under General Williams, to the Russian Army. With Remarks on the Present State of Turkey. *7th Thousand.* Post 8vo. 3*s.* 6*d.*

SCROPE'S (William) Days of Deer-Stalking in the Forest of Atholl; with some Account of the Nature and Habits of the Red Deer. *Third Edition.* Woodcuts. Crown 8vo. 20*s.*

——— Days and Nights of Salmon Fishing in the Tweed; with a short Account of the Natural History and Habits of the Salmon. *Second Edition.* Woodcuts. Royal 8vo. 31*s.* 6*d.*

SCROPE'S (G. P.) Memoir of Lord Sydenham, and his Administration in Canada. *Second Edition.* Portrait. 8vo. 9*s.* 6*d.*

SEYMOUR'S (H. DANBY) Travels in the Crimea and along the Shores of the Sea of Azoff and the Black Sea. *Third Edition.* Map. 8vo. 12*s.*

SHAW'S (THOS. B.) Outlines of English Literature, for the Use of Young Students. Post 8vo. 12*s.*

SHEIL'S (LADY) Glimpses of Life and Manners in Persia. Woodcuts. Post 8vo. 12*s.*

SIERRA LEONE; Described in a Series of Letters to Friends at Home. By A LADY. Edited by MRS. NORTON. Post 8vo. 6*s.*

SMITH'S (WM., LL.D.) Dictionary of Greek and Roman Antiquities. *Second Edition.* With 500 Woodcuts. 8vo. 42*s.*

——— Smaller Dictionary of Greek and Roman Antiquities. *Third Edition.* With 200 Woodcuts. Crown 8vo. 7*s.* 6*d.*

——— Dictionary of Greek and Roman Biography and Mythology. With 500 Woodcuts. 3 Vols. 8vo. 5*l.* 15*s.* 6*d.*

——— Dictionary of Greek and Roman Geography. With Woodcuts. 2 Vols. 8vo.

——— Historical Atlas of Ancient Geography. 4to. [*In Preparation.*

——— Dictionary of Biblical Antiquities, Biography, and Geography. With Woodcuts. 8vo. [*In Preparation.*

——— Classical Dictionary for the Higher Forms in Schools. Compiled from the larger works. *Third Edition.* 8vo. 15*s.*

——— Smaller Classical Dictionary. *Third Edition.* With 200 Woodcuts. Crown 8vo. 7*s.* 6*d.*

——— Latin-English Dictionary. Based upon the Works of Forcellini and Freund. 8vo. 21*s.*

——— Smaller Latin-English Dictionary. Square 12mo. 7*s.* 6*d.*

——— School History of Greece; from the Earliest Times to the Roman Conquest. With the History of Literature and Art. *Seventh Edition.* Woodcuts. Crown 8vo. 7*s.* 6*d.*

——— School History of Rome; from the Earliest Times to the Establishment of the Empire. With the History of Literature and Art. By H. G. LIDDELL, D.D. Woodcuts. Crown 8vo. 7*s.* 6*d.* [*Uniform with* DR. WM. SMITH'S HISTORY OF GREECE.]

——— Questions on Dr Wm. Smith's History of Greece. For the Use of Schools and Teachers. By REV. CHARLES BICKMORE. Post 8vo. 2*s.*

——— Gibbon's History of the Decline and Fall of the Roman Empire. Edited, with Notes. Portrait and Map. 8 Vols. 8vo. 60*s.* (Murray's British Classics.)

——— Student's Gibbon; being the History of the Decline and Fall, Abridged. Incorporating the Researches of Recent Commentators. Woodcuts. Post 8vo. 7*s.* 6*d.*

——— (WM. JAS.) Grenville Letters and Diaries, including MR. GRENVILLE'S DIARY OF POLITICAL EVENTS, while First Lord of the Treasury. Edited, with Notes. 4 Vols. 8vo. 64*s.*

——— (JAMES & HORACE) Rejected Addresses. *23rd Edition.* Fcap. 8vo. 1*s.*, or *Fine Paper*, with Portrait. Fcap. 8vo. 5*s.*

SOMERVILLE'S (MARY) Physical Geography. *Third Edition.* Portrait. 2 Vols. Fcap. 8vo. 12*s*.

——— Connexion of the Physical Sciences. *Eighth Edition.* Plates. Fcap. 8vo. 10*s*. 6*d*.

SOUTHEY'S (ROBERT) Book of the Church; with Notes containing the Authorities, and an Index. *Sixth Edition.* 8vo. 12*s*.

——— Lives of John Bunyan & Oliver Cromwell. Post 8vo. 2*s*. 6*d*.

SPECKTER'S (OTTO) Puss in Boots, suited to the Tastes of Old and Young. *A New Edition.* With 12 Woodcuts. Square 12mo. 1*s*. 6*d*.

——— Charmed Roe; or, the Story of the Little Brother and Sister. Illustrated. 16mo.

STANLEY'S (EDWARD, D.D., Bp. of Norwich) ADDRESSES AND CHARGES. With a Memoir of his Life. By HIS SON. *Second Edition.* 8vo. 10*s*. 6*d*.

——— (ARTHUR P.) Commentary on St. Paul's Epistles to the Corinthians, with Notes and Dissertations. *Second Edition.* 2 Vols. 8vo.

——— Historical Memorials of Canterbury. The Landing of Augustine—The Murder of Becket—The Black Prince—The Shrine of Becket. *Second Edition.* Woodcuts. 8vo. 8*s*. 6*d*.

——— Sinai and Palestine, in Connexion with their History. *Third Edition.* Map. 8vo. 16*s*.

ST. JOHN'S (CHARLES) Wild Sports and Natural History of the Highlands. Post 8vo. 6*s*.

——— (BAYLE) Adventures in the Libyan Desert and the Oasis of Jupiter Ammon. Woodcuts. Post 8vo. 2*s*. 6*d*.

STEPHENSON'S (GEORGE), Life. The Railway Engineer. By SAMUEL SMILES. Portrait. 8vo. *In the Press.*

STOTHARD'S (THOS., R. A.) Life. With Personal Reminiscences. By Mrs. BRAY. With Portrait and 60 Woodcuts. 4to. 21*s*.

STREET'S (G. E.) Brick and Marble Architecture of Italy, in the Middle Ages. Plates. 8vo. 21*s*.

STRIFE FOR THE MASTERY. Two Allegories. With Illustrations. Crown 8vo. 6*s*.

SUNLIGHT THROUGH THE MIST; or, Practical Lessons drawn from the Lives of Good Men, intended as a Sunday Book for Children. By A LADY. *Second Edition.* 16mo. 3*s*. 6*d*.

SWIFT'S (JONATHAN) Works. New Edition, based upon Sir Walter Scott's Edition, entirely revised. 8vo. *In Preparation.*

SYDENHAM'S (LORD) Memoirs. With his Administration in Canada. By G. POULETT SCROPE, M.P. *Second Edition.* Portrait. 8vo. 9*s*. 6*d*.

SYME'S (JAS.) Principles of Surgery. Fourth Edition, revised. 8vo. 14*s*.

TALBOT'S (H. FOX) English Etymologies. 8vo. 12*s*.

TAYLOR'S (HENRY) Notes from Life. Fcap 8vo. 2*s*.

——— (J. E.) Fairy Ring. A Collection of Stories for Young Persons. From the German. With Illustrations by RICHARD DOYLE. *Second Edition.* Woodcuts. Fcap. 8vo.

TENNENT'S (SIR J. E.) Christianity in Ceylon. Its Introduction and Progress under the Portuguese, Dutch, British, and American Missions. With an Historical Sketch of the Brahmanical and Buddhist Superstitions. Woodcuts. 8vo. 14*s*.

THREE-LEAVED MANUAL OF FAMILY PRAYER; arranged so as to save the trouble of turning the Pages backwards and forwards. Royal 8vo. 2*s*.

TICKNOR'S (GEORGE) History of Spanish Literature. With Criticisms on particular Works, and Biographical Notices of Prominent Writers. *Second Edition.* 3 Vols. 8vo. 24*s*.

TOCQUEVILLE'S (M. DE) State of France before the Revolution, 1789, and on the Causes of that Event. Translated by HENRY REEVE, Esq. 8vo. 14*s*.

TREMENHEERE'S (H. S.) Political Experience of the Ancients, in its bearing on Modern Times. Fcap. 8vo. 2*s*. 6*d*.

——————— Notes on Public Subjects, made during a Tour in the United States and Canada. Post 8vo. 10*s*. 6*d*.

——————— Constitution of the United States compared with our own. Post 8vo. 9*s*. 6*d*.

TWISS' (HORACE) Public and Private Life of Lord Chancellor Eldon, with Selections from his Correspondence. Portrait. *Third Edition.* 2 Vols. Post 8vo. 21*s*.

UBICINI'S (M. A.) Letters on Turkey and its Inhabitants—the Moslems, Greeks, Armenians, &c. Translated by LADY EASTHOPE. 2 Vols. Post 8vo. 21*s*.

VAUGHAN'S (REV. DR.) Sermons preached in Harrow School. 8vo. 10*s*. 6*d*.

——————— New Sermons. 12mo. 5*s*.

VAUX'S (W. S. W.) Handbook to the Antiquities in the British Museum; being a Description of the Remains of Greek, Assyrian, Egyptian, and Etruscan Art preserved there. With Woodcuts. *New Edition.* Post 8vo.

VENABLES' (REV. R. L.) Domestic Scenes in Russia during a Year's Residence, chiefly in the Interior. *Second Edition.* Post 8vo. 5*s*.

VOYAGE to the Mauritius and back, touching at the Cape of Good Hope, and St. Helena. By Author of "PADDIANA." Post 8vo. 9*s*. 6*d*.

WAAGEN'S (DR.) Treasures of Art in Great Britain. Being an Account of the Chief Collections of Paintings, Sculpture, Manuscripts, Miniatures, &c. &c., in this Country. Obtained from Personal Inspection during Visits to England. 3 Vols. 8vo. 36*s*.

WADDINGTON'S (DEAN) Condition and Prospects of the Greek Church. *New Edition.* Fcap. 8vo. 3*s*. 6*d*.

WAKEFIELD'S (E. J.) Adventures in New Zealand. With some Account of the Beginning of the British Colonisation of the Island. Map. 2 Vols. 8vo. 28*s*.

WALKS AND TALKS. A Story-book for Young Children. By AUNT IDA. With Woodcuts. 16mo. 5*s*.

WARD'S (ROBERT PLUMER) Memoir, Correspondence, Literary and Unpublished Diaries and Remains. By the HON. EDMUND PHIPPS. Portrait. 2 Vols. 8vo. 28*s*.